TAKKA TAKKA BOM BOM

An Intrepid War Correspondent's 50 Year Odyssey

AL J. VENTER

CASEMATE

Philadelphia & Oxford

Published in the United States of America and Great Britain in 2023 by
CASEMATE PUBLISHERS
1950 Lawrence Road, Havertown, PA 19083, USA
and
The Old Music Hall, 106–108 Cowley Road, Oxford OX4 1JE, UK

Hardback Edition: ISBN 978-1-63624-380-1
Digital Edition: ISBN 978-1-63624-381-8

A CIP record for this book is available from the British Library

Printed and bound in the United Kingdom by CPI Group (UK) Ltd, Croydon, CR0 4YY

Typeset in India by Lapiz Digital Services, Chennai.

For a complete list of Casemate titles, please contact:

CASEMATE PUBLISHERS (US)
Telephone (610) 853-9131
Fax (610) 853-9146
Email: casemate@casematepublishers.com
www.casematepublishers.com

CASEMATE PUBLISHERS (UK)
Telephone (0)1226 734350
Email: casemate-uk@casematepublishers.co.uk
www.casematepublishers.co.uk

Cover image: Bruce Gonneau
All photographs from author's collection unless otherwise credited.

For Lynn,
my lovely *Madame l'Ambassadrice,* who often covered
the same ground in Africa as I did

Contents

Maps

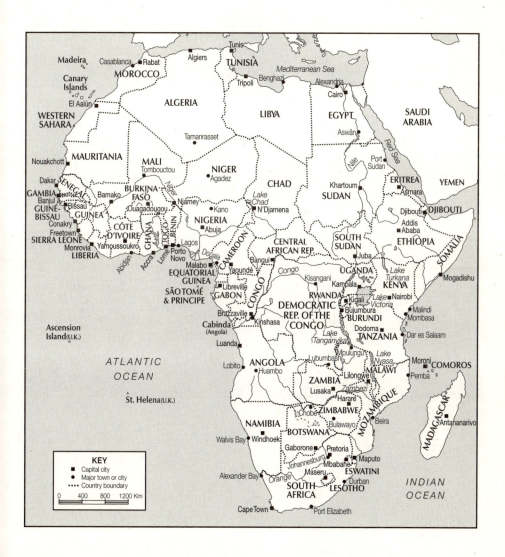

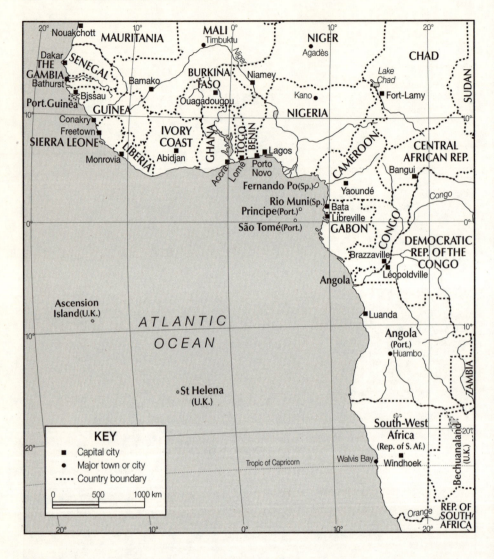

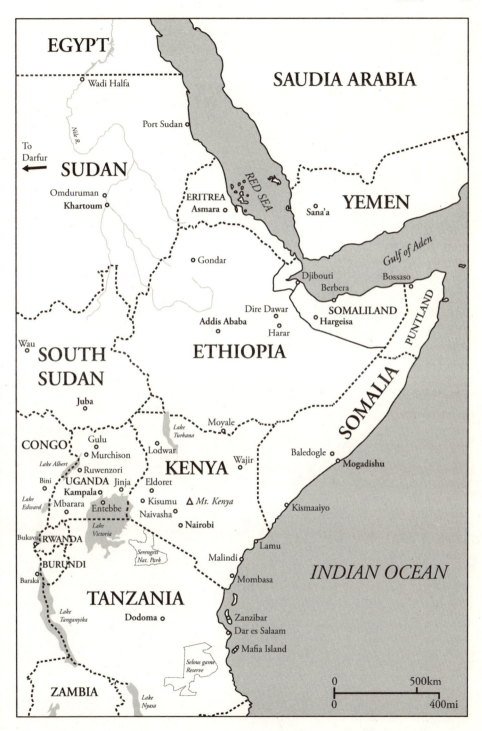

Author's note

A clear case needs to be made in a book that deals in great detail and consequence with Africa and much of its recent history in the immediate post-independence period. Critics will be quick to seek out racial issues from a South African author with an Afrikaner family background. That will happen, so we have to pre-empt with this clear statement of intent: *Takka Takka Bom Bom* deals with recent African history, much of it illuminating and hopeful, but sometimes tarnished by events that might be sensitive or controversial. I recall my own experiences with those issues in much the same way that historical films are screened abroad these days – movies like *Gone with the Wind* and the books of Ernest Hemingway or Evelyn Waugh – where it is usually stated prior to presentation that the language or terminology used is 'of the time' – in other words, the way things were then and not as they are today.

During World War I, or what our grandparents called the 'Great War', when the combined might of Britain and volunteers from London's far-flung dominions joined forces, parts of Africa saw a good deal of action, especially in regions colonised by Berlin.

With his unit, my father was sent to fight in German East Africa, then Tanganyika; their job was to battle the wily and astonishingly innovative German Colonel Paul von Lettow-Vorbeck. This remarkable strategist and his *Schutztruppe* continued fighting for four more years in an unforgiving African bush – his only recourse against a preponderant British colonial force that included tens of thousands of South Africans was his ability to keep a couple of steps ahead of those determined to destroy him.

Together with a remarkable bunch of local troops, listed in his daybooks as Askaris, ambushes followed with the Germans and their loyal African troops ending up running rings around the Allies. It was in that war that the modern-day machine gun came into its own, as it did on both sides of what the newspapers dubbed the 'Western Front'.

The only difference was that von Lettow-Vorbeck's Askaris used their native kiSwahili to clinch an onomatopoeic nomenclature and refer to the old, water-cooled Maxim machine guns as *takka takka bom boms*.

It made sense at the time.

Not an autobiography

In today's world, it would probably make headlines if an eight- or nine-year-old kid was shot at by his drunken stepfather as he ran down the road to the police station after his mother had been severely beaten. It happened several times in Piet Retief – a small town in what was then Eastern Transvaal – in the quiet years that followed World War II where I spent part of my earlier years. I only witnessed those brutalities – and then inadvertently – when I came home from boarding school.

In later years, I reflected that there had probably been many more such confrontations, some of which left my mom with a black eye or two and other head injuries. Of course, I was prepubescent and knew no better. I accepted that kind of violence as par for the course; my immature mind reasoned that if it was happening in my home, others must be experiencing the same.

For many years I hid the actual narrative of my home life from everybody. This is the first time I have written about the matter; mainly because I felt that dealing with the multitude of panoplies that subsequently shaped my life – those traumatic events – belittled both my family and me.

One of my lady friends with whom I was associated for many years suggested that my early childhood mishaps – secreted in the deep recesses of my subconscious – might have triggered the kind of complexities that damaged me psychologically and lasted pretty much into adulthood. She said that scars from such abuses rarely go away and she was probably right.

When I first shared those ghastly events, I was having a few ales with a war buddy in a particularly filthy conflict in a distant corner of Africa that I'd been covering. As the evening lingered on, we became more loquacious, and he confided that he had comfortably handled killing in action. He was pretty candid – as he declared matter-of-factly that he had done so 'quite often', adding that it was usually on Special Forces operations and more often than not behind enemy lines. 'It was a job…I did it,' he stated, 'and who was I to argue?'

'But' he continued, 'it's a very different proposition when you're in those final, critical moments – when everything is down to just you and him, and you're so close to the man you're attempting to snuff that you can smell his breath. You never forget those confrontational moments that end it all,' he whispered, adding, 'It's then that circumstances become pretty intimate, if you get the picture…'

I mentioned that I'd experienced something similar, the only difference being that it was my putative stepfather who had tried to shoot me. I suggested to my pal that some children might be expected to witness their mothers being beaten by their stepdads, and sometimes even real fathers. But, I reckoned, the attacker was more often than not 'blotto'. No question, though, Mom always came out of it damaged.

'All I was trying to do,' I explained, 'was to protect her.' I went on: 'That slobbering old bastard tried to kill me when I ran down the road to call the cops.'

In the process, confused and terrified, I admitted that there were times when the alcoholic shit was so close that I could smell his drink-addled breath. I proceeded to tell my buddy that those experiences involving my mother generated lingering memories that I've never quite been able to shake off. Going back a year or two from being shot at, my mother, having divorced my biological father, married an absolute cretin, then a bank manager in a small town in rural South Africa. Almost routinely, he would get plastered and start beating her. In those moments of mindless brutality that he seemed to thrive on, I would jump onto his back (for all the good *that* did), pummel him and then slip out the front door and run like hell. Moments later, having gathered himself together, he would rush into the bedroom, grab his rifle, head to the front porch, and start shooting at me as I disappeared into the shadows. There weren't many streetlights in the town in those days, and – even sober – the old sod was a poor shot. Lucky me…

Not that trying to tell the officer on duty at the front desk of the police station what had taken place did any good. In those days, immediately after the war in the mid-forties, the four most 'upstanding' men in town were the police chief, the mayor, the Dutch Reformed Church *dominee* and Boet Schoon, the alcoholic bank manager who married my mother. All four of those 'upstanding' social leaders were known to be as close as a bunch of cardinals in an inconclusive papal conclave, each one covering the other's back for a variety of indiscretions. Rumour had it that one of them had been screwing his domestic, a black woman, and made her pregnant. I never discovered the outcome of that impropriety.

In apartheid South Africa, in the simplest of language, whites fraternising with people of colour – as in just about all of Britain's colonies – was taboo. 'It never happened,' the pastors would preach, and the old folk would nod. It simply couldn't, they'd insist, though quite a few of them had probably savoured a few illicit dalliances in their day. More to the point, it happened on a massive scale. How else, after three centuries of colonisation – first by the Dutch and then the British – could South Africa have a community of more than three million people of mixed blood?

Yet, all things considered, this family drama was only an ancillary part of my personal travails at a very young age because the violence to which my mother was subjected went on for a long time. It ended when she attempted suicide. That old bastard had taken me on a fishing trip, which was abruptly cut short mid-afternoon because he needed his booze. So we headed home early, which is when we found my mother comatose with an empty bottle of pills next to her. It was one of the few weekends that the psycho wasn't under the influence; he acted promptly and she survived after having had her stomach pumped – thanks to the speedy arrival of a couple of medics from the local hospital. If not, she would most certainly have died.

Looking back, those experiences meant that very little could be described as halcyon in what was otherwise a fairly typical childhood, except that I was a midge when my mother first sent me to boarding school. I imagine she did it to keep me out of harm's way at home; in the broader view of events, I should have been left with a load of ugly paradoxes but fortunately, I wasn't.

It was significant throughout my earlier years, having moved back to Johannesburg after my mother left the malevolent wife-beater, that I started moving – though still relatively young – into a very different social circle. My new home was in Yeoville, a predominantly Jewish orthodox suburb to the immediate north of the city proper where I managed to assimilate a fair smattering of Yiddish, a delightfully expressive language.

Afrikaans background or not, living in close proximity to this community, it was inevitable that I would assimilate their customs and mannerisms, especially since the parents of most of my close buddies were émigrés from Eastern Europe, as had been my mother. It was the same thing that took place for more than a century east of London's Liverpool Street – the only difference being that South Africa had gold and diamonds in abundance. As with the California Gold Rush several decades before, word got around that money was to be made.

Coupled with that, my mom's dearest friend (with whom she had gone to school) was Dolly Sachs, sister of Violet Weinberg, who – with her husband Eli – served on the Central Committee of the South African Communist Party (SACP); clandestine of course. As house friends, I entrusted Eli to take the wedding photographs for my first wedding, being too naive to fully comprehend the political implications.

I got to know Sheila Weinberg, their daughter, quite well before she went on to play a significant role in Nelson Mandela's African National Congress (ANC) until her death in November 2004. But I was much closer to her brother Mark, who was perhaps two or three years younger than me, even though he was deaf from a car accident at a very early age. That didn't prevent him from qualifying as an actuary and living a normal social life that included nights out at our favourite pub, the Radium Beer Hall on Louis Botha Avenue, not far from his family home.

As with his parents, Mark became vigorously opposed to the racial injustices that had become commonplace in South Africa, to the extent that he refused to travel on segregated buses and would walk to work in the city and back home again to Orange Grove – usually barefoot and in solidarity with the Brothers. He died a tragic death in a gas accident while in the bath, and, since his parents were in prison at the time, it was left to Sheila to lay her brother to rest.

An interesting sidelight here is that while my mother – with Christian roots – was born in Germany, her friends were the Jewish girls with whom she'd grown up: the Joffes, Cohens, Sachses, Bermans, Rubins – and our lovely neighbours, the quiet-spoken Chaitowitzes – together with many others from Johannesburg's northern suburbs.

Like her sister, Dolly Sachs was also a senior member of the Central Committee of the South African Communist Party: it seems the entire family had the Marxist bug. Her husband, Bennie Sachs, was editor of the *Jewish Times* and the uncle of the South African former ANC leader, Albie Sachs, also a card-carrying communist and former KGB operative in his day.

For all the drama, I did learn a few sharp lessons as a youngster; if I hadn't, you probably wouldn't be reading this or even begun to share the multitude of exploits that followed. These included my meeting *le Grand Docteur* Albert Schweitzer at his jungle hospital in Gabon a few months before he died. That event took place not far from the same region where Joseph Conrad meandered at the turn of the century and from where the backdrop to his unforgettable *Heart of Darkness* emerged, with its disturbing depiction of white savagery on black.

And then going into a beleaguered Beirut with an Israeli invasion force led by Ariel Sharon – we called him Ariq – and whom we, as well as quite a few others, acknowledged as one of the classic military commanders of the past century.

Or spending a couple of months in the co-pilot's seat of an ageing Soviet helicopter gunship that leaked when it rained. Our role was to try and shoot rebels using machetes to chop off the arms and legs of children and old women in an utterly dysfunctional guerrilla war in Sierra Leone. We had no difficulty distinguishing friend from foe – the insurgents we sought were generally fuelled by hate, rot-gut gin and dope – most of whom seemed to enjoy dismembering those most vulnerable. That West African civil war left behind a multitude of disfigurements, mainly because there were a couple of hundred thousand innocents involved, the majority targeted by barbarians who often ate their victims.

That horrific custom befell my old buddy, Bob MacKenzie, a former American Special Forces operator and Vietnam veteran. Before he was killed, Bob had fought as a hired gun in various wars – Rhodesia's included – as a SAS operator. He accompanied me to El Salvador to cover another bloody struggle and several other adventures he was reluctant to discuss – because we suspected at the time that another of his paymasters might have been Langley. MacKenzie would definitely have slotted into the role of a valued Central Intelligence Agency asset.

His widow, Sibyl, later told me that after he took the job as commander of a combat force battling rebels in Sierra Leone, Bob was captured by the rebels during a frontal onslaught in that West African jungle and tortured to death. The rebels wasted no time cutting out his heart and passing it around for everybody to have a bite; in their befuddled minds, it was a mark of great respect for an incredibly brave man. I should mention that Sibyl was the daughter of Ray Cline, one of the best-known, long-standing CIA operators and regarded in his heyday as the 'Company's' senior analyst during the Cuban missile crisis.

He was a top man in the agency when Bob met Sibyl – it might have been written that they should meet – when Cline invited Bob to dinner during a brief visit to headquarters from his latest adventure.

In recording people's lives – like mine – I have purposely avoided using the word autobiography because some might regard it as pretentious and, anyway, few are worth more than cursory interest. Oscar Wilde had it right when he declared that a biography is a mesh through which our real-life escapades are revealed – and I suppose that would apply to me.

So, anybody seated within the lonely confines of four walls with only a keyboard for company – and possibly getting involved in an all-embracing stretch of writing that could last several months – needs to have something unusual and captivating to relate to if it is to amount to much. Lose the plot – as legions of publishers who have commissioned what at first appears to be a promising title, and it fails to deliver – and the reader will close the covers and turn on the television instead.

And so, one has to ask, what do minor souls like this nonentity do when they have a story to tell? In my case, it's not so much a single event or a flurry of experiences but rather an emotive series of narratives involving life as it was lived – rarely dull and often unnerving. Apart from time spent covering wars in Africa, the Middle East, Central Asia, and others (and spending time in a few prisons), there were quite a few significant events that never made Page One.

A handful, like the Biafran War, which ended with a million people dead, most of whom were children – and Mali, a conflict I covered in 2021 – were horrific. In truth, I never quite got over the Nigerian debacle because the first thing I did when I got home to South Africa was to write a book on the people of mixed parentage classified 'Coloured' in South Africa, the majority living in the Cape as I did. My objective was to castigate the apartheid government for the idiotic laws to which they subjected these poor souls.[1]

---

1   Al J. Venter, *Coloured: A Profile of Two Million South Africans*. Human & Rousseau: Cape Town, 1974.

In the course of visiting the front lines of some of these conflicts, some were generally fought over imaginary contours drawn in the sand; I rarely trusted the kind of publicity that such events generated. Most times, they were either sourced by well-funded public relations companies, or, more frequently, in later phases, self-serving United Nations press releases. In one instance, relying on supposedly reliable news reports, I was arrested on espionage charges in the Congo while trying to get back into an Angola being ripped apart by civil combat that went on for 30-something years.

There were several such experiences, including gunrunning into the United States or heading into what is today irreverently referred to by some as 'Hezbollahland' in South Lebanon. I returned to the Levant many times as the civil war progressed, in between spending time with Christian forces in a fragmented and all-but-devastated Beirut that was struggling to breathe as Islamic and Israeli bombardments rained mortar bombs and incendiaries over our heads.

I went back there in December 2018 but didn't stay long because so much had changed. I discovered that soon enough because the Jihadists took an unusual interest in my presence in what remains an extremely unsettled zone along the northern border with Israel. As a result, I stayed for a few days at the United Nations base at Naqoura, a lonely place for transients – I was the only guest in an enormous new hotel. That worried me, as did the place's security. I slept, as the expression goes, with one eye open. The following morning, I wasted no time grabbing a cab and heading back to more familiar Beirut environments to which I was better accustomed, where I sensed that a bunch of not-so-discreet undercover tails checked my every move.

Who knows to whom those Shi'ite agents were reporting? There was no question that they knew exactly who I was, even before I had set out to Naqoura from Beirut. In the final stages of that visit to South Lebanon, my taxi was stopped at a roadblock just after we left Tyre. A young man approached and asked me in perfect English, even before I'd identified myself: 'Where are you headed, Mr Venter?'

After all the rigmarole involving military and government offices to obtain the requisite authorities to enter what numerous roadside posters declared a 'Restricted Zone', he would have known exactly where I was going and why. We spoke briefly while he checked my passport and documents, during which time I casually asked him where in the UK he came from.

He didn't turn his head when he answered, 'Kilburn...you know that part of London, I'm sure,' he replied.

Having made his point, he signalled the driver to proceed.

During an out-of-the-ordinary but rather ill-defined career, I'd obviously met a host of people, some in the same game as me and many others, like the young Londoner on a distant and all-but deserted road in Lebanon. The majority were affable, but I also encountered my share of 'hostiles', including several that might have ended things very differently had I not been imbued with an innate suspicion of anyone who took more than a cursory interest in my well-being. Or possibly, the assignment in which I might have been involved with just then.

In my earlier days (also Israeli-linked), I exposed a major KGB operative in Rhodesia, which happened quite by accident, through an Israeli contact who might himself have been linked to Mossad. That caused the suspect to flee back to Europe; had he not done so, the South Africans or the Rhodesians would have iced him. I deal with that matter more comprehensively in a later chapter.

Other notable events included working for – or involvement in one way or another with – several intelligence agencies like the CIA, for whom I produced a film on the war in Afghanistan, then subjected to a Soviet invasion, similar to what is now happening in the Ukraine; South African military intelligence (which, in my case was obvious, because I was born there); the Portuguese secret service; Israel, as well as something of an event that ended up with Britain's intelligence and had long-term implications.

In that little episode, I channelled everything through my old pal, Frederick Forsyth, with whom I'd spent time in Biafra more than half a century ago. What I didn't know until very recently was that Freddie had an equally illustrious series of experiences to recount since he had been working for Britain's Secret Intelligence Service – better known to those involved as 'Friends' (and MI6 to the general public) – a good deal longer than I'd been active.

For obvious reasons, Forsyth's service with Britain's SIS will never be fully told, but like me, he is fortunate to still be around to tell his story, or part of it, anyway. As he said in a letter to me, together with his biography published a while back:[2] 'It is good to see that after a lifetime of (mainly) African hell-holes and danger zones, you seem to have settled, still alive, and against the odds in the warm embrace of an English town.' In closing, he added a typical Forsyth contemplative touch: 'I suspect that we shouldn't still be around. But we are, so raise a pint in the pub to our sheer good luck!' It was no surprise that the letter was banged out on his trusty old Olivetti typewriter – and that in an age when we'd all embraced computers a generation before. But then that's the Freddie I got to know – a stickler for tradition – though he has since taken a computer course and moved on.

I'd imagine that much of what took place in those distant days centred on the adage coined by someone who, probably tongue-in-cheek, declared that life seems to be little more than an endurance test with no prizes or plans.

---

2   Frederick Forsyth, *The Outsider: My Life in Intrigue*. Corgi: 2016.

FREDERICK FORSYTH

29th February 2016

My dear Al,

I was gratified, surprised and very much impressed to receive a copy of your book. It is a tour de force and clearly represents a fearsome amount of work.

There is almost a pretty intimidating amount of references to myself - I have not yet had the balls to delve into them all, but I will as soon as I can and hope they are reasonably benign!!

And as to the dedication, well..... wow and thank you. It is good to see that after a lifetime of (mainly) African hellholes and danger zones you appear to have settled, still alive against the odds, in the warm embrace of a West Country English town.

I enclose a volume of my own recent (September) utterance and I suspect that both books show that, by the odds, we shouldn't really be still around. But we are, so raise a paint in the pub to our sheer good luck!!

All best,

Freddie

CHAPTER I

Africa, the great continent with an appeal all its own

Going from primary school in a small South African town to covering hostilities in a spate of wars in Africa, the Middle East and Central America was an unlikely career choice for someone with an unassuming background who tended towards a bit of adventure. So was my subsequent link to intelligence work for half a dozen nations, including doing 'something interesting' for the Central Intelligence Agency in Afghanistan during that nation's Soviet war.

I was a pretty ordinary kid, underweight and without the sort of muscle needed to handle myself in a scrap. That came later in the South African Navy when our training instructors at Saldanha Bay on the icy Atlantic coast of southern Africa knocked seven or eight hundredweight of shit into us to make men of recalcitrant boys. It was a strict and tough regimen, though it had its moments. Most of us were fresh out of school and thrust in at the deep end of learning about age-old maritime rituals like splicing hawsers, morning parades to hoist the flag, rowing whalers inherited from the Royal Navy, and the occasional 'run ashore' that suggested illicit brews – and, for the first time in my life – mind-blowing hangovers.

We also ran weekly half-marathons in the arid Western Cape countryside – where those who couldn't keep up left their breakfasts on the side of tracks made by the soles of thousands of others before. As one of our smarmy petty officers said when another trainee was hauled off to the sick bay, 'You shouldn't be here if you can't take a joke, wanker!'

My steps towards adulthood were multifarious, but I suppose an inherent stubbornness, distilled by the kind of intransigence that creates rebels – probably inculcated by my German and Boer antecedents – had something to do with it: after all, my forefathers on both fronts had fought bitter wars against the British. Almost all our instructors at the naval base were ex-Royal Navy and were hardly a rum lot because having come through the last war, most of them unscathed – it was only a decade after Führer's war had ended – they reacted with kindness when they spotted a need.

My peregrinations through Africa followed naval service, and writing about the continent north of the Limpopo became easier when I was able to overlook its ructions, especially when it's your own often dubious and rambunctious exploits in focus.

Nevertheless, Africa – a continent that was both volatile and on the cusp of new adventures – mostly in those countries that had recently been granted the right to run their own affairs, free from their former colonial masters – embraced a sometimes-contradictory enchantment all its own. In those distant 1960s days, travel was a pleasure, and we mixed easily with a panoply of African people who were as astonished at the new political order of things as we were. At the end of my many years of travel throughout Africa, I had visited all the countries in Africa, except Mauretania.

Despite its diverse and often intimidating foibles, the great continent has a unique appeal of its own, sometimes lost on city-dwellers. European and American magazines and newspapers are full of Kenyan and southern African wildlife thrills; in reality, there is more to Africa, much more.

For those who have ventured into the pristine, unspoilt wilds and forest country of Africa and inhaled its red dust a few times – usually unconsciously, because that's how it goes – or listened to the mellifluous flow of women calling across the hills from one village to another, sirens of a totally different culture – one rarely forgets those moments. So too with the distinctive whiff of raw wood smoke wafting up from the kraals at sunset.

Lasting sensations – yes, some of which cannot be adequately described in words. They still resonate with some of us though, buried in the distant mist of memories that older folk rekindle when they reminisce about days long past – the legacies of an Africa long gone.

Alan Paton, a delightful man I only got to know fleetingly because he was usually in one part of Africa while I was traipsing around in another, captured it vividly in the opening paragraph of *Cry, the Beloved Country*. That book is still one of the great literary works to emerge from South Africa's troubled, more recent history. He wrote about a corner of South Africa that unfolds across the northern approaches to the Wild Coast, a vast, relatively untamed area he adored. His words were: 'There is a lovely road which runs from Ixopo into the hills. These hills are grass-covered and rolling, and they are lovely beyond any singing of it.'

I have yet to find a more compelling introduction to anything I've read.

I recently went back to the Wild Coast on my way to one of the lodges that hosts the scuba-diving mob that descends on this stretch of coast during the annual Sardine Run each winter. I found that an awful lot had changed there as well.

The road south out of Durban takes you through Lusikisiki, a small town that in its day was as delightful as its name. No longer: the place is a pullulating, overcrowded mishmash of traders and market mammies, the majority drowned in the cacophony of modern-day African music, which bears little resemblance to some of the greats like Ladysmith Black Mambazo, Miriam Makeba, or the more contemporaneous Johnny Clegg, whose life was tragically cut short – we were all sad to see him go.

No question, the continent has its problems and Lusikisiki will always be a small cog in Africa's great multicultural social wheel where little matters more than where your next meal is coming from or who is buying the beer. This is neither Europe nor America; things have never been so bad that some of us *wazungus,* as Swahili-speaking people like to refer to us have not hankered to return. And that despite the kind of contentious issues that only Africa can generate and rarely get adequate mention abroad. I would go back tomorrow, but time, I fear – as the years edge ever upward – simply does not allow it.

As my long-time friend and colleague Mirella Ricciardi – that delightful Kenyan photographer and author – who, as she phrased it not long ago after she'd severed her umbilical tie to the African continent and went to live in London, wrote: 'When you have been born in Africa you are marked by Africa, and wherever you go, you are a displaced person, for you have two identities.'

Conditions are very different today, and whereas it was fairly safe to move about the continent until relatively recently, there are many destinations where it has become perilous. We know about the Congo, Somalia, northern Mozambique, Liberia and Chad, but there are many more.

While covering the war for Britain's *Jane's Intelligence Review* in the Central African Republic in 2019, the commander of the combat unit I was with didn't allow me to go anywhere unless an eight-man bodyguard accompanied me. It was worse in Mali in late 2021, this time for *Jane's Defence Weekly*, where I could not move beyond our base gates unless I travelled in a convoy of three or four armoured vehicles – and with even more troops to guard me.

Issues were graphically illustrated while in Bamako, Mali's capital, where I was required to have a Covid test to fly home. That involved a relatively short drive from our base at Camp Bifrost near the airport towards the centre of that great city that straddles the Niger River. It was once a plum posting in the French colonial epoch, but no longer. It took us 15 minutes to reach the outskirts of the main city on the south bank, but the final 800 metres before we reached the American Hospital (where the test was administered) became a grinding, utterly exasperating and disharmonic shuffle-and-shout of barely moving vehicles, grinding gears, all brutally interrupted by snatched lanes in a chaotic jumble of traffic. That short leg should have taken minutes; instead, it lasted almost two hours.

Our four armoured vehicles, with their requisite complement of eight or ten bodyguards – supposedly for our protection – would not have been able to retaliate had we been attacked because they were effectively 'locked in'. Worse, the Jihadists were perfectly aware of that threat, and it was only a matter of time before they put it to use. My view, I told my hosts, the NATO-linked officers in charge both times, was that the overblown protection routine was counterproductive. I was the only man not in uniform, and white – like most of my protectors – and the enemy would soon know that I was possibly a valuable asset (even though I was only a scribbler, but they didn't know that). So, it would not take their imams long to decide on what action to take. Anyway, we were never attacked, but the next correspondent or TV team covering those West African wars might not be so lucky.

Africa has changed in many other ways. A simple spin through the heart of Lagos's central business district (CBD) on Victoria Island – which soon becomes a very long one and where there are sometimes six or eight lanes of traffic simultaneously going in different directions (or barely moving because of gridlock) – and you quickly come to appreciate the real meaning of bedlam. It's two or three times worse in the Congo's Kinshasa, regarded by just about every diplomat ever stationed there as probably the most chaotic city on any continent in which to drive.

Or trying to persuade a traffic officer in one of Mozambique's towns that you were not speeding, to the point where you would show him on your dash-cam that you were travelling at fifty kilometres an hour (and not eighty as he claimed), usually preceded by a demand for a 'little something to ease your passage' – you get the gist.

It's the same in any one of several dozen sub-Saharan African capitals (with Cairo not far behind), and with decades of inadequate urban planning unfulfilled – coupled with bankrupt exchequers – things are not likely to ever improve. The reasons are basic and start with the reality that just about every major city in Africa is flooded with ever-growing masses of people; the majority have little money, no work, few opportunities and hopeless prospects for the future. Small wonder so many of them are trying to reach Europe.

What is interesting about Africa is that its inhabitants generally tend to put their problems aside once the troubles have passed. More often than not, the residents slot back routinely into their everyday lives. The same with today's generation, the majority entranced by some of the stories that have emerged from family and others over the years: overland treks in the tradition of the American 'Wild West', battling locals for land and the few possessions they had, usually wildlife. There were also ivory hunters and, of course, endless stories about experiences in the bush, which generally started at the edge of the town where most of them lived in the old days.

Peculiarly, notions about Africa are very different in Europe and America, where the focus today is fixated on enslaved people. Yet, few of those protagonists know that most of these poor souls shipped across the Atlantic to the so-called 'New World' came from West Africa, which was eventually dominated by French and British colonial interests. South Africa also had slaves – a legacy of the Dutch who first colonised the Cape – the majority coming from Holland's possessions in the East Indies, which included present-day Indonesia and Malaysia.

Long before that, Arab slavers had already dug deep into East Africa's backwaters for their victims, the majority sent in chains to the Middle East and whose descendants can be seen today among some of the dark-skinned nationals of countries like Egypt, Sudan and the entire Arabian Peninsula which includes the Yemen.

That said, this great continent does have some serious issues that need to be dealt with, but things are hardly ever so bad that people stop going there. Indeed, more foreign passport holders are living in Africa today than in earlier years, and long before the reader has closed the covers of this book, still more will have strolled through the arrivals hall at the Oliver Tambo International Airport in Johannesburg or Nairobi's Embakazi. May it always be so.

Yet it was Africa's discord that initially put this scribe on his personal road to perdition on what Europe's early chroniclers would sometimes perniciously refer to as the 'Dark Continent'. Yes, it was 'dark' but mostly in their perceptions because had it been half as gloomy as they liked to project, Europe would never have fallen over itself to arbitrarily claim vast tracts of it. You need to get into Thomas Pakenham's superlative *The Scramble for Africa* to even begin to understand Africa's often understated colonial traditions.

My own understanding of this colossus was very different from that of most visitors who make an initial acquaintance with Africa. My first overland jaunt probably set the scene for my career. I was at school in Johannesburg, and during a one-month-long vacation, my father – at my request – handed me a rail ticket to visit classmates in Northern Rhodesia, Zambia today.

I took the train north from Jo'burg, together with the rest of my pals at the start of my holidays, but just for the hell of it, when the vacation ended, I decided to hitchhike home – all of 14 years old with very little cash in my pocket. I took a bet that I would beat the train on that almost three-day journey. And that I managed to do, my first real gamble against the odds. The trip was exhilarating from the word go because the road ahead stretched almost 2,400 kilometres from Chililabombwe, north of Kitwe (almost on the Congolese frontier), all the way back to Marist Brothers College in Johannesburg.

Now I reckon I must have had more than a dash of chutzpah to do something quite so outrageous; my parents were appalled. At the time, it seemed to be the kind of challenge that appealed; in later years, such urges came naturally.

I did something similar seven years later when I left the navy, once again using my thumb to hike from Cape Town to Mombasa, where I managed the persuade the first officer of the Norwegian ship *Thorscape* – berthed at Kilindini Docks during its routine run between Canada and the East Coast of Africa – to take me with them to Montreal. That was something you could do before insurance companies started to impose their impossibly draconian legal strictures. And let's face it, you had to be young, impetuous, and just a little foolhardy to do such a thing. Fortunately, I qualified in all three prerequisites.

Later, after finishing my studies in London, I headed home to make a place for myself in South African society, such it was. But in those days – and here I'm talking about the 1960s – travelling by air tended to be arduous, though the old Union Castle Line did offer a sometimes boisterous alternative by sea that could last a fortnight.

If you flew from London to Johannesburg, as I did the first time, it took three long days in a prop-driven Super Constellation passenger plane to travel down the length of the continent. We would put our heads down in nightly stopovers, usually in places with exciting names like Khartoum (of Kitchener fame), Ndola, Kisumu (lying spread-eagled over rows of small hills on the eastern shores of Lake Victoria), or depending on the airline, Douala in Cameroon. There was a stimulating combination of untested adventure in that mix, including the possibility – remote, but it happened in the days of prop-driven passenger planes – of belly-landing in one of Africa's great lakes.

The airline I flew with was called Trek Airways (in itself a somewhat disconcerting appellation), but it was low-cost and, the company had a reasonable flight record, many of its pilots had flown bombers in the war. Their responsibilities centred on eighty of us squeezed tight on board in narrow seats and travelling at a magnificent 482 kilometres an hour in an aircraft developed during Hitler's war. Most were initially built as the Lockheed Aircraft Corporation's answer to the venerable old Douglas DC-6. In our eyes, the machine was massive; most of us had grown up in an epoch of Piper Cubs and Hawker Hurricanes – on home-grown turf. South Africans rarely saw wartime behemoths like the Lancaster or Boeing's B-17 Flying Fortress.

Yet, by yesterday's standards, those antiquated but astonishingly reliable aircraft were perfectly adequate for the journey, even if the Lockheed L-1049's empty take-off weight was only about 30 tons, compared to the almost 300 tons fielded by the Airbus A380 today.

To us simple souls, the journey from Europe to Africa was, if not a challenge, then without doubt the most enlivening experience around for those who could afford it. At the same time, with air safety still in its infancy, the 8,000-kilometre trip was not without risk. In those long-ago days, quite a few trans-African flights ended in disaster. Still, if all went well, the long, cramped and uncomfortable hauls with few amenities were always quite jolly events – even if the privations to which we were subjected were unimaginable by today's super-jet standards.

Three issues of paramount importance needed to be covered for the duration: decent beds for nightly stopovers, loos that worked and, of course, enough liquor to dull imponderables. Certainly, some of the morning katzenjammers on the three-day trip were de rigueur.

Overnight stays in some of the locations en route – attended to by squads of immaculately clad Africans in spanking white suits and red fezzes – were a relic of a colonial tradition that went back a century or two. The flight companies did their bit by offering the passengers food and drink and, if we were lucky, the kind of frivolity that could sometimes go on until the bus arrived at dawn to take us to the airport for the next leg.

CHAPTER 2

Home by five

Looking back on life as it circuitously unravels, it is almost as if it is sourced from a cognitive unwinding ball of string: things go rolling round and round. During the process, previous mistakes are often repeated. All manner of images emerge, some sobering, others quite entertaining – like my father first telling me about *takka takka bom boms* – which he probably did to keep me amused. The concept must have caught my fancy because I recall laughing about it as he sounded off.

Dad was never a cheerful sort, having had a tough life from an early age, being the oldest son of a large brood of indigents and leaving school early to start work to help support his family. He was a resolute type – a quality I suspect I might have inherited. Dad was self-educated – he taught himself shorthand because he believed that skill would come in handy at some stage – and it did, which might be why he progressed rapidly once he'd joined the railways.

Before this, a lot had happened, including the 'Great War' and serving in the army in Tanganyika against the same indomitable Colonel Paul von Lettow-Vorbeck giving Allied forces the right royal run-around. I recall Dad once saying that this was where he first heard the rattle of machine guns for real – his unit having been caught in an ambush somewhere close to Tanga – the biggest German town on the coast, immediately to the east of Kilimanjaro. At that time, a future South African prime minister, Jannie Smuts, was commanding the Allied show against German forces in Tanganyika. This was quite a change from fighting British troops on horseback in the Boer War only a few years before – and despite being well-seasoned in guerrilla tactics – he was never able to get to grips with the elusive German.

London seemed to have other things in mind for Smuts; his admirable attributes as a leader appeared to have been recognised relatively early on. He was soon called to Britain, possibly just as well – that colonel in Tanganyika with his unconventional bush skills became the only German officer in the 'Great War' never to surrender. When the armistice was signed, von Lettow-Vorbeck marched his troops across the border into Northern Rhodesia and laid down his arms before returning to Europe.[1]

Over time, Smuts, now in London, became a close friend and confidant of Winston Churchill and was eventually called on to serve in the British War Cabinet in World War II, having been elevated to the upper echelons of military service as a field marshal in the British Army. Jan Christiaan Smuts was the only colonial officer who achieved that distinction, and the irony is matchless since he had fought a fierce and brutal war against those same imperial colleagues who ended up, if not embracing him, then according him great tribute.

Some curious stories emerged during that period, including Smuts, in his native Afrikaans, disarmingly telling Churchill during a cabinet meeting in London – when he felt that the old bulldog was surpassing himself: '*Nou praat jy kak, Winnie!*' (Now you're talking shit, Winnie!). To Smuts, Churchill was always 'Winnie', and the British leader fondly reciprocated by calling his erstwhile Boer adversary 'Jannie'.

My father, having returned to South Africa after the 'Great War', went back to the railways and must have done quite well because he was soon running complex services that involved freight coming into South Africa from the Belgian Congo and the two Rhodesias. Another major war followed and Dad was tasked with handling shipping at what was then one of Africa's larger harbours, Port Elizabeth, or simply 'PE'. His official title was Port Goods Superintendent, which said nothing about his role as coordinator of Allied maritime convoys heading out of Algoa Bay (where the harbour lies). Undoubtedly a sensitive job, it must have surprised some of his colleagues since he was married to a woman who had not only been born in Germany, but still spoke the language whenever her family came to visit.

For Mom and Dad, the job meant two things: firstly, it gave them the security they had been working towards, together with a lovely big house within the precincts of the harbour. Secondly, I arrived.

My mother was a senior nurse and worked nights. My father's time was taken up with secretive shipping issues; since South Africa was one of the first countries to follow Britain into the war, he had his hands full organising wartime freight. Thus, they were each immersed in their own domains. Only years later did I learn that among his tasks was the shipment of munitions to Britain and Allied forces in Egypt, Port Elizabeth being the country's principal despatch point for those cargoes. He was rarely home before my bedtime, and it's surprising they even had time for procreation.

---

1   James Ambrose Brown, *They Fought for King and Country*. Ashanti: 1996. One of the best books to materialise from that East African campaign (mainly restricted to Tanganyika, a German colony until the war ended). A reviewer commented: 'Fighting under gruelling conditions and against a resourceful foe, the South African soldiers performed admirably.'

Apart from keeping all the freight that passed through the docks moving, Dad had a hand in coordinating major naval convoys that called in at Port Elizabeth, heading to or from Europe, the Middle East or Australasia. This came home rather sharply to this little boy – I was perhaps four years old – when he arrived home one evening totally distressed. He was all nerves and, big man that he was, unashamedly in tears.

Naturally, I was far too young to understand the situation. Still, some of that emerged years later when Dad explained that one of his responsibilities had been to arrange for the transportation of several hundred Italian prisoners of war to a destination that I'd never established: he had to get them on board the ship. Most of these POWs had been taken captive when South African forces – at the vanguard of a significant Allied force based in Kenya – invaded Italian-held Abyssinia and routed Benito Mussolini's pompous *Regio Esercito* legions. One of the architects of that operation, which lasted 18 months and involved tens of thousands of South African soldiers, was Orde Wingate, maverick leader of Haile Selassie's guerrilla-orientated Gideon Force. This was the same man who created the acclaimed Chindit deep-penetration missions into Japanese-held territory during the Burma Campaign.

My father's distress stemmed from the fact that the day before, all the Italian POWs were taken aboard a freighter, and being wartime, hatches were battened – standard procedure when moving troops – both with Allied and Axis naval forces. It was an essential precaution to prevent prisoners from causing problems en route. With everything in place and my father having signed off, the convoy sailed, and the freighter was torpedoed by a German U-boat. It was struck amidships barely an hour after it had cleared Port Elizabeth's roadstead. The prisoners were trapped below deck as the ship sank within minutes – very few survived. I've dived that area often enough to know that sharks would have been another problem for those who had been unable to extricate themselves and swim free.

Once Dad got home, and something was clearly amiss, I was taken to my room by my mother. I vaguely remember talk about the city's King's Beach being littered with scores of dead washed up on shore during the night. My brother, Jannie, who was at school, recalled being driven down to the sea with a group of fellow students for their morning swim and then being turned back as soon as the beach came into view.

Life was not all gloom and doom for this little 'un, living on the verge of an extremely sensitive and top-security wartime harbour. I couldn't have asked for more.

I was still too young for school, and since Dad was busy with wartime work and Mom would sleep during the day because she worked nights, I was left pretty much to my own devices. Though we could afford domestic help, they had their work cut out, so I could wander far and wide into the rail marshalling yards towards the rear of the house. It was a playground from heaven – acres of steam engines chugging about and shunting rail cars, together with staff who knew that I was the boss's son and they should keep a wary eye on what I was doing.

There was a little girl named Claire whose family lived in one of the railway houses on the road adjoining the docks, and curiously, I remember her well as she was my only real friend. And I hers, since there were no other children that I recall. Claire and I decided that her father's old jalopy – probably a pre-war Chevy or Ford – needed redecorating. The two of us obliged with a can of yellow paint we found in the rail yard. That was serious, and I expect my father sorted it out, but it must have cost him a packet. I was reprimanded but not smacked, though I would get cuffed for much less by my mother, who was big on kids being seen but not heard. However, I got the thrashing of my life when she returned home early one morning and found me on the far side of the major road that topped the railyards; Humewood Road, I seem to remember. It was rush hour, and on my own, I'd threaded my way through the heavy traffic.

Following his Port Elizabeth posting, Dad was transferred to Johannesburg, where he headed the largest rail freight clearing centre in Africa at the time, at Kaserne. I recall nothing of the move, except that we lived in a large house in Berea, one of the first residential suburbs north of the CBD. My mother used her talents to put the Edith Cavell Nursing Home on the map, and Dad bought several adjoining houses. I'm not sure why she named it after Edith Cavell, since the Germans had executed that famous British nursing sister as a spy during World War I.

Clearly, my family was in the money because Johannesburg was *the* place for anybody with initiative. Once again, I was allowed to do just about anything I liked, provided I was home for supper at five.

It was also time for me to be sent to a proper school – a kindergarten for Grades 1 and 2. Mom arranged for James, a huge Zulu and my closest confidant, to take me to classes a quarter mile down the road; he'd fetch me again early afternoon, walking in both directions. James was responsible for my evening bath, and I have only fond memories of this lovely man who spoke more Zulu than English. I must have got on well with him – he never raised a hand to me – though most of the nurses at Edith Cavell regarded me as a terror reincarnate.

Apart from some new Jewish friends living in Olivia Road from whom I picked up my smattering of Yiddish, James was basically my only extraneous link with the outside world. I was probably five or six by then. I asked Dad about James some years later. He told me that the big guy had died in a knife fight, quite commonplace in South African cities in those days.

There was one other aspect of life in Johannesburg that, despite being extremely violent and highly inappropriate, I took for granted – an annual Christmas Day occurrence. As with the Aborigines in Australia and America's Indians, South

Africa's Zulus, Xhosas, and other tribes were introduced to hard liquor by the white man. As South Africa moved into the modern period, almost everybody drank. However, for the African community, Christmas meant festivity, and the tribes would drink themselves motherless from the moment they opened their eyes that joyous morning.

After my family's annual festive meal, things started to happen for the younger generation. Lunch over, the adults would disappear for their customary siestas while we kids headed out into the streets to see how many dead people were lying around. There were always dozens, and it was the same each year. Apart from getting sloshed, Christmas also seemed to our inebriated African friends that time of the year to settle old scores, which meant fights galore, some with age-old Zulu *knobkieries* (a large club or cudgel with a big round knob at one end) that was used to land with great force on the head of an adversary. A well-placed blow would cleave open an opponent's skull often with terminal consequences. There was no point calling the police in those days – the cops rarely arrested the perpetrators. At any other time, the perpetrators would be taken into custody, but not on Christmas Day.

In Johannesburg's Berea and Hillbrow suburbs it happened in just about every street, so there must have been many hundreds, possibly a thousand casualties across the city, with bodies left where they lay until the 'meat trucks' arrived. There were also numerous stabbings, but the belligerent Zulus preferred smashing heads. We would come upon these bodies lying in the streets, some barely alive, some not, quite a few with their brains exposed. Later that afternoon, in hushed tones, we children would gather and compare notes about the atrocities we'd just seen. Like who had observed the worst atrocity?

There was never 'anything worse'. It was all horrendous, though we accepted it as par, for no other reason than this bloodshed was a regular annual event until my mother and I moved elsewhere.

I never did follow up on that so-called festive season carnage, but matters must have eased in due course, though every city had its share of unbridled violence. Indeed, all those horrid and bloody events are on record in the country's newspaper and library archives.

My fifth year on this planet turned into a momentous twelve months. Apart from attending kindergarten – I still recall Mrs Short, the headmistress – a kindly lady who ended up having a few unusual problems with me that were not entirely of my own making. I also remember my folks getting the occasional phone call from somebody I'd never met but referred to as my 'Uncle George' and who was, as the colloquialism termed it, 'Up North'. That meant that George, my mother's youngest brother, was a soldier fighting that terrible man named Hitler. My Uncle George was one of 330,000 South Africans of all races who volunteered for military service 'Up North' as it was referred to in the old Union.[2]

The South African military, both the army and an air force seconded to the RAF – followed by a fledgling navy – fought some tough battles against Rommel. Once they had cleared North Africa of Axis powers in the aftermath of the Battle of El Alamein, they moved on to Italy, where the South African 6th Armoured Division came under the overall command of General Mark Clark's Fifth Army. Mom always took great interest in what George was doing which, in retrospect, wasn't all that peculiar because they were of German extraction. This might have been unusual in Britain at the time, but not in the United States, where many Americans of German origin also existed.

That year, a turning point in our lives came when my brother Jannie and I were sent off to my grandfather's farm near Lydenburg. That two-week escapade turned into a disaster because I lost a finger by sticking my hand into the delivery end of a milling machine which promptly sliced it off.

Perhaps twenty minutes after that accident, I vividly remember my grandfather pulling the antiquated single-horse carriage from the shed (it was wartime and fuel was rationed), loading up my brother and me, and heading to the town hospital. A local doctor did a terrible job stitching me up; they had to do it again, this time under my mother's supervision at the Edith Cavell. I imagine that a record of my admission is somewhere in the hospital archives since it was there that I was first taken for surgery.

My parents had received a phone call from the local police station in the middle of the night telling them their son had had 'a terrible accident', which was not the case. Then the line went dead, probably because wartime communications were not what they should have been. For hours, they tried to call back, but nothing worked. By then, my mother was in a panicked state, probably imagining the worst. Finally, totally distraught, she pushed my father onto a train to sort things out.

An interesting sidelight here is that I cannot watch anybody working in the kitchen with a knife ever since that somewhat unheralded amputation. It appears that I never quite got over it. To make matters worse, I was no sooner back at school – the bandages having been removed – than I was fooling around in the playground and opened the wound on a rusty sheet of corrugated iron, which I later heard, alarmed the teachers more than it did me. A phone call brought trusty old James running and my having another procedure.

---

2   The South Africans who volunteered to fight Germany comprised approximately 200,000 whites, 80,000 blacks and 40,000–50,000 Coloureds/Malays. All were volunteers – regardless of whether they were career soldiers/airmen/seamen, mobilised part-time reservists, or hostilities-only enlistments – a truly remarkable achievement for such a small nation.

CHAPTER 3

Heading out into the unknown

My real education started when, as a bog-standard prep-schoolboy and full-time boarder, I was sent to Marist Brothers College in Johannesburg's Observatory, not quite 'top notch' education-wise, but close. That said, I must admit that my notion of school – almost all the way through – was that it was a pretty detestable waste of time, no fault of a fine bunch of teachers, the majority from Ireland, Scotland or England who came to teach in South Africa and imparted some fine classical and literary traditions.

They belonged to the international community of the Catholic religious institute of Marist Brothers – and I should mention that despite my efforts (or lack of them) – they did their best to help this wayward soul who seemed to be repelled by the time-consuming repetitiveness of it all. Unfortunately, my boredom threshold was low, abysmally so.

The result was that I was considered something of a dullard and never excelled academically, something which only happened later with my tertiary studies in Britain. When presented with my school report a few years earlier, where I was placed twenty-fifth out of twenty-six, I recall my mother asking rhetorically – and well within my hearing: 'Have I given birth to a *dummkopf*?' I would console myself with the thought that Winston Churchill – in his early years – was also not the brightest boy on the block and I believed that my time would come.

Fat chance that was…

However, I shared one attribute with that great leader: books, the precious and often-rewarding road to escape. Our school library was expansive, thanks again to the Brothers, who believed in inculcating the likes of Sheridan, Faulkner, Camus, the great Scottish explorer James Bruce (also known as the Pale Abyssinian), Hemingway, Shaw, and of course, the Russians, as well as many others that fit comfortably into a substantial literary curriculum.

There was no television or other diversions like iPods, so it wasn't long – even as a youngster – before I'd read every *Biggles* volume in print and Franklin Dixon's *Hardy Boys*. Baroness Orczy's *Scarlet Pimpernel* chronology, the great O. Henry, Maugham, and many others followed. I devoured them all, some twice over, though some stuff was as dry as rocking horse shit to this immature mind. But I persevered anyway, to the extent that when I met some old school pals years later, they would enquire whether I was still reading as much as I did.

With time – and endless compulsory study hours – my joy in dealing with issues of every possible persuasion in print extended into a new genre of titles that covered the two world wars. I was 14 when I asked my mother to get me some of the works of a celebrated British naval historian, Captain Stephen Roskill RN, followed in 1954 by the first volume in his series, the mammoth 800-page *War at Sea*.

Several more of those historic volumes followed, and I ended up knowing more about the sinking of the *Scharnhorst* and the Battle of the North Cape in the Atlantic, Eniwetok, the Mariana Islands and Okinawa in the Pacific, as well as the capture of Singapore by Japanese forces in 1942 than any Latin declensions or mathematical concepts that I should by then have mastered.

As might have been expected, I'd already become fidgety about being cooped up within the confines of a regimented life at boarding school. While conditions at Marist were not spartan, they were strictly regulated: up at six in the morning, an hour's study before breakfast and two more hours in the evening. The Brothers were stringent about pupils not venturing beyond the school gates, which was why I was expelled for skulking out without permission. Brother Connell subsequently had a change of heart, probably because my father was mainly out of the picture. He let me return with a warning and 'six of the best' – corporal punishment still being the norm.

Being a boys' school, we only encountered girls over weekends when the sisters of some of my pals would arrive to watch cricket or rugby matches. Still, in the kind of seclusion we were thrust into, we had precious little to offer. Some of my pal's young mothers were the original MILFs, but even thinking like that was off-limits.

All these conflicting emotions understandably affected my ideas (and hormones) and what I did during the school holidays. From very early on, I wanted only to get as far away as possible from the stultifying regime that most of the boys accepted as part of their lives, but I couldn't. Instead, at the age of about 14 or 15, I chose to travel during hols and not laze about at home.

My travels took me as far as the annual rail ticket from my father allowed and that brief adventure – hiking back to Johannesburg from the frontiers of the Belgian Congo – was all part of it, including a journey of 1,600 kilometres or more through Africa, totally on my own.

Without a doubt, those frustrations also reflected in my scouring almost anything about 'foreign lands' that came to hand. I would spend hours perusing atlases and imagining visiting strange and exotic places like French Polynesia, where Gauguin had been holed up for many years, or Kwajalein – recognised by the majority of buffs interested in such things – as the coral outcrop where one of the great battles of the war against the Japanese was fought.

After reading the exploits of the Norwegian explorer Thor Heyerdahl about crossing the Pacific Ocean east to west and recounted in his marvellous *The Kon Tiki Expedition*, I swore that one day I would do the same, perhaps not on a balsa raft, but something equally primitive. I also promised myself that I would visit what, to my mind, was still a remote and mysterious place somewhere north of Australia called Papua New Guinea, which, sadly, I have never done. The name alone has tremendous appeal.

I wasn't the only youngster with stifled yearnings for the kind of escapades our parents regarded as over the top. Michael Rockefeller, whose father was the governor of New York and great-grandfather, the co-founder of Standard Oil and one of America's wealthiest dynasties, travelled to Papua New Guinea in 1961 to photograph the Asmat people and collect their art. The 23-year-old adventurer disappeared after the boat in which he was a passenger capsized, but more recent research suggests that cannibals ate him.[1]

Closer to home, I was intrigued by the exploits of Bobby Wilmot, who hunted crocodiles for their skins, for which there was an enormous demand in the fashion trade: ladies' handbags and flashy footwear. He was extraordinarily successful at this, going out at night in flimsy boats, catching the eyes of the predators in his lights and going in to make the kill. At the time, there was a good demand for croc skins in Europe, which meant that Bobby was often in the news. I earnestly desired a piece of his action, so I wrote to him in Maun and asked for a job. He could have tossed this brazen approach from a 15-year-old into the bin, but instead, I received a friendly letter telling me that things were not yet suitable for me to join his hunt and that I should finish my studies.

Disappointed, I then wrote to someone diving abalone off the coast of southern Africa and asked the same question. There I had no response.

Bobby Wilmot's story is all of classic Africa. He came from a family with more than a century of exploring the hinterland, and his son Lloyd is still at it. On my second overland trip across Africa, I visited Bobby at Maun's Crocodile Camp, and he recalled the letter. But the job still eluded me. A couple of years later, he died at one of his safari camps in the Okavango – a black mamba struck him in the face. It was a tragic event that still does the rounds among some of Maun's old hands. Bobby had the vital anti-venom serum he needed in his fridge at the camp, which was some distance from the attack. Undeterred, he hurried back, which, in turn, was counter-productive because it increased his blood circulation. Then, he dropped the vial at the most critical moment, and it broke. Minutes later, Bobby was dead.

---

1   Carl Hoffman, *Savage Harvest: A Tale of Cannibals, Colonialism and Michael Rockefeller's Tragic Quest for Primitive Art*. William Morrow, an imprint of HarperCollins Publishers: 2014.

While still at school, my early efforts to head out into the unknown, either with Wilmot or diving for abalone, kind of did the rounds. It wasn't long before my housemaster quizzed me about what he termed my 'idiotic intentions'. I told him I was deadly serious. He eyed me with scepticism, accentuated by a smile that was anything but wry but said nothing more. He did mention it to my mother the next time she visited with the usual bag of goodies, which was always after classes on Wednesday afternoons during term, but she made no comment.

Though I might not have had much of a family life, there was something else that the old girl handed down that has been of inestimable value throughout my life: music. Whenever I got home, she was usually listening to one of her 'favourites' on a turntable that played long-playing records. That phase, which lasted years, was pivotal to my upbringing because music became the other great love of my life.

So it was, with no effort on her part, that my earliest musical inclinations ran towards Bruch, Tchaikovsky, Brahms, Mendelssohn, Sibelius and many others, which is rarely taught – you either like good music, or you don't. It was one of the reasons, while in the navy, I would head for Cape Town City Hall's Sunday night concerts, probably the only one in the audience in navy Number One's.

In London years later, I even fell in love (obviously at a distance) with Jacqueline du Pré after hearing her play her best-known Elgar cello concerto at the Festival Hall for the first time. While I was in London, I attended her concerts in the British capital just about every time she returned.

Not entirely unexpectedly, one of the first things I did when I got to Britain was to travel to Dorking in Surrey by train so that I could view the house of Ralph Vaughan Williams. I spent hours looking for the place, but there was no Internet in those days that would have told me that it had been torn down in the 1930s. Still on my bucket list, though time is getting short, is a visit to Rock Hill, Aaron Copland's final home at Cortlandt Manor, New York.

However, I digress…

Meantime, back at school, there had been quite a few questions asked about this boy 'who is not quite normal' (my solo hike from the Congo being high on that agenda) and, to be fair, my mother didn't bat an eye. She'd accepted that from an early age, I was an adventurous tyke, possibly because her father – he'd been a hard-hat diver in the Imperial German Navy – was equally unconventional. But it did result in Dad writing a lengthy screed telling me to get on with my studies and not be silly.

A year or so later, still short of finishing my final academic year, I skipped school and joined the navy. I was just out of my sixteenth year, and fortunately, I didn't need my parents' permission, though I was the youngest rating on the ship for almost a year. Captain Stephen Roskill had probably pointed the way ahead in his historic wartime volumes and my eternal thanks are to him.

One also needs to ask how many youngsters emerge from uniform having been put through that figurative mincing machine and then, forever after, talking about the best years of their lives. From school, it was straight to the naval recruiting office, which I visited after a month's vacation. I just couldn't wait to escape from the stifling 'all-school' environment into something different.

Effectively, it meant that I moved from one strictly disciplined environment to another, with very little social activity in the big bad world in between, but that suited me because the navy was different.

Earlier, I'd had my heart set on several of the opposite sex with whom I'd had fleeting relationships but only got to first base after joining my first ship, a Loch Class frigate that dated from wartime service. Built as HMS *Loch Ard* for the Royal Navy, she was transferred to the South African Navy a year before hostilities ended and eventually renamed SAS *Transvaal*.

With an overall length of 300 feet and a displacement of 2,300 tons at deep load, the *Transvaal* was handy as an anti-submarine vessel and everything else this aspiring young matelot could imagine. While beauty might be in the eye of the beholder, on seeing her alongside Durban's Salisbury Island naval base for the first time, for me she was the embodiment of magnificence. Her twin 4-inch guns on the fo'c'sle – set off against the extended quarterdeck – slotted into my concept of the classic British warship class handed down from World War I. In those days, they were referred to as destroyers.

Sea time had to be preceded by three robust months of basics at Saldanha Bay's naval base, which lay along the Atlantic Ocean's West Coast 160 kilometres north of Cape Town. Conditions were stringent: there was no shore leave, no girls, no grog, no malingering but instead, plenty of good food and the kind of hardships our instructors liked to think would make reasonable seamen of us. Our officers and senior NCOs (petty and chief petty officers and warrants) were a disparate lot, the majority British who arrived in South Africa not long after Germany had been defeated. I joined a decade after the end of the war, and most of the Royal Navy traditions were still intact, including, for many of the ratings below deck, the most important tradition of all – the daily 'tot' which, instead of Caribbean rum issued in Royal Navy messes – was good-quality South African brandy.

This customarily came at noon: half a glass and drunk neat, but only for those 21 or older. Naturally, it excluded me, though some of the fellows allowed me 'sippers' on special occasions – like my birthday – which was simply a sip, but never 'gulpers'. It was the one occasion when 'Swain', our coxswain a stickler for 'proper procedures' and answerable personally to the captain, would turn a blind eye.

Other customs arrived with the frigates from the United Kingdom, including having to assimilate naval slang, some of which went back centuries. We knew that the word *matelot* for sailors was French, but it was an everyday term in both the Royal and South African navies, as was plain and simple 'jack'. So too with playing 'silly buggers', a stern reprimand when we youngsters were fooling about. *Chai* was tea and cocoa was *kai*. Also, you 'dhobied' your clothes, not washed them, and we 'went ashore', even if it was from a land-based installation (as with our training camp at Saldanha Bay). If you were going ashore to have 'a wet', it meant alcohol.

We slept in hammocks, strung up on steel stanchions, which made life more tolerable when encountering heavy seas, and all announcements over the intercom were preceded by a bo'sun's call, including 'out pipes' or 'pipes down' at lights out which was a specific instruction and not preceded by the general call.

The maritime force recruited from Britain included some of the best professionals who had initially put their names forward at South Africa House in London after Pretoria had acquired a small fleet of warships. The tally included the three Royal Navy Loch Class frigates and two destroyers – one of which had a young man of Greek and Danish royal extraction by the name of Philip Mountbatten serve as the first lieutenant during the war and who subsequently married the future Queen. There were also several minesweepers and a pair of ancient coal-fired Bar-class boom defence vessels, including the SAS *Somerset* which could manage all of seven knots at full tilt. These warships eventually descended on Simonstown which by then had served as a British naval base for a century and a half.

'Snoekie' – as previous generations of RN salts had dubbed the port – was perched on the edge of a row of hills and seemed like a little bit of England appended to Africa. Even today, Simonstown is a delightful little town on the way to Cape Point, straddling as it does, the main road running north to south. In my time, it was lined by more pubs than any other town in the southern hemisphere, each reflecting the kind of British tradition you might still find in Devon or East Anglia. There was the Lord Nelson (still running), the St George's, the Prince Alfred and several more, all with two bars: one for officers and the other for us lowly ratings.

Opposite the Prince Alfred stood the high-walled Union Jack Club, where ships' crews would congregate on Sunday evenings whenever they were alongside and where you'd get a beer for sixpence. When time was called, Royal Navy ratings would congregate on one side of the bar and the South Africans on the other – many of them ruffians waiting to use their fists. After a particularly nasty punch-up, one of the officers declared, 'It's almost like you silly buggers are fighting the Boer War all over again.'

What I only realised in later years was that all the RN personnel who headed out to South Africa on contract after the war had seen service in the Atlantic or the Mediterranean, some a good deal of it. Most had experienced action in one form or another and a few even had their ships sunk by hostile fire. Yet, in all my time in the navy, I never heard any of them talk about those encounters: it seems that having experienced and survived it all, they preferred to bury their memories.

Among them were some illustrious individuals. My last commanding officer on the frigate SAS *Vrystaat* (originally HMS *Wrangler*, a fleet destroyer whose dual-shaft geared steam turbines could push 32 knots) was Captain (later Rear Admiral) M. R. Terry-Lloyd, who, as a commander, was appointed Senior Officer, Anti-Submarine Flotillas in wartime 1944.

His brother, J. V. Terry-Lloyd (also South African), was a member of a clandestine British strike force that, between them, had garnered four Victoria Crosses (together with 64 other decorations) and linked inter alia to Operation *Source*, a series of attacks involving X-Craft midget submarines. These were deployed to neutralise heavy German warships – including the *Tirpitz*, *Scharnhorst* and *Lützow* – all based in remote Norwegian fiords.

Of all my life experiences, the time spent on board the frigate *Transvaal* was among the most memorable and also the most instructive. A schoolboy at heart, tackling the kind of real-life experiences that included lookout duties when on emergency runs through the sort of heavy seas that have always made the southern-latitude Roaring Forties fearful among mariners, was all part of it. On that frigate, it was usually to bring succour to a critically ill weatherman on the remote Prince Edward Islands, and dodging icebergs was sometimes part of it.

We also visited Tristan da Cunha, part of a group of islands in the South Atlantic Ocean, midway between southern Africa and South America. We took on board islanders and their longboats; they helped our crew members get ashore at the even-more-remote Gough Island, which was to become a weather station.

It was a succession of unusual and oft-times thrilling experiences to my young mind, but there were risks involved, including packs of killer whales, or as these marvellous creatures are known today, orcas. Our small boats would never head out when pulling inshore to the islands without a clutch of hand grenades – one of which, its pin pulled – would be tossed over the side when these predators displayed aggression. While the orcas of the Pacific North West might be the most placid maritime creatures along Canada's Inside Passage, they didn't seem to follow suit in the deep South Indian Ocean half a century ago.

Another problem for smaller craft ferrying men and equipment ashore was the kelp, huge masses that sometimes jammed props, and the men had to row back to clear them. That could become critical if the wind was up, as it was on one trip when Petty Officer Johnnie Bold's naval whaler turned turtle in the swell and he drowned. Relief ships have helicopters on board these days, so contemporary crews experience few dramatic events.

The weather around Marion Island, one of our regular destinations, was always a problem. Summer or winter, it was constantly changeable, with storms blowing up within minutes and the ship having to up-anchor and dash for the lee. Those sometimes furious 120- to 140-kph quasi-hurricanes that turned the ocean surface a blistering foam-topped white could last for days. They occasionally resulted in crew already ashore stranded until the frigate returned.

I was once 'abandoned' there for three days with thirty of my mates who had been unloading stores. There were no beds in the tiny shore camp, only an unheated empty shed. So, we did the best we could and slept in a great big pile to keep from freezing.

Most operational vessels operating out of Simonstown took part in annual Capex Exercises, which involved fighting ships from many nations, including Britain and occasionally the United States. Manoeuvres involved searches for real submarines – detached for the duration – which did not always elude us. I also had a small role in the Action Information Command Centre (AICC) below the bridge. Still, I admit that I have never been able to master the intricacies of plotting the course – either of our warship or the sub we were hunting – primarily done in the dark, with only plotting tables with transparent surfaces lit from below for guidance. Small wonder then, with all those new-fangled systems coming into play, modern navies halted the lunchtime issue of booze.

There is an addendum to my link to the frigate SAS *Transvaal*. The graceful old lady was decommissioned in the late 1970s, sold as scrap and scuttled in 33 metres of water on the western shore of False Bay. I dived on her while making a TV documentary titled *The Wreck Hunters*, which went awry as I had to dive on her twice in succession to complete the sequence and suffered a mild case of the bends, which I didn't believe needed time in a recompression chamber. That was a mistake. All bend cases need some form of recompression, and I had pain in my right shoulder for years afterwards.

Another, even more serious, blunder followed decades later when I again went down to the frigate with a group of casual weekend divers. I did a string of stupid things that I'd always instructed my learner divers not to do, and all but drowned. I was 76 years old, had been diving for almost half a century, but if it hadn't been for the prompt action of two former navy divers, Rod King and Ian Lowe, I wouldn't be around.[2]

One of the most interesting of all my naval experiences was a West African cruise to Luanda, the capital city of Angola, while I was still on board the *Vrystaat*. It was a historic 'showing the flag' occasion and something of a revelation for those who had never been farther north than Rhodesia's Salisbury or Lourenço Marques in Portuguese East Africa. It was also the first time that one of the frigates had gone north into a region some still regarded as 'Darkest Africa'.

One and all, we were astonished to find Luanda, then still under Portuguese rule, quite illuminating. Indeed, it was a beautiful, friendly and modern city, sometimes

---

2   Al J. Venter, *Shipwreck Stories*. Protea Books: 2014. The full story of that minor catastrophe – for that was what it was – appears in Chapter 25, headed 'A Near-Death Disaster and How Not to Dive Wrecks'.

referred to in European circles as the 'Lisbon in Africa'. Our frigate sailed into Luanda harbour on a bright sunny day in 1959 – with me still only 20 years old – on a journey that would shape my life for decades. I returned many times in later years to cover the guerrilla war that followed Africa's epoch of apprised freedom (Angola lasted 13 years). After Luanda, our frigate headed up the Congo River and visited Matadi, the country's largest port; the Congo was still under Belgian colonial administration and about to become independent.

Luanda was a prosperous and cosmopolitan city with all the trappings of a European capital, including modern buildings, restaurants far beyond our meagre earnings and suburbs that vied with those of Cape Town or Johannesburg. That – and the craziest traffic south of Marseille – where, to our astonishment, locals drove on the wrong side of the road.

The navy intended for the ship to stay a week. However, after a first night of cheap booze and licentious broads, coupled with the kind of sometimes-violent disruptions that made headlines back home, our rather ostentatious state visit was abruptly cut short. Much of the fracas was centred on the 'plunder' of several 500-litre wine barrels standing on the quay alongside our ship. There were no barriers or security guards because, as the Luanda police said afterwards, who would bother to steal something as mundane as wine anyway? There was so much it around that even the locals wouldn't pay for it.

My shipmates didn't share that view. Those crew members who had to stay on board used hammers to broach several wooden vats and help themselves, which soon turned into a shambles that eventually involved the police. As we discovered the next day, the alcohol-inspired melee resulted in the arrest of several South African sailors – with the rest of us remanded to remain on board – or, as they say, 'confined to barracks'.

The result was that the SAS *Vrystaat* – to the exasperation of Captain Terry-Lloyd, who had one hellova reputation as a disciplinarian – had been disgraced, and it did not take him long to call it a day. The order from the bridge was to let go fore and aft, and we continued our journey north up the coast towards the final port of call on the Congo River.

Once alongside at Matadi, none of the ship's company was allowed ashore, even though we were there for several days – the reason was that they feared the crew would also turn that harbour upside down. As I established afterwards, there was another reason for keeping the men on the ship. With the Congolese aware that the country would soon become independent, trouble was already brewing in the townships. They had radios, and the locals would listen to the news avidly. They did not need the visit of a warship from a country that practised racial discrimination; even they had heard of apartheid!

And while Brussels sanctioned the visit, they came down hard when Captain Terry-Lloyd sent a message to the local governor telling him he intended to fire a twenty-gun salute on his arrival at Matadi. The colonial administration averred that the locals would have feared that they were being invaded, so it never happened.

I returned to Luanda not many years later. I'd left the navy, qualified professionally in London, headed back to South Africa and decided travel back to Britain overland again in late 1964. That journey involved crossing the length of Angola, by then battling an insurgent campaign across a broad front in the north where the frontier with the Congo stretched across an otherwise un-demarcated map: all jungle terrain with maybe a single border post every three or four hundred kilometres.

In other respects, it was a good year for travel because there was much happening abroad: humans were making strides toward space travel beyond the Earth's orbit, Tokyo hosted the 18th Summer Olympics, the Beatles took America by storm and concurrently, race riots gripped its big cities. Finally, President Lyndon Johnson escalated American involvement in the Vietnam War.

On my second visit, this time as a civilian hitchhiking across Africa, I reached Luanda after a reasonably long haul north from Angola's port city of Lobito, where the local military had arrested me; foreigners travelling overland through Portugal's African colonies were not only rare, but also suspect. The guerrilla war was on the upswing, and somebody concluded I could only have been a foreign spy because I didn't have my own vehicle. Though I spent a night in the cells devoured by mosquitoes, my South African passport and valid visa got me a release the following morning.

On reaching the outskirts of Luanda late the next day, we plunged into the evening rush hour traffic. The truck driver who had given me a lift was in a hurry; he sped through the outskirts into the centre of town and dropped me off adjacent to the city's famous lagoon-side Marginal.

I had been to Luanda before, in a naval uniform, but this time I was a civvy and had no ship to report back to. The result was that from the moment I arrived, I was awed by the astonishing pace of a great city closing shop for the night. Also, I was careful about money because a long road lay ahead, so for some of the time I compromised by abstaining, but at something like a dollar or two for a good bottle of Douro *vinho tinto*, one was easily swayed.

At the same time, the Luanda of the mid-1960s (I was still in my mid-twenties) was somewhat different from what I'd experienced five or six years before while still in the navy. For a start, with an ongoing war in the *Dembos* (the jungles to the north of the capital) only a few hours' drive from the heart of the city, there were troops in uniform everywhere: soldiers, sailors and airmen. I observed a military component in the bars and restaurants that appeared to mix easily with the civilian population, both black and white. The informality of interracial association surprised this newcomer from a South African society just then in the process of shoring up its own racial barriers.

Interestingly, within the predominantly white community that must have been well into six figures, academic and science clubs catered for all demands in just about every suburb, with even a privately owned observatory. So too with traditional and classical concerts, chamber groups, and a small national orchestra.

Overseas artists performed routinely in all major centres, and the lovely Amália Rodrigues, with her distinctive *Fado* following, was regarded by locals almost as a regular. While musical fare was primarily European or American, one of Luanda's elite clubs, Xavarotti, would often engage prominent artists from abroad.

Even the golf course was in full swing. John Miller, the *Daily Telegraph*'s correspondent in Africa tasked with an assignment through the country towards the end of the war, wrote a report that suggested that everything in Angola was fine. This was an understatement because Lisbon's forces on the ground in Africa were not winning the war. In his report to London, he warned that golfers had to 'watch for battle-clad paratroopers dropping on or near the sixteenth hole in routine training jumps.'

Things were cheap in Angola then – partly because tourists (there were hardly any) had not bumped up prices. Portugal was coping with its conflicts, and anybody who wished to visit the country had to have a very good reason before gaining entry. Despite the war, that category excluded the American and European hunting fraternities because Angola then still boasted some of the best safaris on the continent. But that, as the saying goes, was strictly 'big bucks'.

Ensconced in Luanda, I had a clean room in one of the local hotels for about $10 a night and could eat an excellent three-course seafood dinner – which included *Caldo Verde*, my favourite – for about half that. After I emerged from my lodgings in the mornings, I'd saunter down to a huge open coffee house near the harbour with windows as big as barn doors and order a mug of *café com leite*, usually with enough bread to carry me through to lunch…all for a couple of dollars.

The coffee house was the regular haunt of many white Portuguese dockworkers, taxi drivers and trades folk – noisily starting their day on the place's rough-hewn wooden benches, very much as I did.

There was an excellent public transport system in Luanda then, and it was possible to move about the city for the equivalent of pennies. The city was divided into the Baixa de Luanda (lower Luanda, the old town) and the Cidade Alta (upper city or the new part) – the status quo still holds.

The Baixa, with its narrow streets and old colonial buildings – a few dating from the 1600s – was situated next to the port, and it was there that my friends and I spent most of our evenings. If the mood took me, I could get a day job on one of the boats that plied the coast and accept my wages in fish once we got back to port.

This would provide my student friends and me with dinner. Angola was that kind of place in the old days. It was an idyllic life, and I would have liked to stay. But the rest of Africa – and London at the end of a very long road ahead – beckoned.

So, I arranged with my newfound Portuguese student pals to mail my South African passport to me in London. After that, I headed to the airport, British passport in hand, to board a plane to Pointe-Noire, the largest port in Congo (Brazzaville) to the north: no questions asked.

CHAPTER 4

Africa in the 1960s

Leaving the relatively friendly ambience of Angola behind was a wrench. Many of my friends at school were Portuguese and for that reason, I have always felt a strong affinity for the nation.

But just then, I was flying north out of Luanda on a short hop – one of only two flights in the entire trans-African traipse to London – into 'the other' Congo, a quasi-communist country that few people in the West knew anything about. It was always the much larger, wealthier, and more troubled neighbour to the south that made the news, almost always bad.

Congo-Brazzaville (or more appropriately Congo-Brazza) lies on the north bank of the great river that bears its name, with 'Leo' (or Leopoldville as the Belgian colonials called it) directly across the water, a short boat trip away. Leo's name was later changed to Kinshasa, capital of the Democratic Republic of the Congo (DRC), one of Africa's most populous countries. Approximately the same size as Argentina, the DRC in the past half-century has transmogrified into the ultimate failed state.

The number of its people who have died in wars, army mutinies, starvation, disease and horrendous prisons – where I spent a short time a decade later before being rescued by French President François Mitterrand – has run into millions since independence from Belgium in 1960.

Once a remote fishing village in the Central African interior, Kinshasa is a monumental disaster with a population that not even the United Nations is sure of, except that it is the world's largest single Francophone urban area, six or eight times the size of Paris.[1] I visited the city often in later years; one could always be sure that exciting things were happening there. I always paid good money at one of its top restaurants perched on a high-rise to escape the rampaging in the streets

---

1 Geopolitical statistics put the total population for Kinshasa (there has never been an official census) at about 17 million. Diplomats who have served there, reckon it could be considerably higher. As with Lagos – even more populous – the two cities keep on expanding. Their inhabitants exist under the most severe, hardscrabble conditions and infant mortality is off the accepted 'civilised' scale.

below which allowed me to view Brazzaville's twinkling lights – and a decidedly more peaceable ambience across the water.

My main concern on leaving Luanda was that by going to Congo-Brazzaville, I was entering an African state that had rather fondly embraced Marxism. The Soviets persuaded its leader that their 'historic and ultimately superior' political creed was an effective antidote against all the colonial ills it had inherited from France as well as Belgium in August 1960 when both states became independent.

Paris had entrusted Alphonse Massamba-Débat, its leader, to establish a democracy. Instead, like several other radical leaders of the time – Guinea's Sékou Touré and Kwame Nkrumah of Ghana – he believed the best way forward would be a one-party state. Effectively the country had become a dictatorship and an excessively cruel one.

Débat published his dogma on what he called 'Scientific Socialism' early on, and it made about as much sense as Nkrumah's 'Consciencism'. Since its tenets went over the heads of most of his subjects, they eventually decided that they'd had enough. Alphonse Massamba-Débat was arrested and executed by firing squad.

However, before that took place, Moscow, Havana and Beijing flooded both major Congo-Brazzaville cities, the capital and the country's principal port, Pointe-Noire – where I was headed – with thousands of military advisers and their respective political and intelligence agents. I had no idea what kind of reception would be waiting for me when the plane eventually landed, and it didn't help that I'd been told by someone in Luanda that the country I was headed for was a 'bit like Cuba'.

It was not, and I needn't have worried. The immigration officer at the airport, an older man with a severe countenance and a regulation pair of Ray-Bans (even though we were in a dimly lit immigration hall), barely glanced at my passport, and no questions were asked. I was surprised he didn't quiz me about what I had been doing in Angola among what locals referred to as 'Fascists'.

So I changed some currency, grabbed my bag, and took a taxi into town. Phew!

There is something of a story behind my heading into a totally alien political environment upon leaving Luanda. I grew up in a part of Africa that had been dominated by European-orientated or 'white' governments for three centuries. Angola, the country I had just left, was then a Portuguese colony and also 'white' orientated, though some people in Lisbon today might refute that.

South Africa had been colonised – first by the Dutch as a halfway station on the sea route to the Spice Islands of the East and thereafter, during the Napoleonic Wars. I was intrigued and fascinated by what I might encounter once I crossed that invisible line on the map between Black Africa and White and frankly, I wasn't disappointed.

Pointe-Noire, the country's only deepwater harbour, was the antithesis of what I'd been expecting. Not a big city, everything centred around the miniature equivalent of a Grand Central, the western terminal of a rail link with Brazzaville 480 kilometres into the interior.

Unlike Luanda, there were no cheap hotels. In fact, there was no cheap anything: I was white, and the locals expected me to behave like a European in a black man's country. It meant that meals were expensive, and there were no low-priced hotels unless I checked into some miserable *hébergement* in the townships, which could have been decidedly dodgy because of security (or lack of). Never mind more mosquitoes than anybody thought possible, and bedbugs: air-conditioning had arrived in Africa by then, but it cost, so the townships managed with mosquito nets.

I didn't have the funds to travel conventionally, so wherever possible, I cut costs to the bare minimum. This was an excellent 'financial' investment in terms of journalistic returns over the four-month journey.

Interestingly, those second-rate hotels that I gravitated towards because of cost had some interesting quirks. The most striking were their beds, usually all-metal, with their pods standing in small tin cans that contained paraffin oil or kerosene. When asked about this, one patron told us it was about the 'creatures of the night'. She said that scorpions and centipedes, some between 15 and 20 centimetres long and boasting massive sets of poisonous pincers were prevented from joining you between the sheets by the hydrocarbon, topped up when needed. It worked very well too, she reckoned, 'though you cannot stop the spiders' (from descending onto the somnolent) from the ceiling.

I wasn't to know it yet, but those same issues followed me across the continent for the rest of my trans-Africa safari. Though I slept in the open often enough and sometimes woke with a scorpion almost always near my head – for some reason, I was never bitten or stung. I'd spent a month on the road, with roughly ninety more days still to go.

Then I had to tackle the question of getting around. Europeans, Americans, Canadians, and others who take the plunge into those far-flung domains often expect to stand on the side of the road and hitch, which rarely happens in Africa if you're white or Asian. You pay – simple as that.

In Francophone Africa, it was the *taxi brousse* or bush taxi. In Nigeria, you hailed a mammy wagon – a large truck, open behind the cab where wooden benches were secured for seating. It might not have been comfortable, but it cost very little to cover long distances, and entire nations willingly used them.

Transients were gullible enough to pay more to travel 'first class'. I never did because that seat was dubbed the 'suicide chair' because of the astonishingly high accident rate on African roads. Sadly, that was the way it was then and frankly, it's even worse today.

It says a lot that Neall Ellis – a veteran of many African wars as well as three years' operational flying support missions in Afghanistan – always maintained that while he frequently came under fire, it wouldn't be enemy bullets that would get him in the end, but much more likely some nitwit doing something stupid on the roads.

Still, I was now on my own – my budget was constrained – and, as the saying goes: one has to take one's chances. So, once north of 'white-dominated Africa', I did what I could and stuck to whatever roads lay ahead. Some were good ones, though few had been paved or maintained – and many, beyond city limits – were little more than improvised tracks carved through heavy bush.

Occasionally, I'd dig deep into my pocket and take a short flight, such as the one out of Luanda and then again from Libreville in Gabon, after visiting Albert Schweitzer. That was a short flip to Douala in Cameroon because I'd been warned about 'unfavourable conditions' in some areas I'd have to traverse, which could include 'bandits'.

There were also times when I'd travel by dugout canoe, the occasional boat or barge. After Gabon, I was stuck on the Anglophone West Cameroon coast for a few days and was rescued by a young man with a makeshift canoe – we did an overnight crossing in his open boat to Calabar in Nigeria. The trip was fine, but he insisted on taking me to his shack, where his wife greeted me with a look that suggested something along the lines of 'Who the fuck are you, and what do you want?'

But that was rare; I rarely encountered animosity. In both Nigeria and Ghana, I was feted as a 'tame' South African from the 'Racist South' and then handed a beer or a jug of palm wine. Most times, I was regarded as a curiosity piece, crazy enough to be venturing across remote regions that were still beset with perils in the minds of most. I seldom encountered any. Politics did enter the equation now and again, which usually involved several South African stamps in my British passport.

A month later, I was forced to make a run from Ghana to the Ivory Coast after receiving a message from the local police to return to Accra to 'answer questions' about what I'd been doing in South Africa. That resulted in my taking a hurried gap involving a four-hour paddle in a dugout, with two extra pairs of strong arms hired for the purpose. A couple of anxious Peace Corps girls accompanied us on the journey, seated towards the rear, but I didn't mind because it meant splitting costs.

On that memorable trip, six weeks after my Brazza sojourn, we set off from a tiny village called New Town in the extreme western corner of Ghana, travelling across an inland sea that went on forever. God knows what would have happened if we'd been caught in a storm – there were plenty at that time of the year. Perpetually short of cash, I didn't waste time after that long haul in an open boat in my bid to head up the West Coast of Africa towards Europe.

On arrival in Congo-Brazzaville's main harbour of Pointe-Noire, I was faced with several options: continue north through some of the densest tropical jungles on any continent or go by sea. Both options were loaded with imponderables.

The road went eastwards from the coast for about 125 kilometres to Dolisie and then north through the famous (or infamous) Mayombe Forest that stretches more than 3,000 kilometres from Angola to Cameroon and is sometimes called the Second Amazon. I was told I would eventually end up in Gabon if I went that way, but it'd take a week, possibly two if the rains came.[2]

Also, this was uncertain terrain. Several aircraft had disappeared into the Mayombe, and some had never been found. And, until I reached Gabon, I would be one of the very few whites in a region that was as backwards as it was primitive. There were very few towns, certainly no hotels and were we to have an accident, which was another warning I was handed, I'd be lucky to find either a doctor or a clinic.

'So, what's the diffs?' said one young African student with whom I shared a couple of beers after a few days in the country and who questioned me keenly about Europe. He was erudite, reasonably well educated in the French baccalaureate tradition and, after Portuguese Africa, not afraid to challenge a white about his views. His final words to me came with a broad smile: 'This is newly independent Africa, my friend – enjoy!'

I learnt languages fairly quickly, so I could speak basic French by this time. Things improved with time, and some years later, when I started filming in the former French colonies, I became fairly fluent, if not fully conversant.

So in Pointe-Noire I made the most of it and savoured my first French beer at a little café just off the main square: it was a Kronenbourg, and in that heat, a refreshing change from warm bottled water that sometimes came from the taps.

Finally, I listened to good advice. Instead of going by road, I grabbed a cab for the docks, where the captain of a steamer took a while to size me up before deciding whether he would take me north – he was headed for Port Gentil in Gabon. After some lengthy pauses, he told me it would cost me US$200, and when I accepted, the skipper – a couple of hundred bucks richer, no questions asked – pulled a bottle of cognac and two tumblers from his desk.

Thus was I to become the unlisted supernumerary on board a freighter whose name I have long forgotten. I had my own cabin when the ship sailed to its next port of call, where it was taking on a cargo of Gabonese timber. I could even join the crew for meals, at no extra charge. After almost a week's delay sleeping rough in Pointe-Noire, my new home was clean, tidy and secure. Also, I had a real bed with sheets that hadn't been slept in before. I felt that I might have been welcomed on board the *Queen Mary*.

---

2   The mammoth Mayombe Forest covers roughly two million square kilometres of Africa – or almost four times the size of France: gargantuan by any standards. It includes parts of Angola, Congo-Brazzaville, the Democratic Republic of the Congo, Gabon and smaller portions of Cameroon, Equatorial Guinea and the Central African Republic.

Before we sailed, there was a day's delay, and I used it to ramble around Pointe-Noire. The city, a former French colonial outpost, was well organised, with buses that ran regularly and traffic officers to control the flow, together with a polite and friendly society that knew what queues were for and weren't nearly as pushy as the Nigerians. More importantly, there were no officious goons around, as I had anticipated.

Unexpectedly, I wasn't the only traveller. On that long journey, I would bump into pairs of youthful American men, neatly dressed, hair short back and sides, similar to Mormons that one often encounters in Midwest cities promulgating their version of the creed. Only these two, staying at the same hotel as I did on my first and only night in Pointe-Noire, were not into religion. They were businessmen, they said, 'We're here to check out prospects in Africa.'

It was all bullshit, of course, because even in those faraway days, I could spot an operator, especially an amateur. It was common knowledge that the CIA was sending squads of its people into areas where the Soviets were active. Their opposite numbers from Moscow and Havana would definitely not have missed them either.

The steamer, its ancient engine grunting and steaming, took a day and a half to reach Port Gentil, the second city of oil-rich Gabon. On getting there, it became the first 'new adventure' day of the rest of my life. The navy was behind me, and I'd travelled almost 3,200 kilometres to reach another former French colonial possession, but this one was very different from the last. Indeed, Port Gentil, for me, stood on the cusp of a totally new African experience, something I'd always wanted to do when I pored over travel books and maps at school.

On my previous crossing of Africa from Cape Town five years before, I went as far north as Kenya, which was a remarkable experience because I went by road (such as they were in those days) because the Great North Road was not yet totally surfaced.

But that was already old hat. In the five or six weeks there – before sailing for Montreal – I'd acquired a solid understanding of the country. I was elated by the kind of experiences that few of my contemporaries had the resources or the ability to explore. I used my time to travel widely, from the mouth of the Tana River and Lamu in the north all the way down the coast southwards to Shimoni a delightful little settlement near the Tanzanian border. There I dived and had my first real shark experience.

Inland, I'd gone even further and touched base at what early pioneers had listed on their charts as Lake Rudolf (today Lake Turkana), together with half a dozen magnificent game parks which formed the backdrop to that marvellous film *Out of Africa*. The movie included images of many of the places I'd visited: Thompson's Falls, Tsavo's twin parks on both sides of the main road linking Nairobi with Mombasa, the Mount Kenya Safari Club, Naivasha and its settler community – both British and Afrikaner (from an earlier epoch) – as well as the Great Rift Valley. Heading up or down East Africa's great escarpment was always exhilarating.

There can be no better introduction to Africa than what was once called British East Africa, but on arriving off Port Gentil in Gabon that early morning, what lay ahead appealed the most.

Before me, I had the real, raw Africa that in the mid-1960s attracted few tourists, and one of my first impressions was that West Africa seems always to have been somewhat shuttered. Partly, I suppose, because of the catastrophe that defined the Congo on independence, along with a succession of coups, revolutions, and army mutinies that started to infect the continent like the pox. The prospect of experiencing it all at close quarters was little short of a consuming anticipatory grist for my rather overactive imaginative mill.

My first impressions of Port Gentil are as vivid in my mind today as they were then, as I stood on the bridge alongside the skipper as we waited to draw closer to the roadstead so we could enter harbour. There were kilometres of logs floating in the swell, all held intact by chains – some clusters as large as football fields – each one destined for ships like ours to take them to the other side of the world.

Over time, it's likely that numerous storms and hurricanes that swept in from the Atlantic caused some of those hardwood conglomerations to break free. This meant that logs were scattered along every beach in sight, thousands of them, and obviously worth good money. Evidently, there was nobody blessed with enough initiative, energy or cash to pay for the labour needed to gather these assets together again and most would probably rot there. The tropics, lethargic, soporific, and totally unforgiving was as unscrupulous then as it is today.

There was no question that there was a ready market abroad for some of these logs, most a metre in diameter and some double that, they included precious hardwoods like ebony or the local, relatively accessible okoumé trees along the Middle Ogowe (or Ogooué as its residents spell it) and the surrounding lake region.

As the history books tell us, lumber was the key factor in attracting European traders to West Africa, but it couldn't have been easy because the locals had their own views; '*le roi okoumé*', they would nonchalantly declare, 'is a fickle patron.'

I found Port Gentil (then, before the oil rush) – about the size of a small French provincial town straddling the estuary of a great river – an appealing settlement. It had its own cathedral and qualified in European terms as a city: the beautiful *Cathédrale* Saint Louis, a truly beautiful creation – surrounded by palms – could have been taken out of context from the Côte d'Azur.

Though the country had already been independent for five years, it still had many of the attributes of a colonial backwater: broad clean streets, the sprawling, jumbled, central market together with almost too many bistros and boulangeries – the majority still owned by French expatriates who appeared to have little inclination to return home.

Interestingly, the French writer Georges Simenon travelled to Libreville before the war and used the town as a scene-setter for his *Coup de lune* (*Moon Stroke*), a lucid, cynical and ironic detective novel published by Fayard in 1933. He described Libreville as having an indefinable uneasiness that 'was not only due to the oppressive humidity of the climate'. As one literary type elaborated, 'moon stroke' (read 'blues' and madness) would, in equatorial latitudes, be comparable to 'blue's stroke', a condition aggravated by alcohol. This might explain the behaviour of many of the whites sent to Africa and the Far East to 'administrate' the native populations.

The old Hotel Central where Simenon stayed was still standing when I got there, though it was already dowdy, something that happens soon enough in that almost consumptive heat. The country lies on the Equator and I had mushrooms growing on my bedroom carpet, so I could sense his frustration. That did not make clear why the French author was somewhat repulsed by Africa – though he might have found, as I did in Nigeria, where I eventually ended up working – that the West African expatriate community tended to be snottily aloof towards new arrivals.

But for all the problems, things were happening in the harbour by the time I got there. Oil had been discovered offshore, and hopes ran high among the locals, both black and white. Unlike other Third World oil capitals, prices remained modest, which suited me because it took a little while to find a boat that would take me into the interior.

My destination was the old French colonial trading post at Lambarene straddling the north bank of the great Ogowe River where Albert Schweitzer built his jungle hospital. The region, then still known as French Equatorial Africa only changed its name to Gabon when Paris handed the country its independence.

Shortly before the first Great War, Schweitzer and his wife Helene travelled from Port Gentil on a primitive raft and took thirteen days to cover the 320 kilometres. With all the stops at what seemed to be just about every village along the way, my journey upriver lasted three days.

CHAPTER 5

Matilda and Albert Schweitzer's jungle hospital

It took a little longer than I'd expected to find a suitable boat to take me to the old Schweitzer hospital at Lambarene, not that I had many options. Most of the vessels were derelict, the owners broke, or they needed to 'fix things'.

I made the effort to check out a few and judging by the condition of some – either with busted engines or wooden hulls with holes in them – we'd be stranded within hours. Some had rotten spars kept intact, or almost intact, with wire. That much could be observed from the surface: what was happening below the waterline with a woodworm infestation was what mattered.

Finally, I settled on a sizeable single-level barge that looked secure and was fitted with a sturdy roof. It mattered to me that her engine was new, and the man running the show seemed to have his act together. The downside was that half of Port Gentil was as eager as I was to buy a seat.

Named *Matilda*, she was a biggish craft, all wood with place for about sixty, everybody sitting in long rows that stretched from fore to aft. Before we got underway, the owner allowed eighty passengers on board, each with luggage. The problem was that there was no stowage space, so we had to hold on tight to our belongings until we pulled out into the stream.

All good, except that an untold number of goats, pigs, chickens, one or two monkeys, and poultry apart (with their legs tied) were brought on board. The animals ran free or hid under the benches. While we humans could relieve ourselves at a single improvised 'toilet' way aft – a wooden seat with a central open ring that hung precariously over the water and secured to the transom with a cord – the animals merrily defecated anywhere. We simply had to manage, which was fine the first day, but with time, things became frantic, especially since there were also several children.

I settled my mind to the inevitable and secured a reasonably decent seat next to the helmsman near the bow, and of course, it cost me. I resigned myself to three days of Dante's Ninth Circle of Hell. What I hadn't counted on was 'stink fish', the name for a ubiquitous West African culinary 'delight' – composed solely of something taken from the sea, salt-cured on wooden drying racks left out in the open for days. That meant that this appalling concoction was partially fermented – and indeed – it stank. Terribly!

I lasted perhaps an hour in my much-cherished seat before I headed onto the ferry's roof and stayed there for the rest of the trip, a wise decision due to the animals shitting at random below. In broken English and French, I was told by fellow passengers shortly before I debussed that I was a very lucky person because it only rained half a dozen times. At that time of the year, I was to be told later, it could be wet for weeks. I didn't respond…

The end result of that experience was that from then on, I have never been able to bear that noxious odour. I encountered stink fish almost everywhere I went in West Africa over the next four or five decades, including when I lived and worked in Nigeria. I could detect the pong at fifty metres, and it still makes me gag.

My fellow passengers were a delight, having long ago learned to handle hardship, and their friendly approach to most problems compensated for my many woes. These included getting stuck in clusters of long reeds and hanging trees that occasionally threatened to overwhelm us while trying to approach a remote village. With kids crying and porkers making discordant noises that could rouse the dead, everybody coped; we simply had to.

I seldom detected a harsh word, except once from the captain when one of the boys fell overboard, and he had to turn the boat around. I had visions of us recovering a body, but the youngster could swim – and I certainly wasn't going to volunteer any rescue attempt – there were crocs that disappeared into deeper water as we approached.

As the only 'whitey' on the journey, I naturally elicited interest, but communications were convoluted as I hadn't yet mastered much French. The only English my fellow travellers had heard came from occasional American sitcoms at street-side bars. Those impromptu English lessons happened reasonably often since more than half a century ago most language dubbing lay well into the future.

I was offered food dozens of times but rarely accepted because, frankly, some of the dishes looked revolting, though I relished the bananas and mangos they gave me. My refusals were always accepted with grace because I would indicate that I was nauseous – pointing to my gut – which, in fact, I was.

Things stayed that way until I reached Lambarene.

For all that, the journey was not only remarkable, but it also remains one of the most memorable three days and nights of my life. The river presented a plethora of first-time moments that can only be described as extraordinary, even though the Ogowe River – at 1,200 kilometres – is only a quarter the length of the great Congo waterway. Yet, for most of its final journey towards the ocean, it is just as broad and as fast-flowing. In places, the great river is one and a half kilometres wide.

In truth, you'd have to go far to find anybody who has even heard of the Ogowe, which seemed always to have been a mysterious and out-of-the-way entity in those faraway days, much the same as it is today. Both the Amazon and the Nile offer boat cruises, but there were none on the Ogowe in the 1960s (except for the likes of the *Matilda*).

There was nothing simple about navigating this river in either direction. Once on the water, there was no discernible shoreline; just a dense, clinging jungle mass topped by gnarled, overhanging trees, lianas and creepers – some thirty or forty metres tall and which sometimes blotted out the sunlight as we passed below. This was also some of the most expansive jungle in Africa and, as one guidebook claimed, outside the Amazon Basin. The Ogowe remains the densest vegetative world that has still not been properly explored by man.

Jungle sounds emerged from those dark shoreline depths that would be impossible to replicate in any studio, ofttimes ominously deep in the jungle and just out of sight. The chorus of growls, barks, howls, roars, squawks and squeals most times defied classification, and I thought it peculiar that we rarely saw any large animals. They were there, of course, like the great pods of hippo, hundreds strong, that would materialise from nowhere, and the occasional snake swimming from one bank to the other, some as thick as my arm.

As we passed, we could hardly miss the occasional trumpeting of elephants somewhere in the distance or the jarring screeches of chimpanzees. The presence of our boat must have been infuriating, intruding on their domain as they spied on us from their lairs. But of the troops themselves, invisible.

It was the same with birdlife. We saw thousands of feathered couriers decked in every possible colour imaginable – so exquisite that they defied description. To my untrained eye, some seemed not to belong to either the parrot or waterbird families, and we rarely got close enough to take individual photos.

I would sit on the roof of the old craft, isolating myself from the racket below and couldn't help but be enthralled by all those sounds – the bird cries were like music, joyous and ravishingly beautiful as great flocks winged across the water in their version of graceful African unison. One could imagine the great primal order of life that had been building in isolation since the beginning of time – at first glance it might have seemed chaotic – but in the great natural order of such things, it sometimes overwhelmed.

My journeys on the Ogowe River – there were two trips – up and downstream over different years, were something I never did again. Though I have travelled great stretches of the Nile – from Khartoum to the Mediterranean, and the Zambezi – neither shares Central Africa's primordial seclusion. My weeks on steamers on Lakes Victoria and Tanganyika pale by comparison.

The thought often crossed my mind while chugging into the interior of a verdant tropical Africa was what would happen if we had to make a dash for it – if the *Matilda* were to capsize or strike a rock. The prospect of trying to reach firm ground through the tangled mass of jungle and putrescent undergrowth would have been horrendous. Then, once ashore, could there be any way through? More to the point, would anybody even come looking for us?

Joseph Conrad had the measure of this unsettling primeval world – that sometimes had a detrimental effect on people's minds – when he wrote about the Congo River, another tremendous African waterway, perhaps two hours by small plane south of our location. Conrad's opus, *Heart of Darkness*, is a compassionate description of life as it was then in this remote wilderness. He recorded those thoughts in ink more than a century ago, and the truth is, almost nothing has changed. It was, he declared:

> Like travelling back to the earliest beginnings of the world, when vegetation rioted on the earth and the big trees were kings. The air was warm, thick, heavy, and sluggish. There was no joy in the brilliance of sunshine. On silvery banks, hippos and alligators sunned themselves side by side. The broadening waters flow through a mob of wooded islands; you lost your way on the river as you would in a desert...this stillness of life did not in the least resemble a peace. It was the stillness of an implacable force brooding over an inscrutable intention. It looked at you with a vengeful aspect.

What is also notable is that this specific corner of Africa – spread out haphazardly along the Ogowe – was penetrated only a decade or two before that illustrious Pole experienced the vagaries of the Congo for himself.

Pierre Savorgnan de Brazza, an enterprising French explorer – and the man who put Brazzaville on the African map – made his way up the Ogowe in the 1870s. In turn, it is said, his diaries inspired the American author Edgar Rice Burroughs to write about John Clayton II (Viscount Greystoke), a fictional archetypal feral child called Tarzan – who had been raised in the African jungle by Mangani great apes.

Indeed, we were heading straight for that original fictional setting.

Though initial impressions are deceptive, both banks were home to hundreds of villages – the majority out of sight from our boat – and probably just as well. Later, I learned that there was a good deal of friction between the tribes living there, usually over hunting rights.

Our helmsman would be guided in by local travellers on board who were headed towards their forest communities. From what I could observe, it took considerable skill to get in and out of the narrow channels – you'd probably miss them on Google Maps. We'd linger briefly as the transient and his family disembarked and then cast off again. More than once, it occurred to me that I could have used a brief session in the water for an improvised bath but was deterred by crocs. Those predators were everywhere!

The rainforest inhabitants always appeared to be aware of our imminent arrival. Routinely, we'd be greeted by youngsters in their dugout pirogues, often throngs of them. Ebullient, they'd shout and splash with their paddles, gushing with delight. It was their idea of a waterborne greeting and it worked splendidly.

As we drew close to the riverbank, we'd hastily supplement our supply of forest leaves – some a metre wide – to be used as dinner plates, after which they'd be thrown overboard. There were also smooth-surfaced plants that were almost silk-like and used as toilet paper; just as well because there wasn't any available. I kept my paper rolls hidden because I wasn't sure when next I'd be able to buy any.

At night on the river, mysterious drums of distant and unseen settlements in the carpet-thick woodland would resonate into the jungle, and it was eerie. They seemed to be calling out to us, not improbable – one village talking to the next – with the drums communicating in their own language. Several times I fell asleep to distant throbbing beats.

I repeated that journey, travelling downstream many years later with my son. That trip, however, from Lambarene to Port Gentil was on board an open metal barge. I paid good money to enjoy the luxury of us being the only passengers because I could not have handled *Matilda*'s jarring cacophony again.

The boat dropped me on the south bank, almost within sight of the Schweitzer hospital on the opposite shore. That meant hailing another craft to take me across, but it wasn't all that easy. Gathered around me were the survivors of a recent road accident that had left two dead and four people seriously injured.

I was surprised that the wounded chose not to go to the spanking new government hospital in the middle of town – recently built with French government aid money. But no, each one of them demanded to be taken to *le Grand Docteur*. So, we all waited until a bigger boat came along.

Without ceremony, we were finally deposited onto an open stretch of beach. We'd hardly landed before that venerable old man hobbled down the steps from his dispensary towards the river's edge. With his distinctive features, he needed no introduction. Dr Albert Schweitzer greeted me cursorily, told me to go ahead and find the French nurse – whose name I can't remember – she would show me my room. He turned and focused his attention on the patients who were being helped or carried ashore.

What struck me about that event was that I knew he was born in 1875 – putting him on the cusp of his ninetieth year – yet he was still working. The doctor died on 4 September 1965, which must have been about eight or nine months after my visit to his hospital. If I'm hazy about the actual dates, that is to be expected because I was travelling alone, with no shortwave radio of my own. It meant that I couldn't keep abreast of current events – his passing could have been only weeks after I'd finally reached London.

Only after his death did it emerge that he had been diagnosed with a terminal illness caused primarily by cerebral vascular insufficiency. Yet it never stopped him from doing what he could to help others.

The sunny afternoon when I first shook the hand of this great man was indeed a momentous occasion. It left me feeling elated – at long last, I had met Albert Schweitzer. I had previously read one of his books, which I confess I found tough going.

Once the car accident emergency had been dealt with, and though not granting me anything close to the amount of time I'd hoped for, I still spent several hours with him, on and off, during my week at what was then one of the most famous hospitals in the world.

One morning, he donned his customary white 'colonial' pith helmet that had not only seen better days but had holes in it, and accompanied me on a visit to the leprosarium – quite a distance from his main medical centre or *Clinique*, as he called it. The leper colony was spread out in a deep forest setting that could house 200 long-term patients. Several Japanese doctors were in attendance, working and living on site. They effectively ran their own show under the auspices of the doctor, and, from what little I could observe, it must have been harrowing. Still, he told me, this dedicated group was doing what they termed 'personal penance' for some of the excesses committed by their fellow countrymen in their Far East conflict. It was evident that he appreciated the help.

I recall walking along the forest track and coming upon a long line of army ants, much larger than the typical variety but seemingly quite disciplined. With a quick movement of his arm, Dr Schweitzer stopped us both in our tracks and in a quiet voice, said that I should be careful where I put my feet: 'You don't want to hurt those little creatures,' were his words.

It was all part of his long-advocated 'Reverence for Life' philosophy, though Schweitzer would use the German noun *Weltanschauung*. He was emphatic: his doctrine meant *all* forms of life and one of the reasons why he was a vegetarian. Curiously, he had no objection to insect repellents, including mosquito sprays, and some claimed that he often enjoyed fried liver on Sundays.

The good doctor was thoroughly familiar with South Africa. He asked me in English (he would have preferred French or German) how things were going there. For many years South African doctors had made regular treks northwards to the Equator to offer a hand at Lambarene. Their expenses were covered by Harry Oppenheimer, son of the Johannesburg gold-mining magnate, Sir Ernest Oppenheimer of Anglo-American fame. Dr Jack Penn, a plastic surgeon of international repute who had done excellent work on wounded soldiers, was another of his friends. As a sculptor, he had done bronze busts of both Schweitzer and Harry Oppenheimer.

An unusual aspect was that the hospital used a fleet of pirogues to fetch and carry patients, usually from across the river. They sometimes covered vast distances, almost always without the help of outboard motors, though things have changed since then. New arrivals would have their presence announced by an antique bell – still there today – alongside his old tin-roofed residence, which has become a museum.

Many of Dr Schweitzer's things have remained, and the last time I visited Lambarene to make a TV documentary on Gabon – which included the hospital – the film crew was shown around. Our escort, one of the ex-pat nurses, told us that some of the doctor's personal items had been stolen as souvenirs, including his reading glasses.

'People!' she exclaimed in disgust.

As for the Tarzan legend – and whether Edgar Rice Burroughs had possibly set the scene for the legendary wild man's actions somewhere in the Ogowe vicinity – the doctor smiled and said that I had no idea how many times he'd been asked that question.

Someone else there mentioned that it was possible that Burroughs, born in the United States in the same year as the doctor, knew about the jungle clinic and had spoken to people who had visited the hospital. This might have given him a platform on which to base his Tarzan concept though obviously, Albert Schweitzer never came into any of it.

Anyone who spent time at the hospital was invariably regaled by some of the doctor's aphorisms – not necessarily by him personally – but more than likely by members of staff with whom we constantly rubbed shoulders.

One favourite frequently bandied about reflected strongly on the man himself (as well as everyday life in the compound): 'There are two means of refuge from the miseries of life: music and cats.' Another, I recall, was quite simply, 'Do something wonderful, people may imitate it.' Both maxims give the visitor a pretty candid idea of the man, even if he could be gruff at times.

More salient, in the words of that maverick commentator, Gregory Corso, author of CooperToons Books, 'He was gentle, cantankerous, kind, *ornery*, and a great humanitarian.' Corso continues, and I quote:

> Just as Albert [Schweitzer] had taken on the *Quest of the Historical Jesus*, even in his own lifetime, writers and journalists began taking pot-shots at the man himself in their Quest for the Historical Albert. That wasn't hard to do, since even as a young man, Albert had a demanding and, as some would say, self-centred character. That said, I know of no other medical practitioner who remained the ultimately dedicated professional into his tenth decade.

The hospital has an interesting history. Albert Schweitzer, among other accomplishments, was one of the great minds of his epoch, and still relatively young when he became a world authority on the music of Bach. He was awarded the Nobel Peace Prize in 1952, inter alia for his altruism and tireless humanitarian work.

He was well into his thirties when he qualified medically, having gained an MD at the University of Strasbourg in 1913. His wife, Helene, of Jewish extraction, took up nursing after they'd married the year before and, within months, set off for Africa at his own expense. She was to become his anaesthetist.

One anecdote that emerged from that period was the stop made by their ship in Dakar, then a French colony. In strolling about town, they came upon a man brutally beating a donkey that had been hitched to a cart with a load that was patently beyond its physical capabilities. Dr Schweitzer berated the man for cruelty and promptly bought the donkey, though there is no record of what he did with it.

Lambarene followed, and from the start, things were difficult. The couple set up shop near a local mission station and briefly lived in a shed formerly used as a chicken hut. They wasted little time in constructing a corrugated-iron hospital, with Schweitzer doing most of the heavy work including laying bricks and fitting a roof. The structure had two rooms: a consulting room and an operating theatre, with a dispensary and the sterilising area below the broad eaves.

The Schweitzers' bungalow was then constructed, also in a simple style, and they employed Joseph, a French-speaking Galoa as their assistant. He'd arrived at the outpost as a patient, liked what he experienced and stayed. What made the place different from most other West African clinics was that Schweitzer had to accept that many of his patients – having heard of the remarkable wonders he could do for the sick – had filtered down from many isolated villages in the interior. Trusting only in good faith, they travelled hundreds of kilometres to Lambarene, almost always with their families in tow.

He found a simple solution that suited everybody, at least for a time. Funds were low, and the facility was blessed with very few staff, so patients were housed in huts that were partially open to the elements. They were not much different from where these folk lived in their villages, which suggests a strong element of prescience on the doctor's part.

It was accepted that the families accompanying the patients would tend to their needs, including ablutions, washing, cooking, and feeding. The hospital provided raw food, primarily vegetables, while families prepared their traditional dishes over open fires. If they had a few francs, they could buy a chicken in the nearby town.

As for toilets, there was no money to construct them. Schweitzer solved that problem by building several 'long drops' at the edge of a small precipice adjacent to the living areas. These were still in use the first time I visited and were my only recourse for the necessary. Both the living conditions of patients and the by-now institutionalised sanitary conditions came under fierce fire once the international press started to arrive.

Journalists were aghast that at the bottom of the communal toilet pit – clearly in view from above – human waste was being very competently dealt with by zillions of maggots. This primitive system had worked perfectly well for decades, as it still does in much of the African continent, but the media found fault. The squeamish were repulsed, and many went into print, accusing the doctor of unsanitary and unhygienic principles.

The same charge was levelled at the hospital's open-air wards, but as Helene Schweitzer pointed out, the very idea of putting someone who had just emerged from the jungle – and had no experience of the civilised world – into a bed with sheets and pillows and in a room with nothing but frames and painted walls, would undoubtedly have had an adverse effect on many. For a start, she declared, they would be deprived of the faces and immediate presence of those they knew and loved, never mind the costs of caring for people whose needs were basic. Food would also have been a problem – most of those poor beings would neither appreciate nor enjoy hospital fare on stainless steel trays.

As Madame Schweitzer told one outspoken American critic: 'You are trying to impose European standards on a society with absolutely no experience of such things. We try to keep everything as basic as possible…ultimately, it works towards a better healing process.'

Dr Albert Schweitzer did not need to clarify to his critics that most of those who emerged out of the most primitive overgrown forest imaginable had never known anything but the village witch doctor (nowadays called a natural healer). Not only was the infant mortality rate among the tribes in the interior appalling, but few of these folk had ever seen anything as basic as a light bulb. It was axiomatic that they would hardly have understood sterilisation.

Proof of that pudding came with the tens of thousands of ordinary people who, over a couple of generations, emerged from the harsh interior and headed straight for the cluster of low buildings with their distinctive corrugated iron roofs. They wanted the familiar and trusted, that which they knew and accepted as having proved its worth. Like the four people injured in the motor accident when I arrived, they preferred methods that had been successful innumerable times in the past.

I spent a week at the hospital and was mostly left to my own devices, moving freely among the buildings and patients' huts to see and do what I pleased. Most of the European staff could speak English, and they didn't object to my presence: the lone visit of this occasional scribbler went on to become a flood in later years.

I slept in one of the guest rooms. Instead of conventional glass windows, all were open gauze to allow for ventilation and keep out mosquitoes; here, too, air-conditioners still lay years ahead. Each room had a bed, a small table with a washbasin, a towel and nothing more, though we were warned to shake out our shoes in the morning before putting them on because of scorpions. We were also told to check the path for snakes when returning to our quarters in the dark.

Meals were enjoyed communally, with *le Docteur* in attendance. After dinner, he would occasionally sit down at the old foot-peddle organ and play his favourite Bach. It was enchanting, but that tradition would soon end; nobody present knew just how ill he was. Then, having eaten and played for his supper, he would push back his chair. Almost like clockwork, we would all stand as he headed off alone to his bed; Madame Schweitzer had died a few years earlier.

It is on record that in the first year of working with the sick, Dr Schweitzer and his wife Helene treated more than 2,000 patients. It could not have been easy because most of the ailments were tropical, of which neither – in the beginning – had any experience. The most common affliction was malaria, followed by yellow fever, but the Schweitzers were never struck down by either, and if they were, there is no record.[1]

There were also cases of yaws (a chronic infection that affects the skin, bone and cartilage), scabies, amoebic dysentery, heart disease, sleeping sickness, typhoid, tick bite fever, strangulated hernias and more. The most common everyday injuries he dealt with were open wounds, sometimes gruesome and caused by machetes in man-to-man confrontations, and which would sometimes elicit an offhand comment from the doctor to nobody in particular, like '*C'est l'Afrique.*'

Until the Japanese arrived to atone for their nation's sins, the husband-and-wife team had to treat leprosy cases themselves, again at personal risk, even though the afflicted were restricted to a distant corner of the compound to avoid cross-contamination. And if that were not enough, a report stated that they were sometimes faced with problems of a hostile tribal nature that included deliberate poisonings. These could be quite cunning because obscure bush potions were employed in bids to stymie the doctor's success rate. Add to that little imbroglio fetishism and cannibalism, of which one tribe – the Mbahouin – were not particularly averse.

It was not surprising that in 1923 Helene – following the birth of their daughter, Rhena – had a 'breakdown'. She felt that she was no longer able to live in the tropics.

No wonder: the average day on the banks of the Ogowe in the early period was taken up – apart from her role as the only anaesthetist – by tending to more severe cases, overseeing laundry, the provision of fresh bandages, dispensary work as well as personally sterilising the clinic's surgical instruments. Helene Schweitzer was the ultimate general factotum.

In addition, she had a home to manage, which included dealing with an infestation of snakes, a constant war on ants and spiders (despite her husband's view on such matters; she was the pragmatist in their remarkable relationship), as well as keeping the peace among warring factions along the Ogowe River. On top of this, she was an

---

1   Jo and Walter Munz. *Albert Schweitzer's Lambarene: A Legacy of Humanity for Our World Today.* Penobscot Press: 2010.

inveterate letter writer. The diary she kept of their first two years in Africa eventually ran to 300 pages, which begs the question: where did she find the time?

With his wife in poor health, the now-ageing doctor moved the family to Baden-Württemberg, where he built a house before returning to Africa, this time on his own. Albert Schweitzer would regularly return to Europe, but the solitary life must have been difficult. Also, he was totally cut off in Africa for the duration of hostilities.

There were numerous reports of his links in later years to a Viennese-born American socialite, Erica Anderson, who became a regular visitor to Lambarene as a photographer and film producer. Wealthy, she made nineteen trips to the hospital over several decades, and in 1958 Mrs Anderson won an Oscar for her documentary, *The Life and Times of Albert Schweitzer*. Aged 62, she died in September 1975 in Great Barrington, Massachusetts, just over a decade after the man who had meant so much to her had passed. She asked that she be buried in Lambarene, where she was finally interred.

I returned to the hospital in the late 1980s while making a TV documentary about Gabon. Naturally, the man and his remarkable clinic had their place. I was even able to take a photo of his grave. Not much had changed except for several new structures – effectively a new hospital – erected a little further into the interior and away from the river. However, the old red-tin-roofed structures below remained intact and, I'm told, are still standing.

What had altered was the hospital administration which seemed to have imposed many of its European strictures on the establishment. This was rather shabbily reflected by my film crew being treated with a disdain that fringed on aggression – it was almost as if we were harbingers of the Ebola virus. I'd hoped we could stay in the original guest cottages, but this was declined, and we were shown the door, presumably because I did not pave the way with greenbacks.

Clearly, we were not welcome, and we felt it keenly. What to do but find somewhere else to stay, though since then, the hospital has made provision for paying guests.

I found a comfortable little hotel in the downtown area of town, appropriately named the Albert Schweitzer Hotel. The *gérant* was an imposingly tall man with a shock of white hair and the distinctive swashbuckling moustache of, I supposed at the time, his late father. He was neither black nor white, but one couldn't miss the implications – and what a delightful host he was.

Little had changed in Lambarene town on that second visit though, judging by recent photos, the place has grown substantially, even though conditions on the country's roads had deteriorated, which I experienced personally. It happened while attempting to persuade our driver on the road out of Libreville to the old hospital that he should not overtake a lumber truck while another was coming straight at us from the opposite direction at great speed. That idiot was in stitches, giggling hysterically because we hadn't been hit, which was when I told him to stop the car and I took the wheel.

Along the river itself, many of the original double-storey colonial trading houses that lined the water still stood – much that took place during regular working hours was focused on the market area. There were scores of boats of all descriptions scurrying noisily about and, as might have been expected, pirogues (some with high-powered outboard engines) to the fore. The place was just as busy as it had always been.

Several oil barges lay alongside a new improvised quay. Some of the oil craft, thirty or forty metres long and made of steel were either headed towards or returning from Port Gentil. Of the old *Matilda*, nothing. She had been replaced by a few fairly modern ferries, though the basic infrastructure of some remained the same – row upon row of hard seats and no doors or windows. I expect that if I ventured onto the river again, I'd definitely end up on the roof again.

More recent reports suggest that several entrepreneurs had brought in larger modern craft that were faster and could cover the distance from Port Gentil to Lambarene in hours. What had not changed in the Gabonese interior since my previous visit two decades before, were the snakes. Very literally, they were everywhere. We'd stroll up Lambarene's main drag along the river and observe those reptiles – some eight or ten feet long – slithering past and impervious to the presence of humans. I would have thought that it would matter because this was now a reasonably busy town.

Those snakes within view were the ones we could see – there must have been thousands more secreted behind logs, culverts, irrigation ditches, drains, basements, or possibly in or under buildings. Yet locals rarely gave them a second glance because most townsfolk had grown up with this spectacle.

The situation was not peculiar to this stretch of the river. It applied to the entire country – and those beyond its borders – the inhabitants had to cope with similar predicaments, though probably not quite as severe.

On the offshore islands of São Tomé and Principe, including the former Spanish colony of Equatorial Guinea (previously Fernando Pó), conditions were just as bad, if not worse (I spent time in them all). As one resident commented drily when questioned, 'Who cares? The snakes get on with their existence and we with ours... we try not to disturb each other.'

Small wonder that vast West African regions are not, as the brochures like to phrase it, 'tourist friendly'.

CHAPTER 6

Plantain and palm wine in Libreville

The road ahead was uncertain once I'd reached the coast and Libreville, the bustling Gabonese capital, which lay a couple of hours by bush taxi to the west of Lambarene.

The name Libreville comes from the place along the African coast where France freed several thousand enslaved people it had rescued from illegal transatlantic traffickers on the high seas. The Royal Navy had released its slaving victims on the shores of what was to become Freetown, the capital of Sierra Leone. You got it: '*town of the free*'. American ships put their freed slaves ashore on a peninsula in present-day Liberia. The liberated reciprocated by calling their capital Monrovia, named after the fifth American President, James Monroe.

More to the point, those rescue efforts of enslaved people by the various navies – as commendable as they were – continued well into the 19th century. Most people then – and even today – believed that the British had abolished slavery in 1807, but that was not the case. That Parliamentary edict affected only the trade in humans and not the institution itself.[1] In the Caribbean alone, there were still three-quarters of a million people in bondage. In the Indian Ocean, the Portuguese continued selling those poor souls – the majority Mozambicans – to the French, who put them to work in sugar plantations on their La Reunion Island colony.

In theory, my four-hour, cross-country journey from the hospital to the coast should have been a dream, but our driver constantly battled logging trucks which rarely gave way when they roared past at 110 kilometres an hour. Quite a few times we were forced to swing hard into the heavily overgrown periphery that lined the route. It was either that or head-on, which was a problem I encountered almost everywhere I travelled on Africa's roads and for those who have visited Africa more recently, the situation is even worse.

---

1   King George III signed the Act for the Abolition of the Slave Trade into law on 25 March 1807, banning trading in enslaved people in the British Empire.

Reaching Libreville for the first time was a delight, characterised by broad, palm-lined streets, tall buildings going up and the kind of joie de vivre that enveloped much of the continent in the 1960s; the city hummed. With independence from France, a burgeoning logging industry and a mega-million-dollar oil production facility taking shape, Gabon was attracting oodles of foreign money from Europe and America. Naturally, prices soared; simply put, my shallow pockets couldn't handle the expense. I suspect that the spate of new embassies was partly to blame, but so was France, and it started with the country's leading diplomat.

Not to be outdone by the Americans or the Soviets, Paris chose the most prestigious spot in Libreville – an immense wooded park overlooking the city – for the splendiferous residence of the French ambassador. The residence was just off Boulevard de l'indépendance and is still one of the most striking in Africa. It was also the annual social event on 14 July (Bastille Day) where in one of the grandest events on the calendar, ministers and opponents of the local political hierarchy, with champagne in hand, joyfully laid aside their differences to toast the Franco-Gabonese friendship. It was also an alcoholic excuse to forget colonial differences – and the French were good at that.

President Léon M'ba, the country's newly ensconced leader never encouraged the old colonial guard to head for home. Because of the flourishing logging industry and oil about to take off (which made him an Élysées Palace favourite), the majority were firmly entrenched within the country's economic, government and social infrastructures and he was hardly going to rock that boat.

It was no secret that the portly M'ba viewed events in the Democratic Republic of the Congo – then battling a full-scale civil war – with distress. Army mutinies and revolutions across Africa had become too commonplace for complacency and the one reason he approached Israel was probably to provide him with the kind of Praetorian protection that ensured longevity. I reckon there must have been more Israeli agents in Libreville at one stage than in any other country in Africa. It was hardly coincidental that the same situation held for President Félix Houphouët-Boigny's Ivory Coast.

I took film crews to both countries to make documentaries about modern Africa in the 1980s. Squads of security personnel, headed by Israeli officers in mufti, would swoop down on us and demand to see permits, which, fortunately, my 'fixers' had always arranged. Very professional and polite, the head of each team would address us in English; satisfied that we were who we said we were, they'd bid us *adieu*.

Twelve or fifteen years before, though, nobody took much notice of this youngster in a bush hat and short pants ambling restlessly about Libreville – as I did for several days – rather desperately searching for a means to head further north. For a start, I avoided European-style restaurants because even a small *salade verte* could put you back ten dollars, so I gravitated towards the fringes of the African townships. Soon enough, I acquired a taste for plantain and seasoned goat stew dishes, together with something else quite novel – palm wine. I even tried a cane rat concoction at one stage – they're as big as cats, and yes, they eat sugar cane – and I suppose you could say it was passable.

My objective was to reach Nigeria as soon as possible. But the overland route was blocked by Spanish Guinea, part of which comprised a mainland enclave called Rio Muni, spread-eagled outwards from the coast and bigger than New Jersey. Madrid discouraged visitors to its equatorial possession (today listed on maps as Equatorial Guinea), and the main 'highway' to the north out of Libreville – by all accounts still not surfaced – was in rough shape.

If I went overland, I was told I'd have to circumvent that colonial relic and make a wide detour into the jungle. I was cautioned that, as with Pointe-Noire, it might take me a week or a month to cover the distance. So reluctantly, I bided my time and reverted to hope.

About a dozen years later, Libreville became integral to my life when I headed into a tiny rebel country in eastern Nigeria – it had declared itself independent – and renamed itself Biafra. I spent a good time covering that war, and I'd like to think that as a consequence one of my best books eventually emerged.[2]

But to get across those land-locked frontiers, stringently controlled by the Nigerian Army and Air Force, I – like everybody else who either wanted to cover the war or deliver supplies – had to enter the rebel state on a relief flight. Most of those clandestine flights originated out of São Tomé, then still a Portuguese colony. Still more aircraft, mainly French and loaded with weapons and ammunition, operated out of Libreville airport.

That placed me in a quandary on my arrival in Gabon on my next visit in 1969. Before flying into Biafra, I had applied for a visa and been given one by the Biafran diplomatic legation in Dar es Salaam. Everything should have been hunky-dory; however, on arrival at Libreville, I was put under 'house arrest' and confined to the airport precincts.

There was no hotel or guest lounge, so I slept on benches and got enough food to stay alive from a two-bit hamburger stand that also served beer. While I protested volubly, the Gabonese officials I was brought before maintained that they knew absolutely nothing about Biafra, even though a dozen or more flights were heading there every night from the self-same air terminal to which I was restricted. As I discovered later, my British passport had caused the glitch. Someone in Gabon's foreign office had questioned what 'my true intentions' were. They probably had good reason for doing so because Whitehall did all it could to stymie Colonel Odumegwu Ojukwu's Biafran liberation cause.

---

2   Al J. Venter, *Biafra's War: A Tribal Conflict in Nigeria that Left a Million Dead*. Helion: 2016.

It was oil, of course, that did it, since nine-tenths of Nigeria's oil resources – the second or third largest deposits of crude on the continent – lay under Biafran soil. Moreover, considering that companies such as British Petroleum were involved in Nigeria and Gabon's start-up oil industry, Libreville had reason to be cautious.

One evening, after days of kicking my heels at what is today the Léon M'ba International Airport, I wandered across the tarmac to the control tower. I got talking to a French air traffic controller who asked me in perfect English where I was from. Cape Town, I told him, and produced my 'other' passport, which was my South African passport. I'd made a habit of packing it into my briefcase whenever I flew into Black Africa because I never knew when it might come in handy.

The flight controller and everybody else at the air terminal was familiar with my having been detained and with a sigh of relief, he exclaimed, '*Voila!* Why didn't you tell those bastards that at the immigration counter before? They all thought you were linked to the fucking Brits.'

The following night I found myself on a battered old DC-6 loaded with baby food headed across open water to Biafra. I use the word 'battered' advisedly because the Douglas Aircraft Company in the United States had long since stopped building those planes – the last one came off the production line in 1958 – and our machine was well past its use-by date.

We came under fairly heavy fire on the way into Biafra. Still, I'll leave that for a later chapter, together with my dealings with Frederick Forsyth – we covered the war together with the famous Italian lensman, Romano Cagnoni.

One of the first problems I faced on arriving in Libreville following my departure from Albert Schweitzer's jungle hospital was where to stay. I simply did not have the money for the hotels where most ex-pats gathered, so I settled for a *gîte* in the townships. The owner, a rather broad, perpetually smiling mama, was more pleased to see me than the reverse, for no other reason than the place was decrepit. Also, it worried me that her house lay adjacent to a slum.

My new *hôtesse* – for want of a better word – was one of those friendly old dears one regularly encounters in Africa, and she assured me that the place was relatively safe. Then she did the unexpected – the good lady decamped into the only other room in the house and gave me her own – with a freshly bedecked bed. I was understandably perplexed, but there was no ulterior motive. She merely wanted to please me, which is how things often happen in Africa.

Meantime, my peregrinations in and around Libreville took me just about everywhere. I tried the bus station where they said, yes, vehicles were heading north, but nobody could say when – or if – they would end up in the Cameroon. I tried the harbour several times, and while occasional small ferries were heading out, including several going to the Portuguese islands, none were going north.

Finally, I met a young Israeli shipping agent who thought he might be able to help. He said that flights were going to Douala, but they were irregular. What he didn't tell me – and which I only discovered after I had boarded a Super Constellation – was that the aircraft had recently delivered a shipment of fresh meat from Rhodesia. It was en route to Douala to pick up a different load, species unknown but urgently needed by Ian Smith's rebel government.

My 'ticket', he declared, would cost me US$100, and I wasn't going to argue. My new Israeli pal gave me no details to start with but sensing my need, he suggested that I could sleep in one of his company's warehouses on the city's outskirts: it would have to be on the floor because there were no beds. There was a caveat, he warned. He'd have to lock me in at a reasonable hour each evening and return in the morning to let me out. There was no charge; frankly, I had to accept because my money was going fast and I still had the long run across West Africa.

What made my sleeping quarters different from before was that while I was safe from human intrusion, the storage shed backed onto a mangled jungle backdrop, with its share of larger creatures moving about in the dark. That included a variety of primates prone to screeching loudly if any threat presented itself, probably one or more of the big cats. I raised this with the Israeli, who confirmed that the jungle started just beyond the city and was still pretty wild. He confided that there were constant reports of domestic dogs disappearing at night – nothing remained except splotches of blood in the streets. Even today, leopards still live on the outskirts of some large African cities like Nairobi and Bangui. Libreville couldn't have been any different, but at least the critters couldn't get into my shed.

Once I'd bedded down that first night – after snuffing out the candle that my Israeli friend had kindly provided – I quickly discovered, judging by the noise, that there were an awful lot of smaller creatures living under the same roof. I have no idea how many snakes there were, except that there must have been quite a few because on waking each morning, I'd spot them peering out at me from behind bags of cement and boxes of who-knows-what and several were whoppers. But like the cane rats (some as big as alley cats), as well as scorpions and tarantulas that were big enough to cover my hand, none of these creatures ever bothered me.

I spent three or four nights in my new dwelling before being picked up early one morning and taken to the airport. Without having my passport checked or encountering a single Gabonese official, I was shunted onto the aircraft with my kit in hand and minutes later, we were airborne. There was a single seat at the back of the empty plane. It occurred to me that the meat hulks, probably unloaded in Gabon, must have been transported from southern Africa on hooks hanging from the aircraft's topmost spars because the entire fuselage was covered in dried blood. Douala, my destination, was a droll place and, by all accounts, still is – a not much-cherished destination by anybody who has been there.

The city lies on a large river surrounded by vast tracts of swamp, mostly mangrove and fringed by jungle. Unlike Libreville, the heat – soporific and coupled with an extremely high humidity level – is more intense than just about anywhere else in West Africa. The mosquitoes are almost overwhelming all year round.

It's the rain that does it. There is rarely a dry season, and the rainfall sometimes reaches four metres a year, unbearable to the average European or American. One old missionary was in the habit of telling his congregation to forgive the rain because it did not know how to go up.

Douala has also been the site of several aircraft accidents, including several passenger planes that, if not inexplicable, were unexpected – most went down immediately after take-off. That included, in 2007, Kenya Airways Flight 507, a Boeing 737-800 with 114 passengers and crew on board. It ended up in the sodden jungle a few kilometres out of town, like the others. As with two commercial flights from way past, conditions were so torturous that it took recovery teams three or four days to bring back the bodies, many partly devoured by crocodiles.

The city has several other claims to fame. Cameroon (Kamerun as it was called when Kaiser Wilhelm held sway) – and any mention of the place in the old days was usually prefaced with 'fever-ravaged' – was one of Germany's larger African colonies. It took British forces several severe military disasters – and eventually French help – to conquer the country.

That was essential because, like Togo, farther to the west along the coast and also a German colony, it had a radio transmitting station that could connect directly with Europe. They were used to relay messages from German East Africa and present-day Namibia (or *Deutsch-Südwestafrika*, as it then was) and German ships operating in the Indian and South Atlantic oceans. Germany lost all its African colonial possessions after the 'Great War'.

In 1919 a League of Nations mandate divided Cameroon unevenly between Paris and London: control of the larger eastern portion was to be administered by France and the smaller western chunk was supposed to be Anglophone and administered by Britain. In the years that followed, there were several insurgencies, centred mainly on who owned or controlled what. This indicated that the arranged marriage was unhappy from the beginning.

The biggest gripe – and the reason for a current low-intensity guerrilla war – is that in the pre-independence period and after that, the use of English was all but ignored by the country's preponderantly French capital, Yaoundé.

Ambling about downtown Douala in the mid-1960s, I was astonished by the number of older people who still spoke German – many of whom hankered after 'yesterday's traditions' – and the distinctly Teutonic architectural style of government and residential buildings. The majority have been torn down, but the German influence remained prominent for decades.

I spoke to an old man who offered me a few life-sized Foumban metal masks that were outstanding and I still have in my collection. Before taking the best of the bunch, I asked if he spoke German. He placed his basket on the ground before answering and nodded in the affirmative. He told me that it was going back almost half a century and that his language skills were partly forgotten.

'Age,' he made clear, drawing himself erect: '*Es ist mein alter*' – was the phrase he used.

Then, in perfect German, he recalled those 'happy days' as if they were something quite recent. I asked him to continue in English because my German wasn't nearly as good as his.

'They were strong,' he declared, adding that the Germans had been fair. 'They played good to us, but if our people went against them, they could be hard…we understood that.'

'You were sorry to see them go then?' I asked.

'Yes.'

'What is it that you miss the most about them?'

'They were straight, they meant what they said, and kept promises. Also, they followed the teachings of the Bible and paid us well for our labour…there were never disputes about money.'

There was sufficient work, he justified, and if their children became ill, German doctors and nurses helped. He held the view, possibly old-fashioned and hardly politically correct today, that if they were beaten (which was often), it was always for a good reason.

'We understood that and accepted it…it was the way.'

He continued: 'The French here today call me *M'sieu*, which means mister. But you never really know what they are thinking…it was different with the Germans… they could look you in the eye.'

While reality is often filtered through the hazy lens of patriotism, I could sense that he was not fond of the French, who had ruled Cameroon since the end of the 'Great War' and only permitted that vast country, after roughly forty years, to declare independence in 1960. I left it at that because the dignified old fellow suddenly became reluctant to continue. It was a chapter of his life from years before that was closed, and I didn't wish to embarrass him further.

I was to discover often enough, traipsing across that vast continent, that its inhabitants were sometimes blessed with long memories. Though they would not say as much, they could hardly hold in high regard a society with a history of almost deifying the man who said of black people, 'I am for the whites because I am white.'

Napoleon was, of course, referring derogatorily to one of the great military leaders of his time, Haiti's Toussaint Louverture – a black general who gave both French and

British military forces a run for their money. Louverture, on the orders of Bonaparte himself, died ignominiously in prison after he'd been captured.[3]

It is interesting, apropos that quiet chat in Douala about early colonial days, that years later – while passing through Tanzania – I again met an old fellow sitting on a bench overlooking Dar es Salaam harbour. It had been a long day, and after exchanging pleasantries, I recall telling him, on being asked, that I had a British passport.

He turned towards me and asked: 'Oh my goodness, that is good to hear, but when are you British coming back?'

'Back?' I queried.

'Yes, to run our affairs here…we've had enough of all this Socialist rubbish. You people did a very good job when you were here before, and many of us want more of it.' And that was two generations before the woke paradigm took over.

He was clearly not a fan of Julius Nyerere and had experienced British colonial rule in his country, then Tanganyika. Before that, like Cameroon, it too had been dominated by the Imperial German Army.

I remained in Douala only a few days. I didn't have a visa for my next stop and couldn't take the chance that I might be refused one by the local Nigerian consul. Word had it that it was not difficult to acquire a visa, but it took a while. However, things speeded up if you discreetly secreted a solid denomination banknote inside your passport when you applied.

I wasn't exactly broke, but I still had more than 3,200 kilometres ahead of me if I were to reach London, so any form of bribery was not on. If I were refused entry to Nigeria, it would mean a 1,600-kilometre detour. I'd have to travel north overland to Chad, then west through the former French sub-Saharan colony of Niger (which many people confuse with Nigeria) until I arrived in Dahomey (the present-day Republic of Benin).

That might not have been too bad – Bruce Chatwin's *The Viceroy of Ouidah*, was still decades ahead – and the country, another former French colony, had an intriguing history that included being home to an all-female regiment called Amazons. All the women were from the country's Fon Tribe, and their primary role until 1904 – or thereabouts – was guarding their king. Over the years, they repulsed many attacks from hostiles, doing so with a fury that became legendary.

The 19th-century explorer Richard Burton visited the country after he'd reached West Africa and sought out this formidable band of female warriors. His take was that 'they were mostly elderly and all hideous,' with his book including etchings of

---

3   Sudhir Hazareesingh, *Black Spartacus: The Epic Life of Toussaint Louverture*. Allen Lane: 2020.

these warriors with Winchester rifles slung across their backs. He added, almost as an afterthought, that their officers were 'decidedly chosen for the size of their bottoms.'

'Elderly' or not, they were a ferocious bunch. At one time, the women attacked the city of Abeokuta in present-day Nigeria, and that in the days before Africa's most populous state was colonised by the British. It appears that Abeokuta had attempted invasion many times, so the Amazons decided to retaliate, which they did in 1851. They concluded their war rituals and marched on Abeokuta.

Historical accounts handed down by word of mouth say their leader ordered her warriors to cover themselves in red and black body paint with an animal fat base. She made them swear never to sleep, rest or eat until Abeokuta was conquered. The prize for each warrior was skulls, as many as they could take back home. The question begs: how exactly did they manage that? The Fon homeland in Dahomey was – and still is – several days' march from Abeokuta, and in that heat, the stench of putrefying human flesh had to be overwhelming.

There were apparently two motives for that onslaught – still celebrated every year. The first was revenge; the second, almost certainly, was slaves. Gezo – king of the Amazons – depended on his women warriors to bring back as many slaves as possible, which he sold to European traders. Those captive humans were his primary source of income, and he had a string of willing buyers along the coast waiting to buy and make their packets – among them some renegade Brits, Portuguese, Spanish opportunists and – of all nations – Danes.

The main captive slave-gathering point lay in Porto Novo, specifically founded to trade in captive humans by a malevolent Brazilian entrepreneur, fictionalised two centuries later by Bruce Chatwin in *The Viceroy of Ouidah*.

The Danish connection is interesting because Copenhagen likes to portray its history as a culture with no historical blemishes. That is not so because several slave forts in present-day Ghana were Danish, and so were the slavers who lived there.

The British called the region the Gold Coast because much of the precious metal that went to Timbuktu and Mansa Musa's historic Mali Empire which lasted five or six centuries came from there. Some of the old Ashanti mines are still productive and, like most of Africa's commodities, in foreign hands.

I did go all the way north through Dahomey at a later stage and spent weeks in the Niger Republic where I made a TV documentary. In the colonial period, both countries had been linked to Paris and not London and while I could pay my way by then and we stayed in the best hotels and hired quality 4x4 SUVs, the latter stretch of road in the arid Sahel became a rather other-worldly experience.

Distances were vast. It took us two days to cover the thousand miles of desert from Niamey, Niger's capital, to Agadez, with only one decent-sized town in between and only a single 'hotel' that claimed to have modern comforts. Though the place looked fine from the outside, the beds had neither mattresses nor bedding, its owners probably concluding that with temperatures hovering in the mid-forties, we wouldn't be needing them.

If that wasn't enough, the shower cubicle had been used as a toilet and nobody had bothered to clean up. While hotels in Niamey, the capital, were what one would expect of five-star establishments, the few we stayed in on our three-day safari to Agadez, on the northern reaches of the country were doss-houses by comparison.

Stuck in Douala, I gathered from others who had travelled the region – including several Peace Corps volunteers – that the Nigerian frontier was lightly guarded. They told me it might be possible to sneak in by boat if I could find someone to take me.

I needed to make my way by road to what was then still called Victoria, the capital of western Cameroon since renamed Limbe, which lies at the foot of Mount Cameroon, at 4,095 metres the highest point in sub-Saharan West and Central Africa, towering over the region. To the immediate south, Victoria was and still is, after Douala, the country's second-largest port. A lot was happening in the local harbour where I was headed.

As I did later with Kilimanjaro, I'd considered climbing the peak, a still-active volcano. The West African mountain was a 'two days up and one down' trek, which meant porters (two to every aspirant climber), so I gave it a miss. Apparently, it was a brilliant trudge, as recounted by Lynn Goodfellow, who took a few days' leave from her posting at the British Embassy in Yaoundé to do the climb.

As she recounted, 'Once we reached the middle heights, we found the remains of aircraft that had smashed into Mount Cameroon, of which there had been dozens over the years. We saw at least eight or nine, but there must have been more, with local natives removing the aluminium detritus to sell as scrap and the tyres to make flip-flops.

'Though close to the Equator, the cold – in the rainy season – when on the ascent and at altitude was punishing because we hadn't thought we'd need a sweater.'

One of the worst aviation disasters in that area was an Air Afrique Douglas DC-6B that struck Mount Cameroon in May 1963 and was Cameroon's second-worst air disaster. Headed for Lagos, the plane lifted off from Douala shortly after midday and slammed into Africa's fourth-tallest peak, just 800 metres below the summit.

Unsure of how to proceed, I hung about several bars on Victoria's waterfront until I met a young Nigerian named Richard. He had arrived a few days before with his fish catch, preferring to market it in Cameroon, where prices were better than back home in Calabar. I asked him about the possibility of hitching a ride on his boat, and suddenly things went all cagey.

'Ya got na visa, heh?' His English verged on Creole.

I nodded. Then he laughed and said that I should buy him a beer so we could talk some more.

Richard and I chatted and joked well into the night. We also polished off more beers than were healthy for either of us, and finally, he said that if I filled the tank on his fishing boat, he'd take me with him. We were to depart the following afternoon to cover the roughly 160 kilometres, more or less in time to arrive in that eastern Nigerian town before first light the next day.

'That time, no police to greet us,' he joked. 'They all asleep, like babies.'

He stated that our destination was not that far away, but there were always problems in those waters. He wouldn't be drawn on what they might be, except that we would be headed for a lovely rural harbour in eastern Nigeria, named Calabar by some long-forgotten buccaneer. It was also one of the most hazardous journeys I'd ever completed on an open boat.

After loading several cans of bully beef, two bottles of French red rotgut, and bottled water, we headed to our destination which lay on both sides of an inland creek just above the estuary of the Cross River. The British had established one of the first landmarks after the Royal Navy had penetrated that coast at Calabar – Lagos having already been acquired by force of arms in the 1850s.

Richard took us straight out to sea, ostensibly on a fishing trip. The more distant we got from the shore, the more concerned I became. His boat was seaworthy, but only just, and his antiquated engine not much better. That meant that once we progressed into deep water – to avoid naval patrols, he said (though I never saw a single police or navy craft) – the more I worried, especially as storm clouds were building around us.

We had to chug quite close to the island of Equatorial Guinea, an erstwhile Spanish colony and today rated as the ultimate prize for the worst place in Africa. For decades, after Madrid granted Spanish Guinea its independence, it was also one of the most xenophobic of Africa's nations.

Things weren't helped when, in 2004, a group of South Africans headed by former British SAS officer Simon Mann led a bungled attempt to overthrow the government. Essentially, the raid was launched in a bid to grab Equatorial Guinea's oil assets, and some of those involved ended up in the island's notorious Black Beach Prison on the island, where several died.

The strike force, led by former South African Special Forces operator, Nick du Toit, seemed to botch everything from the start, including timing and security. He served almost six years of a 34-year sentence before being released.

The most famous Black Beach inmate of them all, Simon Mann – a business partner of fellow conspirator Mark Thatcher, son of former British Prime Minister Margaret Thatcher – was held prisoner in Equatorial Guinea for several years. However, it has since emerged that the conditions under which Mann was held were very different to those endured by people like Nick du Toit, who admits today that he's lucky to be alive. Money talks, and the Mann family, of brewery fame in Britain, have a lot of it.

The rest of the journey was uneventful. We approached the Nigerian coastline in the dark, and my youthful fisherman friend, with no compass, started navigating by what one might regard as 'feel and touch' because the night was as black as a raven's bum.

I never once considered that we might get stranded – in fact, we never had the time because the sea was rough enough to keep us both busy: if he wasn't fixing the engine, I was pumping the bilge: the old vessel was all but porous. From early evening we were soaked from the spray, and tropics or not, I was frozen for much of the journey.

Several times, spotting the lights of villages I suggested that we pull in till morning. Richard laughed it off. 'We get there…you see.'

Sometime after midnight, when every light had disappeared – their owners asleep – he ran headlong into an enormous cluster of jungle foliage hanging low over the water. It wasn't a single tree but more like a forest that seemed to stretch in every direction, and several times the boat held fast in a vegetative grip so we couldn't budge. Since we couldn't see which way was which, we had to sit that one out. Richard said the tide was falling and rather than try to hack out with a machete, which could draw attention to our plight, he preferred to take his chances.

A few hours later, we were heading up a narrow inlet, and a faint glow from the east showed the skipper the way. Half an hour later Calabar, quaint and picturesque in those untroubled days immediately after independence, lay dead ahead.

Richard tied up alongside a cluster of huts with tin roofs and woke his wife. That was when she greeted me with an ugly look that made me wish the worst of the journey was ahead. I wasn't even offered coffee – or possibly there was none – in the boondocks, it was primarily a white man's drink.

CHAPTER 7

Nigeria: 'Crazy, but I love it!'

The first time I visited Nigeria was undoubtedly the most compelling African experience of my life. The country had been independent for only five years, and what a vibrant, exuberant society it was. In one report that I sent to the Argus Africa News Service, I referred to the place as 'Crazy, but I love it!'

I entered clandestinely, not even getting my passport stamped after spending a few days in magical Calabar. During the next few weeks, I paid my way around by travelling in bush taxis and mammy wagons, British Army Bedford trucks that ruled the road and sold in Nigeria as war surplus. I spent next to nothing in Nigerian Nairas to travel from Calabar, through Port Harcourt, Onitsha and Benin across the land to Lagos, where I promptly went down with malaria.

Wherever this white boy from South Africa went into what was to become the Federation of Nigerian States, I was feted, fed, fooled with and displayed to all who were curious to know what somebody from the 'Racist South' was like. Everybody knew about apartheid and having 'emerged' from there, the consensus was that they had to check whether I had horns. Some touched my skin and hair to make sure I was real; others plied me with enough Star beer to set up a roadside stall, to uncover whatever I might have secreted. And when that didn't work, they tried palm wine.

It was significant that I never once encountered any hostility throughout my Nigerian peregrinations, political or otherwise. Indeed, Lagos was then among the most secure cities in Africa. We were out every night, often on foot, moving around the bars on Lagos's Victoria Island or up Yaba and Ikorodu Roadway – often until the wee hours. A mugging was as alien a concept to the average Nigerian as flush toilets in their still-primitive wooden huts, but my! how things have since changed.

Though I never gave it a second thought at the time, I recall that many of my new Nigerian friends, almost all reasonably well-educated, were quite proud of their colonial heritage. The fact that both Nigeria and Ghana were at the core of the transatlantic slaving industry for several centuries was never as much of an issue as it is today.

Instead, they would parody those British people they met, where class consciousness was an almost obsessive trait. The presence of low-life creatures like me and my colleagues was hardly acknowledged beyond their social domain. It caught on with quite a few Nigerian swanks, especially within the upper echelons of their society, as I discovered when I eventually returned to work in Lagos. They were often more British than the Poms themselves.

You'd encounter them at diplomatic functions, company cocktail parties, or music recitals that could bore the paper off a wall. One and all, Nigerians would reminisce about fond days spent in the 'old country', though few then had done much more than attend one of the universities, almost always on state-aided scholarships. Moreover, it was invariably Oxbridge to the fore and hardly ever anything Red Brick.

Were you to become intrusive and ask questions about people with whom they might have been familiar, or places visited, more than likely you'd be met with silence – or the need to slip away to the bar and 'get another drink'.

So, while moving freely about a string of West African cities, I was handed from one group of Nigerians to another. It became not only an exhilarating social experience but also an introduction to the kind of gastronomic experience one didn't find outside Africa then.

I might initially have been wary of some of the cuisine to start with, but being bold, I uncovered a range of food that the rest of the world knew very little about. There was *gari*, a popular *fufu* recipe in Nigeria, customarily processed from the cassava root. Then yams, that to the unsuspecting might have been a new brand of tuber, though I quickly found out otherwise.

While most whites in West Africa tended to stick to European dishes, I made a point of seeking out the best in ethnicity. When I'm in London, I still look for the occasional restaurant that offers a quality Asaro yam potage with Yoruba origins. The same with Nigerian peppered fish, though one must be cautious of too much chilli, which can burn your throat.

Some of my European pals who followed were unsure about the hygiene, which we all agreed could be dodgy. When travelling in Africa, the dictum was explicit: if you can't peel it, don't eat it.

My time in Nigeria on that first exploratory West African journey set the scene for the rest of the trip. It continued by road, with no flights to ease the rigours, of which there were many.

I had no idea what lay ahead, and border crossings (generally arduous), were only part of the problem. My main concern was the cost of accommodation because I could rarely afford a night in a decent hotel. Though there were moments when I thought, the hell with it, I need a few nights' good rest.

There were many small lodging houses along the way, but one needed to choose carefully – many were termed 'doss-houses' – paid by the hour and rarely unaccompanied. There was almost always the usual unfriendly strong-arm around who, if you checked in, would go through your luggage the moment you slipped out for a bite. Fortunately, that was only at the lower end of the social structure.

Sanitation became a regular issue because some people didn't bother to clean up after themselves, and there was nothing you could do about it except travel with a bottle of bleach. In truth, I never could adapt to Muslim-style latrines, which are never anything more than a hole in the floor with a tap affixed to the wall. Give me a Western-style, high-level WC any day.

Toilets, or lack of them, did present problems on the road. Most times, when somebody needed to 'go', the driver would be asked to stop, and a few discreet steps into the bush would suffice. There were no lions in that wilderness, so the prospect of encountering anything fierce didn't exist. Except for the snakes, so you had to tread carefully if you took a leak.

We often saw these reptiles on West African roads, particularly in southern areas where the country was engulfed by jungle or forest. When a giant snake came slithering by, the entire vehicle would erupt with whistles and whoops, and the driver sometimes chided for not running over it.

In Africa, I'd make a point of not travelling after dark. While the roads were busy day and night, most accidents happened at night, partly because some drivers seemed to be easily night-blinded by oncoming traffic.

On one journey in Ghana between Takoradi and Accra some years later, my wife and I were stuck with a fairly old 'chauffeur' who cost us plenty but seemed unsure of the road after the sun had set. After turning straight into oncoming traffic twice, I was forced to grab the wheel to avoid an accident – my reliable second sense had suggested that I sit in the passenger seat – and I took over from him. It was then that I found that his brakes hardly worked.

I could count myself lucky not to have been involved in collisions, though we had our share of near disasters. At the same time, most journeys were light-hearted and uneventful: in those days, there were almost no military roadblocks (how different today, guns and all!). That was the norm almost all the way to Dakar, 3,200 kilometres away across regions where 'roads' marked on the map could be deceptive: some were nothing more than tracks through forest and bush.

Yet I was pleased that I'd got that far, so I continued, always arriving early at the next bus or mammy wagon stop to be sure of a seat. The trip usually took ages; there were halts at every town – sometimes hours-long – waiting for passengers who were often 'no shows'. During these pauses, I would go into town to see what was on offer – usually in search of a meal and, most times, leaving my bag with the driver. I wasn't robbed once, but that was then, and things have changed radically.

Usually, I'd be offered the seat up front, but because of the number of accidents we passed, I preferred the relative safety of somewhere towards the rear, not that this would have made much difference had we hit something. Then I discovered something quite disturbing – whenever we came across an accident, the average Nigerian didn't go anywhere near the dead or injured. Blood in any form repulsed them, which meant that it could be hours before an ambulance arrived. Their resources were minimal, and it sometimes took days to collect the deceased.

Safe travel in Africa means: don't take any chances, check the vehicle's tyres and, more importantly, ask to see a valid driver's licence. Fakes are easy to spot because most look handmade. And in the event of having an accident, the first thing likely to disappear is your wallet, even then. So, most of us hid our cash on our bodies, in our underpants and so on.

These days one must accept that being involved in an accident on African roads is always possible – I rarely travelled from Uganda's Entebbe Airport to Kampala without seeing at least one serious pile-up – bodies would be placed on the side of the verge to await collection.

I would ask my travel companions what they would do if they needed urgent medical treatment; the American Peace Corps and British volunteers mostly had their own doctors, usually based in big cities. The medical attention required after a smash wouldn't be available in the interior because it would take medical personnel too long to arrive at the accident scene. In those cases, emergency flights were available for anything life-threatening. American aid workers or British NGO victims would be flown to Europe by military transports, if necessary. In my case, I simply had to hope that I would manage, which I did since my pile-ups were minor.

The other issue that bothered me was tropical diseases, malaria especially. I created my own emergency kit that included enough quinine for a platoon, strong painkillers and, most importantly, two litres of saline drip should I need blood. But first, I had to be shown how it was administered.

When I did go down with malaria, I turned to the vicar of the Anglican Church in Lagos: I'd been given his name by somebody along the way as he had a reputation as a Good Samaritan.

Undeterred by my raging fever, he took me to a room at the back of the vestry, and I was well cared for and fed. It took a week before I was up and about again, though physically, I was left weak, as is usually the case with anything tropical. But I was a tough bugger and pulled through soon enough and went on my way.

Malaria was an affliction that happened often enough during my meanderings through the wilds – in my case possibly a dozen times over the more than half a century that I was active. The peculiar thing though, was that I religiously took my tablets (I'd lost too many pals not to have done so). In the 1960s the regimen was something like one Chloroquine tablet a day and another, possibly Camoquine, once a week, but they didn't always work. In the 1970s it progressed to two tablets. By the 1990s it was probably five a day and five a week, I forget. But all those pills played havoc with your liver. Now there is new medication that stops malaria in its tracks within 72 hours.

These days you are treated with the herbal-based, three-day Artemisinin-based cure (or one of its derivatives) which was an enormous relief when I contracted malaria in Zambia. Down I went and three tablets later – one taken each day – and I was up and running.

The other big concern throughout was hepatitis. While working in Lagos in the mid-1960s, following a hectic weekend in Cotonou (the next largish city on the main coastal road west), I did the unthinkable when I woke early one morning with an enormous thirst and drank unfiltered water. To be fair – I had a hangover from Hades, it was five in the morning, the patron was asleep, and I needed liquid.

So, I turned on the tap in the garden outside and drank my fill. Days later, I was hit by hepatitis, which took me years to recover from. That attack of jaundice, complete with the whites of my eyes turning yellow, inhibited my drinking alcohol and necessitated a visit to a GP in West Africa – easily as expensive as in the United States – especially when the doctor is an ex-pat. Mine was a kindly Greek professional who had seen and done it all. Apart from a course of medication – pills by the dozen – liquor was out!

'Nothing alcoholic! *óchi alkoól! Nada! Nyet!* You understand?' he demanded.

This was not to be taken lightly. In that part of the world, there were, in his view, three primary causes of death. The first was malaria, as might be expected. Then came hepatitis because the water in Third World countries is often untreated, and then tetanus, commonly known as lockjaw.

'I suggest you take this very seriously and follow my advice,' were his parting words.

I did argue since I was on my lonesome. I explained that I was not into little boys or little girls (though I adored big girls). Nor did I shove any powders up my nose – but I told him I had that single 'vice' – and couldn't cut out liquor altogether.

It was a conundrum he considered for a few moments before he declared: 'OK, but no beer. If you really need a drink, only two tiny tots of a good-quality Scotch. No more.' I stuck to that regimen for a couple of years, but it took a decade before I could drink beer again.

I was sceptical of what he said about tetanus, though I recall that it was the first injection you were given on arriving at ER when you were young. The reality came home when I moved to Lagos and took an apartment in the suburb of Apapa. My nearest neighbours were an English couple – the wife regarded by everybody as 'certifiably mad'.

It took me a while to find out why. A few years before, while living in Liberia, both their pre-teen sons had died from lockjaw.

My first journey along Nigeria's southern tropical route had taken me to the north and back to the east before I finally left the country. During that time, I learned that Britain's 'Jewel in its West African Crown' suffered from a single legacy that took years to put right.

Since the southern road was mainly east to west and not far from the sea, there were many rivers along the way to cross. To compound matters, there is a stream or a large river at the base of just about every hill in Equatorial Africa.

The colonials built passable two-lane roads throughout the country, but the bridges over almost every stream were single lanes, probably to save money. So, when travelling in the country's southern regions, the driver would reach the top of a hill, and spotting a car heading his way at the crest of the opposite rise, he would very often increase speed so that his car or truck would be first to cross. Basic logic: the first vehicle to reach the bridge would not be forced to yield.

The results were catastrophic, and it went on for decades. I doubt whether a single bridge between east and west Nigeria was not littered with the debris of road disasters, including buses and fuel tankers that levelled the bush for several hundred metres when their cargoes exploded.

Nigeria is the only country where I have *twice* encountered fuel tankers that had been involved in head-on collisions. It sounds absurd, yet it still happens. Trucks carrying hi-octane fuel were something else when they overturned. Villagers in their hundreds would descend on the wreck from all directions, carrying every possible container imaginable, including pots, jars, water bottles, buckets and even beer cans, to haul away free gasoline. It was there for the taking, so why not?

But more times than I care to venture, there would be somebody who'd arrive with a lighted cigarette between the lips. A simple Google search will reveal many such instances.

As an interesting aside, I was able to visit Nigeria's ancient city of Benin in the mid-west. In 1852, the original town was plundered by a British naval force, and the traditional king (he was then and is still referred to as Oba) was arrested and banished. During the attack, the soldiers stole hoards of historic treasures, many of which are now in the British Museum. For almost a century, the Nigerians have been trying to get London to return their national heritage, but like Greece's Elgin Marbles, the cause, though not lost, has been muddied.

When I went into those same historic Benin strongholds in 1964, it surprised me that I was free to move about where I pleased. There were Benin bronzes, both of traditional Obas and their queens (Binis), and large ivory carvings scattered all over the place. I can only surmise how much more was filched before somebody secured the remains of what was once one of Africa's most valuable collections of historical art.

As colonisers, the British went to great lengths to create a succession of towns in Africa that they hoped would compare with anything similar in the United Kingdom. They aimed to emulate what had been achieved in places like Manchester or Blackpool; obviously impossible. But they did achieve a great deal by constructing decent roads, complete with roundabouts and drainage systems for the storms encountered in the deep tropics. They also built libraries, hospitals, schools, universities, and a lot more.

Those days you went to Africa to work in the mines or as a teacher, town planner, medical practitioner, or administrator – most of these dedicated souls contributed substantially to the country's infrastructure and few came home with much money saved. In the process, the British and the French built good roads across most of their possessions and many rail links, some of which were torn up after independence (as in Sierra Leone – the steel rails connecting Freetown, the country's capital into the interior, were sold to China).

Not surprisingly, nations operated fairly efficiently under British and French rule: trains ran on time, there was transport galore – even if a mammy wagon or mini taxi was not to everybody's liking – roadworks, administrative procedures, and communications were secure. If you mailed a letter to Outer Mongolia, it might take a while, but it would get there.

While it might have taken half an hour to cash a traveller's cheque at the local branch of Barclays, you weren't dealing with today's slick-handed felons who are determined to separate you from your money. Without a doubt, Africa today is very different from when *Rule Britannia* was sung on New Year's Eve in just about every colonial bar stretching from the Cape to Cairo.

All of this suggests that after Thomas Pakenham's 'Colonial Epoch' became a reality in the 19th century, many African countries emerged with a newly enriched purpose – though not without faults – but demonstrably progressive and growing in both hope and strength for the future. The late Jan Morris, one of my personal heroes, forfeited a cushy job on *The Observer* after telling its anti-colonial editor David Astor that the British Empire 'on the whole, is a force for good in the world'.

The one thing the British town planners who had been seconded to African municipalities could not find an answer to was how to handle the complex sewage problems of large conurbations like Lagos, Freetown, or Accra. They managed very well in Cape Town, Nairobi, and Johannesburg, so did the Portuguese in their cities – but on the West Coast of Africa, those issues seemed insurmountable – the first being volume.

In Lagos, as a result, a fair proportion of the city's sewage was dumped in a horrendous dark brown pile that we viewed each morning from Carter Bridge while driving to work; it eventually topped ten or fifteen metres. A primitive conveyer belt powered by a two-stroke engine was used to move the muck deposited by night carts – hundreds of them – to the peak of this noxious, always pending catastrophe; essentially, that is what it was. If the engine broke down, which it did quite often, well... At the time, it was the single biggest mountain of shit in the world and curiously, that didn't seem to bother most people living there. However, there were ructions when one of the night carts – towed by small tractors by the time I arrived (it had been donkeys before) – would overturn on the approaches. Then we'd be stuck, literally, with a man-made, quasi-liquid crap carpet covering the road for roughly a kilometre in both directions.

While the Nigerians could become vocal about the mess, we expatriates had to mind what we said because criticism of Nigeria was either evidence of an imperial throwback or, more directly, racist.

One infamous event involved a young American Peace Corps female volunteer sending home a postcard that mentioned the country's disgusting filth and slums. Of course, it was an indiscretion on her part, and after a clerk in the post office in Lagos passed it on to somebody in the government, all hell broke loose. The poor woman was kicked out of the country, but the Nigerians were still not satisfied – the issue was kicked up the line to Washington with demands for apologies at government level. They got it.

For all that, the standard of governance in Nigeria was exemplary for the first few years. Things worked, and these included finances. After completing a spell with the British group, Holts, I shipped all my goods and chattels to South Africa when I left Nigeria. Several months later, a cheque arrived in the post in Johannesburg for money that, the accompanying statement revealed, was a refund for taxes overpaid.

In those days, most people could freely express their political opinions; the all-encompassing security apparatus for which Nigeria became notorious in subsequent military governments only came later. British author Frederick Forsyth told me thirty years later when we got together at my home on the Columbia River in Washington State, that he still didn't dare visit the country: 'I'm pretty sure they'd kill me if I did,' he averred, referring to the time he spent covering the civil war from Biafra, rebel-side.

There was a more sinister aspect to what lay immediately ahead in a country attractive enough for me to decide to work there again, and that was (and still is) oil. Indeed, the absolute exploitation of the country's disputatious oil resources began immediately after the Biafran War.

Money had started to arrive in the nation's coffers, and the figures were staggering, symptomatic of what was taking place in other oil-rich countries. With it came graft, malfeasance, greed, corruption, and repudiation of the original colonial administration that initially put this West African state on the international map. Once it started, Nigeria's war was brought to a staggering halt only after three years of heavy fighting that left a million dead, the majority innocent women and children starved to death.

We will return to that horrendous historical chapter of modern African slaughter later.

A fascinating aspect of that journey, and others in West Africa that followed, was encountering the widespread use of pidgin English; something I found entrenched within the greater part of society. While peculiar to your or my ear, the language is comprehensible only after familiarising yourself with the basics. It has always caused problems for the uninitiated, which included the best part of colonial society.

For instance, in Sierra Leone, you greet your friends by asking: 'How di body?' Their answer would be, 'Di body fine.'

Similarly, somebody 'not on seat' in Nigeria (if you're calling by phone) means they were out. 'Chop' is food, and please is 'abeg', while 'Una dey mad' in pidgin English translates to mean that those people involved are crazy.

Then you have the Lord's Prayer, which has numerous variations. The one that drew my attention came from a Presbyterian church near Ikeja (where I ended up manning my company's offices after returning to work in Lagos). It went something like this:

> So makuna pray laik dis: 'Awa Papa weydey for hevun, wi praiz yor name. Mak yor Kindom kom, mak wetin yu wont, hapun for dis wold as e bi for hevun. Giv us di fud wey wi go chop evriday, forgiv us all di bad-bad tins wey wi don du, as wi sef dey forgiv odas di bad tins wey dem du us. Nor alow us enta temtashon bot mak yu save us from bad tins.'

Critics have scoffed at some of the fundamentals involved, but in reality pidgin – confusing to some – comes down to the basics that allow a vast section of society to communicate effectively. There is nothing chic or classy about it, and in the broader societal context, pidgin works.

Indeed, I found aspects that were melodious and quite charming.

From Lagos, I continued along some of the main highways towards the west, crossing the border into what was then listed on contemporary maps as Dahomey (Benin today), followed by the Republic of Togo, like Cameroon, a former German possession.

I had no entry stamp into Nigeria, and the immigration official at the Dahomey border post accepted my word when I said they'd forgotten to stamp my passport when I entered from Cameroon. A sizeable bank note helped spur the transition.

Cotonou, the former French colonial capital, was a disappointment. It lacked character and was expensive. I'd considered going by train to the north and completing the journey to Dakar through the Sahel, thereby avoiding Liberia's uncertain jungle interior where people were said to have mysteriously disappeared, but some aid workers warned me off.

I didn't stay long, and interestingly, Dahomey's history soon became a good deal more chequered after I'd moved on. Graham Greene's classic film, *The Comedians*, starring Richard Burton and Elizabeth Taylor, followed soon afterwards. It would have been too risky to consider Haiti (the book is set in Port au Prince) as a filming location. Greene's plot was critical of Haiti and black rule. It highlighted the iniquities of the tyrant 'Papa Doc' Duvalier and his Tonton Macoutes, a real-life bunch of homicidal gangsters. Somehow, the Dahomey president was persuaded by the film's producers to let them use Cotonou as the unflattering venue, and the film had mixed reviews. One critic declared, 'Mr Greene's characteristic story of white men carrying [the burdens of black people] cheerlessly and with an undisguised readiness to dump them as soon as they can get away from this God-forsaken place is no great shakes of a drama.'

Dahomey had another side to it about then: insurrection. In 1977, one of my old pals, French soldier of fortune, Bob Denard, led a band of his cutthroats in an airborne bid to topple the Dahomey government. The venture was codenamed Operation *Crevette*, with the mercenaries trying to sneak in by plane, but the army was waiting, the attack having been betrayed from within. The debacle was a disaster from the start and, as Denard told me many years later, he was fortunate to get out alive.

With one of Africa's busiest roads leading towards the west, a trip to the Republic of Togo followed. Though no great guns, I always enjoyed my visits because I'd got to know some of the Lebanese traders in Lomé, the capital.

Like Dahomey, Togo – a bit smaller than Ireland – had also been a French colony, but it also had a troubled history, its leaders not always agreeing with neighbouring Ghana's demands. Since the former British colony was more extensive, with a bigger army, Accra expected its demands to be met. That ended with the assassination of the country's leader, Sylvanus Olympio, three years after Togo had been cut free. The plot was said to have been masterminded by Ghana's President Nkrumah, and whatever the consequences, it was Africa's first post-independence coup d'état.

My Lebanese friends in Lomé were into just about everything above and below board that the country had to offer – and topping the list was gold.

Ghana, one of the biggest producers of the precious metal in the region, was by then undergoing the strictures of Nkrumah's radical domination. It was to be expected that almost anyone would buy gold on the black market and smuggle it abroad and the principal recipient for much of it was Togo, Ghana's nearest neighbour.

If not simple, the system worked and was used by most smugglers. Gold acquired in Ghana would be melted and fashioned into eight- or ten-inch bars, about as thick as your thumb. These would be inserted into one of the body's orifices and the carrier would attempt to slip across a heavily patrolled frontier.

Those involved in the trade knew precisely where to dispense their wares, to the extent that a bottle of bleach would be handed over on first calling at one of the Lebanese shops. The recipient was ushered to the toilet and expected to do the rest.

It probably wasn't the most sophisticated operation, but my Lebanese pals had ingratiated themselves with the responsible parties in the Togolese government, and they got their cut. As with diamonds in Sierra Leone, smugglers could board the Air France flight out of Lomé with unusually heavy holdalls that somehow never got checked.

I took photos of one such cache after my friend Mustapha had extricated it from his safe – a shoebox-sized wooden box filled with thin, long glistening pieces of gold.

It didn't take Ghana's security services long to latch onto what was happening. In later years, many passengers departing the country on international flights were subjected to the indignity of 'intrusive body searches'.

That continued until a black American university professor of considerable prestige in the academic world was put to that unsavoury test. On arriving home, he went public and complained that only black people – not a single white – were being targeted. 'I saw and experienced this myself,' he declared.

Togo had one other pursuit in which I was particularly interested: voodoo, juju or, in less arcane terms, black magic. West African witch doctors profess it to be a mysterious and restricted age-old tradition using magic to communicate with supernatural spirits and dead people.

When dealing specifically with Africa, most guidebooks on the subject point to the Akodessewa voodoo market in Lomé, regularly visited by tourists who are curious about such esoteric issues. But that's small fry compared to a significant voodoo hideout some distance down the coast, a dozen times as large.

I included a ten-minute segment on the place in one of my TV documentaries, and of all the films I've produced, this was probably the most disturbing. I went there with my camera crew, and we found approximately a hundred stalls, every single one filled with the remains of dead animals, birds (parrots especially, by the thousands), reptiles and much more. There were even some stuffed horse heads.

It has been said that if you have the right connections (and money), you can buy the remains of a human child, possibly apocryphal, but not beyond the realms of probability.

The market is famous, or rather infamous, but not in the accepted mode. You cannot get in there with a camera (my permission to film cost me plenty), and once filming was underway, I couldn't wait to finish. The entire market reeked of nauseating putrefaction that I have never since experienced. The place was rank evil – and we could feel it.

With so many dead creatures not properly cured and stacked out in the open, that was to be expected, but the stench didn't seem to bother those manning their stalls. In French – and in big block letters – some were named, 'A Christian Enterprise'.

The market was known to legions of witch doctors, medicine men (and women), healers, mountebanks, shamans, *sangomas*, quacks or just plain fakers along the West African coast. Its reputation extended into the Caribbean, Brazil, Cuba and elsewhere; by several accounts, some buyers are even practising in New York and Los Angeles.

There is also a huge following in other African regions and many Third World countries, predominantly Nigeria and Jamaica.

In my brief call at Albert Schweitzer's hospital, he admitted that he had an endless battle persuading his patients to accept his system of healing and not theirs. Many had travelled long distances to seek his help, but there were still a few who would succumb to other influences, mainly witch doctors when his 'cures' were not instantaneous. There were always a few of these scoundrels lurking around Lambarene, and he had his work cut out to chase them off the property.

From the days of slavery and human sacrifice in the last century (then a common practice), and possibly even today, Togo has been central to this practice. Several colonial diaries suggest that those interested in this rigmarole would arrive in droves, even as recently as a hundred years ago.

CHAPTER 8

A peripatetic existence

One of the ancient sages once said something about every journey being a little bit of hell. That might apply to present-day Africa, but in the mid-1960s, while not all was elation and joy, travelling around the continent generated the kind of excitement I have rarely experienced since.

The thrill of anticipation of the unknown became a powerful motivator, mainly because I rarely encountered any real danger. Things took a double turn once I'd started putting my neck on the line as a war correspondent, but that was still to come.

Each day during that four-month journey up the West Coast of Africa – except for the week in bed in Lagos with malaria – I was presented with fresh challenges, images, experiences, cultures and, quite often, historical traditions that one never finds elsewhere. In Nigeria, every lengthy road trip was initiated by emptying a bottle of gin over the front end of the vehicle we were heading out in. That pleased me – rather on the driver's radiator than in his gut.

There were shrines, some as tall as buildings, that would receive homage, perhaps only for a minute or two, but reverential. Time and again, I sensed a distinctly strange and unseen force at work. I found, in Badagry, a town west of Lagos on the road into Benin, that every photo I took of fetish shrines came out blank – and that on a roll of 36 slides where all other images, having been processed, were intact. That was certainly quite strange…

Most travellers I encountered offered nothing but friendship, and I was given support when I needed it. More remarkable were the assurances that the exciting surprises awaiting me at the other end were endless. These were the kind of expectations – not including appalling standards of driving – that could only be welcome because it was their world, not mine. 'Africa is yours, so enjoy,' (or words to that effect) was also a constant.

I relished those exchanges, but what astounded me was that I encountered very few First World fellow transients along the way. It seemed that only two decades after the end of World War II, Africa was a world – to most of the international community – that remained mysterious, unsullied, and potentially hostile when, in fact, it was not. That well-beaten ground had been trammelled since the mid-1960s by legions of young people trying to improve things for the people of Africa.

Something not often commented on was the significant numbers of American and European youngsters who were prepared to give time and effort – and occasionally their lives – to create a 'better' Africa. The Peace Corps, the brainchild of President John F. Kennedy, took a great initiative in terms of numbers involved, as well as Britain's Voluntary Service Overseas (VSO), both still active today. So, too, with many professionals from France, including doctors and nurses, such as those who went to Biafra at their own expense to tend to the wounded and dying.

The VSO was the forerunner. It began its work in 1958 when Alec and Mora Dickson recruited and sent sixteen British volunteers overseas in response to a letter from the Bishop of Portsmouth. He had asked for people to assist in teaching English abroad.

I met many inspiring individuals, especially French doctors in Biafra, whose vigour and enthusiasm were admirable, considering the limited resources they had available. Some of the surgery they allowed me to witness took place without anaesthetics. Very often, it was a piece of wood clenched between the teeth and two strong men holding the patient down while amputations and other procedures took place.

More of that later…

What I did discover was that in the early days of independence – except for the Belgian and Portuguese colonies – Africa was a relatively happy place.

The majority of job-seekers usually found them if they had a reasonable level of education, generally from schools founded by British and French missionaries, clinics had staff on call, the municipalities worked, and the police quickly responded to calls because the rule of law was firmly entrenched. Essentially, most countries were secure until a succession of army mutinies and revolutions began to roll in. Meantime, I, and everybody else of my genre could travel from one country to the next – from Gambia and Dakar on the extreme Atlantic West Coast to Somalia and Kenya straddling the eastern shores of the Indian Ocean – and in comparative safety.

It is worth mentioning that of my roughly 120 days and nights travelling through West Africa during late 1964 and early 1965, I would gather my few possessions and make a bed for myself in an alleyway or the grounds of one of the schools or larger hotels. The security guards barely gave me a glance. That suited me as I was more concerned about scorpions than robbers and thieves. As for snakes, they were always around, but I'd learnt that if you left them alone, they wouldn't bother you – or so you believed – with more than a modicum of hope.

There were times when I would pay my way, like joining one of the fishing crews in Half Assini, a small town in the extreme southwest of Ghana. A Ceylonese teacher doing voluntary work at the town school offered me accommodation 'for as long as you like'. I offered my services to locals who ran one of the large Kru boats used to take out their nets – they'd push off from the beach shortly after dawn every morning except Sundays – a reprieve I came to relish.

We had to paddle hard to beat the surf, and once beyond the breakers the net would be spread. After that, we'd row back to shore, the return trip taking a while. Then came the hard part – hauling in the nets – a job that needed a dozen or more pairs of strong arms, depending on the day's catch, but the nets were always teeming with fish because the effects of overfishing hadn't yet begun to take effect.

I'd be presented with a sizeable Atlantic cob, snapper, or jack for my labour. We'd always take a shark or two, but I'd give them a miss since my host did the cooking on an open wood fire and that wasn't his game.

On that trip, living as I did on a day-to-day basis, not knowing what the morrow would bring, there had to be a few downs – everybody welcomed strangers but some local folk preferred to keep their distance. This was to be expected since I was living the equivalent of a vagrant's peripatetic existence, and to all intents and purposes, I lived frugally. It showed because I was usually barefoot.

Occasionally the inevitable racial element would emerge, for the simple reason that white people working on the continent did not readily mix socially with Africans. Their presence was acknowledged, and while most would treat blacks in a friendly or respectful manner, the prospect of meeting for a pint after work seldom happened as it might have if they had been 'back home'.

In Lagos, where I returned to work a little more than a year after my first West African sojourn, it was immediately noticeable that the European community had their own social clubs. Occasionally, Africans were welcome, though this was not the norm. While some might refute this, race relations in Africa more than half a century ago were, as it is phrased today, 'of its time' and socially accepted by most.

The 'system' such as it was, was firmly ensconced within the respective communities, and apart from those who had regular daily interactions, whites did their thing and blacks did theirs – and don't let any hard-bitten West African old-timers tell you otherwise.

There were exceptions. Several of my friends, as well as a close colleague at John Holt, married into Nigerian families and were content and happy – their children were delightful little souls. Others went, as we called it 'bush', a relatively obscure inclination to observe juju or fetish rites, which included shrines at the back of the house where daily offerings were made.

One of these was Harry Whittaker, a mid-level manager within John Holt. He had reached retirement age, and I was sent to Nigeria to replace him. He had been living on the coast for decades, and it took me a while to realise that the last thing that Harry wanted was to leave Africa. His very soul had become entwined with some of the more obscure (to white people) traditions it inculcated. I got the impression that his embrace of the supernatural must have gone deep – rumour had it that he kept a voodoo shrine in his house, but whether or not he made offerings to it was another matter.

Those anomalies apart, my presence heading up the coast in 1964 constantly offered fresh revelations. It was only weeks into the journey when I came to accept that I was regarded as something of a curiosity piece, mainly because, unlike most 'whiteys', I was inclined to accept most people at face value.

Also, I enjoyed African company. As a child, some of my first playmates were Zulu kids, yet as an adult in South Africa, I had no social interaction with Zulu people. The only exception was with my very dear compadre, former political leader Mangosuthu Buthelezi – he and I shared some precious moments. The result was that the Gabonese, Nigerians, Ghanaians, and others were intrigued by my rather novel approach.

This has probably been shared by generations of aid workers who came to Africa, the majority hugely apprehensive to begin with. It doesn't take them long to discover that while there are always differences, it's really a bit of a gas.

Without a doubt, there were distractions, one or two unpleasant. On my first West African expedition in Abidjan, I found a 'hangout' in the Plateau – an upmarket African township across the lagoon – which meant I had to cross a bridge each time I wanted to go there. I must have drawn someone's attention because one evening, on the way into town and to my favourite bistro, I was accosted by a well-dressed young man who asked for the time.

Within seconds, he'd forcibly grabbed my arm, having decided to look at my wristwatch himself. Naturally, I resisted and pulled away, at which point he thumped me hard in the face. When I went down, he jumped onto my chest, started pummelling and shouting that I was a racist. It was a clever move because a small crowd had gathered and was growing fast – the last thing on earth I needed was an altercation based on race – which was when I tried to cool it and succeeded. The man eventually desisted, helped me to my feet, shook my hand, and we parted ways. It was only when I tried to settle my dinner bill that I discovered that my wallet was gone.

I reported the matter to the local police station, and the first reaction of the gendarme on duty, on hearing my story through an interpreter, was: 'Oh no, not another one.'

In my assessment of the situation at the time, Ghana was the one country that I still had to cross and which might have presented a problem or three.

I was born in South Africa, a country that had imposed harsh racial laws on people of colour. We knew that Ghana's President Nkrumah was a vociferous critic of Pretoria and at the forefront of advocating 'Africa for the Africans'. He subsequently invited South African blacks to head there for military training so that a revolutionary army could be forged to wage a liberation war. Before crossing into Ghana, I reasoned that I might well be questioned about my reason for visiting the country.

The Ghanaians were right to be suspicious of newcomers from the African 'Deep South', especially since the media had exposed the murderous antics of mercenaries executing rebels in the Congo. Those idiots had mounted their victims' heads on stakes and taken photos of themselves as 'victors'. It was obscenely bizarre, but it happened.

Therefore, I had to tread lightly once I'd crossed the border from Togo and be especially wary of anyone who might be more than casually interested in my South African background. That included a relatively large body of British radicals – mainly academics – who had been encouraged by Nkrumah to decamp to Ghana. They were offered all sorts of inducements to head his ideological quest of transforming Ghana into Africa's first genuinely socialist state: large homes, servants, travel – things most of them could only dream about. That bunch ended up influencing and publishing some of his more radical treatises.

On a practical level, since I had a British passport, the Ghanaian government couldn't arrest me on any charge in particular. However, they might expel me – which would have meant sending me to either Britain or back to South Africa – thereby putting an end to my slog.

Ultimately, that was not how things turned out. After crossing the border into Ghana, the first person I met was a delightfully buxom woman named Mama Makola. She sauntered across the busy road, took my hand, and said I looked famished. I was. I'd travelled long and hard and had had several lengthy delays. Bouncy and effervescent, Mama Makola had sparkling eyes that laughed and a smile that might have belonged to the original African Queen when she said the two words I most wanted to hear: food and beer.

Mama led me to her stall, a ramshackle affair that stood open to the element. A rusty tin roof said it all, and as she declared, 'It might be modest, but it's mine!' At that, she thrust a plate lined with banana leaves and a cup into my hands. I didn't argue.

Arriving in Accra for the first time was a bit like being abruptly thrust into a never-ending African Mardi Gras. Highlife music at maximum decibels and bustle, together with traffic of an Asian intensity stultified. Also, the tropical humidity was something to be endured, or you went home. Hardly anyone in those days had air-conditioning, and no question, fetid and intrusive, the average Ghanaian seemed to enjoy the kind of climate that can turn leather green in a week.

Though I've been back many times, very little has changed in this modest West African state over the years. The people are always ebullient, laughing and smiling – but so were the smells – which could vary between a rugby club change room after a match and a crowded London Underground on a summer Friday evening. The smells often could be nauseating and repugnant, the open drains especially.

Other sensations were timeless, especially the music, which included catchy African pieces starting to come through from the Congo. Even vultures scavenging over garbage pits on the outskirts of town could make for something new, and the medicine men and their stalls where all manner of magic ingredients were sold.

In a sense, Accra today is the same rambling, accessible, rambunctious friendly place it has always been, probably because the Ghanaians do their thing, and their pride shows. For a start, the city has never had that emaciated, debilitated look found in other larger African cities like Lagos, Bamako, or Dar es Salaam.

I visited Black Star Square in the Ghanaian capital, where Nkrumah made some of his more dramatic exhortations, including escalating guerrilla wars throughout southern Africa. He was never discreet about where the help to achieve that aim would come from since his ties with Moscow and Havana were strong. *Osajefo* (Nkrumah's popular name) was vocal in declaring that socialism in all its forms was the only way ahead.

I made contact with a senior member of the Anglican hierarchy in Accra – the majority alumni of the London School of Economics – Nkrumah's trusted British advisers and wasn't surprised to be extensively questioned about my intentions while in Ghana (I couldn't hide my accent, so they knew where I came from). That prompted me to take the gap and head into isolation in Half Assini and temporarily, at least, become a fisherman.

An American Peace Corps volunteer I met on my first day in the capital told me that to see and truly understand Ghana, I should go to the bus station off central Accra's Barnes Road. It's a dirty, dusty stretch of real estate, she cautioned, but it would give me what I needed.

'Look for a *tro-tro* heading down the coast towards Winneba, pay your Cedis and sit tight!' she advised. Once clear of the city, another world would emerge, and as it happened, she was spot on.

As I headed along the coast towards the west, the commotion of city life soon retreated and gave way to clusters of stalls and chop bars where the homemade *kenkey*, fish, and goat soup were all regular fare. Social obligation seemed to dictate the pace, but most striking was that everybody seemed – if not happy – at least content. Many of these folk wore threadbare clothes, and only the mammies carried excess weight, but life seemed good. Beyond the bright lights, the atmosphere was more relaxed.

There were other variances: like the costumes of some of the locals and the complicated regalia of elders, or the occasional cane rat – some as big as dachshunds (they call them 'grasscutters') – strung up on bamboo stakes and for sale along most of West Africa's roads. Though rodents, cane rats are highly prized for providing a distinctive flavour to *gari* stews, as in Benin, Togo, Nigeria, and Cameroon farther east. As we sped past, I would sometimes spot the tiny charred, black, almost human-like carcass of a vervet monkey strung tight over charcoal coals.

Of course, it was the people that made the place, and it says a lot when the prestigious *Lonely Planet* handbook reckoned that if there were an award for the friendliest nation in Africa, Ghana would be a powerful contender, 'especially if budget travellers are doing the voting', it declared in an early edition, and for good reason.

Part of the country's charm lies in the reality that this modest West African state – approximately the same size as Britain – is not yet part of the full-blown international tourist circuit, and compared to more familiar haunts, the place is cheap. Meals at roadside stalls start at a couple of dollars, though that's pushing it. You'd be wise to give the stalls a miss because nobody knows how long that meal has been exposed to the elements and invariably hosting some of the biggest green flies on any continent.

Interestingly, more and more African Americans, disillusioned with their own country on the far side of the Atlantic, are heading for that little corner of Africa.

The Ivory Coast, Francophone, gained independence in August 1960, the last of the great pro-West colonial strongholds: to this day France maintains a permanent military presence. My immediate problem was that the country was expensive, so I gravitated to Abidjan's *Quartier Africaine* in Treichville, across the lagoon from the city's CBD.

In that once-beautiful West African city, I encountered a culture that has always been the exclusive preserve of the French, from the hypermarchés and patisseries on almost every main street to the baguettes served for breakfast in the best hotels, together with a facsimile of that morning's *Le Monde*, direct from Paris.

Even today, the European influence – still fringing on the neo-colonial – runs deep, particularly within the city's black middle class, who prefer to speak only French and no indigenous African language. This meant it was not easy to find traditional African food, except at a *maquis* (open-air restaurant).

Situated in the plush and leafy Abidjan suburb of Cocody, I visited the palace of Felix Houphouët-Boigny, affectionately called 'Papa Houphouët' by his people. My intentions were not to see how this famous black leader lived – I knew he also had a farm in France – but rather to get up close to some of his art that was open to the public. These included mainly French masters, many contemporary, and several of Bernard Buffet's huge butterfly oils that covered entire walls. Since the country's upheaval, that area has been blocked off.

I often returned to the Ivory Coast with my film crews, which was always a pleasure. We covered almost the entire country from the coast towards the arid north and were never hassled by officialdom or tribal groups – just about everybody was delighted to help. But, even then, we started to detect some of the problems that would arise after *Le Vieux* (The Old One, as Houphouët-Boigny, was dubbed) had passed on.

His career is worth a mention. President Houphouët-Boigny, in his early years as a medical aide, planter and trade union official, remains one of Africa's most notable post-independence success stories. Installed as head of the Ivory Coast by

France in 1960, and with very little political opposition, he developed the country into one of the most enterprising open market economies in Africa. He despised Nkrumah and his communist ally, Sékou Touré, and, as might have been expected, that sentiment was fully reciprocated.

Also, his affection for his former colonial masters, having established a policy known as *Françafrique,* was legendary, so it was not surprising that he was elected to the French Parliament. Western politicians often referred to him as the 'Sage of Africa' and others as the 'Grand Old Man of Africa'. It must have helped that he severed diplomatic relations with Moscow in 1969 and refused to recognise the People's Republic of China until 1983.[1]

Totally committed to foiling Soviet efforts in Africa during the Cold War, he became a favourite of many Western governments, the United States especially. Consequently, it might have been expected that he was unequivocally opposed to Luanda's Marxist rulers trying to destroy Angola's UNITA (The National Union for the Total Independence of Angola) movement. Throughout, he maintained a discreet level of contact with South Africa's white-ruled government, which only emerged after his death.

Once he had passed, conditions soon deteriorated in that West African country. After his death, the Côte d'Ivoire soon devolved into strife, and there were several coups between 1994 and 2002. A devaluation of the French-backed CFA franc followed, as did a full-scale civil war in 2002 involving South African helicopter gunship pilots, many of whom had seen action in other African wars.

The root cause of all that mayhem has come to haunt many other African countries. Since then, Jihadists have tried to gain power by force of arms in most nearby West African countries, usually spearheaded by al-Qaeda or Islamic State. As with other conflicts in sub-Saharan Africa, the Islamic north attempted to seize control of the Christian and animist south.

There are numerous examples of these hostilities in Mali, the Niger Republic, Burkina Faso, the Congo's eastern provinces, Nigeria, Somalia, Mozambique, and the Central African Republic. That list increases by the year.

But that's something for another book.

---

1   It took President Houphouët-Boigny almost twenty years to normalise relations with Moscow, re-establishing diplomatic relations in 1986.

CHAPTER 9

Rib-eye and red wine in Abidjan

One notable event about that long journey across Africa was that Abidjan was the only place during a long and industrious life where I experienced what I believed to be a heart attack. It happened in the late 1970s, a long time after my four-month overland trek from South Africa to London.

I'd returned to the Ivory Coast with a film crew to make a TV documentary on the country, something I was looking forward to. I always made a point of staying at that magnificent tourist edifice, the Hotel Ivoire, Africa's snazziest hotel – super-upmarket, splendidly tropical – with the only ice rink in Black Africa. Nothing cheap there, though all things considered, that is what one pays for.

I arrived in the Ivory Coast with three nagging problems: firstly, I'd taken a circuitous route to Abidjan from Beirut through Paris, a frustrating dog's leg of a journey. I had been in the Levant covering the civil war with the Lebanese Force Command – all Christian Arabs – the majority of whom were fighting a rearguard series of battles along the Green Line. It was harrowing, and more than once, I came as close to getting taken out as I'd ever been. Effectively, that was my first problem. My nerves were shot, I wasn't sleeping properly, and I had an underlying fear that I'd bitten off too big a chunk…more about that later.

Secondly, not content to be filming only in Africa, I had another team active in Central Asia. They were picking up a good deal of aggro in Afghanistan, where the Soviets were fighting a last-ditch action, and in Pakistan, where those in the business are aware that unforeseen things tend to happen, if only because that's how it works in countries that can barely run themselves.

My third problem was not quite as much of a single issue as a series of 'withdrawal' symptoms (which, I suppose you might call it). I had given up booze and red meat for three months, something I did from time to time, believing it would be beneficial to my health: more likely, that self-imposed abstinence was getting to me. This abstinence might have been acceptable under normal circumstances, but – as I was about to discover – it works the other way around when you are gadding about the planet under the kind of stress that can stymie one's best efforts.

When filming in the Ivory Coast, I always employed a 'fixer' – as it is known in the trade – because that individual is indispensable. These are people who assist film makers in foreign countries and are not only required to be familiar with local conditions, language, places, travel and risks, but also be good organises and familiar with the ruling hierarchy. That meant facilitating the authority I'd need to make the kind of television documentary I had in mind.

My guy – let's call him Pierre because he is still living in West Africa – while inordinately expensive, was one of the best. He is French and career-wise played an influential role in establishing Air Afrique. This pan-African airline was then robbed blind by its staff and, if not actually bankrupted, eventually had the rug ripped out from out under it by its major shareholder Air France when things got totally out of hand.

Case in point: I once had to travel from Niamey in the Niger Republic to Dakar, a lengthy flight and it surprised me that we were offered nothing to eat, not even a bread roll. On disembarking in Senegal, the head of cabin staff marched past me with a plastic bag four feet high filled with rolls, originally meant for the passengers: all would go on sale at his local marché the following morning. So, too, with the soft drinks that never came around.

Pierre symbolised the approach of many French nationals who remained in Africa with their families after France had vacated its colonial possessions. Pierre and his wife even bought a plush apartment in Cocody, anticipating only good things ahead. Nobody thought the Ivory Coast would have to suffer the travails and bloodshed of two civil wars, with some of the violence ending in their street in the capital. But that was still to come.

Pierre arranged a meeting with the Ivorian Minister of Tourism at his office. We needed to chat about the film and – as was (and still is) the custom throughout much of Africa – to hand over a not-so-small *cadeau* to ease the process.

Everything went well for the first few minutes of meeting that eminent man, who wore a classy pair of ostrich-skin loafers and a suit that might have flashed the hallmark of one of the flagship showrooms along Paris's Avenue Montaigne. Then, quite unexpectedly, things went toes up. I'd been in his office barely five minutes when I was struck by massive chest pains that caused me to collapse in a chair. Pierre told me later that my face had gone grey and that I was struggling to breathe.

No question, this was a disaster for us all – Pierre saw his fixer's fee go out the window, and there would be no gift for the minister. Nor the customary 'big eats' and champagne that usually followed such meetings, where else but at the Hotel Ivoire.

What to do? Pierre shuffled me into the nearest elevator and into his Peugeot, and we rushed off to what he said was the best cardiac clinic in the country. It was already getting dark when I asked whether it would still be open because you never know about such things in Africa.

'Yes,' he replied, by now equally stressed as he dodged traffic in the evening rush hour. 'This is Abidjan…everything works very well…'

It took a little while, but we eventually turned off the highway into a road lined by jungle giants and stopped at a building that looked suspiciously like the kind of bunker that Hitler might have built along his Atlantic Wall to prevent the Allies from invading.

Though I was preoccupied with my imminent death, I don't recall much else or even whether the place had windows, except that it was a very low in structure, all brick and with a flat roof. A single bulb was suspended over the main entrance, barred by a steel gate. It crossed my mind that this was not the kind of image I'd expected of a leading clinic, but I was in the Frenchman's hands, and he would know the ropes. My buddy helped me to the main door and knocked hard – no answer. He tried again…still no response.

Through cracks on the side of the entrance, we could see that there were lights on inside, so he tried again. Finally, the main door was pulled slightly ajar, and a face somewhat hesitantly appeared.

Pointing to the 'patient', Pierre told the man – who hadn't bothered to identify himself, so we had no idea whether he was a doctor or one of the porters – that he had to let us in so that a doctor could examine me. It was all in French, of course, and after many years of trekking through West Africa, I had a good handle on the language by then, so I understood perfectly.

'What's wrong with him?' the man asked, still hiding behind the door.

'We think he's had a heart attack,' Pierre answered.

'So?'

'So, we need him to be admitted.'

It seemed that someone else had arrived on the other side, and we could hear them talking. Instead of throwing the door open, they slammed it shut it in our faces. Pierre looked at me and shrugged, puzzled. After a minute or so, he knocked again.

This time somebody different came into view. The door again opened about six or eight inches.

'What do you want?' he asked in a perceptibly angry tone.

'Hasn't your colleague told you?' Pierre responded in exasperation. There was another delay, shorter this time when the newcomer said in a loud voice: '*L'argent*.' He demanded money. What else?

Faced with a somewhat delicate situation that Pierre did not want to exacerbate for fear of us being turned away, he asked in a quiet but emphatic voice, 'Are you crazy…we have a man here who has had a heart attack, and you are demanding cash.'

The man behind the door again said: '*L'argent*.'

We were getting nowhere, even though Pierre asked him to at least let us in the door so I could be seated while things were sorted out. But the fellow was adamant. '*L'argent*,' he declared once more, gruffly this time.

'How much?' Pierre asked, and the man gave him a figure in CFA francs, the currency used by eight former French territories in Africa and roughly equivalent to about $250.

Finally, having made clear that he didn't walk around with that sort of cash – nobody in Abidjan does because the capital boasts some of the most accomplished pickpockets on the continent – he would have to go back into town and fetch it. Respectfully, he asked whether I could be allowed inside to wait in comparative comfort while he went to fetch the money, indicating with a gesture that I was not well.

The response was abrupt: 'No!'

Pierre headed into the city to draw cash from an ATM – it took almost an hour because of the traffic.

Finally, I was allowed into the inner sanctum of what could easily have been a prison cell. Escorted to a bed that seemed reasonably clean, but the linen was definitely not fresh; this started to look ominous…

'Lie down,' the man ordered. What to do but comply?

Pierre asked the man whether he should be addressed as *docteur* – he was as curious as I was to know with whom we were dealing. Though in green hospital garb and clearly a staff member, he replied that *monsieur* was okay, which Pierre had been doing anyway. At least now we knew that we were *not* dealing with someone in real authority, though he did say that I needed to have an electrocardiogram (ECG) when he wheeled a mechanical device on a small trolley into the ward.

Anybody who has ever had an ECG will know that various terminals leading out from the core of the device need to be affixed to specific points on both the torso and the arms. They will also recall that these fixtures customarily need a small blob of oil or liquid to provide accurate readings.

Unfortunately, my new hospital didn't have any oil or, for that matter, anything else that might help.

That meant that Pierre again had to head out to one of the al fresco sidewalk stalls in his car and buy a small quantity of raw olive oil from one of the women seated on her patch of the curb. Like me, my friend was shocked, but he did it anyway.

Meantime, waiting for Pierre to return, I could look around from where I'd been deposited. The 'hospital' was not a large institution; it was relatively compact and probably boasted half a dozen small wards. Also, I wasn't alone, because against the opposite wall lay a seriously ill young woman. She would scream in pain from time to time, a discordant shout that must have reverberated throughout the building. *Monsieur*'s reaction each time was to come running and very loudly order her – both in French and some tribal dialect – to shut the hell up! Frankly, that bothered me because he didn't offer her any medical assistance or even a single pill to tide her through and I didn't think she'd make morning.

When Pierre returned with the oil, the only thing that went well was the ECG. Neither of us said anything about the results or whether the readings were good or bad. *Monsieur* glanced at me several times while reviewing the graphs, which was scary.

Finally, he called my friend aside and rather ominously said he would have to call one of the specialists. He stressed that it was night and that it would be expensive, everything stated in low, conspiratorial tones. Pierre didn't protest.

An hour later, there was a knock at the front door, which we could all hear, and moments later in breezed the only other white person apart from Pierre, with whom I had any dealings that entire day. European, she introduced herself as a cardiac surgeon (thank God) and went over the details of my perceived affliction, listened to my story about the flights, the war, my temporary aversion to liquor and red meat. She took my pulse, did another ECG and sat herself down at the end of my bed.

'Mister Venter,' she said, and her smile surprised me, 'I am going to discharge you back to your hotel.'

'Now?' I asked, my relief palpable.

'Yes, right now. You grab your things, and off you go. And when you get to the Hotel Ivoire – they have one of the best steakhouses in all of West Africa – and you order yourself a big rib-eye, which is always top class because I often dine there. You do that, together with a couple of glasses of red wine to round the evening off.'

'Is that all?' I asked, puzzled.

'Yes, and tomorrow you will be fine. But I suggest you get back to your normal diet because to my mind, all this,' she said, with a wave of her hand, 'is your body protesting.'

So that really was *it*.

Pierre dropped me off at the hotel, and I went straight to the restaurant, rather sorry that I hadn't asked the doctor to join me because she was quite a dish.

While life was reasonably comfortable for this transient on my way north in 1964, I decided to crack what I was told would be the most demanding leg of the entire journey – an overland trip through unknown territory to reach Monrovia, the Liberian capital. That meant a trip of about 1,250 kilometres, the last third through primitive Liberian terrain that has not been adequately mapped, even today.

Bush taxis would take me through Yamoussoukro in the heart of the country and then west. At one point, I was supposed to swing north towards the city of Man in Ivory Coast's Dix-Huit Montagnes, which in those days was more of a large cluster of market stalls than anything substantive. My flawed deduction was that it might be better to follow the more direct route towards what was still the only African country that had never been colonised.[1]

I found a 'main road' that was little more than a single track through the bush to Toulépleu, another nondescript little town that was to become a focal point of the civil war that followed more than thirty years after I had passed that way.

Throughout the week-long journey, most of which was spent trying to navigate my way through some exceptionally heavily foliaged country in the extreme west, I was faced with problems like finding places in the jungle to sleep and in the latter stages – before I reached anything like a proper throughway – something to eat, for the simple reason that there were very few settlements along the way.

While I knew there were few predators left in West Africa and probably no lions, it was not so much the animals that were of concern but my ability to survive. I was also fearful of contracting malaria again as well as any other tropical disease because there were no doctors for hundreds of kilometres had I needed to alert anybody in case of an emergency.

Eventually, I reached a village where a Greek trader and his wife sold me cans of Chinese corned beef that were hardly edible. But I got some of the protein my body needed, and at least I could sleep on their porch. They were kind, offering me a coffee on both mornings that I loitered there waiting for a lift. Until a Land Rover arrived, I hadn't seen another vehicle for days.

It was a difficult journey, spurred on in part by Graham Greene's epic tale of enduring roughly the same conditions with his cousin in his 1936 West African safari through Liberia, culminating in his book, *Journey Without Maps*, even today – almost a century later – worth a read. That was Greene's first cross-country trip outside Europe and indirectly resulted in his being posted to wartime Sierra Leone as a British secret agent.

Why did the Greek couple battle it out in what I regarded as one of the most primal tropical African terrains I'd seen? Their modest home was in the heart of a tremendous arboreal wilderness where few people lived and even fewer ventured. It must have been rewarding in some way for them to stay put in such a severe environment because their existence was, if anything, quite challenging. More pertinent, they certainly weren't taking much cash from the occasional passing trade. I eventually came to suspect that they might be involved in either in gold or diamonds, the latter from neighbouring Sierra Leone.

---

1   A somewhat disputatious comment because before and after World War II, the Firestone rubber plantations were enormous and became the largest single commercial enterprise in the country. Firestone's role within Liberia's ruling clique was prodigious and reached to the president. More salient, what Firestone demanded it got, even its own form of currency for labour on its holdings, something that eluded French and British financial giants in their colonial possessions in Africa.

Though many people must have known that Liberia was rich in alluvial gold, very few made much effort to extract the metal from the tens of thousands of the country's streams, rivers and ponds. The one man who did was Louis, a former American serviceman who described himself as a 'Hillbilly from Kentucky'. He had been based in Liberia during the war and never went home again. Louis set up a small alluvial mining operation years before I met him but said he had an easier way of finding gold, though it took me a while to uncover his secret.

Apart from the Greek couple that all but saved my life, Louis was one of the first whites I met in the country not long after I got onto one of the main roads leading to the capital. He told me that life had never been better, and, as he said, 'I've had many wives, none of them my own.' All were local women who must have produced dozens of his children over a couple of decades. I drove around with Louis most of the time I spent in Liberia, and we were constantly being waved at by young and old who called out his name as we passed. That was one very popular buck!

Louis was initially cautious about how he lived and where he got his cash until he admitted one day, having topped off a bottle of Bourbon – that he was a grave robber! Not ordinary graves, he insisted, but ancient burial sites dating back centuries. Many of the dead were buried with beads, bangles, and various forms of jewellery – a good deal of it iron but quite often solid gold. In his mind, the fact that they were hundreds of years old made it less of a crime, and he wouldn't accept anything to the contrary from me. He admitted that if any of the tribal folk in the areas he plundered tumbled onto what he was doing, they'd kill him, 'probably in the blink of an eye', but that just seemed to add spice to his wobbly existence.

What was sad was that Louis could probably have made good money selling those precious historical artefacts to private collectors. There were museums worldwide that would have taken the stuff – even underhand – but the maverick American melted the treasures down, probably fearful of being caught. He sold the gold in the form of homemade ingots.

Louis intrigued me with his tales about the people, particularly those in the jungle around us, every one of them believing in sorcery and witchcraft. In Liberia, he said, it was not simply a matter of a few magical potions or making offerings to a shrine out back somewhere, but the real serious business of sacrifice that could sometimes include humans. He would often stop his Jeep, and we'd stroll down a path in the bush to a point where somebody had fashioned a primitive fence across a stretch of the bush.

'That's "no go" country,' he declared with a generous wave of the hand. He explained that there were many sections of the forest that strangers were prohibited from entering because they were controlled by what the locals called 'secret societies'.

'They come here after dark and perform a series of rituals, thanksgivings to their primitive spirits whom they believe protect them. Quite a lot of it has to do with casting spells on people, good or bad ones...I don't know which is which, so don't ask.'

Louis had tried a few times to get involved, but while he had almost total freedom to do as he pleased in the country, he believed some things were best left alone. Voodoo was one of them.

At one stage, he stopped in a remote area reasonably close to a tall peak sticking out of the forest a couple of kilometres away and pointed: 'Now that's the real thing: "Spirit Mountain" they call it, and you don't go there because I was once told – no holds barred – that if I tried, that would be it! They weren't joking either because it was a form of paying tribute to the so-called "Supreme Power", whatever that's supposed to mean.'

What was sad about Louis, very much alive and an active relic of a war in which he had never fought, was that the African country in which he had made a home for himself – even though he was white – almost celebrated his rambunctiousness. He was happy to fall down drunk wherever he pleased, seduce the wives of just about everybody, secretly plunder historical artefacts, and never think twice about any of it. He could have contributed so much to the people of Liberia, but he never did. Still, not everyone was taken in; some referred to him as a derelict 'white animal'.

On a more personal note, while filming in the country some years later with my crew, we spent five days in a remote region near Bopulo, which lies some distance north of a village called Tubmanburg. President Tubman once spent a night there, though I cannot imagine why. The entire region was – and still is – undeveloped: no towns, not a single hotel or restaurant, just tiny primitive tribal compounds in the jungle.

As suggested by our 'minder' – who was a mandatory government functionary – we took our own food. His sole role was to ensure that none of us stepped out of line by filming 'wrong things' – such as, I assume, dead people's heads mounted on stakes, which were commonplace in the dark interior, or the bodies that lay outside our hotel every morning in Monrovia. That was almost two decades after my first visit on the overland journey, and malevolent forces had taken over the country.

What made the isolated Liberian community we filmed different from similar villages in the Ivory Coast or Ghana was that the settlement was not only primal but almost archaic. The people living there had seen white people before – one old man had even worked on the rubber plantations – many, though, had never spoken to a white man or even come close to one.

What was disturbing was that they had some weird traditions, like burying their dead beside their huts. That meant there were graves practically everywhere – not conventional burial places like in cemeteries back home – but piles of large rocks surrounded by smaller ones topped with a small shrine on which offerings were made.

Though most film people would laugh it off, my three-person crew refused the offer of huts in which to get their heads down. Instead, they returned to our VW Combi each evening after we'd had a bite, drove it up the road a few hundred metres and slept in the vehicle. I slept in the village and each morning, I could report that nothing untoward had happened, though the mosquitoes were a menace, even with a net.

Another issue raised by Louis was that cannibalism seemed to be, if not commonplace, a reality. Again, under the circumstances, it was not the sort of thing you asked questions about because of the hostility such interest might generate.

There were quite a few instances of cannibalism that we knew about and involved conflicts in two parts of West Africa: several in Sierra Leone during the civil war and others in Liberia. In the former, regular reports of troops being involved in such practices on both sides of the front were underscored by a headline: 'Cannibalism/Ritual Murder Hits Freetown' in the capital city's *Weekend Spark* on 4 August 1995. More evidence of this revolting practice followed the death of the former Liberian President Samuel Doe. In his *Spectator* article, Canadian columnist Mark Steyn mentioned that parts of his body were eaten by the soldiers that killed him:

> They removed His Excellency's genitals and then fought over them, believing that the 'powers' and 'manhood' of the person whose parts you're eating are transferred to the eater.[2]

---

2   Mark Steyn, 'The White Man's Burden: "There is a case for intervening in Liberia, but it is not one being urged by American liberals."' *The Spectator*, 2 August 2003.

CHAPTER 10

Kids with machine guns and water for fuel

If Lagos is the filthiest city on the African continent, then Monrovia, the Liberian capital, must be the most dissolute.

American town planners must have had a hand in its creation because it was initially laid out like a small Midwest town. The image of contemporary Monrovia is of a grossly overcrowded city with interminable rows of thousands of overhead electric wires that crisscross the city's streets. That, and more bar room joints than you can count and enough neon signs to possibly light up all of Africa.

Even the city's cops were dressed in dark uniforms, almost as if they had just stepped straight out of one of New York's twenty-seven precincts. Police cars were two-tone, as in the United States, with lights affixed, modern style, to their roofs.

It was indeed what some might call 'Little America', but there was another aspect to it. Those Liberians with close ties across the Atlantic could, if they had the money (and many did), fly back and forth to the United States without formal restrictions: no visas, no residency, nothing, though things might have changed since I was there. A century ago, Liberians had been accorded honorary American citizenship, which was why their currency for many years was the US dollar. That courtesy was revoked after some Liberians became involved in a spate of money-laundering conspiracies on behalf of Mexican drug cartels and the Mafia.

On the negative side, it has long been accepted that Americo-Liberians regard themselves as several tiers above the rest of the population. They created a separate community that sees itself as superior to the country's tribal people, a kind of 'apartheid' dictum among black people – harsh but true – and one of the causes of a succession of civil wars a generation or more ago.

To qualify for the much-aspired 'upper echelon' bracket, your forefathers should have been among formerly enslaved people, liberated at sea by American warships and deposited on Monrovia's beaches approximately two centuries ago. Other Africans already on American soil when slavery was abolished were offered free transport back across the ocean, but there were few takers.

Nevertheless, for this newly arrived country boy from down south, it was a novel experience. One of the first friends I made in Liberia was Lamar, a young African-American who was spending his sabbatical, as he phrased it, 'getting to know my roots'. On hearing that I had come from South Africa, he intimated that he and his friends back home in Chicago had gotten together at one stage to find a way to 'nuke' the apartheid regime. He was deadly serious; he told me, 'If I could, I would.' He'd even bought a subscription to the *Bulletin of the Atomic Scientists* to stay abreast of developments.

Lamar took me in tow in his jalopy, and between beers, we did the rounds, which included Liberia's presidential palace, probably the most opulent on the West Coast of Africa. American contractors had built it, and its reputed 108 rooms were all furnished by Macy's Department Store of New York, and at American taxpayers' expense.

We even had a drink at the Ducor Palace Hotel, one of the most prominent buildings in the country at the time, a nine-storey structure built in 1960 by Israeli architect Moshe Mayer. What set the Ducor aside from other hotels in the country was that from its roof – if you woke up early enough – you were able to witness the morning swathe of villagers on the far northern shores, tens of thousands of them, entering the sea to 'do the necessary' since only people with money in Liberia had proper toilets.

The hotel was so luxurious that President Félix Houphouët-Boigny, on visiting it for the first time, was so impressed that he commissioned Mayer to erect a 12-storey luxury hotel in Abidjan. The stunning Hotel Ivoire emerged three years later. During a state visit to Liberia, the former Ugandan dictator, Idi Amin Dada, swam in the Ducor pool with a handgun strapped to his trunks. Sadly, the Ducor Palace is no more; it was destroyed during the civil war that followed the fall of Sergeant Samuel Kenyon Doe in 1990.

Despite all its problems, many of which involved its formerly enslaved people, the country has a fascinating history. Liberia's president, who was in office when I first arrived, is now acknowledged as the man responsible for bringing Liberia to international prominence in the 1960s. A delightfully convivial figure and a good friend of President John F. Kennedy – his name characteristically harked back to America's southern states – William Vacanarat Shadrack Tubman, even though he was himself a true-blue Liberian.

He was cherished with unabashed affection and called the 'Old Man' by his people who held him in high regard. Born in Maryland, Liberia, Tubman was always referred to with great reverence by his people.

President Tubman served for seven consecutive terms, which gave him the longest tenure of any modern president just about anywhere. He expanded the American side of his heritage by marrying a woman from Atlanta, Georgia. He went on to maintain other US traditions such as a congress, a senate, and a supreme court that would probably have fitted comfortably within the precincts of 1 First Street, NE Washington DC.

Throughout his rule, Tubman was regarded as 'the Great Unifier' of his country, 'From the darkest jungles in the interior to the great city that makes our capital what it is.' Or, at least, that was the plan. Yet in truth, his presidential opponents never garnered more than a tiny proportion of the national vote, which meant that the 'Americo-Liberia Pioneer' community – a minority – held political sway and kept the majority of the country's indigenes at bay, a situation which eventually caused an army mutiny and brought Master Sergeant Samuel Doe – and indigenous tribesman and not one of the 'cherished few' – to power.

Despite protests to the contrary, all hinterland counties – economically and politically neglected for a century or more – were unofficially relegated as second-class citizens. While gradually brought into the national framework, they wielded no real power.

Nobody took much notice of these shenanigans. Some American diplomats warned that if things were not put right in 'this developing age of egalitarianism' and most of the population not made more representative in decisions that affected their lives, things would go badly awry. So they did.

The worm turned in April 1980, when a belligerent master sergeant in the Liberian armed forces – a tribesman from the Krahn ethnic group – seized power in a dysfunctional army mutiny that somehow succeeded. President William Tolbert, by then the twentieth president of the country, was murdered in the same palace that Macy's had furnished; another thirty or more of his political grandees were killed. The man responsible was Master Sergeant Samuel Doe.

The execution of the rest of the country's leaders, including cabinet members, followed. They were taken to a local beach and shot by a firing squad. There was no lucidly polished anything there – nationality, politics, ethics, or anything else commendable.

Sources present at the shootings, some of whom took photos, recalled that the murders turned into a disgustingly bizarre spectacle. Most of the troops were too drunk to aim straight, resulting in the victims being wounded several times before somebody despatched them with a pistol shot to the head. Tragically, the troops ran out of ammunition halfway through and sent for more and that took over an hour.

Doe, the great 'overnight' leader (because he emerged, literally one evening from the ranks) with more than a few apples short of a picnic basket, didn't last very long either. Having elevated himself to the rank of general, he was ousted by a former American gangster, Charles Taylor, who was on the run from the FBI. Taylor survived his overthrow and is currently in prison following a human rights trial at the International Court of Justice in the Hague for the murder of tens of thousands of his countrymen.

Without elaborating on the ramifications or dialectics of these sad issues, I again need to quote Mark Steyn, a political commentator with an abiding interest in African affairs. I do so because his views share a fundamental bearing on how I was to earn my crust as a foreign correspondent in the decades ahead, mainly in Africa.

In an incisive article for London's *The Spectator* titled 'The White Man's Burden', Steyn declared that there is a 'case for intervening in Liberia'. The commentator is troubled when he states: 'In the sprawling cities of West Africa, for the swollen population of unemployed and unemployable illiterate male youths, stealing and killing are pretty much the only rational career choices.'[1] 'In Liberia, male life expectancy in the last five years has declined from fifty-six to forty-four years; in Sierra Leone, it's down to thirty-two.'[2] He continued:

> The Congressional Black Caucus blames all this on the legacy of colonialism, but it would be more accurate to call it the legacy of post-colonialism or prematurely-terminated colonialism. The first generation of the continent's leaders was the London School of Economics-educated Afro-Marxists who did a great job destroying their imperial inheritance. By the time that crowd faded from the scene, the Cold War was over, and nobody needed African puppets.

For all that, some unusual stories emerged from Liberia during the time that both Samuel Doe and Charles Taylor believed they were keeping things together. Indeed, they were not, but nobody was brave enough to say so because you were never sure whether you might displease these lunatics and be either shot or decapitated.

One event emerged from an old friend, Danny O'Brien, an American pilot with more experience than most in helicopter support missions in Sierra Leone's civil war. There were many aviators there including chopper gunship pilot Neall Ellis – all sticking their necks out and coming under a lot of fire. The bottom line is that that form of conflict seems to attract its peculiar brand of adventurer.[3]

One memorable event involved Danny who, with his crew were operating out of Monrovia at the time, going out on numerous relief missions, usually at the behest of the US State Department. They were flying a beat-up Russian Mi-8 helicopter that had probably seen service with the Soviet Air Force in Afghanistan in the 1980s.

Working for International Charters Incorporated, an Oregon group still active today, Danny took his machine – with about 20 officials on board – into Zwedru, a remote village in Liberia's interior. Recalling the incident at his home south of Seattle some years later, Danny remembered it as having been an unscheduled flight. As he phrased it: 'There was no curriculum, script or template to get by,' adding that it

---

1   Mark Steyn, 'The White Man's Burden: "There is a case for intervening in Liberia, but it is not one being urged by American liberals."' *The Spectator*, 2 August 2003.

2   That was in 2003, immediately after the civil war. Life expectancy in Sierra Leone has significantly increased since then.

3   Al J. Venter, *Gunship Ace: The Wars of Neall Ellis, Gunship Pilot and Mercenary.* Casemate: 2012. Reissued in paperback in the United States and South Africa, 2021.

was one of those typical 'Hey you!' missions that always result in trouble. 'But this was State calling the shots, and we did what they told us.'

When the helicopter arrived at a remote jungle encampment, 400 or more agitated and none-too-happy Liberian guerrilla fighters were waiting on the ground. As Danny recounted: 'The first impression I got was that this was a bunch of rebels who were big-time pissed.'

Apparently, two hours before the helicopter reached its destination, this untidy band of Krahn fighters (all had previously been closely associated with the recently-very-dead, former Liberian leader, Samuel Doe) had come under surprise attack by forces loyal to the opposition. There had been casualties, and as might be expected, the survivors were in a fury.

'We found out later that they hadn't received any word of our heading out in their direction. Our job was to take in a delegation to sort out some political impasse, so they had no idea why a helicopter would suddenly swoop in from nowhere. We could just as easily have been the enemy, so I suppose we were lucky not to have been attacked when we first circled the football field where we eventually put the wheels down.'

Having unloaded his passengers, all of whom went into town under rebel escort, Danny and his crew sat back at the improvised airstrip and waited for them to finish their business and return. Meanwhile, they were attracting attention: the aviators were being observed by a group of irregulars, some of whom were perhaps eight or 10 years old and armed with an assortment of infantry squad weapons that included AKs, RPGs and RPD machine guns.

'One of my guys recalled afterwards that while it was still early in the day, it was obvious that they had been mixing their brew. Either that or they'd been smoking something because soon afterwards, the taunting started.

'They'd wave their Kalashnikovs about like crazies, and we knew that we couldn't hang about indefinitely because things could only get worse,' Danny recalled. But he couldn't simply up sticks and haul out of there without his 'cargo'.

The leader of this crazy band – gimlet-eyed and brutish – stepped forward and used his weapon to indicate that the helicopter wasn't going anywhere. Then the three men were pulled from their machine, beaten and robbed of everything, including their wedding rings. The hapless trio was finally stripped naked, with some women brawling over who would get their clothes. One of the biggest fights erupted over a pair of coloured jockeys.

'Things went even further downhill when the idiots started firing shots between our legs…there was no particular aim; they just let rip. They would laugh like hell each time because they could see we were scared shitless.'

More beatings followed. Then some of the ringleaders argued about whether the victims should be shot or cut up with machetes, and since those doing the talking were deadly serious, this was worrying. Some of them then ransacked the helicopter, ripping out the radio and other equipment, which eventually had to be replaced. Not that they would have any use for the stuff in some dark African jungle, Danny thought.

Hearing shots, Danny and the crew were eventually rescued by the guerrilla group. Their leader, a woman who had been waiting on the ground when the helicopter arrived and preferred to be known by her nom de guerre, 'Attila', which was somewhat appropriate, O'Brien remembers. This formidable lady was rather large in proportion, voice and energy and had earlier identified herself as 'Number Two' within that rebel band.

'Gun in hand, she marched fixed-eyed towards the rioting mob, fired several shots in the air and told her bodyguards to grab the ringleaders. She promptly ordered them to be taken behind some buildings and shot,' said O'Brien.

'Kill them now!' she yelled. That was when the kids, some not yet teenagers, were taken away and executed. Soon afterwards, O'Brien and his crew – without a single pair of underpants between them – were allowed to take the delegation and their helicopter back to Monrovia.

From the Liberian capital, I headed north again, crossing the border into Sierra Leone at a tumbledown shack on a bridge, officially the frontier. That didn't bother the border guards because they were a friendly mob, so I sent somebody out to a street-side stall to buy them all beers. Liquor invariably speeds things up in remote areas.

One of the immediate impressions of Freetown, the first city of Sierra Leone, was the magnificent natural harbour on which it lies. One of the biggest bays on the Atlantic Ocean, the port still bore evidence of its role as a convoy gathering point in two world wars. The remains of a derelict Royal Navy submarine were visible at low tide in Cline Bay, and I was to spot it again decades later while covering the civil war.

In Freetown that first time, I went to the old City Hotel, Graham Greene's unofficial wartime 'headquarters'. It was still standing, and I only managed a single night in an upstairs room before the cockroaches drove me out. Running the place in those days was Freddie Ferrari, a Swiss-Italian national who had married a local woman with whom he had several sons, none of whom pleased him because they refused to work and existed on handouts from their father.

Quiet-spoken and a font of anecdote of the period, Ferrari in his heyday had hosted all of Freetown's colonial notables in his first-floor bar, Greene included. I questioned him over a few ales, and he was delighted to share some of his reminiscences, several of which do not warrant repeating.

In a BBC report, Tim Butcher tells us that the City Hotel, destroyed by fire in 2000, had already 'been a forlorn place of ambitions run to waste'. Greene was more explicit, declaring that it had been a 'home from home' for men who had not encountered success at any turn of the long road and no longer expected it.

Butcher added his footnote: 'Through Greene, the hotel became a literary leitmotif for the late colonial age, not just in Sierra Leone but across Britain's declining empire.'

I found Freetown in late 1964 to be pretty laid back but only in parts; the central city business area was always remarkably vibrant – it was the largest burgeoning commercial centre between Dakar and Abidjan. The country's economy was flourishing, a solid middle class appeared to hold its own, and Fourah Bay University ranked among the best in Africa in colonial times. More relevant, the civil service was unmatched, even in Lagos. Today, unfortunately, both hardly function.

With his dodgy old Mi-24 helicopter gunship, Neall Ellis helped that government win the war against Foday Sankoh's rebels in the civil war that followed. Though he and his crew fought hard for some years, putting their lives on the line, when he left Sierra Leone, the government owed him more than $2 million. He has never been paid.

During that first visit, the country had been independent for only four years, and there was clear evidence throughout the nation that Lebanese-fostered corruption would eventually bankrupt the nation. The Levantines had always dominated trade in Sierra Leone (as they have, with a community of almost 200,000 strong in Nigeria) – and once it became independent, those Arabs took control of the country's diamond fields.

The first casualty was Sierra Leone's rail system, a damnable exercise in sleaze and sold to Chinese interests. It should never have happened, even though many backhanders were involved. From then on, Sierra Leone went the way of almost all independent Africa.

To add an enormous dollop of insult to this ungainly scenario, the massive Lebanese school in Freetown, which I visited – with more than a thousand enrolled scholars – refused to admit ethnic Sierra Leonean students unless they were related to or were the offspring of at least one Lebanese parent. Unusually, this form of racial segregation was not only tolerated but sanctioned by the Freetown government.

As with most issues involving avarice, the rot invariably starts at the top. Sir Milton Margai – the country's first elected leader who took over in April 1961 – did not live long enough to implement stringent checks and balances. Things went seriously adrift when his brother, Sir Albert Margai – also knighted by the Queen, though goodness knows why – controversially took over. Within months he had started to strip the country's treasury.

Army coups d'état followed, the military became a shambled collection of misfits, and the rest is history. The 11-year civil war started in 1991 and only ended after Britain had stepped in and defeated the rebels. By then, tens of thousands of people had been murdered and half the population displaced from their homes.

Sierra Leone's cornucopia of horrors, like most recent developments in Africa, has a track record that goes way back, long before its present travails. One should bear in mind that until relatively recently, this was still a reasonably backward country with only city and mostly town dwellers being educated. Apart from diamonds, it was relatively undeveloped land. Maps of the West Coast little more than a century ago showed sparse detail in the interior – the first big war with Germany forced the pace of progress in Africa, both for Britain and France.

British administrator and author Roy Lewis takes issue with his colonial government in his book *Sierra Leone: A Modern Portrait*, published in 1954, for so effectively 'shielding the tribes from hasty interference in their settled customs'. He pointed out that it was not until 1927 that the international community discovered that London 'still firmly upheld the principle of domestic slavery' in the hinterland.

On my return to Freetown in the summer of 2000, I found that the city had changed, and frankly, transmogrified would be more appropriate. The only reason that Freetown is not the largest slum on the African continent today is that as cities go, Lagos, Kinshasa, Conakry, and Luanda are bigger. Sadly, the Sierra Leone capital is also one of the reasons why tourism has never caught on in West Africa. Millions have enjoyed East Africa's delights, but there seems to be little to attract the visitor on the other side of the continent.

On arrival at Lungi International – clean, modern, and progressive as one would expect of a modern airport – you generally take the ferry across the bay to reach Freetown, and the visitor is thrust into what Peace Corps volunteers have described as the ultimate cathartic culture shock experience (the travel agency I consulted for my return thought it best not to mention the perils). On first initiation into Freetown proper, even today, you are confronted by the filth and degradation of a city of several million people that has been deteriorating for more than half a century.

The stench and open drains are only part of it, and while the people are friendly enough, nobody has the money to improve living conditions, added to government corruption which ranks beyond cure or care.

All that begs the question: while there are a few modern Western-style hotels, what would attract tourists to visit the place? You cannot even go to where the boats come in with their daily catches – the fish are gutted there and then, and the innards left to rot in the sun.

This disregard for hygiene, coupled with two Ebola epidemics in 2014 and 2020, which infected tens of thousands, hardly bodes well for ordinary domestic life, never mind tourism. Nobody has any real idea of the number of people who died in either epidemic because a fair proportion of deaths occurred in the remote bush and jungle areas beyond proper contact; fatalities are thought to have run into thousands.

From the quaint post-colonial, prosperous little settlement that was the Freetown of the 1960s and 1970s, the malaise that followed in the wake of a Lebanese 'takeover' meant that – war or no war – the Sierra Leoneans led ghastly lives. I spent some months there, on and off over several years, but I cannot help feeling that things will not change. The capital of Sierra Leone had become a city of palms – all outstretched and waiting to be greased. The other reason is that the army has overthrown a succession of governments over the years, and it was perhaps inevitable that one bunch of thugs should replace another.

The country's early history reflects a lot on what is happening in Freetown today, apart from being the site of some of the first efforts by the West to redeem 300 years of plunder, slavery, and piracy. As always, the intent was honourable, but as we all know, the road to hell...

Today, there are many nostalgic links to the 'old country' where the Royal Navy deposited formerly enslaved people on Freetown's rocky shores. Some of its prominent landmarks include the Queen Elizabeth II Quay, suburbs commemorating slavery that include Wilberforce and New England, and roads that honour Milton, McCauley, Keats, Charles Dickens, and many others.

There is also a tribute to Lord Chief Justice Sir John Holt, who ruled that, 'as soon as a man sets foot on English ground, he is free.' This evidenced that – almost throughout the country – traditions had not changed much since Queen Victoria buried her beloved Albert, with Sierra Leone remaining a British colony for a century-and-a-half.

Many of the actions that followed colonisation quickly became mendacious. What's more, they took place on both sides of the Atlantic. Take one example: the first strip of land used to set down enslaved people freed at sea was granted to the British government by King Tombo, the Temne chief of the Sierra Leone Mountain peninsula. He gave the British a site in exchange for a load of trumpery that included some rum, muskets, and an embroidered waistcoat.

If it sounds like déjà vu, you've got it!

Freetown does offer a few curious anomalies. One that was personal came when I joined mercenary aviator Neall Ellis in his fight against the rebels. I started drinking water from the city's taps. He told me it was just fine and that he had been doing so for years.

He didn't disclose that he was on a bi-monthly deworming regimen.

A lot of the country's history can be found by just wandering through the city's old colonial graveyards, though one must be wary of snakes. They are everywhere, especially on the edge of towns and some are big'uns.

In one of the burial plots adjacent to Freetown's Tower Hill, I found the grave of Elizabeth Murial Duncan, a mother from a small town in Essex who, at 22, was 'taken unexpectedly'. The 1822 inscription on her grave noted that she had become ill in the morning and 'died of high fever' before sunset.

The mortality rate was alarming; Sierra Leone soon acquired a sinister reputation. In his book Roy Lewis, then on the staff of Britain's *Economist*, confirmed that the colony 'exacted a dreadful toll on lives'. He noted that between 1814 and 1885, 'five governors and seven acting governors died at their posts or on their ships home.'

Harrison Rankin, who wrote *The White Man's Grave* – published in 1847 – recorded a discussion that went something like this: 'One kind friend, more facetious than the rest observed that, since I was bound for such a deadly place, it would be judicious to include a coffin in my equipment, since it might come in handy at an early date.'

Another visitor to this stretch of the West African coast said that in the first years after its settlement, it was quite usual of a morning to ask: 'How many died last night?'

Getting large parcels of diamonds out of the country, until relatively recently, was easy. Sadly, it still is. One of the dealers who remained in Freetown during the war described how he managed to get his parcels of gemstones out of the country.

Each time he wanted to leave the country (with perhaps five kilos of uncut diamonds); he would discreetly negotiate his passage beforehand by going directly to the head of the country's security services. He wouldn't even bother with any other government minister: the responsibility for success was now firmly vested in this senior official. Anyway, the fee demanded by the intermediary was hefty enough to cope with any contingency.

Having settled on a figure, the man would go through the usual pre-flight routines before departure. This could include a physical search for diamonds by a special police agency at either Lungi International Airport or Hastings if it were a short trip. Customs and passport control would follow.

Once through and his flight had been called, he would board with the rest of the passengers. Before take-off, a uniformed officer would board the plane and hand over a package with goods worth millions of dollars.

As he said, 'It was usually given to me with a smile.' Just like that…

On a later visit to Sierra Leone, I spent time with some of the Lebanese. One of them, Hassan Delbani, a Shi'ite militant, was a passionate supporter of the Hezbollah movement in Lebanon; he was also Neill Ellis's side gunner. We often flew together on missions, which could get quite hairy.

Another was Mustapha, who owned a single-engine private plane, and we too would sometimes go up on flips. To protect his asset from theft, he and some others had alarm devices installed in the hangar. An alarm was placed under the aircraft to cover all approaches that had both movement-sensing and infrared abilities. Each time someone approached the aircraft, the system sounded a blood-curdling, high-pitched scream.

However, since Africa grapples with the kind of problems not generally found on other continents, South African pilots who flew a Puma helicopter from Durban and delivered it intact to its new owners on the West Coast took a few extra precautions. They applied tamper tape to check whether cowlings had been opened during the dark hours. 'Part of our daily routine was thoroughly checking our fuel before take-off,' the pilot told me when we had a few beers a year later, including some reports doing the rounds of fuel being siphoned off aircraft and replaced with water.

Ellis, who flew combat for years in many African conflicts, added his two bits' worth by saying, 'It was pretty standard practice in some Third World countries.' He recalled events while flying gunships in Sierra Leone:[4]

> One morning in Freetown, we arrived at the helicopter I'd parked at Cockerill Barracks and found that 900 litres of fuel had been siphoned from the chopper during the night. Fortunately, those responsible were 'thoughtful' enough not to replace it with water.
>
> Another time, our fuel had been stolen and replaced with water. Fortunately, we spotted that aberration during my pre-flight inspection – we had only 100 litres of fuel taken.

I mentioned this to a South African commercial pilot, Jeff McKay, who had flown wide bodies out of Australia to the US and beyond for Qantas. The same thing happened to him, twice actually, while flying commercially around Africa. He'd had an incident at Nacala, one of Mozambique's biggest airports, and also in Kinshasa in the 1990s. 'Luckily, I was operating a Beech King Air and picked it up during my flight checks.'

I heard something similar from Leif Hellström, a Swedish friend and fellow author interested in African goings-on. One of his fellow countrymen who worked in the Congo said one night he wandered into the air force hangar at N'Djili International Airport, Kinshasa. There he found a C-130 military transport plane with long lengths of hose fitted into drain valves under the wings.

'People were scurrying around siphoning fuel into jerry cans, obviously for private sale.' It was a regular thing, he reckoned. He went on: 'The air force had French Mirage jets, which would be towed to a petrol company terminal at N'Djili once a week for filling up, naturally at government expense. All aircraft were fitted with maximum long-range tanks, and even engineless hulks were towed across for the illicit fuelling process. Once they had been taken back to their original holding areas, the fuel was pumped out by air force personnel and sold on the black market.'

Makes you think…

---

4   Al J. Venter, *War Dog: Fighting Other People's Wars*. Casemate: 2005.

CHAPTER 11

Republic of Guinea to London

The last leg of my journey up the West Coast of Africa was by road. I left Freetown early one January morning in 1965, only nine days after Winston Churchill had died in his London home, having succumbed to a fatal stroke.

The route ahead was cut and dried. From Sierra Leone, I would cross into the Republic of Guinea – followed by a long, lonely haul into Senegal, which would take me to the former French colonial capital of Dakar – thus winding up my four-month crossing of a great deal of the African continent.

There was nothing easy about it. Though I'd never faced any real danger in Africa, Guinea presented some challenging obstacles; the first was that its president, Sékou Touré, had turned his back on the West and become a close ally of the Soviets when the Cold War had suddenly become hot. As I had heard on the grapevine in Freetown, people like me, travelling independently – with no specific purpose other than wanting to get from A to B – were not made to feel welcome in a country that had declared itself a socialist republic. The second was my South African background.

Some backpackers had already been arrested as suspected 'infiltrators or spies'. They were released after their embassies protested, but it meant that most young people gave Guinea a miss.

I experienced something similar in Ghana because Kwame Nkrumah was the leading light of the anti-imperialist brigade and despised all things from the 'White South' (which he was entitled to do). Still, I quickly skedaddled into the neighbouring Ivory Coast when I was summoned to Accra to give a reason for my visit.

The Ghanaian president might have been a firebrand, but he never allowed his country to become a military staging post for Soviet and Cuban warships and military aircraft. In contrast, Guinea had done precisely that. President Sékou Touré despised the one man he should have admired – General de Gaulle – who had spearheaded the granting of independence to French colonies in Africa. He had singled out Sékou Touré, a radical trade unionist, to lead the race. Notwithstanding, the young leader viewed de Gaulle with undisguised disdain.

Consequently, Conakry, Sékou Touré's large modern harbour, was to become the equivalent of what Diego Garcia is today for the Americans. The main difference was that in West Africa, nobody could counter that move since Guinea had pretty much severed ties with France.

De Gaulle was not without blame. As with all the former French colonies, Guinea had been given the choice of maintaining ties with the former motherland – including the CFA currency unit (linked to the French franc) – but Touré wanted none of it. He chose to go it alone, though, at independence in October 1958, he almost immediately sought Soviet help to help him through those troubles (there is evidence that he was a card-carrying communist from his student days). One of his more memorable quotes – which rather neatly encapsulates the impasse he had at the time with Paris – was: 'An African statesman is not a naked boy begging from rich capitalists.'

The consequences of that action became shambolic. At short shrift, de Gaulle ordered all French nationals home and declared they should take whatever 'belonged to France'. As a result, his citizens shipped out every moveable piece of equipment and machinery from their privately owned factories – some even stripping their homes of light fittings and toilets.

The two leaders – one black (newly elected), and one white (a traditionalist of the Old European School) – loathed one another to the extreme. Those sentiments were evident to the entire international community, and I was heading into that uncertain cauldron of political furore with only my British passport for protection.

Curiously, I had no problem getting a Guinean visa at that country's embassy in Freetown: I wasn't even asked why I wanted to go there! Conakry, in contrast to Freetown, was something of an anti-climax. I found myself in a pleasant tropical back-of-beyond where there were still French residents and almost no evidence that the country, as one redneck declared, 'has gone all Commie'.

I was decidedly cautious, not flashing my camera when I moved about in a city that, then, might have been about the same size as Rhodesia's Salisbury. Security was tight – far more stringent than anything I had experienced in the previous months – with armed guards at the gates of all public buildings. But, as I discovered in December 2017, on my last visit to Lebanon, precisely the same situation prevails in Beirut today, almost sixty years later, so nothing is new.

What I wasn't allowed to see – foreigners weren't allowed anywhere near the harbour – were two massive Soviet endowments that had arrived with Moscow's good wishes a short while before. The first was a rock-hard mountain of cement 30 feet tall which took up an entire section of one of the quays. The shipment had been delivered in standard-issue paper bags – evidently not waterproof – and unloaded in the middle of the West African rainy season. It makes you ask: wasn't anybody in charge? The result was that the entire consignment mutated into a solid concrete mass and was immovable. That mound is probably still there today, and to call it an error is to understate the scale of the blunder by several magnitudes.

Even worse, the other 'gift' comprised Russian shiploads of snowploughs to a country that likely last experienced freezing in the Pleistocene epoch. Hundreds of these machines were stuck in the harbour until somebody could decide what to do with them. That pair of disasters became a standing joke within both the expatriate and diplomatic communities in Conakry, the inference being that some bright spark in the Soviet Union hadn't paid attention in his geography classes at school.

As with other cities I'd traversed during my journey, I latched onto a small crowd of Americans living in the capital city, all working for the Peace Corps.

The one group, who lived in a fine old colonial villa near the centre of town, had as its putative leader a New England youngster with the surname Vanderbilt, and yes, he was a scion of that famous family. He was 'doing his bit for his country'. He could probably have chosen to go anywhere in the world – his dad knew John Kennedy (whose brother-in-law, Sargent Shriver, at the behest of the president, was the driving force behind the establishment of both the Job Corps and the Peace Corps) – but he chose the Republic of Guinea.

All were young, affable, and fired up by the challenge of working in a supposedly hostile country. They welcomed my presence, especially since I could already prepare a mean Durban curry. However, they did stipulate that there were house rules, one of which involved my not emerging into the street, camera in hand. Also, political discussions were out: I didn't argue because I needed a bed for a few nights while I sussed out the way ahead.

One of my best photos, sitting behind my little Olivetti portable typewriter – complete with leopard-skin puggaree around my bush hat – was taken on their first-storey veranda in the heart of Conakry.

As the days went by, I could explore the city with my camera, which I discreetly disguised in a small rucksack with a few valuables, including my passport. The most daring photo of all was a street-side shot of the local broadcasting station with a giant billboard that proclaimed: *Voix de la Révolution*. I was stupid to take the chance; had I been seen, I would have been arrested since the first target of most African coup plotters, without doubt, is the national radio station.

I left my American friends after four or five days, the last night given over to a party (still one of my best!), though I was left nursing a two-day hangover. This was not made easier by my having to leave the village at first light for the central bus station.

I crept through Conakry just as dawn broke, and while I thought security patrols might stop me, they didn't even notice my presence. I was an early arrival at the bus station, which meant that it was only a two- or three-hour delay before we set off towards Labé, Guinea's second-largest city. I was relegated to an inside seat in an overcrowded *taxi brousse* – it was 'all-stops' en route and took a day to cover approximately 480 kilometres.

I observed that the Guinean interior was not as thickly foliaged as further south, with few farms and most villages in-between, hardscrabble poor. Some more fortunate souls seemed to have discovered that there was wealth under their feet because it wasn't long before Guinea became a major producer of diamonds.

In Labé, I had my first brush with security when I was stopped at a roadblock and told to accompany some uniformed men to the police station.

Dozens of questions followed: the wheres, whys and the whens, as well as where my journey across Africa had taken me, all demanded by a senior man in a splendid uniform who spoke good English. Though it took a while, they eventually released me, satisfied that my destination was Dakar in Senegal and not Portuguese Guinea, with which the Conakry government was at war in all but name.

In truth, that colonial struggle eventually developed into a grim and bitter guerrilla conflict with many fierce battles fought in the Portuguese enclave and people dying every day. I covered it extensively in later years and about which I wrote several books.

Guinea would permanently deny involvement in the colonial Guinea war – even though Portuguese Army prisoners were held captive in Conakry – and later freed in a daring commando raid from the sea.[1]

I wasn't to know it yet, but my route towards the north would take me close to that action, which was probably why I was taken off the bus.

Finally, I reached the small town of Koundara, approximately 35 kilometres south of Guinea's frontier with Senegal, and perhaps several hours' drive by Soviet army wagon from the nearest Portuguese military outpost in the southeastern corner of what was eventually to become Guiné-Bissau.

With little money to spare, a pair of Americans came to my rescue. As with the group of my Peace Corps worker friends in Conakry, they offered me a corner in their modest little cottage. I accepted with alacrity.

Though conditions were spartan, the delay proved to be rewarding. Several houses away, there was a large building with numerous antennae protruding from the roof: without doubt, a radio relay station linked to the rebel army fighting the Portuguese in the neighbouring territory. During the course of several brief discussions, they mentioned that the place was staffed by Russians and that there was a lot of movement in and out of the structure. What also emerged was that the building seemed to have some kind of significance for the guerrillas.

Those goings-on understandably spiked my interest. I'd been in Angola only months before and it was impossible to miss the fact that there was a full-scale insurgency on the go. Precisely that was happening, perhaps 50 kilometres from where I was staying. But conditions in the Guinea Republic made it impossible

---

1   Operation *Trident* featured in both my books: *Portugal's Guerrilla Wars in Africa*. Helion: 2013 and translated into Portuguese under the title *Portugal e as Guerrilhas d'Africa* (Clube do Autor, Lisbon) and *The Last of Africa's Cold War Conflicts*. Pen & Sword: 2019.

to question my hosts too closely, after all, I was a tourist and I couldn't embarrass them with probing enquiries about what was distinctly a military communications control point.

I did manage a few lengthy strolls past the place while I scouted out Koundara for want of anything better to do, but even that was halted when I sensed that I was being tailed and in broad daylight, because we didn't venture out after dark.

The structure, its exact location and its unknown role in the ongoing war in Portuguese Guinea subsequently became the subject of a fairly lengthy discussion at Portugal's London Embassy after I had returned to Britain. The defence portfolio was held by Colonel, later General, José de Bettencourt Rodrigues – a man who would leave a lasting imprint on his country's war in Angola.

Neither of us knew it at the time, but he would radically change the course of my career, a topic I wrote about in my book *Portugal's Guerrilla Wars in Africa*.

I left Koundara on that final leg to the border post, again early in the day. The immigration counter was housed in a small nondescript building, separate from all the others, and things didn't bode well when the official, a big man with a military bearing, motioned me to one side. I was to wait until he had dealt with all the other passengers. When my driver argued that he couldn't wait, I sensed from the official's body language and the response, that he'd told the chauffeur, in French, to blow.

Finally, I became the sole focus of his attention, having called me into a small office at the back. Through an interpreter, he questioned me about my stay, by which time it was evident that he was *Sécurité*. Plainly unhappy with my responses, he literally threw my passport back at me and told me that my travel document was not in order.

'Why?' I asked through the interpreter, bewildered.

He replied that I needed an exit visa, and I was ordered to return to Koundara and report to police headquarters. His menace emanated from just about every pore and to my mind, perfectly fitted the occasion. I was hardly in a position to argue.

I was sent back to Koundara twice more, and the joker, who knew perfectly well what he was doing, showed little compassion. After all, why should he? Throughout the ordeal, he reflected the kind of contempt you would show to a dead rat at the end of a stick.

Eventually, he let me through, but only after I'd been obliged to spend several more nights at the home of my newfound American pals, bless their hearts. Towards the end of my unscheduled stay, I could see that they were becoming apprehensive because what was taking place at the frontier post was unusual. And finally, when I strolled past a large, circular metal disk that proclaimed in large red letters, *République du Sénégal*, I walked on air.

That was not the end of it. Tambacounda, the railhead where I would swing hard left to reach Dakar, lay more than 160 kilometres away, which would take the road to within metres of another country, Gambia, an extreme backwater in the fast-fading British Empire. There I was to meet another European named Marcel, who had 'gone bush' and had made a home on the banks of the Gambia River for himself, his Senegalese wife, and their children.

Marcel could almost be regarded as an offshoot of a cult that the likes of Paul Gauguin might have initiated. Like the French artist, he had lived in Paris, even though it was three-quarters of a century after the great post-Impressionist had left for Tahiti and like him, Marcel had no particular interest in going home. Purely out of curiosity, I hung about for a day and a night in the tiny riverside village near his family encampment, exhausted after my travails in Guinea.

Unlike Louis, the Liberian grave robber, this Frenchman had no real purpose in life, and indeed he and his family appeared to live a harsh, survivalist existence. One evening while we were sharing a few beers, he told me that he was so poor that he didn't have two *sous* to rub together. But he spoke good English, and we chatted well into the night.

Marcel openly admitted that he had embraced Islam and he had no real problems, apart from feeding his family, which he sometimes did by fishing in the river. He also trapped for food: birds, and animals. Nobody in his little world appeared to be hungry or emaciated, so he must have done reasonably well.

'What of the future?' I asked. 'Will you go back to France?'

Marcel shook his head and answered that nobody could predict the future.

'My health is good, so is that of my wife, and – as you see – our little tin and reed shack is modest. We only sleep in it, and the rest of the time, we're out here in the clean air and make the best of it.' His children all attended a small village school where a French volunteer taught the basics. 'I give them the rest: the culture, the history, our people and their traditions.'

I left it at that and was on my way again with a lift I'd organised with somebody working for the United Nations. Dakar awaited us both.

It is worth mentioning that nearby Gambia was one of the first countries I visited once I had set out to make my mark as a scribbler.

That was only a few years after I'd left Marcel and his family camped on the banks of the Gambia River on my way to Dakar. Its capital was Bathurst since renamed Banjul, and what a delightful experience that was.

I wrote something about the place for Argus Africa News Service, stating that Banjul was the only place in the world where I found high school students studying under streetlamps 'because few of their families had electricity at home'. The article went on: 'On my first night in the country I discovered groups of youngsters gathered at various vantage points where the lights were brightest. Those not reading were helping others with more difficult aspects of their homework. If anything, the scene was industrious, and it did indicate how seriously the majority of West Africans take their studies. If they have an opportunity, they use it because there may never be another.'

I recalled that the Gambian capital was also the only West African city where it was possible to see parties of Scandinavian tourists strolling unabashedly bare-arsed along the city's beaches; most were impervious to the stares of a black society whose morals (then) fringed on the Victorian.

'The two contrasts were bizarre, but they did illustrate the refreshingly unsophisticated atmosphere one discovered in this English-speaking enclave, surrounded by the Francophonic Senegalese Republic'. That easy informality started at Yumdum Airport on Bathurst's outskirts, with the arrival of the weekly flight from London, always something of a gala occasion.

'Anyone among these handsome, hospitable people who had any standing in Gambian society made it his or her business to get out there and join in the frivolities. There was bound to be somebody they knew returning from abroad and, as in other regions along this tropical coast, any arrival or departure rated a celebration.'

It was also notable, I recalled, that when you stepped off the plane, Yumdum was the only airport in Africa where you had to ask directions from the laughing throng to get to Immigration. For several years after Gambia's independence from Britain, Immigration doubled as the local bar. The barman, a rotund, smiling, profusely sweating police sergeant in khaki – sporting two rows of World War II campaign medals – was also the local immigration clerk.

Much has since changed along this stretch of the West African coast, including two attempts at overthrowing the Gambian government by force of arms. The first, in 1994 succeeded, and the second which followed in 2014 was thwarted, with several of the conspirators killed.

I only recently discovered one of the notebooks I had with me where I recorded a few of my impressions of that very first visit to Dakar after leaving Guinea. Remember, that was 1965, and the city has changed significantly since. I had no spare cash (as usual), so once in the Senegalese capital, I made do with cheap lodgings and small eating houses that accorded better with my circumstances. I quote:

> It's a big city Dakar, probably the size of Nairobi on the other side of this vast continent and a welcome sight as we emerged from the arid countryside and clouds of dust that stifled because we had to drive with the windows down or suffocate.
>
> Though the country has only been independent for five years, Dakar boasts some of the most aggressive touts on the continent, mostly unemployed (or, more likely, unemployable). They don't ask for money; they demand it, almost as if it's their right.
>
> Being a former French colony, I was expecting something that might have resembled Tangiers in Morocco, but that was possibly pushing it, though some subtle Mediterranean cultural undertones à la française couldn't be missed, interspersed with occasional splashes of metropolitan flair that the colonials had left behind.

Most of the black population follow Islamic traditions, though not staunchly, because many drink. That and whores by the dozen and, for those who want them (the Tangiers touch once more), there are rent boys on every other corner. If anyone is looking for a latter-day version of *The Alexandria Quartet*, Dakar might provide the answer.

All the trimmings of a modern city were there: the Bruxelles *salon de thé*, a handful of first-rate French restaurants discreetly tucked away on back streets, and rustic bars along the waterfront, though a fortnight's garbage waited to be collected and the heat jarred. Dakar's main markets were leviathan then, and they still are (I've been back as recently as 2021).

The main one, Marché Kermel, was a sprawling, jumbled centre of organised chaos where on that first trip, I could get a 'bits and pieces' reasonably satisfying meal for the equivalent of a couple of dollars in CFA francs. As was pointed out, the city has been a gathering spot for traders to sell their wares to European settlers since 1910.

I have visited Dakar quite a few times in the interim and much has changed, not strictly for the better. On my last visit, my taxi driver needed an advance to fill his tank on the way in from the airport, and you made damn sure that your hotel door was locked and bolted when you settled down for the night…no need to elaborate…

There were some more positive changes, including a film industry that has burgeoned over the past quarter-century and produced some of the best movies around – the majority streets ahead of some of Bollywood's meretricious offerings.

And then there is the Kora, an instrument said to predate both the lyre and the guitar and the source of some of the most beautiful music anywhere, played on a calabash with 21 strings. Many musicians are of Sufi persuasion; unlike Sunnis or Shi'ites, the Sufis are regarded as the romantics of the Islamic world. There are a good many West African Kora recording on YouTube, and I find it is always a pleasure to tune in.

Sadly, China has moved into Senegal, as it has in in almost every African country. As one wag put it, the came in almost 'under the radar' with their nationals generally exuding a sense of entitlement, probably because in Dakar, they built one of the largest sports stadiums on the continent. It is evident that the Senegalese government didn't realise it at the time, but with Beijing, nothing is free.

I had two more priorities in what had been France's colonial showpiece in West Africa before I headed to Europe, having cadged a lift on an oil rig tender that was headed for the Canary Islands.

The first was Gorée Island in Dakar's vast, natural bay that in its day was the epicentre of the transatlantic slave trade on Africa's West Coast. Lying just offshore, it was the ideal location for human trafficking, which was how it acquired its name *Maison des Esclaves* (House of Slaves). That terrifying set of dungeons was constructed by Afro-French Métis (Créole) families who dealt in enslaved people in the 1780s.

With my older brother Jannie on a Port Elizabeth Beach.

My grandfather Robert Peschel in the service of the Imperial German Navy under Kaiser Wilhelm II.

Off-duty at one of the shore batteries in Simonstown, mid-1950s.

As a young man in search of adventure in West Africa shortly before I took a job in Nigeria.

Photograph of Dr Schweitzer, dedicated to me. I spent a week at the great man's jungle hospital at Lambarane in Gabon.

In London on my way to work in the snow in 1961.

The *Londoner*, Stena Lines' first ferry service between Britain and France. In 1965 I was tasked by Clarksons to establish the service. (Stena Lines)

The great Sten Olsson, for whom I established Stena Lines' first ferry service in Britain in 1965. (Sten Olsson Family Collection)

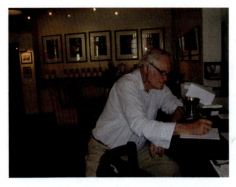

Peter Younghusband, who covered Africa for *Newsweek* and the *London Daily Mail*, and who taught me my trade in the 1960s, taken at his home in Stanford in the Cape. (Courtesy of Peter Younghusband)

Heavy stuff guarding our convoy in Angola's Dembos – jungle country.

In trying to get back into Angola, I ventured into the Congo where I was arrested on charges of espionage.

I visited Monrovia several times over the years and it was always a disaster.

Libreville was one of the best of France's colonial capitals.

One of Ghana's old slave castles.

With my team at the John Holt offices at Lagos airport.

Biafran rocket attack on the Scandinavian freighter *Titania* in Nigeria's Warri Harbour when I was trying to enter the beleaguered enclave.

The one and only Romano Cagnoni, with whom I shared time, food, and experiences in a war-ravaged Biafra.

Biafran battle casualties.

British armour being offloaded in Nigeria's Apapa Docks (I secretly filmed this during a visit to Lagos harbour).

This photo was taken in Portuguese Guinea at the height of that West African colonial war.

War buddies in Sierra Leone – with Cobus Claassens, who was played by Leonardo DiCaprio in the movie *Blood Diamond*. The two men became good friends.

Going to war in a battered old Soviet BMP-2 in Sierra Leone with Executive Outcomes.

Mercenaries at a forward chopper base, in the Sierra Leone diamond fields, notice the Hip in the background.

British SAS veteran Fred Marafano (second right). He spent years battling Sierra Leone rebels, latterly with South African mercenaries.

In the gunner seat during the Sierra Leone war. Sitting under the front bubble of the old Soviet Mi-24 chopper, I got the best photos when we went into action.

One of the RAF Chinook helicopters dispensing anti-missile flares over Sierra Leone during an ongoing jungle operation.

Preparing to fire a Soviet RPG-7. The weapon is a charm to handle because there is no recoil.

With a French TV team before the Ugandan Army chased us out of Gulu in the north.

Mogadishu was a delightful Indian Ocean hideaway before the civil war.

Approaching Mogadishu airport in a U.S. Army Blackhawk.

In Somalia attached to an American chopper unit operating out of Baledogle during Operation *Restore Hope* in the early 90s.

I captured this image moments after Neall Ellis had let rip with a rocket salvo from the Hind at a rebel camp in the Sierra Leone jungle.

Another bush war, another chopper attack, this time in the Central African Republic where I went in twice with a NATO rapid reaction force in 2019 and 2022. The gunship was a Pakistani Air Force Mi-24.

Colonel Ron Reid-Daly, who founded the Selous Scouts. One of my best buddies ever.

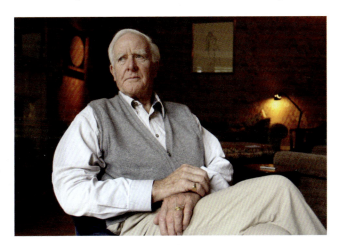

David Cornwell, whose pen name was John le Carré, a good friend.

With the famous Arthur C. Clarke at his Sri Lanka home.

South Angola with American Vietnam veteran correspondent Robert Poos during the Border War.

South African Puma over south Angola. Taken at dawn, this was one of my best operational shots from that conflict.

A South African recce contingent place explosives to detonate a flooded Soviet tank in Angola.

A squad of 32 Battalion operatives on patrol inside Angola. I went out on patrol with 32 operational squads several times during the course of the war.

Lifting a Soviet TM-57 anti-tank mine along *Oom Willie se Pad*, the main highway linking east and west Caprivi, south of Angola. I took this photo while filming in the war zone and admit to it being a somewhat dodgy operation.

This photo was taken when I went into action with a bunch of South African 'Parabats'. It was taken as we were being dropped on the outskirts of Cuamato village in South Angola. Our unit took six casualties, including two KIA.

On the conning tower of one of South Africa's submarines during an operation off the West African coast.

At the nucleus of that hideous business (because that is what it was) sat an eminent Senegalese Grandee who had reached an accord with local people to capture entire tribal communities living in the interior. They would sell them to buyers in Dakar for transhipment. Those poor souls were held as prisoners in chambers behind thick walls that are now a significant tourist attraction. Sad but true.

My other interest in the city was more recent, but just as unfortunate. It involved a clever act of skulduggery by the Royal Navy early on in World War II. The French had built several heavy gun batteries in Dakar, which were then in the hands of pro-Nazi Vichy loyalists, and these weapons were my specific interest because the events behind it all make for a gripping story.

The British knew that France's new battleship, the 38,000-ton *Richelieu* – a superlative warship that packed eight 15-inch guns and could cut the waves at 30 knots – was at anchor off Dakar and, if seized, might be used against Allied convoys. For that reason, the destructive potential of that fine warship – nor any of the others in this strategic West African harbour – could not be ignored. So, in early July 1940, the Royal Navy secretly positioned a strike force, headed by the aircraft carrier HMS *Hermes*, off Dakar and, with their usual sangfroid, launched Operation *Catapult*.

They sent in six antique Fairey Swordfish biplanes, if not to sink the *Richelieu*, then to disable her. It was accepted that the mismatch of biplanes (top speed, a magnificent 224 kilometres an hour) and battleship guns was a gamble, but the vintage warplanes did their job and punched a hole in the battleship's stern.

Dakar's limited dockyard facilities could not repair the *Richelieu*, so she was immobilised and effectively, that African state was all but sidelined for the duration of hostilities.

Arriving back in London has always been a pleasure; it was also this time, though I took a decidedly circuitous route. I travelled steerage class from the Canary Islands to Cadiz, lazed in Seville for a few days – which was to become my favourite European city in later years – and then to Barcelona (third class in the middle of winter, huddled in a coach with no windows). The final leg of my trip was from Barcelona to Paris before taking the Dover ferry from Calais.

It might have sounded tedious, but it wasn't. Once in Spain I was diverted to Casa Campelo near Alicante, where a week with some like-minded young folk with time on their hands, were waiting: I'd met one of their friends on the ship headed to Cadiz.

Some were either flush with hope or aspiring to the impossible – others were either in love or just out of it. The common denominator was that we were all watching our pennies, except for Chuck, who was also the only person 'on' something. Chuck, a youthful American pilot who had been badly wounded in Vietnam, used his monthly disability cheque to stock up on the hard stuff. He became addicted while in hospital in Japan, and since the severity of his injuries guaranteed him a pension for life, he wasn't complaining.

We were a happy, albeit a dysfunctional bunch, which is usually the case when a crowd of youngsters mush together and survive on a series of collective shoestrings. Each morning we'd head out to the market and buy chunks of cheese together with handfuls of olives. If we were feeling light-hearted, we'd grab some Serrano ham slices, which didn't happen often because it was a delicacy and expensive. The carafe of red wine that accompanied our evening meal was a *sine qua non* – all of which put us back about three dollars each.

Evenings would usually be an impromptu gathering at the corner cantina where one of the locals – his speciality was flamenco – would spend most of the night playing his guitar. You could do that on Spain's Costa Blanca then, but no longer. Those long-forgotten memories are impossible to replicate in this modern era.

I would have liked to have stayed, but London was beckoning; prospects were awaiting my arrival. A letter of introduction had already been sent to Clarksons, Europe's largest shipbrokers in the City of London, who thought they might have a job for me. As it happened, they did.

During my train journey out of Barcelona, I experienced my one and only rail disaster – a high speed derailment in which nobody was seriously hurt, likely due to the sturdy construction of the rail coaches then. I must have had a hundred narrow misses on Africa's roads and seen dozens of horrific collisions, but it seemed that I needed to reach Europe to have a genuine accident.

It is one of the realities of life that simple events, and sometimes the long arm of coincidence, end up changing our lives for better or worse.

For me, two things came together: the first was a night out on the town shortly after I arrived in London. That happened in Soho's famous pub known as 'The French' – General de Gaulle was said to drink there occasionally during the war.[2] I was having a pint there when I mentioned offhandedly to my drinking buddy what had happened in Koundara – the obscure little village in Guinea where an obnoxious border guard forced me to stay longer than was necessary. It was the Soviet radio station that intrigued him, *pastis* in one hand and a cigarette in the other. He was curious and wanted to know more. Much more…

---

2   As London pubs go, The French House (formerly The York Minster) is still something of an institution among artists and writers. It is where General de Gaulle is said to have written his speech rallying the French people, *À tous les français*, and Brendan Behan wrote a large portion of *The Quare Fellow*. Dylan Thomas once left the *Under Milk Wood* manuscript under his chair after a splurge. While working on getting the ferry project going in London, I lived in a nearby condemned bedsitter for a while, so I went there often and could observe why it sold more Ricard *pastis* than anywhere else in Britain.

I couldn't help. It had been a cursory event based on a few observations centred on radio masts poking out of the roof of a house just up the road from where I was staying. While with the pair of Peace Corps volunteers who briefly took me in, the Soviet and Cuban presence nearby was hardly ever mentioned: I was left to make up my own mind about what was happening.

Not long afterwards, I received a call from the Portuguese Embassy in London. The caller introduced himself as Colonel Bettencourt Rodrigues – a soft-spoken military man who suggested we should meet for coffee to discuss my journey across Africa. 'Nothing more,' he added, 'just a quiet exchange of views since I too am interested in Africa.'

I accepted, as I was always ready to chat with others who might have shared the same experiences as I had. A week later, we met in his office in Belgravia, a little more than a stone's throw from Buckingham Palace. I discovered the colonel's first name was José and that he was one of those social beings who put you at ease immediately – if he chose to do so. Nevertheless, he remained formal, addressing me by my surname. In turn, I addressed him as 'Colonel'. That first inauspicious meeting was a prelude to events that lasted decades.

After the initial preliminaries, Colonel Rodrigues came to the point. He told me that somebody in South Africa had spoken to him about my trip, specifically Koundara and the radio station. He did not need to clarify that Koundara was directly linked to Lisbon's colonial war in nearby Portuguese Guinea. I realised then that my pal in 'The French' – with whom I'd had a few drinks a month or so ago – was probably involved in intelligence. Presumably, he told one of his contacts in Pretoria about what I had seen. That information was passed on to Lisbon, where others would undoubtedly have an interest.

It struck me quite forcibly that I might have become inveigled in something equated to the murky doings of subterfuge or espionage, and frankly, I was enthralled because this was usually the kind of thing one only reads about. So, instead of heading for the door, I accepted an offer of more coffee, and the colonel pressed on.

He pulled out a sheaf of large-scale aerial photos from his desk drawer. At first, I didn't recognise them as aerial views of Koundara, but the colonel assured me they were and that someone had put his life on the line to get them. He handed one of the images to me and asked whether I could identify the house where I stayed with my American friends. It was not difficult because the town was small, and our house was just off the main central square. I used a thick red pencil to identify the structure.

'Which means that the house with the radio antennas is this one,' he declared, pointing to the building. At this point, he brought out a magnifying glass which he used to scan the images closely.

Satisfied that we were on track, he further surprised me by asking whether it would be possible for me to accompany a 'group of my friends' to Koundara to accurately pinpoint the building. One loaded question it was too, coming straight out of the blue.

I didn't reply immediately because apart from the element of surprise, I had just started working in London. Anyway, such an expedition would have taken weeks, even though he assured me it was all expenses paid. He would personally cover flights: London to Lisbon, then to Bissau in Portuguese Guinea, plus all hotel costs. He further confided that there would also be a 'small gratuity' for my efforts.

Colonel Rodrigues and I met several more times at the embassy over the following months, and – though I was eager for the adventure to take place – it never did. I eventually learnt that I would have had to accompany a unit of paratroopers on a night-time operation across the border to destroy the radio facility.

This brings me to subsequent developments a few years later. By now, I had started writing, and when I returned to South Africa after spending time in Nigeria, I decided it might be a good idea to cover the escalating guerrilla war in Angola. Until then, few scribes had achieved that much because Lisbon was opposed – with the occasional exception – to any media presence in its African wars. Colonel Rodrigues had helped me before to return to South Africa through Angola; possibly, he could do so again.

After having made a home for myself in Cape Town, I dropped him a line since he was still the military attaché in London and asked him on an informal basis whether it might be possible for me to report on that war.

He replied promptly: 'Send me your passport.'

That chance meeting in a London pub a few years before altered the course of my life and changed my career choice. My career in shipping was done; I was about to cover my first guerrilla war – in Angola.

But there was a lot to still happen in both London and Nigeria before I was to have that experience...

CHAPTER 12

The Londoner: my dream of a ship

Arriving in London in early 1965 was almost like coming home. My first visit to the UK had been five years earlier. I'd come in from New York on the liner *America* after six months in Canada and the United States, having spent brief spells as a lumberjack in northern Quebec, on a northern Ontario gold mine and picking tobacco along the shores of Lake Erie – a placid, enchanting stretch of water.

Most evenings after work on a farm in Southern Ontario I'd get a lift to the lake and the prospect of no sharks was exhilarating. Until then, having only swum in the Indian Ocean off the Natal coast and along Kenya's shores (where there had been numerous shark attacks), it was, to me, a unique experience.

For this country boy from a distant, relatively 'unsophisticated' Africa, those first few years in the United Kingdom are indelibly etched in my memory. A bevy of admirably disciplined minds had tutored me at Marist Brothers College, all honed by their respective Irish, English or Scottish heritage – the basics of which they gladly imparted to us young colonials. That was followed, while serving in the navy, by the immersion into still more tradition by British-born chiefs and petty officers, which meant that I always felt comfortable returning to London.

It was always 'Destination Earl's Court' for many of the young hopefuls from the Empire: Canadians, Australians, New Zealanders, as well as a tidy number of South Africans and it worked like this: Many graduates from the major Commonwealth countries were eager to expand their professional backgrounds and experience by working in the UK, usually for two or three years, and then head home again. No visas or work permits were required: you arrived off the boat (before jet travel became an everyday thing), got a stamp in your passport, took the train to London, and got drunk that first night. The following day you started looking for a job.

The first time round, in 1960, I arrived from across the Atlantic on a Friday: bought a ticket for the musical *Irma la Douce* in the West End and on the following Monday morning, applied for a job as a clerk at an office in Upper Thames Street, Billingsgate – for centuries known as the heart of London's traditional fish market. I was to start work the following day.

By the end of the week, I'd registered at the Baltic Exchange to attend classes that would qualify me to become an Associate of the Institute of Chartered Shipbrokers. It was a tough call, but shipping was my game. But first, I had to be interviewed by Mister Sinha, the secretary of my prospective employer. He was a diminutive, bookish individual who spoke better English than I did, even though he initially hailed from the Punjab.

To start with, his approach was tentative, querying my background, family ties and what I'd done in the navy. Satisfied, he took on a more serious demeanour: 'You will appreciate, Mister Venter, that you are now in the United Kingdom and that we have no apartheid here.'

Mr Sinha – I never found out whether he had a first name or not since all management in the UK in those days sat on the left hand of God – listened carefully as I laid out my background and what I wanted. More important, I made it clear that I not only wanted the job, but needed it.

I was flummoxed when he raised the racial issue again, since I'd never expected to be confronted on the subject in London – Nigeria, yes, but not in the United Kingdom. It took a few moments before I could answer, assuring him that a racist I was not. I also mentioned that when I was a youngster, I'd lived in Durban for a while and spent time with Indian friends in Phoenix, one of their townships.

'That's it!' he declared, leaning forward. 'We have no *townships* in this country... you do understand, I am sure!' It was a statement of fact and not a question.

Seemingly satisfied, I was dismissed without a smile and told that I had the job and that the pay was a pitiful 14 pounds a week – it might have been more, though – the exact figure escapes me. I'd already found a place to stay in Putney from a notice posted on a board in the main entrance hall of South Africa House in Trafalgar Square. Three pounds a week for the room that needed a shilling in the meter if I wanted to boil a kettle.

But that was then, and it was some years before I qualified as a Fellow of the Institute of Chartered Shipbrokers, the professional body for all members of the commercial shipping industry worldwide and centred on Lloyds of London. I probably wouldn't have succeeded had the kindly Mr Sinha not given me a job several years before: untried, untested, and like him, from the colonies.

When I landed back in London after the lengthy African haul, after a tough couple of years in shipping back in South Africa, I already had an appointment in the city. Presumably, I'd impressed my bosses in Johannesburg, and they must have relayed good things about me to their British associates. When I called the secretary, she told me a meeting was scheduled at the city offices of Clarksons – once described by the *Financial Times* as 'the undisputed world heavyweight in the international shipbroking market'.

To be clear, a shipbroker deals with ships, while a stockbroker is focused on stocks and shares; Clarksons, then situated in St Mary Axe, deep in the heart of the City of London, headed the former.

Promptly at nine on the Monday morning, I was ushered by a uniformed official into what seemed to be an almost ritual company meeting in the expansive mahogany-panelled office of Sir Alexander Glen, the distinguished chairman. Only later did I learn that this customary meeting functioned almost solely for the directorate, chosen friends and associates to discuss what everyone had done over the weekend. Occasionally, some business would be addressed.

They were indeed a jolly crowd, and this 27-year-old, tanned and healthy from a long journey across Africa couldn't have been further from home, both socially and geographically. Though I was a total stranger and a colonial, I was warmly welcomed by everyone to whom I was introduced – much more so than by the enigmatic Mister Sinha on our first acquaintance some years previously.

As could be expected, I was out of my depth – South African accent and all – since those around me were top-class British leaders and entrepreneurs, several of whom were well-known figures. More to the point, I could hardly figure out where I might fit into a mélange that was both gracious and sociable.

Finally, I was introduced to Sir Alexander, who, by then, I'd observed was called Sandy by his chums. He drew me aside and briefly quizzed me about my trip and my intentions. I admitted that I had none. He then put a hand on my shoulder and asked in a quiet, authoritative tone, 'Young man, how would you like to run your own shipping company?'

It was an offer that came from nowhere, from someone I'd just met and, to boot, a much-esteemed Knight of the Realm. And this from a man (I had done my homework) who'd ended his career in the Royal Navy as a fully fledged four-ringer – and a gong or two for valour!

Without a doubt, I was floored since the implications at that precious moment were imponderable. So were the ramifications – almost impossible to grasp at such short notice. All I could do was stammer a yes, followed by asking what it would entail?

Sir Alexander led me towards his desk and asked somebody to join us. He proceeded to tell me that Clarksons had been approached by a Swedish shipowner of considerable sway and whom he personally knew. The plan was to set up a daily service for passengers and cars between Britain and France.

'It's quite basic, really,' he declared. 'The man is building a large ship that, as we speak, is being fitted out in France.' Compliant, I nodded and asked for his name.

'Sten Olsson, the shipping entrepreneur,' he responded. 'You've probably never heard of him, but you will, I assure you,' telling me too that the Swedish shipping magnate ran his company out of Gothenburg. The ship was almost ready to be put into service, and he'd asked Clarksons to establish a daily ferry service between Tilbury on the Lower Thames and Calais. Essentially, what Sir Alexander was charging me with was to establish the first Stena Line service in the British Isles.

I later learned that Sir Alexander Glen KBE, DSC and a graduate of Balliol, Oxford, wasn't handed his knighthood because he had the right connections – he'd earned it the hard way. During the war, he was one of the hands-on architects responsible for mining the Danube, preventing vital *Wehrmacht* fuel supplies from Romania's strategic Ploesti oilfields from reaching Germany. His book, *Target Danube*, published years later, reads like an Ian Fleming cutaway. This also explains why Sandy Glen, a senior officer in the Royal Navy, was one of the inspirations for the character of James Bond.

I am dead sure that Clarksons would have checked me out scrupulously – enough to be satisfied that I, a total stranger, could handle this mammoth job under extremely challenging circumstances, even though there was a legion of efficient, professional British talent on their doorstep. Through his contacts within Clarksons, Sir Alex would undoubtedly have liaised closely with my MD in Johannesburg, Tiny Musgrave – in his day, a national tennis player who had played at Wimbledon. Tiny gave me the original letter of introduction, possibly to confirm that I was up to the task at hand.

Also, having qualified as a FICS – linked to the same Baltic Exchange in London (through whom Clarksons would channel much of its work) – one might assume that the company had access to my exam results, both at Associate and Fellowship levels. I was told that my marks had been 'quite good', except for accounting. To this day, I've never been able to get to grips with the double-entry system. None of these studies were easy going; professional qualifications in Britain never are.

There was no doubt that I would accept Sir Alexander's offer of a job because I needed a job anyway, and this was, as the saying goes, 'in the pound seats'. There was one provision however: I had 'four months and not a week more' to get the show on the water.

The ship's name was *The Londoner*, designed to take 126 cars and a thousand passengers on board. The intention was, once the service was up and running, that she'd depart each morning from Tilbury moorings in the lower reaches of the Thames, reach Calais about lunchtime, give passengers an hour or two ashore and then head back to British waters. Also, I wouldn't be working for Clarksons, the shipbrokers, but for Clarkson Booker, their travel-orientated subsidiary company. My new offices comprised an entire floor at 35 Albemarle Street, an ideal West End location, barely a two-minute stroll from the Ritz.

There were three immediate demands: firstly, to introduce myself to my future managing director, Ken Holmes, at his offices near the Bank of England; secondly, to estimate the number of staff I would need to fulfil my role, and lastly report back to Sir Alex in a week's time with a draft plan of how I would accomplish these goals. When done, I was to go to the travel desk and have them issue me an airline ticket for Paris. I would then take a train to a shipbuilding yard handling the Swedish contract in Rouen and inspect what would dominate my life for the best part of the year ahead.

The vessel was nearing completion at the Ateliers et Chantiers de la Seine-Maritime in Le Trait, on Rouen's outskirts. My first introduction to her, on arriving at the gates at seven in the morning, were tumblers of hard grog being handed out to staff about to start their shift. In those days in France, that was the way things were done.

I found Ken Holmes to be pin-sharp and opportunistic in his approach to most matters. He clearly appreciated a few of the esoteric delights of somebody of his status, like having a Morgan +4 built, which came with a fibreglass coupé body. The first time he mentioned it, I thought he was talking about a boat and was accorded the appropriate response. But then I was a colonial and got away with it.

We got on well from the start, though had I not been up to scratch, I'd have got my marching orders from him early on. More importantly, he let me get on with things without demanding that I report back at every stage – an enormous relief; it seemed he was confident that I could handle the task.

A month or so after the service had been inaugurated, the ferry developed engine problems and departure was delayed in Calais. I got a call from the ship's master saying that there were passengers who had to make rail connections and didn't have the money to overnight in hotels. I had only one option: charter two passenger aircraft and bring back those with urgent needs. It was an expensive exercise, but Ken didn't blink. That touch of chutzpah even got us a mention in Fleet Street!

My next big undertaking was staff. The Albemarle Street office had space in a general office for about fifteen, plus a smaller cubicle for me and my secretary, who was English and lived south of the river. The immediate problem was to find more than a dozen willing hands that were demonstrably keen, clever and innovative – considering that we were going to create this brand-new entity from the bootstraps up – with only four months in which to do it.

One immediate problem was that Britain, in the mid-1960s, was beset with trade union problems. While I could hire easily enough, dismissal was another story; firstly, three written warnings had to be issued. That would take time and could be subject to conjecture if, God forbid, feelings were hurt, and legal action followed.

Time was short, so I couldn't allow anything to impede our progress. This included a complete travel plan for the daily service to France and back, creating booking lists for the year ahead, liaison with travel agents, ongoing workshops with a weighty firm of advertisers, as well as getting heads together with one of the most prominent public relations combines in Europe. We even had to design our tickets, day trips, week-long returns and so forth – an around-the-clock effort...and we did it!

To achieve all this, I had the answer: the Overseas Visitors Club in Earl's Court. Each new batch of arrivals from Canada, the Antipodes or South Africa brought a fresh crowd of enthusiastic young people looking for work, even temporary employment of the kind I was offering. Thankfully, the majority were well educated, which suggested an inculcation of academic discipline, which suited me well.

I employed, among others, an architect, a librarian, two legal minds, an accountant from Fiji and someone who had worked in homicide in Toronto – an incredible gathering of Commonwealth nationals. My second-in-charge was an Australian who will remain nameless because he shagged my secretary and ended up with the clap. Most salient of all was that not one of them was a nine-to-fiver. They'd been briefed on the background as well as the end goal, and all agreed that if overtime was needed, that was fine. They were only too grateful for a job, and eventually, everybody enjoyed bringing something to fruition, which may not have happened under different circumstances. We worked, as the adage goes, our butts off. There were many nights that instead of going home, I pulled out a sleeping bag and a pillow from the cupboard and slept under my desk.

A rather humorous sidelight was that occasionally, to avoid the long trip home, I slept at a friend's place overlooking Hyde Park. He had a strikingly beautiful Israeli girlfriend who would help with the rent. When he was short of cash and the landlord called, she'd strip down and stark naked, throw open the door and plead for more time. Apparently, she was fairly successful.

The chairman of Clarkson Booker (our travel division) carefully monitored our progress, a wonderfully amiable gentleman who was adored by all. Admiral Sir John Eccles, a tall, strikingly handsome man – elusive about what he did in the war – but we knew about one or two things, including the fact that he had been involved with the Royal Navy's ultra-secret X-Craft midget submarines. Also, he spoke fluent Japanese and had been the captain of HMS *Durban* on the China Station immediately before the attack on Pearl Harbour.

The Japanese had detained a British cargo ship, *Marie Moller*, and without fuss, he sent a handwritten note in Japanese to the local Nip commander requesting her release. The Japanese were so delighted that they immediately sent the vessel on its way, which basically sums up the man who was to play such a significant role in my life.

The admiral came to Clarksons, bringing with him his also-retired former flag lieutenant, Tom Gullick – and sad to say, things didn't work out with him peering over my shoulder when the mood took him. Gullick made no bones about treating me dismissively as a lower being – probably because I was South African – even though I was running the single biggest Clarkson Booker project at the time. He became a notable birdwatcher, though Gullick, as a younger man, was an arrogant twerp, and the staff avoided him.

The next big step was meeting the man himself, Sten Olsson – then a relatively unknown factor in our lives – and what a pleasant surprise it was. Sten, as I got to know him, though a multimillionaire (he died a billionaire in 2013), was one of the most unassuming individuals I've encountered in a long and productive life that has taken me to five of the six continents. When meeting Sten for the first time when he was on an unexpected visit, someone in the office exclaimed:

'That's one really nice man,' with which we all agreed. Though not ostentatious, Sten always stayed at the Savoy when visiting London – the same Savoy Hotel used by that great actor and musician Richard Harris. During his later years, Harris took a turn for the worse – and when being rushed to hospital on a stretcher – he had the presence of mind to raise himself while being carried through the hotel lobby to exclaim to shocked guests in a loud voice: 'It was the food! It was the food!' A wicked sense of humour to the last…

Sten mixed easily with us all, whether it was a meeting with the admiral or at the swish West End offices of Batten, Barton, Durstine & Osborne or BBDO as we all knew it, one of the great advertising agencies of the time that handled our account together with a budget which ran into six figures.

He had a rather novel way of introducing the British public to *The Londoner*. There were 50,000 tickets printed which offered bearers a day trip to Calais – all circulated among hundreds of pubs in the city – and handed out free of charge: still more tickets went to Manchester, Newcastle, Canterbury, and other cities. BBDO's job was to put the word out in the media that this freebie was available, but only for a stipulated time. The gesture floored just about everybody because nothing like that had been done in Britain before, but there was more than a modicum of method to Sten's madness.

At one of the meetings with our public relations firm, the issue of the freebie was raised as being nonconformist. Sten agreed.

'Of course, it is,' he declared, 'but remember that we have a casino on the ship and dozens of slot machines that gobble up money as fast as passengers can insert their coins.'

I soon came to understand his somewhat unconventional logic, and, later, when I raised the matter, he confirmed that gambling, bar none, was his single biggest money earner.

Not strictly hands-on, Sten was a nonconformist in other ways. He liked to have important issues brought to his attention. As UK manager of his company, I sat in on many meetings with him when he came to London and that also meant getting together after hours for a chat and probably more good-quality single malt than was good for either of us. Where else but at the Savoy? It got to the point during the last month or two that Sten and I went skedaddling more often than I have ever done since.

Clarkson Booker took better-than-average care of me personally while I was involved in the project. I had use of a large new Rover limousine which, being fully automatic, took some time to get used to. Occasionally, Ken Holmes would come by the office and suggest that we were 'going out'.

Before we grabbed the car, he would instruct me to draw £500 from petty cash, in today's terms, probably the equivalent of a couple of thousand quid. 'Leave the details to me,' he declared. 'Just go and get the money.'

So, I did. Ken would book a table at one of the most expensive restaurants in London, from where we'd swan off to a casino. That, too, was an introduction to things new – I've never been a gambler, nor ever will I be. Halfway through the evening, Ken would sidle up and ask if I had any cash left, and I'd fish out a bundle of notes. I tried making money on the tables but never ventured betting more than fifty or eighty pounds – Ken taking the rest. He'd lose it all, of course.

Sten was different. Always dapper and slightly balding, he wasn't a big man but was strongly built: he made an effort to keep himself in good shape. Moreover, he always dressed as if he were about to step out for an audience with King Gustaf, his beloved monarch.

Sten and I sometimes went to a casino – not really to gamble – but more to experience the flow, the exhilaration and the atmosphere, punting something here and making a few bucks there. Money wasn't his objective: beautiful women were.

He'd met my girlfriend several times and taken us out to dinner. Sten wanted to know if others within our social circle were in the same mould. Naturally there was, and her name was Vivienne – not only a looker – but she lived in the same block that we did with a man who tended to violence. She didn't quite know how to extricate herself from the relationship, or possibly lacked the courage.

Vivienne accepted the offer of a night out on the town when her man had disappeared up north. The dinner went splendidly at one of the Savoy restaurants that had live music and we left them there about midnight. When we returned home the following evening, she came down and showed us what had arrived at her office; 'something' from Asquith's – a magnificent pair of diamond earrings. That was the Sten I got to know: certainly no gadabout because he took his relationships very seriously indeed.

My Swedish entrepreneur friend apart, everyday life for me in London then was totally fixated on making a success of the new Stena Line – to the extent that I would occasionally go to Calais on board *The Londoner* and meet my opposite number in France, Henri Ravisse. Henri, a big man in height and girth, would entertain me – possibly too sumptuously – because I've never been a big eater. If Sten came along, we would head down the coast to one of the superior restaurants in the region.

On occasion, I'd get to the ferry at its Tilbury berth after dark, sleep in a cabin set aside for my use, and head out to France for a short break to remove the splinters in the windmills of my mind.

The biggest night of the year was after the ship had been commissioned, completed sea trials, and sailed up the Thames to anchor overnight in the Pool of London. This was Sten at his best because it was his idea of fun and the PR blokes thought he was a genius.

It wasn't all that easy. The event needed a warrant from the Port of London Authority – but he'd cleverly invited all their big wigs to a shindig at the Savoy by way of introduction. They couldn't refuse because the man was contributing a valuable attribute to the city and had spent millions of his own money achieving that objective.

After the annual Oxford–Cambridge boat race, the launch became the gala event of the year on the river. On the evening of 30 June 1965 – within the shadow of Tower Bridge, the 700 guests we'd invited were ferried to *The Londoner* by a fleet of small boats. I'd imagine that Sir Alexander would have seen to it that everybody worth his oats in the shipping world – and Lloyds – would have been invited to that understated riot of colour, quality background music and top-of-the-range champagne.

I invited my entire staff – they deserved it – and all my Earl's Court mates – including my two best pals with whom I had been at school, Kevin and Larry O'Donoghue – who cumulatively probably drank as much of the bubbly as the rest of the entourage. That was the last time I spent a night on the ship that was not the focal point of my life.

Months later, I made a career change and never looked back…Nigeria was waiting.

CHAPTER 13

Looking for wars and learning to write

Even with *The Londoner* on course in its daily cross-channel slot, I was far from done at Clarkson Booker. While secure in the job, I was suddenly stuck without a project.

A couple of days after the official launch, Ken Holmes called me in to offer a word of thanks. At the end of that little session, walking out the door, he motioned me back. 'One last word, young man – before you do anything else – go to the travel desk and have them issue you a ticket to any destination in the world where you'd like to spend a month.'

'Anywhere?' I asked.

'That's what I said – Hong Kong, San Francisco – wherever.'

It was the kind of offer of which dreams are made, but while I flew high with setting up the ferry, my pay packet was always half-empty. I lived like a lord, but by 1965 standards, I was still below par and hadn't saved a cent. I suppose I could have shoved £100 into my back pocket when I was out gambling with Ken – nobody would have been any the wiser – but it never occurred to silly old me.

I took up the travel offer anyway, but instead of heading out to an exotic destination like Tahiti, I asked for a return ticket to Casablanca, which I knew was both cheap and friendly. I had yet to experience the Arab world, and this was an opportunity, even if much of the Moroccan tourist-orientated culture was faux-Arabic.

A week later, I was back at Ken's office, eager for the next challenge, which he'd confided earlier was twofold. There was an upcoming trade fair in China (in the days before President Nixon had opened that door) or, even better, getting an iron ore project off the ground in Cassinga in southern Angola, which would have been my first choice. As it happened, neither panned out. It was possibly just as well about the African option because Cassinga became a strategic South African ground and air target in the military struggle that was then developing in Angola – even if it was still more than a decade ahead.

I'd handed over the Albermarle Street offices to my Australian deputy and, in the process, quietly suggested that he didn't hump any more secretaries. At Ken's suggestion, I went home to wait for a call. And then I waited some more. At the end of the month, I headed back to his office for news, but still nothing…

'Be patient, Al. You've done one good job, and there'll be others,' he declared. 'Tell you what; I'll give you a raise, which should make you happy.'

The extra cash was welcome, but I was still frustrated. When I went into the offices later in the month on an extraneous issue, I bumped into him again and drew another blank. I was pleased that he sensed my frustration and, as a result, got another small raise, obviously to keep me content. When that didn't work, he tried something else.

'You like to write, young fellow, so why don't you go back to doing that because it is satisfying when you're having your work published.'

It was indeed, and the approach surprised me because I wasn't aware that he'd been keeping tabs on me. He didn't know that almost all my writing was work-related. I was still getting articles published in the Argus Africa News Service and United Press, while also writing for several shipping magazines, including some no longer around, like *Playfair*. I was pleased with the exposure because it meant I was doing something right.

Then I had a piece published in *Blackwoods*, a literary magazine that featured travellers' experiences, together with the occasional adventure story. The editor accepted something I'd written about my time in the navy when the SAS *Transvaal* visited Marion Island and one of our boats capsized with loss of life. I was chuffed. Now, for the first time, I was in good company because historically, the magazine had published the likes of Conrad, Eliot, John Buchan and Thomas de Quincy. Unfortunately, it folded not long after I came along, which I feared was something of an omen.

So, I went back to my digs and wrote some more, usually reading several books a week. Then my rejection slips began to multiply, and by the end of the third month, still with nothing at work forthcoming, I decided that while I was reasonably comfortable and being paid a monthly salary, I was going nowhere. Something had to give.

During those months out of the office, I had not realised that – because I was obliged to write (there was really nothing else to do, and I was getting paid for it) – the experience ended up paying a dividend or two. As one of my editors on the *Daily Express* would say while stringing for that newspaper years later, 'There is only one way to learn this craft, and that is to write, write and write some more.'

Go at it long enough, he'd tell me with the kind of Scots enthusiasm that he liked to bestow on all his charges, 'and it'll all come together in the end…you'll see that for yourself eventually, young feller.' He was right of course, though it took me a while to accept that kind of rationale. I expect my covering world shipping trends helped because that panoply was advancing all the time – the 'container era' had just started, which was another complex story, just as interesting.

Throughout this phase, I travelled an anxious and frustrating road to get my work into print. It was relatively easy to start reporting on maritime matters after the navy – I was interested in such things – but the 'anxious' part hung heavily because I was never sure whether the articles I was working on would ever be published. I had no mentor or tutor to show me the ropes, and in retrospect, even a limited period spent in the newsroom of one of the dailies would have helped immeasurably.

My real problem was that I'd never had any kind of formal journalistic training, so it was essentially a case of trying to 'feel my way'. There was nothing intuitive about it as some like to believe – that only comes with time – or, as some scribes say, after your initial 2,000-hour apprenticeship. I realise today that, most of all, I lacked the kind of confidence usually imbibed by starting off as a lowly cub reporter chasing ambulances and moving on from there.

My reading, still omnivorous, helped because I covered a diversity of literary disciplines. It kept me abreast of what was taking place because I was also reading the BBC's *The Listener*, the intellectual counterpart to the BBC listings magazine, *Radio Times*, and one of the great literary magazines of the era, sadly now defunct (it ceased publication in 1991).

I learned more from *The Listener* than any other contemporary publication, including *Paris Review* and *Granta*, though the *New York Review of Books* comes a good second. As Jean Seaton, professor of media history and official historian of the BBC wrote, '*The Listener* was where the British did their thinking. Literate and engaged, it had the mild irony of all the best of British culture.' She added, almost as a postscript, 'the only thing you signed up to when you bought *The Listener* was informed scepticism and wit.'

On reaching London, I discovered other attributes and started to include the likes of Synge and Shaw, Sheridan and others – all viewed in a fresh, classical light because I could see some of their works on the stage at the Aldwych and Haymarket theatres. But speak to the average journalist today about *School for Scandal* or *Uncle Vanya*, and the majority wouldn't have a clue. Football or rugby, yes, but very rarely anything repertory. The same for art: how many of them could tell the difference between a Manet or a Modigliani?

As for my writing, I've never been blessed with the God-given talent of a John Steinbeck, but with time I accepted that perhaps he and I did share a few traits. As a war correspondent, he covered conflicts that deserved attention. More importantly, to my mind, that Nobel Prize winner never stopped sending himself off on expeditions, always trying to better understand the world he wrote about. That kind of angst, I fear, hangs heavily over my head as well because I've never stopped looking for new missions, or the occasional war.

In truth, some things never stop. I covered one of my last conflicts in 2021 when I spent a month embedded with a NATO tactical air detachment in Mali's Jihadist war. Before that, in late 2019, I went with a crack group of Portuguese Paratroopers into the Central African Republic, a country in a perpetual state of upheaval, and again in 2022.

I never saw much action in my later years, but being with an eager group of professional fighting men was invigorating. It was like renewing old acquaintances because the grandfathers, as well as some fathers of most of the youngsters I was with, had fought in Lisbon's colonial wars in Angola, Mozambique and Portuguese Guinea (Guiné-Bissau today).[1]

Also, I could identify closely with the concept: 'Why the title "war correspondent" should carry so much glamour, I don't know?' Here I'm quoting an old friend and colleague, Chris Munnion, after his years of covering Third World emergencies for the *Daily Telegraph*.

He said: 'Reporting war has been the most dispiriting, soul-destroying experience I have ever had, especially in Africa. Ordinary people in a war behave very differently… it does de-humanise all concerned and carries no glamour whatsoever.'

Veteran BBC correspondent Jeremy Bowen goes a step further about conflict in his report on Middle East wars when he declares that wars are not just huge, noisy engines of destruction:[2] 'They also seep into lives like a virus… When war takes hold, it does not simply break bodies, hearts, and minds. It poisons the future.'

From early on, I was drawn to John le Carré's books, starting with *The Spy That Came in from the Cold* and, much later (one of my favourites), his first post-glasnost spy novel, *Russia House*. I was captivated by that masterful wordsmith's grasp of the subjects – esoteric, astonishingly insightful, and deep-rooted – that he covered so well because he'd worked for British intelligence. It intrigued me how he structured his characters and their unusually complex roles in the murky world of 'spooks'.

Curiously, David Cornwell – John le Carré was his pseudonym – spoke very much as he wrote, his memory sharp and always drawing readily on anecdotes and events past. Eric Homberger did good service in his obituary, published in *The Guardian* in London on 14 December 2020. He wrote that le Carré went about the business of being a novelist with journalistic care: 'Every potential location was scouted and conversations, tones, accents, dress, and the feel of a location found a place in his travel notebooks. The immediacy of his observations gave his novels an extraordinary visual precision.' I tried to emulate that in later years, but let's be frank, there really was only one John le Carré.

---

1   I wrote several books as a result of those assignments half a century ago, some fairly recently, including the best-known *Portugal's Guerrilla Wars in Africa*, which has gone into several editions (Helion, UK). There is a Portuguese edition, under the title *Portugal e as Guerrilhas de Africa*, as also *A Guerra de Libertação de Angola* (Clube do Autor, Lisbon).

2   Jeremy Bowen, *The Making of the Modern Middle East: A Personal History*. Pan Macmillan: 2022.

David Cornwell is undoubtedly one of the finest novelists that Britain has produced in the past century. When I eventually met him – he'd asked me, on a short visit to London to give him a hand in something he was working on that dealt with mercenaries – I discovered a quiet-spoken, totally understated individual who could captivate the moment with just a few words.

While it was kind of cloak and daggers to start with, the Cornwells always avoided publicity (except when there were book launches to attend). He and his wife Jane were waiting for me at a rather swish restaurant in Hampstead – and while I imagine the food was great – I recall none of it. Instead, I was captivated by the conversation.

After that, we walked to their house where, in the middle of a large study, stood an enormous table bedecked by all sorts of books, papers, maps, files and much else. We spent an hour going over some of the details he was searching for because David knew exactly what he wanted, and though it took a while, we finally got to it. That little get-together gave me an insight into his methodology, from which eventually emerged *The Mission Song*, together with a few words of thanks in his Acknowledgements.

One of the tips he gave me during that visit – in answer to a question – was that he rarely used adjectives in his work. 'If I can get away with it, I like to make the verb do the work.' That kind of guidance from a master stays with you.

At one point I took a brief break and ambled over to his large wooden desk by the window, which was covered in papers. I sat down for a few moments, relishing the opportunity to be able to share that space with someone that I would never have met under ordinary circumstances.

An interesting observation during my visit to their house was the number of nude female studies, all beautifully framed, that decked the walls of their home, and I surmised that none were of Jane. That surprised me, as it had too when I had visited Paul Johnson, another famous writer, at his London home a few years earlier. There were even more beautiful ladies on display on the walls.

For her part, I found Jane to be a great help over the years. I'd occasionally approach her for something, and she'd always come out tops. It was not generally known, but Jane, a prominent editor in her own right for many years, played a decisive if somewhat backroom role in her husband's work. He would write mornings, and they would go over the day's work during a stroll later where he'd read to her, and this strong-minded woman would contribute. It is sad that her participation in the creation of the novels, which was constructively editorial, has too often been overlooked.

He once said of his wife: 'I find her compassionate, understanding and remarkably intelligent.'

David's death was a surprise because we'd compared notes about keeping fit into old age. He confided that Jane would regularly drop him off about a mile from their home at St Buryan in Cornwall near Land's End, where they owned a lengthy stretch overlooking the sea. He would trudge home along an uneven track which he called dour, though it might have been to detract the curious. That wild stretch of shoreline, undeveloped and quite spectacular in summer and even in the harshest of winters, must be one of the finest hideaways in the British Isles. Fit and strong, David Cornwell almost made 90, and sadly, Jane passed away not long afterwards.

Before John le Carré, the author that made an enormous impact on my long road in recording personal experiences was Jan Morris, or James, as he still was when I read *Venice*, one of his/her early books. I eventually communicated directly with Morris to try and persuade her to do a chapter on an African theme for a book I was putting together, for which both Paul Johnson and Lionel Barber had contributed chapters.[3]

She responded kindly from Wales, saying that she had retired and couldn't help. That letter got lost when I moved to the United States, but her reasoning was sound as she was getting older and needed to decide very carefully what she would or would not write about in the limited time left to her.

Jan Morris died shortly before David Cornwell, aged 94, in November 2020, and I can do no better than reflect on what inspired me about her output and what I would have liked to achieve but never have.

Colin Thubron wrote a wonderfully evocative tribute to both the individual and her work that appeared in London's *Daily Telegraph* within days of her taking that long last long walk, declaring that Jan Morris's writings struck him 'with hopeless admiration'.

He continued: 'It shone with all the literary gifts of this remarkable writer: the lightly worn knowledge, the panache, the verbal touches of magic and surprise, the undercurrent of irreverence…' While still with us, he recalled, she liked to do a thousand paces a day in the Welsh hills, no matter the weather. Thubron's tribute is masterful. But then, like both Cornwell and Morris, he too is one of the ultimate craftsmen of the genre.[4]

At Clarkson Booker, one month followed another, and while Ken Holmes tried to keep me focused on good prospects, I was getting, if not desperate, then fraught.

Writing was fine if that was your life, but at that stage, it had not yet reached that juncture. All I wanted was to be able to work, put things together, and create new things out of virtually nothing, as I had done with *The Londoner*. I saw good progress once that lovely ship started its regular rounds and did so with more than a tinge of resentment – that had been my 'baby' and force of circumstances unkindly separated me from the familiar.

---

3   Al J. Venter (ed.), *Challenge: Southern Africa Within the African Revolutionary Context*. Ashanti: 1989.
4   Colin Thubron, *Daily Telegraph*, 24 November 2020.

It was about then that I started to scratch around at a few other options, and it was inevitable that I would look back fondly at my recent journey across Africa, particularly Nigeria. I reasoned that since I was now well qualified and had the Clarkson group as a backup, perhaps I could head back to that tropical stretch of coast. Also, many British firms were active throughout Africa, including several majors in Nigeria, so I took a giant step and applied to the three most prominent. That resulted in good responses from them all.

I settled on John Holt, which had one of the most prominent shipping outlets in Anglophone West Africa, and I was offered the position of shipping manager. The money was good. I would be given accommodation (rent-free) with a 'steward' to look after my needs (the word 'servant' having given way to one less demeaning). Part of the deal included a brand-new Ford Corsair.

There would be a month-long holiday 'back home' (always 'home', never as Britain or England), all expenses paid. Not a bad package, so I took the job. Ken wasn't happy to see me go, but he didn't think I would last in the tropics and said he'd be waiting for me to return.

CHAPTER 14

A bloody battle and a narrow escape in Lagos

I flew into Lagos's Ikeja Airport (Murtala Muhammed International Airport today) early in 1966, only days after a bunch of dissidents, mainly southern Nigerian army officers, had seized power in what was to become one of the most violent military takeovers Africa had yet experienced. Looking back today, Nigeria's Christian south was countering the country's more populous Islamic north. However, a few northern officers had thrown in their lot with the plotters because they regarded the government as irretrievably corrupt.

In retrospect, the coup was well planned, and – though there were unnecessary deaths – reasonably well-implemented, theoretically as well as literally, and interestingly, that format of coup d'état is still studied today in some Western military establishments. It is worth noting that until independence in 1960, Nigerian tribal enmities – previously kept firmly under control by the exiguous British administration – were now becoming serious.

But even then, things just muddled along...until the putsch.

Among those murdered were Sir Abubakar Tafewa Balewa, the first Nigerian prime minister and one of Africa's truly revered elder statesmen. Also killed was Sir Ahmadu Bello, a much-admired (especially in Britain) conservative Nigerian statesman who used remarkable tact and zeal to mastermind Northern Nigeria through its independence process in 1960.

Dozens more prominent people were slaughtered, the majority in their beds, including politicians, senior army officers (their wives weren't spared either), and sentinels on protective duties.

My God! I thought as I stepped off the plane at Lagos into an airport surrounded by throngs of troops who swung their rifles around in abandon. What was I heading into? Everyone in the arrivals hall was demanding travel documents and asking questions, the first being:

'Who are you and what do you want in Nigeria?'

Some welcome...

The Nigeria of January 1966 was very different from the one I had left fifteen months before when I hiked up the West Coast of Africa to get to London.

The expatriate community, of which I had become a member while working in Lagos, was a mixed bunch and, in some respects, little to shout about. Many were there because they couldn't succeed elsewhere. Others were outright scoundrels though, to be fair, there were a lot of good blokes flying the flag high.

The Nigerians, by and large, were aware of their shortcomings. The colonial misfits – the majority ensconced in relatively easy numbers – were referred to somewhat deprecatingly as 'white trash', and I suppose quite a few warranted the affront. Looking back, there was no question that quite a few were chancers, rascals actually. Their interests rarely extended beyond working the system and making a few quid on the side, cheap Nigerian hooch, and floozies.

The majority were British, though there was a fair sprinkling of Australasians, Canadians, and other European nationals. There was even a South African technician at Ikeja Airport who was doing specialised work keeping planes aloft, so the Nigerians let him stay. However, there was no other contact with the 'Racist South' except that the mail got through.

Our status was dictated strictly by the given terms of our contracts. Indeed, the 'tween-ranks pecking order was maintained by a system that smacked of militarism, a tradition that went back a century or more in this part of Africa, both in erstwhile British and French colonies. Upper ranks simply did not mix with those from lower decks.

Yet, for all that, life was good. Accommodation – according to your status – came as part of the deal. Higher echelons got houses, while those in lower rungs, like me, were given apartments. A manager could have three or four servants if he had children or entertained a lot. Many did.

There was a complicated array of perks: a free flight home each year and two for those who qualified. A highly prized perk was for the firm to pay for your children's education at public schools in Britain. Their travels – two or three times a year between Heathrow and Lagos, Kano or one of the Eastern 'stations' – were part of the package.

The foremost ex-pat event of the week in Lagos, Kano, Port Harcourt and elsewhere was the Sunday curry lunch at the club. It was a grand, boozy traditional kind of do to which few locals were invited.

In the old days, the clubs had been fairly vigorously segregated along racial lines, even if nothing was defined and certainly no by-laws that stipulated that blacks were not welcome. It was argued that it was just the accepted thing and that Nigerians had their own clubs anyway. It should be mentioned that while this racism was subtle, it was undoubtedly manifest, and you wouldn't get away with it today.

That soon changed once the military took over because it simply had to. When a Nigerian soldier arrived at my 'local', the Apapa Club, and ordered a Star or a

Guinness, he was served with a smile and did not have to pay. Word quickly got around the barracks.

There were other distractions. The most important of these centred around the fact that there were few eligible females from 'back home' in these outlying posts. Those there worked in the embassies or with various aid or religious missions. Quite a few were Peace Corps or British VSO.

There were many married women, and if you were 'lucky', you hit a homer. But in a small, thoroughly integrated social environment like Lagos of Kano (or in the Francophone countries: Abidjan, Brazzaville, Yaoundé in Cameroon and elsewhere), such liaisons rarely lasted long before people started to talk. Indeed, it was challenging to have a secret life in the former colonies, no matter the lingo – because every one of us was under some kind of surveillance – if not from our bosses, then from the government. As a result, you either cooled it or were sent home in disgrace.

There were any number of local girls, but in those days, it was just not done to be seen with one on your arm in the club. Upcountry, yes, but not in your parlour…

These things were happening, but always well away from expatriate residential areas and almost always within shadowy confines. Anyway, most of my associates did not advertise their predilection for 'something dark'. That came later in the evening at any one of hundreds of little open-air clubs along Ikeja and Ikorodu roads, Yaba, Ebute-Metta or on Victoria Island. Those that did chose African girlfriends were discreet about it because, let's face it, Britain had only recently emerged from an age when black people were regarded as inferior.

Yet, some of my colleagues were married to black women, the majority, as to be expected, quite lovely, charming and often boasting a mission-led education. Their spouses weren't any worse off: in fact, they were welcomed within the broader strata of society, though I sensed that their children sometimes suffered.

In the meantime, I'd settled into my new job in Lagos, and there were some exciting developments following an army mutiny that had caused me a few problems from the start.

It did not take long for the primarily British expatriate community to settle back into its traditional role of running the various private consortiums active along this stretch of the West Coast, but then some uneasy undertones started to emerge after the coup. More worrying, the Nigerian armed forces were no longer in the background: they were everywhere, and roadblocks had become commonplace. It was worse outside all major centres, where troops manning checkpoints were often drunk or drugged and reports of bribes being demanded to be allowed to pass started to emerge. This was definitely not the Nigeria of old.

My designated office was at Ikeja Airport, and though I didn't know it yet, it was there that a group of Muslim army officers plotted retribution for the January murders. This all took place almost under my nose, and I wasn't sharp enough to catch a glimpse of what was happening. Granted, I spoke neither Hausa nor one of the Fulani dialects, so an outsider would have found it difficult to detect any form of subversion.

From my office, adjacent to the main airport apron, despite it being open to large numbers of commercial airlines – including the old Pan American Airways that ran a weekly service between New York and Johannesburg – I was able to observe first-hand the Nigerian government starting an arms build-up of its own in anticipation of expected trouble.

However, we hadn't the foggiest from where that would emerge. The first evidence of this trend was the arrival, complete in Nigerian Air Force livery, of a squadron of Czechoslovakian Aero L-29 Delphins. Some of these small jets were parked just beyond my office windows, and I had a grandstand view of the goings-on.

NATO strategists did not regard the eight Delphins bought by the Lagos government in the mid-1960s as a sophisticated aircraft – on the contrary, it was a trainer. Its development resulted from the Soviet Air Force needing a jet-powered replacement for its fleet of piston-engine instruction aircraft and the L-29 provided the answer – a Warsaw Pact jet trainer. It was also Czechoslovakia's first locally designed and built aircraft, powered initially by Bristol Siddeley Viper engines, first flown in 1959.

For the first two or three months following the delivery of the Delphins to Ikeja Airport – also the most significant operations centre for the Nigerian Air Force – those planes were given so much attention they were almost mollycoddled. Each one was carefully washed down and polished every morning, and at day's end, someone would emerge from the hangars, meticulously shut down the cockpits and add additional canvas covers so that nothing would be damaged if it rained.

Soon, probably because there had been a change of command, the covers disappeared. A month or two later, nobody even bothered about rain or whether the cockpits stood exposed to the elements. The fighter-trainers did not remain either pristine or operational for very long, though some did see service in the civil war that followed after a bunch of Czech technicians arrived and worked hard to spruce them up again. But by then, Lagos had already been shopping around and eventually bought Soviet MiG-17s, which came into the country with a large contingent of Egyptian MiG pilots and technicians.

During this period of service with John Holt in West Africa, I travelled a good deal, always by car, which was the accepted way of doing things in Nigeria at the time, inevitably accompanied by a Nigerian member of staff.

Most of all, I enjoyed heading towards the east, near the Cameroon frontier. Though unsettled because of developing uncertainties – it had been eastern Ibo troops in the main that murdered the northern leaders – this was still the most ordered part of the country.

When I initially entered Nigeria – impecunious and overland from 'Down South' a year or two before – Calabar had been my Nigerian touchstone, partly because the town nestles like a cherub at the head of a river inlet. The second time around, it was still fresh in my mind: a tropical hideaway, distant from all the country's travails and where I had made friends with a lovely bunch of British and American volunteers.

As with most of these communities, a newcomer was always welcome, though volunteers were paid only enough to survive, even if they had recourse to their embassies or had problems. As with most aid contingents, they had excellent medical backup, to the extent that seriously ill Peace Corps members would be flown to the American military hospital in Frankfurt should the ailment or injury warrant it – road accidents being the biggest culprit.

With little money, you could easily lose yourself in Calabar for a week or a month because everything you needed was either home-grown or caught and consequently cheap. More importantly, while northerners in the Sahel tend to be distant from us infidels, these southerners were friendly, and until then, I'd never experienced anything like it.

Also, a charm was Jos, a prominent place in the interior with its tin mines and strange, primitive tribes who wanted only to be left alone.

Then the north: places like the ancient Kano, an historic Hausa capital a millennium ago, Maiduguri, Sokoto and others – were pleasant enough, at least when people weren't slitting each other's throats. Throughout the inter-tribal pogroms after the military uprising, whites were regarded as separate from that kind of violence, but still, once things started getting nasty, you simply could not escape the drama or the tension.

There was much debate in the country, not only about the mutiny and the senseless killings but also about the Eastern Region increasingly turning itself into a military stronghold. Politics during that phase was in a state of confusion, as is usually the case after a revolution. Nigeria was no exception.

Because I was travelling extensively and meeting people from every possible stratum of society, white and black, in uniform or out, I could follow developments in post-coup Nigeria better than most foreigners. I'd get to some northern cities and make a beeline for ex-pats who worked for John Holt or one of their many subsidiaries.

I didn't have the kind of money to entertain them or their families, but I would always arrive with a few beers, and invariably a new face was welcome. Some thought I might have come from headquarters (John Holt's Nigerian headquarters was in Lagos) to check on what they were doing, but generally the reception was amicable.

Still, I met many folks who sensed that Nigeria had turned the corner, not necessarily for the better. Those who would confide anything would mention exceptional hostility towards easterners for murdering the country's northern politicians, almost all Muslim. They would also talk about 'long memories' of a society that neither forgets nor forgives.

During the imperial period, when London ruled, the Northern Region, was largely left to govern itself – a legacy of what was termed Lord Lugard's 'indirect rule'. That clearly showed that the Islamic faith was held in great respect in the Nigerian colony, and the British never meddled with it. That the Ibo easterners, of all people, should have perpetrated such acts as killing their leaders was insufferable to Muslims everywhere, but in those days it took them a little longer to react. The murders were to cost those Christian southerners dearly.

Islam, we all know, is a profoundly conservative religion. Even then, Muslims were not happy with 'progressive' Western social norms, especially concerning sex. The education of northerners was almost exclusively Koranic and considered 'backwards' by their fellow southern countrymen and by many in the Western world. In truth, though, few would publicly voice that opinion.

The Ibos, in contrast – a bush and village people – had no such comprehensive Arabic culture as the north had enjoyed for more than a thousand years. Southern communities, in any event, took readily to education offered by mainly British mission schools. It may have been limited, but at least the London Missionary Society and other Christian religious bodies turned the Ibos into employable clerks and government servants. Those schools spread throughout the north, and Islamic people – with exceptions, of course – offered little in the way of competition.

Northerners had to see good steady jobs filled with what they regarded as detestable aliens – taking the bread out of their children's mouths, as it were. Consequently, a series of violent outbursts in the *Sabon Garis* (Strangers' Quarters) of the old walled cities of Kano, Zaria, Katsina and quite a few smaller towns followed. I was to visit Kano's Ibo areas several times and was eventually to see places that had been gutted and plundered, stalls burned, and their original owners dead or gone. That was only the beginning and regarded by the majority as a sociological matter rather than a political storm that most believed would pass.

Then came Independence, that blessed word. And not long afterwards, oil was discovered on the coast of the Eastern Region; looking back, it seems always to have been a curse, but most of all, it certainly made the Ibos greedy.

Case in point: at the time of Britain's handover, only about 15 per cent of Nigeria's officer corps came from the north and the west, and most of those who replaced former white officers were of Ibo extraction. To avoid friction between the three regions, it was then determined that the army should be recruited by quota: 50 per cent from the north and a quarter each from the Ibo east and the Yoruba west. But by 1965, easterners still filled nearly half of the places offered by the British to Nigeria at Sandhurst.

Once again, the Ibos showed that they were pushier than the rest, thereby becoming even more hated. The fact that they seemed to be taking over the whole Federal Army was regarded by some Nigerians, northerners especially, as positively dangerous.

In the event, the officers responsible for the first military insurrection in January 1966 disclaimed any tribal motive for the insurrection. All they wished to do, they said, was to get rid of a corrupt government. Their entrenched view was that only the armed forces could be trusted.

After my travels, I would return to Lagos and meet with my colleagues, sometimes at a formal dinner when somebody from London or Liverpool arrived, and I'd mention my fears. I even suggested that there were more rumblings afoot, and, to some, that was unjustifiable and unwarranted 'revolutionary talk' that ended up creating some big problems for me. The very idea that there might be another military disturbance was preposterous. It couldn't happen…it would *not* happen!

Indeed, the very suggestion that there might be another coup was unthinkable, and I was labelled an agent provocateur, and even more disconcerting, in their midst. More peculiar was that to my mind, from personal observation 'out there' while on my many trips, the downturn was blatant. The writing was not exactly on the wall, but most whites in the southern cities of Lagos and Port Harcourt had almost no social contact with black people, and, not surprisingly, any form of emerging subterfuge went over their heads.

Precisely the same took place with the British and American diplomatic missions. Nobody – least of all their intelligence staff – had the vaguest notion of what was happening behind the scenes in Nigeria in mid-1966. Then it happened – as some of us knew it would – though most got the timing wrong.

Notably, I had predicted that another revolution was in the works in some of my published articles. Since some of these lucubrations appeared in print a month or so before the second army mutiny – following that bit of introspection – I could do no wrong. I had predicted what many of my Nigerian pals believed was impossible in two major reports: the first for *News Check*, then run by my old friend Otto Krause; followed shortly afterwards by *Huisgenoot*.

Both were my first cover stories, the one in English and the other in Afrikaans.

Then it happened. Suddenly on the morning of 19 July 1966, as I was on my way to work, I found myself in the middle of what had been – less than an hour before – a bloody battle for Ikeja Airport. I had just turned off the main road from Ikorodu to the airport toward my office when I saw bodies strewn along the roadside. There were armoured cars, Nigerian Army troop carriers and civilian vehicles, some burning, others capsized, lying all over the place.

Unfortunately, I had already made an almost fatal mistake by turning off the main road into an area about a mile square where there had been some serious fighting only an hour or two before. That effectively meant that I was directly in the line of fire of troops holding the airport, though the shooting had stopped by then. I could, of course, have turned around immediately. But that would have drawn attention and possibly worse to follow.

So, I did the only thing I could – I drove slowly and deliberately ahead towards my airport office, precisely as I had done every morning since I'd arrived in the country. Despite the carnage on both sides of the road, I acted as if it were a familiar daily occurrence, even though there were still some wounded calling for help, their cries desperate.

I had absolutely no option but to drive on, the car radio turned up loud, and my elbow resting on the open window as this was before air-conditioning became universal; casually, I tapped on the wheel in time to a Highlife tune. I also twisted my face into what I hoped might be interpreted as a smile. What else to do?

Then, quite unexpectedly, for I hadn't seen another soul, there they were – dead ahead – half a dozen soldiers prostrate on the ground gathered around several heavy machine guns.

There were probably still more troops behind the tree line, but I could only observe those in my immediate vision. I had no idea what kind of weapons they were nor their calibres – but they looked pretty formidable from where I was, perched at the wheel of my Ford – because all the muzzles were pointed at me. Worse, I had to go past them before I could make that final turn towards the airport. The army unit manning them had chosen positions at the side of the road, and I suppose I could have driven over them had I been crazy enough to do so.

Once abreast of the troops, I lifted a hand and waved. 'Good morning, gentlemen,' I called loudly, still smiling. 'Everything OK?' I asked, trying to be jovial as I kept my free hand aloft.

Not one reacted; all were grim-faced and silent. I'm sure that they were totally baffled since I must have been a phenomenon that did not fall within the scope of their simple instructions – kill anything and everything that approaches the airport.

I knew that there had been plenty of killings and murders during the troubles in the months after I'd arrived in Nigeria. But this, on my veritable doorstep, seemed to be a regular pitched battle and these youngsters – few of whom could have been out of their teens – were responsible.

Then, to my astonishment, they let me pass – no roadblock or officer with a raised hand – and I was allowed to continue driving.

My office, John Holt Shipping Services in Apapa, knew I had gone to work that morning, but the phone lines were cut, and for several hours they couldn't establish whether I was one of the about twenty-odd people killed in the ambush on the Ikeja Road. One of the dead, an expatriate, was a Lebanese businessman.

I took no chances on my return that evening, not having dared to emerge from my office all day. This time I got permission to go back through army lines to the main road that would take me home to Apapa. The officer in charge, a cut-and-dried Hausa captain who was immaculate in starched khaki and had spent time at Sandhurst – he was quite exuberant and said that he had loved it – escorted me back to the main road. To my surprise, he spoke fondly of the rugby he'd watched back in the UK. He had even been to Twickenham…

By the time we reached that same stretch of road where the original battle had taken place 12 hours earlier, every single body as well as wrecked or destroyed vehicles had been removed. It was somewhat sinister because all seemed so peaceful once more. It would have been difficult to believe that at that moment, Nigerian soldiers were in the process of attempting to slaughter just about every Ibo in the country who had not fled.

Pax Britannica was only a distant memory for the majority on both sides, and Africa was its old self again. And let's face it, for those who know the West Coast, there are occasions in Nigeria when things can be deceptive.

It was to the Apapa Club that I went on the morning after my 'escape' at Ikeja. My office told me not to go near the airport and I didn't argue. Nothing like that had ever happened before, and by all accounts, private and public, the first coup d'état the previous January was a Wednesday afternoon exercise on Salisbury Plain by comparison.

More ominous with the latest uprising was that the Nigerian Army was everywhere. The British High Commission and other diplomatic missions encouraged us to keep a low profile. Most of us gathered at our clubs and compared notes – though, as the beer flowed – the stories did improve with each telling.

By lunch on the second day, I decided to have a look at things for myself. Wilf Nussey, who ran the Argus Africa News Service out of the offices of *The Star* in Johannesburg, had been calling and wanted to know what was happening. But because I didn't have my usual easy access to Ikeja, I couldn't file copy, and anyway, all post offices were shut. Indeed, I didn't have the facilities of Reuters, the BBC or any of the other news agencies based in Nigeria. I was still very much a backroom boy, which suited me fine for the moment.

Discussing it with my mates at the club, I decided that since the largest naval base in the country lay adjacent to Apapa Docks, perhaps a kilometre from the club, I believed it might be possible to learn something by visiting the place. Why not? After all, the Nigerian Navy was regarded as the most disciplined and best ordered of the Nigerian armed forces.

Since I was living there, I had a rough idea of how to get to the base, even though the roads in the area were a jumble. They had been laid over what had once been a swamp and followed no set pattern or grid.

After a couple of wrong turns, I eventually came to a stretch of road that led directly to the Nigerian Navy base, about 500 metres from where I made my final turn to reach it. Its steel gates were shut, and the towers on either side, from what I could see, appeared to be manned. It didn't exactly look welcoming, and I was unsure of what to do next. Also, I'd stopped in the middle of the road – another mistake.

While contemplating whether to go back, a siren sounded. The gates suddenly opened, and a squad of about a dozen soldiers – all armed – rushed out. An officer appeared and called loudly: '*You there!* You come here, or we shoot! *Now!*

I hesitated a moment. Then a shot rang out. It was the officer, pistol in hand. He was firing in my direction. That decided it. I drove ahead slowly, again trying the pasted smile and elbow-on-the-window routine, but it was a little more challenging this time. My car moved forward, possibly too slowly, and instead of accepting that I was complying with his order – a lone civilian driving a sedan, the officer became more animated. I could see by the bars on his whites that he was a lieutenant commander, and at that point, he was already ahead of his men, waving his pistol in the air.

'Come!' he shrieked. '*Right now!*'

What next? I couldn't even make a run for it; the road was too narrow for me to turn around quickly. Anyway, by now, he was just ahead of me.

Perhaps 20 metres short of the gate – which I now saw had machine-gun emplacements mounted – I pulled up. The officer was in front of the car shouting something incomprehensible and even more disconcertingly; he was foaming at the mouth. Looking at him closely – I had no option but to do so – I saw a crazed look in his eyes. The man was smashed.

'What you want? *What you want here?*' he shouted, his voice rising an octave or two each time. I was terrified, though I dared not show it. In varying stages of undress, rage and stupefaction, the rest of his troops surrounded me, probably under the impression that the naval base was under attack. Some, now in a state of severe agitation moved right up to the car, surrounding it. A dozen rifles pointed at my head, and another three or four muzzles pressed against my body.

'Get out! Get out!' the officer shouted. Anywhere else in the world, the situation into which I had suddenly been thrust would have been regarded as farcical, but just then I thought that I was about to be shot since the expatriate community had already taken half a dozen casualties the previous day. In 1966, for no apparent reason, many lives were lost in Nigeria, but we, the public heard only rumours, which were often exaggerated.

The reason was simple: the moment the military took power, they occupied radio stations and the editorial offices of the country's newspapers. As a result, none of the events that should have been in the news was reported. Rumour, of course, tends to feast on its own excesses, which didn't help either.

'Lykes Lines…' I called loudly. I had seen the offices of the American shipping line on an adjacent road as I approached the navy base; it was my only option and a desperate one at that. The officer stepped back a pace. He hadn't a clue what I was talking about.

'Lykes Lines. The American shipping line,' I said again, louder. The man was befuddled, and it showed.

The word 'America' must have made an impression. Washington had not looked kindly on the antics of General Aguiyi-Ironsi, and his Ibo goons following the first military takeover, and the State Department had been quite vocal about it. The Nigerian press had reported the events of the first coup because they were allowed to do so.

'What you mean? Lykes Lines! Lykes Lines! *What you mean?*' The man was screaming again. I began to get out of the car since he'd ordered me to do so earlier, and I was simply complying, but he moved quickly forward, pistol in my face and forced me back into the vehicle.

'Stay there…stay where you are! Do you hear?' There was no argument. It's not only in Africa that you don't argue with a man pointing a gun at your head!

Then, in a more direct approach, I again mentioned the American shipping line, again pointing towards the company's building across the way. The Nigerian officer turned and looked in that direction, and thank God, there was a big Lykes Lines sign on the road.

By now, all the soldiers around me were gesticulating wildly and screaming. One of them shouted: 'Kill him! Kill the bastard! He's not supposed to be here!' Another sailor with a sub-machine gun – he'd already stuck the muzzle in my ear – demanded to know why I was spying.

'Who you spy for?' he shouted. It was all so predictable and, I admit, darned intimidating.

Looking back, I realise today that none of it had the ingredients of a stage play or a film; it was all too bizarre…also noisy and damnably repetitive.

Since then, with the kind of work that I do, I have been involved in similar situations half a dozen times, and each time my skin crawls, as it does now writing about it. Each experience I had to accept seemed worse than the last: the wild, hysterical rantings of soldiers, often high on some substance or other or drunk and most times out of control. There was no possibility of reasoning with them – once they had made up their minds, that was that!

Additionally, a white man in a black man's country in the middle of a revolution didn't ease matters either. I was on my own.

I was unprepared for what was happening along that lonely stretch of road in Apapa and knew that if I didn't keep my head, I could easily be killed, even by accident. By their actions, some of these idiots seemed to believe that I was up to no good, probably a mercenary. The papers were full of ghastly stories of hired guns killing black people, and events in the Congo were alive in the minds of some because the newspapers were full of what was happening there at the time.

There was a solution of sorts, I suppose, but it took a while. I found over time that it is often better to counter this kind of hysteria with an offhand, friendly nonchalance. Any other approach, even the vaguest suggestion of antagonism, could only lead to disaster.

After I'd mentioned the name Lykes Lines a dozen times – becoming quite animated in my protestations, even though I smiled throughout – the officer eventually put his hands in the air to silence his men.

'Get back…get back,' he shouted at them. 'You!' he pointed at me. 'Get out of the car. Now!'

I did and stood beside it with my hands in the air. Then, for the first time, I saw that both machine guns on the turrets beside the main gate had been pointing directly at me. It had been that way probably throughout this horrible pantomime; though, had they opened fire, they would likely have killed half the lunatics in the road around me. I prayed those manning it were sober – or at least, less drunk than the naval officer questioning me.

'You say, what is your business?' I could now smell he had been drinking, and I knew I had little time in hand because his attention span was wavering.

Again I did what he demanded, and in as few words as possible, I explained that Lykes Lines was an American shipping company, and that was where I was headed when I made a wrong turn in the road. I also told him that its ships regularly called at Lagos, and pointing towards John Holt export documents on my back seat, I said that I was a shipping man. I had taken the more important papers from my office at Ikeja the day before, just in case.

The officer looked carefully at me, incredulous, and then peered into the car again through the rear window. What he saw seemed to placate him, and we went through the rigmarole again.

It took fifteen or twenty more minutes of convincing talk to get him to believe me. Even then, he did so grudgingly, but I sensed too that my smile and apparent nonchalance helped. I had to convince him that I wasn't a threat to the nation's security, and in the end, I succeeded.

Eventually, he allowed me to turn my car around. I did so very slowly, all the while under the barrels of the pair of heavy machine guns on the turrets. His men were still pointing their weapons in my direction, one or two with their barrels pressed into my back before I pulled away.

I could still feel the aggression as I drove those last few hundred metres away from the base. I was glad to get away!

When I told them at the club, some of the more experienced Old Coasters agreed that I had been extraordinarily lucky. They told me several Apapa residents had been threatened by troops in the dock area earlier that day. One was wounded by rifle fire for no specific reason except that he was in the wrong place at the wrong time.

Nigeria had been nothing like that the first time I passed through the country on my overland journey. I wouldn't have gone near the place if I'd known how things would eventually turn out. Sadly, not much has changed in almost half a century.

We were all a lot more cautious afterwards. My steward, David, an Ibo, kept me informed of what was happening using his tribal grapevine as a conduit. Young Ibo males, he confided, were being pressured to return home and undergo military training, even though the Biafran war was still a year away.

With the assassination of General Ironsi in the July coup, his place was taken by a 30-year-old Army Chief of Staff, Lieutenant-Colonel Yakubu Gowon, possibly one of the most amiable of all Nigeria's post-independent leaders.

As we got to know him, Jack Gowon was the original 'Mister Nice Guy'. Uncharacteristically (for a Nigerian), he was short on pretension and pomp and believed implicitly in the direct approach. His only flaw – if that be it – was that he was a Christian in a Nigeria that almost overnight had become dominated by the Muslim north. Gowon was the son of an evangelist from the Plateau area of the Middle Belt. He was overthrown five years after the end of the War of National Unity (as the war in Biafra was euphemistically phrased by Nigeria's military leaders) and went back to university in Britain.

CHAPTER 15

Another close call

I was to spend a month at Ikeja after that historic battle, which ultimately changed the face of Nigeria for all time.

Ikeja Airport was also where I started writing seriously – one of few who was doing any freelance reporting – because the military junta prohibited the international media from entering the country. It went so well that I could barely keep pace with demand.

There was no shortage of stories and quite a few unexpected 'scoops'. Also, getting my missives and photos out of the country was not a problem, bearing in mind that these were times when the fax machine – though invented – was not yet in general use, certainly not in West Africa. Never mind cell phones...

Each time I had something for one of my editors, I'd sidle up to a departing Pan American passenger waiting to check his or her baggage. Totally unassuming, I'd ask them to take my little package out of the country: it would usually contain a roll or two of film and, of course, my story. But they did not know that, and nobody ever refused.

I would say something about my mother not having heard from me for ages 'because the army had taken over', and that I wanted to show her that I was alive and thriving. I'd also hand over a slip of paper with somebody's phone number at the offices of *The Star* newspaper in downtown Johannesburg who'd already been briefed about the procedure.

'My brother's number,' I would tell my newfound 'courier' and that he'd send someone to their hotel to fetch the packet; it worked like a charm. Not one of my reports went missing – but I don't suggest trying that at any airport today.

Those were indeed interesting times. Apart from the Argus Africa News Service, I cut my teeth as a budding journalist on stories that went to United Press International in London, Otto Krause's *News Check*, and several other magazines, which, for a cub reporter – which was really all I was – meant quite something.

Being the only person with access to what was going on at the time in Nigeria, and something of a rarity – I was willing to risk smuggling reports and photos out of the country – I not only made a packet but also learnt a good deal about the news-gathering game.

My situation was unique because the new military regime in Lagos embargoed all information about the second army mutiny, mainly because the violence and killings continued unabated. In some parts in the north of the country it got worse, which forced millions of southerners to flee. The last thing Nigeria's new cadre of revolutionaries needed was for images of the dead or wounded to be splashed across the front pages of the international media. It says a lot that they were remarkably successful. While those massacres made headlines in certain quarters, they were not supported by photos, gruesome or otherwise. Had they been, the West might have taken more appropriate action.

While I had a camera and took pictures as I moved across the land in my work for John Holt, I was always cautious about entering hostile areas after the last two fracases experienced with the military. I'd quickly learned the first basic survival rule: keep your distance.

Finally, a few of Fleet Street's more prominent figures began to arrive in Lagos, but they were kept on a short leash and stayed that way until the start of the civil war. In contrast to the army mutiny, the Biafran War – as the international community got to know it – became Africa's first great tribal conflict in modern times, followed by quite a few others. Frederick Forsyth, then still a journalist, was one of the first despatched to report on what was going on in Nigeria for the BBC. He and I spoke about it years later when we spent time together at my home in Chinook, Washington State.

Freddie, as I got to know him while we covered Biafra a couple of years after the second coup, was writing his novel, *The Afghan*, at the time. As with David Cornwell, I gave him a hand with some local colour which involved plot settings in the Cascades, a mountain range that stretches way north into Canada. A team from Washington State Parks drove down to my place at Chinook, and, as was Freddie's custom, he gathered all he needed from those who knew that region well.

I used that opportunity to question him about his experiences in Nigeria, especially his time spent in the rebel Biafran enclave and later used that information to expand my book, *Biafra's War*, which I dedicated to that good man.[1]

As an outstanding foreign correspondent, Frederick Forsyth got to know and talk to many of the leading Nigerian players, including coup leaders and families of those murdered in the first army mutiny and, after that, in Biafra itself. He was one of the last to leave what was left of the rebel state in 1969 and arrived back in

---

1   Al J. Venter, *Biafra's War 1967–1970: A Tribal Conflict in Nigeria That Left a Million Dead*. Helion: 2018. Extracts also used in *Barrel of a Gun: A Correspondent's Misspent Moments in Combat*. Casemate: 2010.

London broke but not disheartened. Decades later, he confided that he dared not return to Nigeria, 'Not even today,' he declared, 'because they'll kill me.'

Yet he never forgot his old friend, Biafran supremo Colonel Odumegwu Ojukwu, who, in a sense, had 'nudged' him on the road to success as a novelist. *The Day of the Jackal* was published within a year of his departure from West Africa, followed shortly afterwards by *The Dogs of War* which was inspired by the mercenaries who were fighting in Biafra when he was there.

In this regard, the always-generous Frederick Forsyth was unusually forthcoming. He would invariably fork out when asked to do so, which meant that for years after Ojukwu had gone into exile in the Ivory Coast, he regularly supported the former Biafran leader with some substantial handouts. He was able to do that, having achieved international status as a best-selling author.

That's the Freddie I know because he helped me too when I relocated back to Britain from North America. Few people have as thorough an understanding of what went on during the Biafran War as Forsyth, and some of his comments are worth repeating. These asides are from my interviews with him at the time:

> As far as the coup leaders were concerned, their approach after taking power was that they could run the country behind Colonel Yakubu Gowon. So too with Sir David Hunt, the British High Commissioner: the Nigerian Army officer was the perfect choice for them all.
>
> Sir David liked that Gowon would snap to attention whenever the British High Commissioner walked in – it pleased the old Brit no end. In contrast, there were those among us who regarded the Nigerian military leader as an overgrown boy scout. He recalled, too, that Sir David's relations with Colonel Odumegwu Ojukwu were frosty.
>
> The British High Commissioner was very much a product of the old British Colonial establishment, and he viewed black people in their proper place. Ojukwu didn't fit that mould – he was the product of a British Public School education – and presented as a black Englishman. He'd been to Oxford, played a good game of rugby, his father had been knighted by the King and was a self-made millionaire. This was a man of substance.

Ojukwu, in turn, recalled Forsyth, regarded Sir David Hunt with the direst suspicion, well-merited as it eventually turned out. From the outset, the British High Commissioner detested the Ibo military leader, and the sentiment was thoroughly reciprocated.

On Hunt's part, he maintained, there were two reasons. Unlike Ojukwu, Hunt was not expensively educated, despite a brilliant classical brain demonstrated at Oxford. However, he *was* a simply crashing snob and a covert racist. Two, he divorced his wife and married Rio Myriantusi, the favourite niece of the mega-rich, Lebanese-Greek Nigerian-based tycoon, A. G. Leventis.

'What complicated matters there,' said Freddie, 'was that she had been Emeka's [Ojukwu's] girlfriend, with the younger man vastly better endowed!

'As a career army officer,' he recalled, 'Colonel Yakubu Gowon was very different, though he was a contemporary of the rebel leader Ojukwu. The two men served in the same units on occasion and knew and understood each other's quirks, which could have been why the Biafran leader believed that he could pull off his wager.

'Indeed, they were poles apart. Gowon wasn't one for publicity. It took us an age to get our first interview with a man who I always found extremely reserved and quiet-spoken. He was reticent to talk about his own life, and though he could have claimed one of the presidential palaces as his own, he never did. All his successors did, most times with excessive brass and hoopla. Gowon, in turn, preferred to stay on in the barracks with his family, possibly because the presence of his own soldiers offered better security.'

Eschewing the limelight and controversy, General Gowon was different in other respects. The media made a big thing about his training at the Royal Military Academy, Sandhurst, and in Ghana. The truth, says Forsyth, 'is that while it sounds like the full three-year permanent commission background, it was actually a three-month summer course where Commonwealth officers literally couldn't fail.'

Gowon had another attribute: a ruthless (and some say, a pragmatic) side that went unheralded. He was the first African leader to hire foreign pilots to fight his war: firstly, Egyptians to fly his MiG-17s and thereafter, a batch of South African and British mercenaries who eventually played a prime role in turning the war around. Gowon was also powerfully opposed to any direct humanitarian aid going into Biafra without the aircraft first landing at Nigerian airports to be checked. Consequently, he was implacably opposed to organisations like Oxfam and Joint Church Aid, which flew their planes into Biafra from the offshore Portuguese island colony of São Tomé or Libreville in Gabon.

The outcome was unpredictable and volatile in the political climate of an unstable Nigeria; General Gowon couldn't last. The army deposed him while he was on a diplomatic mission to Uganda in July 1975.

Biafra, too, was very different because it was a colonial war that eventually evolved. After leaving my job with Holts, I covered that conflict by coming in from abroad because nobody could enter the rebel territory except with the Nigerian Army. It was also no secret that the Lagos High Command regarded journalists with great suspicion.

The only difference with other African wars (the Sudan's Darfur excepted) was that the 'imperialists' involved were black. The devil in disguise here was the Nigerian government itself. We all knew that the Ibo leader and his people tried to break free from Federal Nigeria after tens of thousands of easterners had been massacred at the hands of Hausa and Fulani militants. Men, women, the frail, the old and the halt – and children of all ages – were targeted. Nothing mattered as long as they were Ibos.

Ojukwu, whom I had known before the war, watched these events with dismay and voiced his fears aloud. He declared that the north was systematically trying to kill off his people. 'If the murders do not stop,' he said in a broadcast to his nation, 'the Eastern Region must take appropriate action.'

The idea of secession was already being discussed in the country's east, even while I was still working out of Ikeja Airport, particularly in Enugu and Onitsha. It was generally agreed that the newfound oil resources in the east would give the Ibos the economic power to secede from the Nigerian Federation. It also emerged about then that these future rebels had already begun to buy weapons from Europe.

Effectively, though none of us knew it, Ojukwu's people were no longer part of the Eastern Region of the Federation of Nigeria – they were, as he himself proclaimed, 'Biafra'.

It was with my John Holt colleague Silas Anusiem – of Ibo extraction, so he was also at risk moving about – that I had my last serious adventure in Nigeria, at least before I returned to cover the Biafran War on the 'other' side. It was to be a long road journey through the east, out towards Port Harcourt and Calabar in the months before concerted hostilities started. I'd visited that part of the country before and found it to be a very different region from the rest.

The people were friendly and much more exuberant than northerners because something was always going on, like a Highlife session or a feast with palm wine. Additionally, among the Ibos, thing got done: they were always willing to help, and though it cost some, you didn't mind sticking your hand in your pocket for achieving results.

In Lagos, in contrast, the lifestyle was an endless round of haggling, delays, cancelled appointments and very little managed without 'dash', the universal system of crossing palms with silver or – increasingly – with large denomination Naira banknotes.

Our route this last time took us across the Niger River at Onitsha and then towards Owerri and Port Harcourt, both crucial cities in the troubles to come. We were on the second day out, and so far, it had been an uneventful journey, having reached the small town of Nsokpo about 20 kilometres from Port Harcourt. Quite unexpectedly, we came upon a crowd, several thousand strong, effectively a solid mass blocking the road ahead.

It was not a pretty sight. The crowd was demonstrably angry because the Nigerian Army – by then despised throughout the east because of northern massacres – had shot some demonstrators a few hours before. Silas suggested I park next to the road and wait for him; he'd go ahead and see what was happening.

Shortly after I'd pulled up, I spotted several youngsters throwing stones at cars that arrived along the same road we'd just used. Being white, they ignored me – it was local fat cats they were after – and most of those people, sensing the danger, turned around and roared off. Then an army truck with about a dozen soldiers on board approached in our direction. The mob surged towards them in a fury of roars and obscenities…this was one angry bunch of dissidents.

As a single bloody-minded mass, they converged on the troops, a frightening, shrieking, hysterical horde. I thought I knew Africa, but I'd never seen anything like this because the mood had become utterly menacing, so I turned the car around and moved back down the road a short distance. I was afraid that the situation would deteriorate further, but I had no option but to wait for Silas to return.

I waited half an hour, then an hour, and still no Silas. By now, I was worried. Also, I was hungry. We'd been on the road for half the day and hadn't stopped once.

Why not take a photograph? I thought. There was evidently a reason for the troubles, and, who knows, there might be a good story somewhere. UPI would undoubtedly use it. So, I pulled out my camera and, for good effect, climbed onto the roof of my car. I was just starting to focus when a couple of young men near me noticed what I was doing.

'No pitcha!' they shouted; their arms raised above their heads.

Thirty or more young men around them heard the cries and turned in my direction, and they too started shouting. Fists in the air, they too screamed: 'No pitcha! You no takka pitcha!'

I smiled, waved, and went on with what I was doing. By now, I was attracting a lot of attention because there were two or three hundred people volubly disapproving of my actions. A minute later, it had become a thousand, or it could have been a couple of thousand because I wasn't counting. Except there was an ocean of black faces in front of me, and there wasn't a man or woman among them who wasn't screaming furiously.

It probably went something like: who the hell is this 'whitey' that has so rudely intruded on the ground where some of our people were gunned down earlier? That I wanted to take photos compounded the issue, for such is the volatility of Africa at a time of crisis.

Just then, this massive surge was heading straight towards me. The cry 'No pitcha!' became a roar. Some of the youngsters alongside had started to rock the car. Hell! This was serious, exemplifying the homily that nothing can go wrong until it goes wrong.

I jumped to the ground just before the first wave of protesters reached the car, and even then, I tried to say something to those closest, but it was useless – a lone voice against thousands. What had started as a few calls to desist had become mass hysteria?

I probably saved my life by jumping into the car at about the same time those nearest to me started beating on my windscreen with their fists, the mob shouting at me in their African lingo – none of which I understood, except that everybody around was apoplectic. I knew too that if I didn't scoot damn fast, they'd haul me out and drag me away. There was no way I could reason with an incensed rabble.

In a single, fluid motion that comes with practice, I started the engine and simultaneously released my brakes. A split second before, I'd shifted the car into gear: everything happened in a blink and a screech of rubber. Some of this enormous throng was directly ahead of me, but I went through the crowd without hitting anyone. That was the moment when I knew that if I had to run someone over to get clear, I'd have to do so. I was fifty metres down the road before the first rock hit my back window, shattering it.

Strangely, the car had been giving trouble on the trip up. Once or twice, I'd had difficulty starting it, usually in the mornings. Had it stalled then, I would have been killed; the mob was out of control. As it happened, the engine took in a flash, and I heard later that with me gone, they turned on another group of soldiers that had just arrived in a troop carrier, slaughtering some and burning their bodies.

Of Silas Anusiem, there was no word. He was gone, swallowed up by chaos, and frankly, he would have been both brave and stupid had he tried to rescue me. By then, I'd foolishly stopped about 200 metres farther down the road to wait for him possibly to catch up, but the mob kept coming, and I decided it was too dangerous to stick around.

Silas and I had agreed beforehand that should we become separated, we would meet at the Cedar Palace Hotel in Port Harcourt. He got there at about ten o'clock that night. What had happened, he told me, was that the army had shot a group of striking students at Nsokpo earlier in the day. A riot had developed, more soldiers arrived, and still more people were killed. The troops involved were northerners. Then the mob cornered some troops. Though the army held its own for a while, every one of them was overpowered, disarmed, and killed. It was a ritual, limb-by-limb procedure, as those poor souls were ripped apart. By the time we arrived, the mob had gone berserk. Undoubtedly, said Silas later, if our car had stalled, I would have been slaughtered. The mob was frenzied, and nobody was thinking rationally. Conditions stayed that way until the first Nigerian Army armoured car arrived.

I was never able to discover how many people died in that riot on the road to Port Harcourt. It must have been a reasonably hefty tally because the Hausas were making dramatic examples elsewhere in the country of southerners who voiced dissent. None of that ever appeared in the Nigerian press.

Many lives were lost in Nigeria in 1966, in the months before I left the country. Notably, not all victims were Ibo because things just seemed to emerge from nowhere. As with most revolutions, rationality is usually the first to go.

Nor was there anyone who would or could do anything about it. We, the public, heard only rumours, the majority of which were exaggerated – that sort of thing is invariably embellished with every subsequent telling – which didn't help either.

I left John Holt and Nigeria that July, only months before war broke out in the east and was pleased to go. The company suggested that I move on because some of my earlier predictions about more trouble in the offing came to pass, and they didn't like it. One of my bosses described me as a 'rabble-rouser' – the last thing they needed on staff.

John Tappenden, my managing director, did not know that I'd decided some months before that I would clear out and that I had persuaded Tony Cusack, one of my colleagues from Liverpool to join me. We'd decided to head for South Africa, not quite overland but close to it, going via Fernando Pó, then the capital of the colonial island of Spanish Guinea, and by ship. Cameroon would be next, then we'd continue south and traverse the Congo to get back into Angola.

Our visas for Angola were handled by my new friend at the Portuguese Embassy in London, Colonel Bettencourt Rodrigues. I'd written to him from Lagos asking whether he could organise permission for us to travel through Lisbon's West African colony and a positive reply came back within days. From Luanda, we headed south by road into South West Africa (Namibia today).

It was a delightful experience all around – starting in Lagos harbour when we boarded a Spanish liner that took a couple of days to reach Fernando Pó. The island itself was Iberian throughout, and still today, many locals speak Spanish. So were the hotels and restaurants in those far off days – it was like emerging from a hell-hole after my Nigerian travails. There was even a little bistro where a Spanish friend strummed his guitar.[2]

The only hiccup came when Tony was pickpocketed in the Congo's Leopoldville (now renamed Kinshasa), and all our travellers' cheques were stolen. That form of currency was the norm when you moved about in remote parts in those pre-credit card days because large sums of money made you vulnerable. We got our money back eventually, having reported the theft to American Express: someone in Beirut had tried to cash them.

---

2   Spanish Guinea was granted independence by Spain in 1968 to become Equatorial Guinea. Fernando Pó was renamed Malabo when this tiny nation of one and a half million people was discovered to be sitting on one of the biggest undersea oilfields on the planet. It ended up ruled by a psychopathic madcap, Francisco Macías Nguema (called Macías), remembered today as one of the most brutal dictators in history because he enjoyed watching people being tortured to death. Did the West ever protest? No!

CHAPTER 16

Getting the job done

Even though it was early days at the start of my new career as a journalist, I decided to grab my passport and head toward Nairobi. With several names and phone numbers given to me by the 'boys', I was sure I would find something interesting to write about in East Africa.

Number one on my list was Jim Penrith, British and a former Royal Navy veteran. He was the Argus Africa News Service's bureau chief in Nairobi – the same group to whom I'd been sending reports from my office at Ikeja Airport. An enterprising journalist, Jim wasn't afraid to put his balls on a block to get a scoop, and he did so regularly. Wherever he went, Penrith was usually preceded by his reputation and the ability to drink us all 'under the table'.

He took me in hand and introduced me to a bunch of his colleagues, including Ronald Robson, who was the BBC's man-on-the-spot in East Africa, as well as Eric Robbins, Africa correspondent for *Time* and *Life* magazines (he'd been expelled from Rhodesia, now Zimbabwe, the year before).

A day or two later, I met Mohamed Amin – who, together with Peter Younghusband, played a monumental role in my life as a developing scribe – Amin in East Africa and Younghusband approximately 4,800 kilometres to the south. A few years younger than me, Amin owned Camerapix, then still a modest but fast-growing news and TV agency that was to make its mark many times over in the years ahead.

Called 'Mo' by his colleagues (an abbreviation of his first name) – many didn't know that family and close friends addressed him as 'Amin', the proper way in his culture, which initially stemmed from Pakistan; I stuck close to Amin from the beginning because we immediately 'clicked'. Married to Dolly, a former beauty queen from Dar es Salaam, they very literally took me unto themselves – and from then on, when in Nairobi – I would stay in their small apartment near the city's present central bus station. It was fine then, but today it's an area I wouldn't even stroll through – never mind sleep in. We were all short of cash, but somehow we managed.

Amin's parents had immigrated to Kenya years before, settled in Eastleigh, a Nairobi suburb, today all but taken over by a million Somalis, and then moved to

Dar es Salaam in Tanganyika, which had Imperial German roots. His formative years were spent in the city that eventually became the capital of Tanzania.

Our relationship could be regarded as somewhat peculiar. I was white, from a racist country and a *Kaburu*, the disparaging Swahili word for Boer; he was Asian, from a society that Kenya's all-white colonial hierarchy had almost always disparaged. I expect that it all had much to do with our shared interest in finding things to report – he with his cameras (he would usually have three or four Nikons slung around his neck) before he turned to television – and me with my portable Olivetti and single Nikon, but with an array of lenses.

There was another side to the man that few of his associates were aware of, mainly because Amin was always so intimately involved with his craft. He had many friends, but few that he got close to and in this regard, I was fortunate. Once he'd made a friend – I would soon discover – it was for life, exemplified by an event that would have tested any friendship.

On 5 July 1969, Tom Mboya, a prominent up-and-coming Kenyan politician of Luo extraction, was assassinated in a Nairobi street. I'd been staying with Amin and Dolly and had made plans to go south into Tanzania with a group of professional hunters – we'd head out from Nairobi in their safari wagons and camp out along the way. I'd leave them on reaching Dar es Salaam because I wanted to get to Zanzibar.

Mboya's assassination – he was shot at close range – took place about noon on a Saturday, roughly the same time we were leaving the city, which means that we missed the security rumpus the murder created; in fact, I didn't hear about it for days.

I had met Tom a few times, generally over a few Tuskers, usually at the Norfolk and found the man an engaging fellow; friendly, personable, and unlike most Africans in those early post-colonial days, he was willing to mix with blacks and whites.

Amin and I knew that Mboya was causing ructions among many of the functionaries within President Jomo Kenyatta's primarily Kikuyu cabinet; some thought the young fellow might be getting too big for his boots. We also knew that politics, almost throughout the African continent, is usually all about which tribe rules the roost, so there was friction based on ethnicity: Luo against Kikuyu.

Indeed, Tom Mboya was way ahead in the leadership game, especially when compared to most of the largely mediocre Kenyan political hopefuls. He'd travelled widely, met a range of American and European leaders, and was generally pinpointed as the natural successor to Mzee Jomo Kenyatta. The latter, we all knew, would have to step down at some time because of age.

What I didn't know was that somehow or another, I would figure both prominently and disconcertingly in a plot hatched by Kenyatta's cronies, probably because I was an irregular visitor to Kenya, and my South African background was no secret. I was to be arrested on my return to Nairobi for Tom's murder, something I only discovered much later and which I compromised after I directly accosted the

British intelligence officer handling the investigation – I proved that I was with a group of hunters en route to Dar es Salaam at the time of the murder.

On my return to Nairobi, Amin told me that the police wanted to see me. He didn't need to say why because I'd already guessed. Nor did he need any prompting because Amin, even at a young age, was a wily fox, wise beyond his years and familiar with the kind of political machinations that originated in State House.

I went straight to Nairobi's central police station, where I immediately accused the British official of trying to frame me, loudly enough for just about everybody in the surrounding offices to hear what was going on. The authorities had not expected this, though they knew damn well that I had nothing to do with Tom Mboya's death. Their tone changed abruptly when I suggested calling London and getting the *Daily Express* involved.

What was apparent was that the planned link-up had gone wrong, badly so. I told the man that they knew exactly where I was headed (I had mentioned the Dar visit to Amin) and that it would have been a simple matter to call the police in Dar es Salaam and have me arrested. I could have been returned to Nairobi within a day or two. Instead, the Kenyan police did nothing and waited for my return.

With the accusation still lingering, I decided it would be best not to return to the Amin household and instead booked myself into a small hotel. That lasted two days when my young *Rafiki* came by on the second evening and told me to grab my things: 'We're going home,' Amin said. That was the nature of the man, putting the reality of any situation ahead of everything else.

Amin knew as well as I did that I had been cleared as a suspect, something he had checked out for himself. We both agreed that had things gone wrong, implications could have been serious: a compelling chapter in our lives at the time.

Amin was always the ultimate action man. He was imbued with a rather impetuous youthfulness that some would call pep and certainly one of the reasons he took so many chances. Even before I met him in 1967, he'd already been through several scrapes, including having a grenade hurled in his direction in Djibouti by a French legionnaire, which almost killed him. He was left with a severe leg wound, which was the reason he walked with a limp. By the time he died in an air disaster in 1996, he had survived almost 20 car accidents.

Life in Nairobi was not all grind (though it sometimes came close to it), and the two of us would occasionally go into the bush, usually to hunt, but more likely just to get away. We'd often have predators around our camp after dark, and it never bothered him – he was quite amused by what could easily have turned dangerous. Being a devout Muslim, he never drank, though he didn't mind me removing a bottle of good-quality white wine from the cooler bag.

Possibly this attitude is best encapsulated when he learned to fly a few years later. During one of my visits to Nairobi, we headed out to Wilson Airport on the city's outskirts, and he said he would take me for a 'spin'. I had no idea he'd qualified as a pilot only weeks before, but we went up anyway. After take-off, he did a wide swing around the Ngong Hills and headed towards the Rift Valley Escarpment before coming into land. I admit that it was one of the most terrifying experiences of my life. Early on, I could see that he was coming in too fast and too low; our wheels must have brushed the fence around the airport perimeter before touching down. It was that close. He offered me the option to go aloft a week later, and I told him what he could do with the plane.

Many of his colleagues were unaware that Amin started taking his news photos in 1963, the same year he and Dolly founded their company. A year later, in January 1964, the Tanganyika Army mutinied, an event that followed a full-scale revolution on tiny Zanzibar Island in which several thousands of Arabs were slaughtered. The ruling Sultan ended up fleeing back to his ancestral home in Oman.[1]

The coup was averted by the prompt action of the British Army and the Royal Navy. HMS *Centaur*, then patrolling Indian Ocean waters on the watch for illegal Rhodesian cargoes, was ordered to Dar es Salaam and landed a Royal Marine force, ending the rebellion with support from British troops based in Kenya.

Even though the British played a dominant security role, the event did push the recently elected Julius Nyerere over the edge, and he invited the Soviets to his East African state to train his military forces. The country's name was also changed to Tanzania (a combination of Tanganyika and Zanzibar).

Amin, still in Dar es Salaam, sensing a unique opportunity that would provide good copy and photos, jumped to it.

Without the necessary documentation, he took a boat to the Spice Island and started taking pictures of East German and other Soviet instructors putting the newly revamped Tanzanian Army through its paces. He was arrested within days, but not before smuggling some rolls of exposed film to Dolly in Dar es Salaam. He survived several tough weeks in prison before he was released, the British High Commission in Dar es Salaam having played a forceful role.

Amin would always say that with so many Arabs and Asians having been killed on the island only a short while before, he was lucky indeed that he hadn't been one of them. He reckoned that his body would have been disposed of offshore, as had happened to many other victims of the purge.

As Allen Pizzey of the American CBS network – another good friend of Amin's – commented long afterwards: 'Getting killed was a very real possibility in the days we [news-gatherers] showed up in African war zones, without so much as a Band-Aid.' No one thought about things like insurance, Pizzey added: 'You just did it.'

---

1 Zanzibar had been part of the overseas holdings of the Sultanate of Oman since 1698, after the defeat of the Portuguese at Fort Jesus in Mombasa, Kenya. In 1832, the Omani ruler Said bin Sultan moved his court from Muscat, Oman, to Zanzibar's Stone Town on the African island, establishing a ruling Arab elite that used slave labour for their plantations. The Omanis were also heavily into the slave trade abroad.

Professionally, Mohamed Amin was probably the most competent photojournalist in Africa for many years, mainly because of his focus, his dedicated work ethic and, most vital, his contact list. You cannot do this work if you cannot speak to the people who matter.

Also, being a devout follower of the faith, he didn't touch a drop of the more potent stuff and that alone gave him a head start because he worked twice the number of hours most of us could manage. He usually got by with four or five hours of sleep a night, with Dolly saying that he'd often leave for the office around three on many mornings. For all that, he had time for just about everybody in Nairobi who called at his office; there would always be people waiting, quite a few expecting handouts for favours.

Additionally, he built up a vast network of connections throughout East Africa and, later, further afield. He would supply cameras and film to people in places like Uganda and Somalia – and there would be a constant flow of material coming in, much of which was processed and sent abroad – usually a dozen photos with a few hundred words per packet. This unsolicited material went to many major newspapers and magazines, the majority in Europe and America initially, and eventually to Asia.

Being topical, his freelance submissions were often used, and editors who might have ignored his stuff before began to take notice. For instance, Idi Amin Dada's anti-British rantings out of Uganda were hardly newsworthy, but because they were sometimes quite ridiculous, publications abroad started wanting more. The same with Somalia after that country went cathartic after the first army mutiny.

Starving millions in Ethiopia followed, and indeed, it was Mohamed Amin who put that debacle on the world's television screens. That only happened because the man was usually first on the scene. As the *Irish Times*[2] reported a few years after his death: 'For three decades, Mohamed Amin chronicled the sad, bloody unravelling of African dreams, a time chockfull of two-bit wars, mad despots and unspeakable acts.'

That was followed by one of Africa's great tragedies, this time in Ethiopia. Amin's filming of Michael Buerk's BBC report of the 1984 famine brought immediate attention to the crisis that went global. It helped start the charity wave that resulted in the Live Aid concerts. Buerk said at the time, 'I needed to say very little to convey the desperation and the suffering.'

After that, the media world beat a path to Amin's Nairobi office door, resulting in his company, Camerapix, becoming a significant factor in African news-gathering. In between, he would continue to contribute exclusive photos of African developments, like the fall of Uganda's Idi Amin following that country's invasion by Tanzania, and another tyrant, Mengistu Haile Mariam of Ethiopia, fleeing to Zimbabwe after being charged with genocide.

---

2   *Irish Times*, 28 November 1998, Dublin.

It is not generally known that 'Mo' was one of the first non-Arabs to cover some of the actions of the Palestinian Liberation Organisation (PLO), including infiltrating the border into Israel in an abortive raid in which he almost came short. After that, in September 1970, he covered the Palestinian Black September uprising to seize control of Jordan, which also went toes up. Essentially it meant that he could move among these radical forces where Western journalists could not.

Each time I got to Nairobi, I would clock in at his office, and after that, we'd dine out at his choice Chinese restaurant, where he would relate his most recent drama. Dolly was always present to prevent us boys from getting out of hand. Other times, to avoid the crush and rigmarole of the Kenyan capital, we'd head out into the bush and usually bag an impala or two. He was not one for needlessly killing animals – in fact, he was at the forefront of the anti-elephant poaching campaign in East Africa – but he was comfortable shooting for the pot.

I started writing his life story but was caught short by a crisis back home, so somebody else ended up doing it. With other successes, including one of the most beautiful books ever produced on Mecca and its annual Haj, it was axiomatic that bucketsful of fame would follow. He was feted by several American presidents, many European and humanitarian leaders, and the Pope.

During one of my last visits to Nairobi – Amin, by then, was spending more time in London, which had become a focal point of his TV production business, when he told me that he had been subjected to a thorough Harley Street medical – partly to settle Dolly's mind that despite working so hard, he was fit and well. Every aspect of his lifestyle and work was examined, followed by blood tests and the rest that were probably the most extensive he'd ever experienced. He was totally candid, telling the specialists about going to the office in the early hours and needing very little sleep.

The doctor's report was astonishing. Not only was Amin in excellent health, but he seemed to thrive under excessive pressure under conditions where many lesser souls would yield. The doctors couldn't give any reason for it, nor did they need to. Dolly got what she wanted, though one of the medical people did make the point that he patently enjoyed everything he did, a solid basis for his success. Everything made good sense.

About then, things started to go wrong, beginning with a trip to Ethiopia with Michael Buerk in 1991.

Amin told me later that he and his Kenyan soundman, John Mathai, had taken up a position on a hill overlooking Addis Ababa when a nearby ammunition dump exploded. Mathai was killed outright, and Amin's left arm was severed at the shoulder by shrapnel, and as he had to admit, it wasn't pretty. Buerk survived reasonably intact and was airlifted back to London.

Because Amin had been contracted to film the Ethiopian debacle by one of the major American networks for whom he had been active for years, they wasted little time or money to have him fitted with one of the first bionic arm prosthetics. When somebody with a bionic arm flexes muscles (or what is left of them), special sensors detect tiny naturally generated electric signals, which are converted into intuitive and proportional bionic limb movements.

Mohamed Amin was back at work with his bionic arm within a year and became remarkably adept at configuring the new limb to do the necessary, including holding the camera. Always the joker, he would often, following a shoot – which in Africa always draws a crowd – return to the vehicle, strip down, take off his bionic arm and place it within clear sight of the crowd.

The resultant uproar from the crowd would stop traffic!

Amin's sad end came on 23 November 1996 after a visit to Addis Ababa with, a colleague with whom we had both worked for years. They had been on a visit to the publishers of the Ethiopian Airlines in-flight magazine, a long-standing Camerapix contract.

Together with 175 others – passengers and crew – he boarded Ethiopian Airlines Flight 96, which, shortly after take-off, had its cockpit stormed by hijackers who forced the pilot to change course towards the Comoros archipelago. Reports afterwards disclosed that the pilot had warned his attackers that he didn't have enough fuel to reach Grande Comoros, but they persisted. The result was that the plane was forced to ditch in shallow waters off the northern tip of the first land mass encountered. More than a hundred people, including Amin and Tetley, were killed. Also revealed was that Amin had played a prominent role in trying to persuade the hijackers to see reason, but they weren't swayed. Apparently, even with only one arm, he tried to tackle one of the leaders in the final moments: that was our Amin, true to form!

As my dear, departed old friend Chris Munnion of London's *Daily Telegraph* said in *Banana Sunday*, a marvellous book that encompasses a wealth of stories that he collected over the years from journalists who worked the African beat – as well as other Third World outposts of the former empire – getting the job done in Africa was a heroic effort.[3]

Some of the yarns that surfaced remain legend decades later. So are a few of the hangovers, and only occasionally was there a head or two banged together. As Chris commented in inimitable Munnion style: 'Scribes rushed about from riot to revolt, from the back-and-beyond to the front, from palaces to prison cells to telegraph, telex, phone, pigeon post and the use of many other ingenious ways to get the unfolding story of Imperial Retreat back to their newspapers.' They seemed to do so with impunity and rarely with any loss of life.

Munnion was spot on; the old order of those days – the 1960s and the 1970s – has long since gone. It's been replaced by much distress and violence. Indeed,

---

3   Chris Munnion, *Banana Sunday: Datelines from Africa*. Ashanti Publishing: 1991.

things are much worse now than in the earlier decades. In the early days following independence, the international community was genuinely interested in what was happening in independent Africa, with Europe and the Americas, by choice, directly engaged. They trusted the new black leaders of Africa: Nkrumah, Tubman, Hastings Banda, Jomo Kenyatta, Julius Nyerere and Modiba Keita of Mali – in retrospect, sometimes a bad mistake.

In the new millennium, the game changed again. For a start, the Cold War was over or was supposed to be. There was no need to gratify the demands of some idiotic tyrant because if you didn't help him, the Soviets would. Few gave a hoot if the deaths in the Congo were measured by thousands or millions. It was all old hat.

That was followed by headlines twenty years later that were more concerned with shrinking budgets, the latest farce in the White House, or possibly chaos in Myanmar or some obscure outbreak of violence south of the Urals. If Africa did get a mention, it was usually because some company's commercial or mining interests were threatened. Africa had reverted to darkness and old night.

Into the third decade of the millennium, things had changed again. China had followed Russia's lead in entering the African continent, not so much to help, but rather to grab whatever opportunities were available. As we go to press, all the great powers are falling over one another to get at strategic and precious minerals, hardwoods and – in the case of Moscow mercenary Wagner Group – wealth, to be taken by a combination of force and cheap labour. The 'recolonisation' of Africa has begun…

From a sufficient distance, the continent's troubles still rarely make the news, and it can sometimes be quite disturbing as cultures clash and egos need to be nursed. New wars have started, and violence has returned, if not with vengeance, then with vigour.

The decade ahead, I fear, is likely to belong to Islamic Jihadists. Mark these words.

Jim Penrith, my Nairobi acquaintance of the 1960s and 1970s and one of the last of the Old Africa Hands, recalls how easy it was to become a mercenary when parts of that vast continent were in turmoil, which was exactly how it was during my first journalistic visit to Kenya. The Congo was in an uproar, and a bunch of mercenaries had decided to set up a rebel government in Kivu, to the east of the country, adjacent to Rwanda and Uganda. The unforeseen tragedy in Rwanda was to follow a few years later.

Penrith had already been working for the Argus Group of newspapers for several years, and characteristically, he'd developed the knack of telling it like it was. He did so again shortly before my visit. I've told Jim's epic tale elsewhere, but it is so good that it's worth repeating.

He recalled walking into the bar in Kampala, seeing this fellow downing *waragi* (the local gin) like there was no tomorrow, grimacing when the potent banana-based firewater hit base. You needed a copper-lined gullet to drink that rough stuff, and my pal shook his head when he had the bottle waved at him invitingly. Jim takes up the story:

I looked around the White Gardenia bar, my favourite watering hole in the Kampala of the late 1960s, and seeing no one I knew, sat down at his table. This guy had already made a serious dent in the *waragi*, but he appeared perfectly sober. I noticed that his heavily muscled forearms and bush jacket collar had a fine coating of red murram dust: he'd evidently driven a long way on border back roads.

'So, *mon ami*, what are you doing in Uganda?' he asked. I knew from experience that the quickest way to terminate a conversation in jumpy Uganda was to admit to being a visiting journalist.

'Just looking around...opportunities,' I said.

He asked whether I'd ever been across the border into the Kivu province of the eastern Congo. 'No,' I replied, but I'd been in Katanga when the Congo blew up in June 1960 after the Belgians abandoned their colony overnight, taking even the electric plugs and light bulbs with them.

I mentioned several other places I'd visited in Central Africa over the years and let drop the names of some of the better-known mercenary officers I'd bumped into. I didn't actually lie and say I'd been a mercenary, nor did I mention that I'd been there as the Nairobi bureau chief of my newsgroup. 'All that was in the days before things quietened down,' I said.

He leant across the rickety table and gripped my arm. 'The Kivu, *mon ami*, is about to take fire, and I am looking for men to join the force of Jean Schramme.' He was talking about 'Black Jack' Schramme, commander of the Congo's 10 Commando, staffed mainly by Belgians or French officers and NCOs, with a sizable African contingent.

The *waragi* now seemed to have loosened his tongue. I listened attentively as he outlined the plan that would see Schramme and his mercenaries drive Mobutu's *Armée Nationale Congolaise* out of the province and take over the primary administrative centre of Bukavu on Lake Kivu. He said he was authorised to recruit throughout East Africa and offer generous pay in US dollars, deposited in a bank anywhere in Europe.

I said I was interested and he asked me to meet him again in the bar in a week. The Kivu rebellion was scheduled to start two weeks after that.

Back in my office in Nairobi, I fired off a cable to London for transmission to Alan Syer, then head of the Argus Africa News Service in Johannesburg and told him of the planned uprising. I said that I intended to drive from Nairobi to Shangugu in Rwanda to wait for the mercenary offensive to begin and reckoned that I would be the only journalist on the spot when Schramme and the men known as *Les affreux* ('The Frightful Ones') stormed Bukavu.

The response that I received a day later astounded me. It said that the paper's London office had checked with their sources and could find no hint or whisper that anything was likely to happen in peaceful Kivu. In effect, the Argus was discounting the report of its own representative in Black Africa. Instead, they had listened to the mandarins thousands of kilometres away in Europe.

A few days before Schramme's planned uprising, I set out for Shangugu anyway. Within 48 hours, I was sitting on the veranda of a hotel perched on a rise, looking out across Lake Kivu and down on the narrow bridge linking the sleepy little Rwandan village with the road into Bukavu. All seemed peaceful, so I walked across the bridge into the Congo. One and a half kilometres further on, the road turned around a bluff, and I could see the sprawl of Bukavu. The next minute I was staring into the barrels of half a dozen Kalashnikovs held by Congolese soldiers who were screaming at me in a language I didn't understand but whose meaning was quite clear. I turned around and slowly strolled back down the way I'd come. It was the longest walk I've ever taken.

Back at the hotel, I joined a knot of locals drinking beer under covered awnings waiting for the war to start. It was like sitting at a drive-in cinema. First came hordes of Congolese soldiers pouring pell-mell down the road, tearing off their military insignia and throwing their weapons into the lake as they raced across the bridge to the safety of Rwanda.

Half an hour later, the sun shone on something that was pure cinematic cliché, a scene that US movie maestro John Huston would have been proud to have directed.

Round the bluff and etched across the skyline came the rag-tag mercenary column, a single line of Jeeps, each with a heavy-calibre Browning machine gun mounted on the back. Flying from an aerial in the lead vehicle was the familiar old flag of Tshombe's Katanga.

Once again, I hurried across the bridge to hitch a lift with the convoy as it wheeled and headed back to Bukavu. In a plush suite in a deserted hotel, I drank looted wine with the mercenaries while waiting to interview Jean Schramme. That chat with the chain-smoking war dog was everything a journalist could ask for. Punctuation was provided by a couple of loud crumps as the Bukavu bank vaults were broached with explosives. The Frightful Ones were collecting an advance on their pay.

As I'd predicted, I was the only newsman at the fall of Bukavu. I wondered how the 'experts' in London were elaborating on this coup.

As usual, Jim always related a good story, and what is even more interesting is that it was exactly how it happened. I was to discover that for myself on a subsequent visit. Only this was on a trip that almost went toes up.

Throughout my budding years as a scribe, I probably did many stupid things as well. But few raised chuckles the way an overland journey from Burundi to Kampala did several years after the Schramme debacle.

On that trip, I was keen to get from Lake Tanganyika to Entebbe as soon as possible, but I couldn't get onto a flight from Bujumbura, so instead, I hitchhiked overland. It was hard going; the roads were terrible, and there were few vehicles, especially at night. Bandits had become a problem in some parts.

A truck dropped me by the side of the road about 800 metres from the lodge of the Kagera National Park in Rwanda, southeast of the legendary Mountains of the Moon in neighbouring Uganda. It was early evening but already quite dark when I arrived, perhaps eight o'clock. There was no moon, but I could see the road leading up to the lodge, where the lights were on. I humped my gear and set off at a good pace.

When I walked through the door into the reception building, a French woman tourist sitting with a small group looked up at me in disbelief and almost dropped her glass. For a few seconds, everybody gaped at me. Then one of the men came forward, a Belgian, the camp's manager. He said he hadn't heard me coming and introduced himself as Luc.

'Where is your car?'

'I have no car.'

'So, how did you get here?'

'I walked. How else?'

'From the road? All the way?'

'Yes, of course.'

Silence...

One of the women in the group suggested that I was kidding.

'Look outside and see where his car is, Luc,' she suggested. The Belgian did just that and came back.

'No car!' he said flatly. I asked what this was all about.

In the past week, he told me, a pride of lions had been terrifying the countryside around the lodge. Three of their staff had been eaten. Everybody in the area was terrified, and nobody budged at night except in a vehicle. It was simply too dangerous, he told me.

'Why don't you shoot the brutes?' I asked, perturbed that I had been exposed to such a danger.

'Because we haven't got a permit to shoot them. We've asked, but this is Africa... you know the scene.'

I suppose I was just lucky that night. Or possibly the lions had already dined.

CHAPTER 17

Independence and revolutions

Africa in the 1960s was a completely new experience for most of us writers who descended on the capital cities of Africa. With the independence of dozens of former British and French colonies – together with a handful that had been ruled from Madrid and Brussels – the continent had suddenly taken a giant step or rather a quantitative hopscotch series of strides.

Those were exuberant, heady times, and as far as most of us were concerned, things seemed to bode fairly well for the future. The machinations linked to Uhuru – the Swahili word for freedom – might have been complex, but they did involve a fresh, optimistic, and reasonably well-educated ruling class.

More salient, the newly created African states had inherited relatively strong economies together with efficient and trustworthy banking systems, coupled with healthy budgets. Of necessity, these were tied to European currencies and their markets, though most preferred to give the pound or the French franc a new body of names. The Euro only followed later.

It was of consequence that every one of these countries, on achieving independence, eased democratically into power under the auspices of carefully delineated constitutions. These were not dissimilar to those enforced by their former colonial masters and in most cases, happened in less than a decade.

Their legal systems, too, were carbon copies of those used in Paris and London for centuries. In the Anglophone and Francophone African states, most people had come to trust those who safeguarded the law: in fact, to be a police officer was both honourable and the force generated respect.

There was absolutely no reason why those transitions should not have gone smoothly: they had previously worked very well in other former British colonies – Australia, Canada, India, New Zealand, South Africa, et al. Indeed, these same governing systems would – or rather should – be easily implemented in those African countries cut loose from the former motherland.

Good roads and communications, a working rail system, reliable school systems and enough hospitals and clinics to keep the populous happy rounded off the functionality of the so-called 'New Order'.

In 1965, when I travelled through Nigeria by road, roughly five years after Africa's most populous nation had been accorded the right to manage its own affairs, the nation was still on a dizzy high. I moved from one city to the next and it seemed like the entire country was as energised as a Saturday night hop. I wrote an article on this enormous cheerfulness for the Argus Group and United Press International, rating it as not only the friendliest country on the continent but also the most confident. This was one of the reasons why I returned to work there – it seemed like an excellent choice.

The kind of joie de vivre I encountered in Lagos, Onitsha, Ibadan, Jos, and Kano was like nothing I'd experienced up or down the east or west coasts of Africa, which I would have known because I'd already spent time in many of those conurbations. It was also no surprise that many African countries were attracting young people from the so-called 'Developed World' – students, academics, qualified individuals, and others who wished to contribute their two bits' worth – including Britain's VSO and the newly founded Peace Corps leading the pack.

As might have been expected, among this social and economic mélange there was a bunch of opportunists who had spotted some of the more unsavoury prospects related to these developments and tried to muscle in for a piece of the action, often illegally. Generally, they were after precious stones and rare minerals and those parameters expanded once oil and natural gas deposits were discovered in Nigeria, Gabon and elsewhere.

When going to Africa from Europe or the Americas, most of us news-gatherers liked to believe that we were heading into something fresh and novel, which was how independent Africa was depicted abroad in the 1960s. There were a few hiccups, as might have been expected, including the first army coup d'état in Togo in January 1963. That was less than three years after France granted the country independence. Another revolution followed four years later. For some of us, that did not bode well.

The new Togolese president, Sylvanus Olympio, French-educated and a graduate of the London School of Economics and Political Science, was overthrown and murdered. His trusted friend Emmanuel Bodjollé was then installed as the chairman of the country's appropriately named Insurrection Committee.

Not long afterwards, Nigeria's twin mutinies followed. I was living there when the second insurrection took place – well planned and coordinated – and suddenly, with Ikeja Airport (where my office was situated), right there at the heart of it. Things weren't so good anymore.

In the decade that followed, almost two dozen African governments were toppled by unconventional means; a revolutionary virus seems to have unleashed a plague on the continent. As many of my colleagues were to discover, some parts of Africa suddenly became a very different proposition to what the majority had been up against in Europe, Asia or the Americas.

Some countries, such as Sierra Leone, the Central African Republic, Uganda, Sudan, or Congo-Brazzaville, had several revolutions in a row – a few experienced six or eight or more. There were also some rather nasty civil wars, and the carnage continues in some countries – like the Congo, the Sudan and Chad. It was our business as foreign correspondents to report on these convulsions and we sometimes found ourselves in awkward situations, but not all that often. When we discussed our experiences later, it was with great compassion because it was almost always the innocents who were dying.

Almost overnight, various anomalies emerged: governments run by soldiers who knew little about the rule of law or human rights, never mind following the basics of democratic processes installed by their former European overlords. Valentine Strasser had just turned 25 when he seized power in Sierra Leone in 1992 and became the youngest head of state in the world. He was a druggie, addicted to heroin, which meant that for most of his rule, he hadn't a clue what was going on in his country – even though there was a full-scale civil war raging in the interior, which eventually spread to his capital, Freetown. He was ousted in another coup in 1995, and in 2000 – still unable to control his addiction – he applied for asylum in Britain but was rejected.

Continent-wise, there were other changes, including capital cities turning into strongholds (like Khartoum, where in July 1969, I was arrested for taking a photo of my hotel and marched at gunpoint through the centre of the city), coupled with roadblocks, top-heavy with firepower and where people were being shot by accident, as happened several times in Harare after Mugabe took over. Sad to say, and this is an indisputable generalisation because those manning them were either drunk or drugged.

Basic principles such as road safety were abandoned, and traffic officers shunted either into regular law enforcement – by now a misnomer – or the military.

Politically, these were tricky times. We had *Osagyefo* (the Akan word for 'Redeemer'), Kwame Nkrumah, a British-created demagogue in Ghana who started well but eventually became preoccupied with inciting revolution among his neighbours. This was an issue the media of the day was not prepared to flag because African leaders 'could do no wrong'.

Today, decades later, Nkrumah is a hero to his people. They forget his conspiracies and the grinding down of the healthy economy he inherited in search of a socialist Nirvana and is instead praised for his radical politics. There was also his self-elected leadership of the Non-Aligned Movement, an international body of 'uncommitted nations', almost all exponents of radical dogmas, in its day almost pro-Soviet. Among them were Sukarno's Indonesia, Egypt under Gamal Abdul Nasser, Nyerere's Tanzania and the Republic of Guinea, headed by another admirer of the Soviet system, Sékou

Touré. The economies of most of those in Africa by the time this body was founded were in tatters.

One needs to examine the substance of Nkrumah's Consciencism-philosophy that he tried to impose on his people. The same with Milton Obote (another tyrant who ruled Uganda and cost many lives) and who was succeeded after an army mutiny by Idi Amin Dada, the biggest lunatic of them all.

Though much of Nkrumah's book, *Consciencism: Philosophy and Ideology for De-Colonization*, is gibberish (judge for yourself, it is still on Amazon, with a preponderance of five stars awarded by readers), even though some pages of the original version were printed sideways, it is no secret that most of the content was fed to *Osagyefo* by his British advisers, mostly LSE stalwarts, a relatively large group of lefties, who had inveigled their way into his confidence.

However, the Ghanaians are not fools. They stuck with the man for a while and the cherished 'Redeemer' was unceremoniously dumped – together with his radical British advisers – in a military takeover while he was in Singapore attempting to charm fellow Commonwealth leaders. That was when a defiant Rhodesia was threatening to declare a unilateral declaration of independence which ultimately resulted in a civil war that, on-and-off, lasted 13 years. These are all interesting chapters of African history for correspondents gadding about the continent in search of a story.

But before any of those events, there had been the enormously convoluted human drama that emerged within days of independence in the newly emerged Democratic Republic of the Congo, a former Belgian colony. That sad country erupted into the ultimate case study of murderous African mayhem that some authorities today maintain cost between four and six million lives.

We are all aware of the Holocaust, but few people knew what was going on a couple of decades later in the Congo or even that this vast nation has been in a state of on-off-on civil war for several generations.

To his credit, that venerable old hand Ted Koppel did a series on the horrific aftermath of its independence for his ABC Network. Not that it made much of a dent in the average American's conscience; however, Koppel did declare that he was personally ashamed that this matter had never been adequately addressed by those professionals with whom he worked his entire professional life – the dreaded media again. His words were, and I quote:

> [It was] a tragedy of historic proportions. A war that has claimed more lives than all other current wars around the world, but outside of Africa, no one seems to have noticed… Fighting in the Congo has involved as many as seven nations, displaced hundreds of thousands of people and killed millions more.

These programmes were broadcast for five nights as part of ABC's '*Nightline*' series. They ended with the comment that it all took place 'at the heart of the continent which lies on the richest patch of earth on the planet', with Koppel declaring that 'the armies [involved] were drawn by wealth, plunder, rape and killing…the people fleeing the soldiers are dying in the jungles by the hundreds of thousands'.

Beyond United States frontiers – nobody apart from a bunch of African boffins – seemed to have noticed any of those goings-on, he declared, and very few in Europe were willing to highlight such a horrific situation that has yet to be equalled…

One can blame a still-unrepentant Belgium for that one. Brussels, having mindlessly abandoned its responsibilities for an African colony it had first took charge of in 1908 – though actual colonial rule, personally handled by that country's King Leopold – began in the late 19th century. Brussels opted out of all responsibility – without notice or ceremony – and with no consideration whatsoever for the horrific consequences.

More importantly, which country would grant independence to a nation with possibly only a dozen university graduates, a civil service that had been reasonably efficiently run by European expatriates and a government system that, though exploitative, worked. And that for a country with a population of forty or fifty million people – possibly more, because nobody in Brussels had been able to do a proper census in a country twice the size of France, Germany and Great Britain combined. As soon as it had been promulgated that the Congo would become independent, the Belgians wasted no time – they grabbed their families and headed post-haste back to Europe.

Thousands of Belgians did remain in the Congo after the mandarins in Brussels had hurled their African subjects, as some put it, 'under the bus'. Those who stayed – the majority at mission stations located deep into the country's triple-tiered forests – had been ministering to the populace before Joseph Conrad made his way up the Congo River late the previous century.

For those interested, a lucid picture of that horrific tragedy has since come from Adam Hochschild in his 'without fear or favour' – *King Leopold's Ghost: A Story of Greed, Terror and Heroism in Colonial Africa*, undeniably one of the best analyses of that colonial epoch. As the American Historical Association declared in 2008, '[the work'] has had an extraordinary impact, attracting readers worldwide, altering the teaching and writing of [African] history and affecting politics and culture at national and international levels.'[1]

After the declaration of independence in June 1960, many expatriates stayed, in bids to salvage some sort of order; most of them dedicated and trusted by all. Yet many of them were slaughtered by mobs. Sadly, it mattered little at the time that most of the nuns attacked in their missions were brutalised and raped, nor that those

---

1   Adam Hochschild, *King Leopold's Ghost: A Story of Greed, Terror and Heroism in Colonial Africa*. Picador Classic: 2019.

Holy Mothers who found themselves pregnant in the aftermath of this carnage were prohibited by Rome from termination.

My old pal Edward Behr – a journalist and war correspondent for *Newsweek* then – had been covering the Congolese debacle and wrote a book about it, titled *Anyone Here Been Raped and Speaks English?* It remains a good read for anybody interested in what was happening in some parts of Africa in the not-so-distant past.

His book's title, phrased as a question, might appear to be ludicrous, but it was hugely appropriate under the circumstances, uttered when Ed boarded a ship about to sail to Europe from the Congolese port of Matadi. He addressed hundreds of Belgian refugees waiting to depart and, by all accounts, had a good response. The New English Library published a new edition recently, apparently still selling well.

The ultimate irony was that the European Union should have chosen as its de facto headquarters – of all places – Brussels, with its atrocious African human rights record that in its contrails on departing Africa left millions dead.

While many of these events are bizarre, the 1960s and the decades that followed were like nothing else happening globally at the time. This was the Africa into which my colleagues who reported the news (and occasionally wrote a book) and I were thrust, even though Vietnam, the Middle East, Central Asia, and the Cold War remained the prime focus.

There were approximately fifty African states that eventually demanded to run their own affairs and make their final break from Europe. Three more under Portuguese control had already turned to guerrilla warfare to achieve their aims, triple insurgencies that lasted more than a decade. Clearly, we all had a stultifying continent-wide scenario in which to earn our crusts, and a good deal of it was to become my little professional hotchpotch for the next half-century.

Wars, revolutions, being shot at from time to time, twice blown up by Soviet landmines, tropical illnesses – like malaria and typhoid – as well as personal dangers. Taken all together, these made for a combination of exciting times for a youngster still in his twenties.

There was the instance of a whore, when I rejected her advances, attacked me with a blade so sharp it sliced clean through the sweater I was wearing at the time. 'Hell hath no fury...'

What is also true is that working in Africa often presented some unusual opportunities, the majority linked to getting around successfully under challenging circumstances. At the same time, it wasn't a cakewalk either. In 1974, together with a French journalist working for *Le Monde*, I was jailed for espionage in the Congo. We were arrested while trying to get back into the Angolan debacle. It was only a bit of luck, and a hastily scribbled note on a piece of loo paper smuggled to the director of a local mining company, that eventually got us released. Details were forwarded to the French Embassy in Kinshasa, and President Mitterrand pulled a few strings.

Other times I would buy a decrepit old Renault 4 in Nairobi, usually for a few hundred dollars, join the Kenyan Automobile Association to apply for the necessary carnet documents (even though I was not a permanent resident) and take the long overland haul southwards to Tanzania, Malawi, Zambia, Rhodesia and finally home to South Africa. There were always problems along the way, but generally, one adventure followed another, and I was paid good money to write about these events.

For those of us working in Africa to earn our crust, many issues had to be dealt with, though rarely anything as severe as some of those currently crippling the continent, Jihadist insurrections included.

Take an isolated example from the old days. Imagine trying to describe to a border guard in a remote region south of Lake Tanganyika that the metal object that I had in the trunk of my car, which kind of resembled a bomb, was something that I would strap onto my back to breathe underwater. Or, as we've already seen, being sent back from the frontier to the nearest immigration office – 35 kilometres away, three times in a row – as happened in Guinea. That was in 1965, and one of my contacts who went through there recently says it is now a lot worse. Following another revolution in Conakry in late 2021, led by a former French Foreign Legionnaire, Mamady Doumbouya, the country's military leaders fear another coup, this time led by mercenaries.

It is instructive that Colonel Doumbouya went straight from a United States Army training session for regional Special Forces commanders in Burkina Faso – a distinctive commendation in itself – to orchestrating the putsch on his return home. No patsy, he is a veteran military man, having served in Afghanistan, Ivory Coast, Djibouti, Central African Republic, Israel, Cyprus, the UK and Guinea during his 15-year-long career.

On a different tack, some of the ramifications of Ramadan, the Islamic holy month when the devout allow nothing to pass their lips between dawn and dusk, were another matter – and it initially surprised me that most of my pals gave moving about in West Africa in that month a miss. For instance, in Nigeria, where I travelled across the country from east to west after leaving Cameroon, some believers took things a step further and did not even allow their spittle down their throats. That meant when seated in open mammy wagons – as I did because I was broke – you were at the receiving end of the spray of anyone ahead of you who was truly sincere in his or her belief. I don't think I need to elaborate.

While Kenya was always a charm, things could sometimes get a little tight in Tanzania (for years under the Soviet mantle), which plainly tells you where President Julius Nyerere's sentiments lay. As a result, one was never sure whether you were under surveillance or not, which could cause problems because I needed to move up and down the East African coast from time to time. Obviously, with Dar es

Salaam slap bang in the middle, that city and its excellent natural harbour became a requisite stop.

After Tanganyika gained its *Uhuru* in 1961 and the *Mwalimu* (Teacher) – as Nyerere liked to be called – apparently decided that all the whites in southern Africa had to go, it got worse.[2]

Even though I travelled on a British passport, my origins lay in South Africa, which sometimes complicated things. It also affected others because Tanzanian immigration and security personnel were scrupulous, and most of their senior operators were trained by the Stasi, East Germany's secret police.

Of course, they knew exactly who I was and would not have missed that I lived permanently in South Africa. However, it did matter that I was writing for various overseas publications at the time, including London's *Daily Express*, NBC *Radio News* and *International Defence Review*, then headquartered in Geneva, which might be one of the reasons why they let me get on with it.

On one visit to Dar es Salaam, I even formally applied for my visa on behalf of the London *Express* to enter Biafra, doing so at the local embassy of the rebel state. That meant having to edge past a bevy of security gooks who asked questions before I could do so. I succeeded in the end, but it was a bind for more than an hour, the official in charge continually returning to a supposed South African connection in his questioning.

There was good reason for that suspicion. South Africa was a significant ally of Portugal, then fighting a guerrilla war in the broad expanses of Mozambique, which lay across the southern reaches of Tanzania, the country providing the rebels with all the military hardware they needed to fight that ten-year war.

In less stressful times, being a sports diver helped; I used that excuse to visit many of the more popular underwater spots along the Tanzanian coast. Nobody took much notice of underwater enthusiasts and I could travel freely just about everywhere without being questioned, except when I tried to take my diving gear across the frontier between Tanzania and Zambia…

---

2   Tanganyika only became Tanzania in 1964, after an attempted army coup was thwarted by the British Marines and the Royal Navy and linked up with Zanzibar.

CHAPTER 18

Subterfuge

Life can be a funny old game when it is your job is to cover unusual or controversial events, get paid good money to deliver the goods and, as we sometimes see, the boss ignores the obvious. I saw that happen in Nigeria while working out of Lagos in 1966 when it was made as plain as day for me to see that a second army mutiny was imminent. Nobody took any notice, and then it happened.

As a news-gatherer, I experienced little of that, though occasionally I would stumble on something that the boffins involved with such arcane issues – intelligence in the lingo – might be interested in, and attempt to write about it. There again, I'd end up with my views or opinions ignored because the plain fact was, in the minds of people who did not know or understand Africa, much of what was happening often did not make sense.

For instance, how do you explain the traditional African practice of *lobola* (it means bride price) and other traditions in contemporary Zulu society, something unheard of in Western culture? The gesture involves payment of cattle to the bride's family for the hand of their daughter.

Or the primitive horrors of a clitorectomy, better known as female genital mutilation (FGM) which, though not commonplace in Africa and some Middle Eastern expatriate communities abroad, is still practised at a horrendous level in many North American and European cities. I've been campaigning against that barbarous practice for years and even included a chapter on this criminal activity in one of my books.[1]

In truth, you don't have to be black to embrace Africa and its good (and sometimes bad) vagaries, as most white Africans – like those living in South Africa, Zimbabwe, or even Kenya – will agree. Indeed, that's the way it often goes with sensitive stuff: as a news-gatherer, you have a better understanding of what makes things tick, whereas the people who read (and judge) your copy back at the editorial offices, do not. Case in point is today's Middle East social imbroglio with all its multifarious customs which date back millennia.

---

1 Al Venter and Friends, *African Stories*. Protea Books: 2014.

While still resident in the United States, I occasionally communicated with former CIA case officer Bob Baer shortly after he had resigned from Langley. I was to discover an individual whose life had become something of a revelation because Bob is one of those rare characters who immersed himself in his job over many years, living and working in the demanding environs of the Eastern Mediterranean.

Although true-blue American – in his younger days he had been a ski-bum in Colorado – Bob was eventually able to pass himself off as a Lebanese Arab. What emerged, quite forcibly as it turned out, is that that would never have succeeded had he not mastered the intricacies of everyday Arabic, an incredibly complex language in both speech and script. More to the point, how many Westerners do you know who can understand even basic Arabic?

Time spent in quite a few Middle Eastern regions allowed Bob to ingratiate himself into those ultra-suspicious societies, to the extent that the Arabs with whom he socialised came to view him as one of their own. In doing so, he uncovered sensitive issues that even Westerners ensconced on the fringes of Arab society were unaware of, most of which he passed on to headquarters, as his job demanded. Obviously, Bob's reports to Langley were not only unusual but often disturbing, if only because it was quality, top-level stuff to which only an insider would have access.

All went well for several years: he had penetrated so deep into the enemy's backyard that he came to be regarded by some of his bosses as possibly over the top and taking too many risks, even though quite a few had served in that quadrant. Some questioned his findings, though there was rarely any logical reason for doing so. This underscored a regular problem in this line of work – the frequent tension between those out in the field and headquarters.

Most salient, he was one of the first to suggest that much of the terror and violence then creeping into the Eastern Mediterranean arena had Iranian origins. That was followed by reports that an insurgent group that called itself Pasdaran (with whom I had a few contacts in the years I spent swanning about southern Lebanon) was directly under the command of Tehran's Islamic Revolutionary Guard Corps (IRGC) – Iran's primary instrument of exporting the ideology of Islamic revolution worldwide. Centred on Shi'ite Lebanon, the movement was subsequently renamed Hezbollah.

For all that, Robert Booker Baer, born in 1952, became one of the CIA's top field officers of the past half-century or more. After retiring from the service, he recounted his career as a ground soldier in the CIA's war on terrorism, running agents in the back alleys of the Middle East in his bestseller, *See No Evil*. An outstanding work of intrigue, espionage and survival, it is certainly one of the best of type to emerge since the end of World War II.[2]

---

2   Baer speaks half a dozen languages, won the prestigious CIA Career Intelligence Medal, with *See No Evil*, written after his retirement and was then all but hounded out of the agency. That was followed in 2004 by *Sleeping with the Enemy*, a savage indictment, published by Three Rivers Press.

Bob on station, either in Beirut, Damascus, Cairo or elsewhere in the Arab World, was the ultimate specialist in spy craft, to the extent that he was able to inveigle his way into the upper echelons of several insurgent movements then active in the region. Once on the bookshelves, the rest of the world started to take notice, so it was not surprising that his memoir became the basis for the 2005 Academy Award-winning Warner Brothers motion picture, *Syriana*. The film's character Bob Barnes, played by George Clooney, is loosely based on Baer.

More significantly, the book would never have emerged had Bob Baer not left the agency, as he told me, in utter disgust. He had come up trumps on the gathering storm of Jihadists in the Middle East more times than he liked to remember, but some of his desk-bound Washington superiors, would not listen. This was partly because they believed they knew better, or more likely, there were probably a handful among them who resented his success.

At one stage Bob Baer even had Osama bin Laden in his sights. He reported back to base and asked for authority to 'pull the trigger' and waited for instructions. None came, even though the matter had been referred to President Clinton. The order that eventually came from the White House was to stand down.

Something of an insight into the problems encountered in this type of enterprise was given by John le Carré in his book *The Little Drummer Girl*. That work excels in explicating the long, slow burn of running intelligence-gathering operations, especially in the Arab world. It also nails the frustrating lack of operational and moral clarity that so often characterises the task at hand.

On a far more unassuming scale, something similar happens often enough in journalism, though it is rare for scribblers to get involved with anything like espionage.

Still, there are times when a potential page-one lead is perused by some sceptical editor and the story – as we say in the trade – is spiked. Naturally, it is possible to take the matter further, but then, how does one respond without becoming entangled in an issue that treads on toes and potentially jeopardising one's job?

So, it goes in the news-gathering game, where I am often asked whether I have uncovered issues that could have been sensitive to governments or individuals. Do I respond? I very rarely do, because the much-maligned Fourth Estate is supposed to be above such things. We deal in facts and very rarely base a report on supposition, even when there is a smidgeon of intrigue involved. In other words, we are scribblers, not spies – though I must confess that I have had my moments.

Now and again during a lengthy career, something notable can emerge, a story that possibly shudders with potential and here, by way of illustration, the notorious Watergate scandal springs to mind. On the night of 17 June 1972, a security guard in the Watergate office complex in Washington, DC called the police when he found a door repeatedly taped open. That incident went on to be dubbed 'Deep Throat', nurtured by American journalists Bob Woodward and Carl Bernstein who kept the identity of their source or sources secret for decades.

Right or wrong, the event is entrenched in American political folklore because President Richard Nixon, in the face of almost certain impeachment and removal from office, resigned, the only president ever to do so. That said, as somebody commented, it is axiomatic that though intelligence might be the best-left arm of government curiosity, it can end up changing history.

As we have already seen, my first real brush with gathering intelligence – the kind that might have military or strategic connotations – took place at the end of 1964, while I was traversing Africa from north to south. I was in Koundara, in the Republic of Guinea when a Peace Corps couple with whom I was staying pointed out a nearby house being used by Soviet agents to monitor messages emanating out of nearby Portuguese Guinea. That country, then a Portuguese colony, was eventually to become Guiné-Bissau after Lisbon had pulled all their forces back to Europe a decade later.

I'll go briefly over the facts again because not only are they important, but they had long-term implications for my career, resulting in a 180-degree change of direction. From a highly qualified professional businessman who had already made his mark in shipping, I opted for the tribulations of a novice reporter.

Upon my return to London, I mentioned that Koundara event to an old friend in a Soho pub and shortly thereafter got a call from Colonel Bettencourt Rodrigues (later, one of the most enterprising generals in the Portuguese armed forces). At that time he was the military attaché at the Portuguese Embassy in Belgrave Square. Although nothing came of the meeting, I did not write about it because I was working in shipping in London.

But we did stay cursorily in touch and eventually, out of the blue, I asked the colonel for permission to cover his country's war in Angola. I'd already spent time in that country three times and because of its colonial war, believed there was a story – or a series of stories – waiting to be told. He granted my request, possibly as a quid pro quo for a minor service rendered in London years before.

What the gesture did achieve was to provide me with the option of either continuing with my shipping profession (by now, I was highly experienced) or pursuing a totally new career in journalism. Without any formal training and with minimal experience, except that which I had garnered in Nigeria during its upheavals, I took the risk and opted for the more interesting alternative.

Let's face it, had I not done so, you probably wouldn't be reading these pages! Like Bob Baer, the thrust of my first real intelligence break also had Middle Eastern connotations, in this case, Israel.

Over the years I spent what could cumulatively have been years either in the Holy Land or in Lebanon, that by then had become a seriously embattled country. I was then that I met Colonel Yoram Hamizrachi, an Israeli intelligence officer who not only became a good friend but who was helpful with some of the work I was doing at the time in southern Lebanon.

The average journalist rarely forgets those rare moments when accorded the kind of lead that makes the front page. My moment of truth came with the unmasking of a Soviet spy in my house in Johannesburg in the early 1980s. Force of circumstances caused me to keep the event under wraps for decades.[3]

It was certainly what some would call a 'dark encounter' involving what we subsequently presumed to be an Eastern Bloc espionage agent using a plausible French background as a cover. While active in Rhodesia, from where he operated, he'd befriended some of the most important people in the country: military and political.

The operative's name was François Darquennes, who identified himself as a French national, though there were several other players. These included a former Israeli Defence Force colonel who had been involved in a series of shady operations in Lebanon, as well as the spy's girlfriend, a South African beauty queen, Karin Pretorius. This strikingly attractive erstwhile university student headed abroad and spent several years in London doing promotional work. She had worked as an investigative journalist in Johannesburg, so one must accept that the man had style. I'll give him that.

Most relevant to these shenanigans was Lord Richard Cecil, a 30-year-old soldier-turned-journalist and second son of the 6th Marquess of Salisbury, who became good friends with Darquennes. The Rhodesian capital had been named after the Salisbury family – one of Britain's most illustrious – so there was much to interest him in this southern African colony then engaged in a protracted guerrilla war.

His title, which he rarely used, was a courtesy bestowed on all sons of marquesses, nor did he make much of having been educated at Eton College, followed by spells at Oxford and Sussex universities. Thereafter he joined the Grenadier Guards and did several tours in Northern Ireland. In April 1978 that enterprising young adventurer was killed in action while working with a cameraman on a documentary film on the Rhodesian civil war.

The main focus of events before the untimely death of Lord Cecil was Darquennes (the supposed Frenchman) with whom I had split a few beers at a bar in Hillbrow earlier on, several times, in fact. This was not unusual since there were said to be more Soviet and East German agents operating in Johannesburg at the time than anywhere else in Africa. The difference was that François Darquennes passed himself off as both a true-blue Frenchman and a professional news photographer, and in the process managed to ingratiate himself into the upper echelons of Salisbury's political elite.

---

3   The last time Darquennes and I exchanged words in my Johannesburg office, he was emphatic that my accusing him of being a Soviet agent was a lie, but as he stressed, damage had been done (whatever that was supposed to mean) and repercussions would follow. I forget his exact words, but it was something along the lines of 'It might take a very long time but we will get you in the end.' It was the 'we' part of the threat that worried me most.

Because he and the young Cecil had become close friends, he was a regular visitor to the home of the Rhodesian Minister of Defence Pieter ('PK') van der Byl and eventually managed to inveigle his way into the Salisbury family at their palatial home in Britain.

That suggested visits to Parliament and meeting more important people, including cabinet ministers, Saudi princes and one or two notable members of the exiled Persian monarchy. It was a notable achievement for a low-key Soviet intelligence operative and suggests that he could be utterly charming as well as manipulative. In a sense, Darquennes was probably very much like Kim Philby – not someone customarily associated with Soviet espionage.

For me, personally – though I wasn't aware of the ramifications until afterwards – the situation was grave for several reasons: firstly, that the Soviet KGB or one of its Eastern Bloc associates was involved, and secondly, I had no idea what I'd got myself into.

My wife Madelon, who often travelled with me to Rhodesia and on one of our visits, had introduced Darquennes – tall, dapper, well-built and with an off-blond shock of hair – to Karin, who became his girlfriend (she was working in Salisbury for the Afrikaans press and radio). By the time the 'Frenchman' disappeared, they had been together almost two years, and within Rhodesian media circles the couple was considered 'quite an item'.

Denise Munnion, wife of the *Daily Telegraph*'s correspondent Chris Munnion who was working in Rhodesia at the time, considered them 'a lovely couple all round, a strong team with her writing the articles and him taking the photos.'

Finally, by way of a denouement, I was – unknowingly, let it be said – instrumental in exposing this agent. Enter the enterprising and experienced Israeli intelligence officer Yoram Hamizrachi.

I'd spent time with Yoram at his Israeli headquarters in northern Israel and he'd given me the authority to go on ops with an unconventional bunch of Christian Arabs, usually in their surplus M113 armoured personnel carriers or captured Egyptian T-34 tanks – almost in the shadow of the ancient crusader Beaufort Castle. By the time the war ended, Israeli jets had blasted it into a 1,000-foot pile of rubble. There was no concealing the origins of the M113s that I was moved about on while visiting this disputed region – Hebrew labels were plastered all over these machines, as were their steel ammunition boxes.

It was Yoram who pulled off the coup de grâce.

I should start at the beginning. There is a sequence of events which eventually came together, first in Israel and later in Rhodesia.

My assignments had taken me to the Middle East several times, and it was inevitable that I would meet up with Colonel Yoram Hamizrachi, this maverick military colonel, who kept a close watch on whoever entered his fief. I'd even taken my wife along to visit the Jewish state because I'd got to know the country so well – in between some noteworthy experiences, either attached to Israeli Army patrols in places like Bethlehem (then partially in radical undercover Palestinian hands) – or along the fortified frontier with Lebanon.

There was also a week on an Israeli *Dabur* gunship patrolling Lebanese harbours, which involved pulling into the port of Tyre for a break, though we never went ashore because of snipers.

Nine of those assignments came easily, but when they happened, the Israelis sometimes took me into the thick of it, such as when I went with Ariq Sharon during the Israel Defence Force (IDF) invasion of Beirut.

The bottom line was that the Israelis knew me, could trust me and allowed to me to work with them, all of which would have been passed on to Colonel Hamizrachi, who I gathered, was also involved in intelligence. He could speak several languages, having lived and worked in Paris and was married to German-born Beate Zahn. He was also fluent in Arabic and Russian. If there was ever a Mossad candidate, he would have made the grade, but then in the Middle East one does not ask questions about such matters.

The most interesting experience for us both came towards the close of our first visit after I'd contacted that remarkable IDF reserve officer. He took Madelon and me 'unofficially' across the border to the then-Christian South Lebanese town of Marj'Ayun (today Ain Arab Marjayoun), with most of the Christians killed or driven out by Hezbollah.

Hamizrachi and I stayed in touch, and having retired from the military a few years later – one of his first excursions was to South Africa where he stayed with us in Johannesburg for a few weeks.

At the same time, I was still going into Rhodesia to cover the war, my wife sometimes accompanying me, though she would remain in Salisbury while I did my thing in the bush. It was then that she befriended Karin Pretorius, and in turn, I'd made contact again with Darquennes. He and I had handled a couple of assignments together, one of which included a helicopter operation bringing in a casualty.

Not unexpectedly, François and Karin were introduced, and their relationship flourished, to the point where months later, she was seriously thinking of getting hitched. François, she told us, came from a family of upstanding Parisian stalwarts who dealt in antiques, owned a place in Brittany and a good deal more. He was quite specific about their property in Paris: their apartment was above the shop.

Apparently, after about a year into the relationship (and possibly with the help of a bit of nudging), he also suggested that he might not be averse to tying the knot with this beautiful Afrikaans girl from Cape Town. Karin was ecstatic. We had put the couple together, so we were the first to be told, though other issues constantly seemed to intervene.

One of them was Darquennes becoming acquainted with Lord Richard Cecil and as we now know, the two became fast friends, with the Frenchman and his girlfriend eventually sharing his house in Salisbury.

The British aristocrat invited the Frenchman to visit Hatfield House, the elegant family home of Lord and Lady Salisbury on London's outskirts near St Albans. A historic structure, it is today a National Trust property that includes what was the original royal palace of Hatfield, though all that remains of the old palace where Queen Elizabeth I briefly lived (and that Anne Boleyn would also have known), is the Banqueting Hall.

Things became more complicated when the two men decided to fly back to Salisbury from London across Africa in a small plane, quite a feat on a continent then starting to unravel. Apparently, with Rhodesia having asserted its Unilateral Declaration of Independence (UDI as it was better known) in 1965, and still at war, flight plans lodged at various airports along the way never mentioned Salisbury as a destination. Instead, it was always listed as Swaziland.

For Darquennes, linking up with an old Etonian, it was a rather distinctive achievement. Their backgrounds were hardly complementary, with Lord Cecil having served in Ulster as a captain: he was cited for gallantry in 1973. Interestingly, he openly expressed the view that the loyalty of British soldiers in Ireland was being severely tested because they were prevented from taking tougher countermeasures.

In the Rhodesian war he experienced a good deal of frontline action, quickly gaining the trust of the men serving with him in the Rhodesian Light Infantry, which happens often enough in small unit operations.

Rhodesian author Chris Cocks who wrote *Fire Force: A Trooper's War in the Rhodesian Light Infantry* – an excellent account of those hostilities – when I quizzed him about the connection, told me that Lord Cecil was never one for mixing it socially 'with the boys.' Instead, he tended to stick to himself when not on active duty. Many British nationals were serving in the Rhodesian military at the time. The aristocratic adventurer, after leaving the military, went on to report on the war between nationalist guerrillas and the Rhodesian Army, making no secret of his sympathy for the country's white minority. He was also a freelance contributor to British newspapers, including *The Times* of London and the *Telegraph*.

That chapter did not last long before he was killed during a contact, having gone into battle in deep bush country near the Zambezi with the Rhodesian African Rifles (RAR). What this sad closure tells us is that Cecil thoroughly enjoyed a scrap.

For his part, the Frenchman never claimed to be much more than a photographer, and a successful one at that. He was marketing his images through three of the biggest photo agencies in Europe; Agence France Presse, Sygma and Sipa Press – the latter, one of the most prestigious international photo agencies in its day – since relocated from Paris to the United States.

His personal approach also helped him move up the social ladder because he was never shy to reflect a positive approach towards the Rhodesian cause. Several of his friends recall him talking about Prime Minister Ian Smith as a 'personal hero'.

With time, François Darquennes was increasingly allowed access to wherever there was action in the Rhodesian war. That took him on several operational sorties where he would have made personal contact with those involved, including senior army commanders. He was one of the first of the media contingent at the scene of one of the two Air Rhodesia Viscounts downed in the Zambezi Valley by Soviet SAM-7 missiles.

For all his protestations to Karin about constantly being broke – which meant that she was always left to pick up the tab whenever they went out to dinner – Darquennes travelled a good deal. He was constantly flying to Johannesburg, invariably after he'd received secretive midnight calls behind closed doors which he refused to talk about. The little that she could pick up was that the language was neither French nor English and admits that it made little sense at the time. Not being politically orientated, Karin thought little of it until after he'd disappeared.

The many flights, she concedes, did worry her, especially since Darquennes was constantly claiming to be skint. But she adored the man and didn't protest. Questioned about his travels at the time by her, he bluntly told her: 'It's none of your business.'

Something similar happened when they were in the wilderness at the Leopard Rock Safari Lodge near Mozambique. It was a special event they'd planned with the Rhodesian Tourist Board, writing articles for the South African press, trying to market the landlocked country during sanctions. As she recalled: 'Suddenly, he received a call one evening and we had to cut everything short because he was urgently needed in Johannesburg... He wasn't at all forthcoming about it, even though, being wartime, it involved a massive palaver getting a fuel permit and the rest – not a word of explanation.'

It was about then that my Israeli friend entered the picture, whether by chance or with purpose, we will never know, though aware of his Israeli intelligence connections, I suspect the latter.

Yoram Hamizrachi, now retired, stayed with Madelon and me in Johannesburg for several weeks, and there was a constant flow of his friends to the house. While it was pleasant enough, he had a predilection to make long-distance calls from my landline. The only problem was that I was picking up the tab.

The big day came when François Darquennes knocked on my front door and it was opened by Yoram. The two men knew about each other through me but had never met; in any event, I hadn't been too effusive about my links with the Israeli or even that he had run his own military show in southern Lebanon. Madelon came up with drinks.

The four of us settled down to a quiet chat and it wasn't long before the Frenchman and the Israeli found common ground, both speaking English. Yoram gave no indication of being familiar with the French language, Parisian culture or its politics. We left them for a while, sat by the pool and when we returned, they were still talking.

We hadn't been back in the room for long when Yoram pulled himself up from his chair and moved across towards Darquennes. Looming over the Frenchman, he declared in a stridently loud voice: 'You're a fucking Soviet spy, you bastard!'

At that moment, nothing made sense except that the Frenchman was as astonished as we were. His jaw dropped visibly.

'What do you mean calling me a spy?' Darquennes demanded.

Yoram responded by addressing him in fluent French.

The discussion petered out shortly afterwards because there was not much more to say. On reflection, Darquennes had just succeeded in ending his career as a Soviet undercover agent and though that prospect might have eluded him just then, he was going to have to answer to someone.

Moments later he grabbed his coat and without bidding even a cursory goodbye, he left.

Hamizrachi didn't need to explain much in the aftermath, except that he seemed to have trapped his adversary into mentioning a few of his cultural activities in the French capital which, he said, were radical. In those days, the French Communist Party was still a potent force and exerted a pervasive cultural influence in the theatrical and in particular the literary world. Only somebody who knew Paris really well would have known that a certain theatre staged regular ultra-left productions.

Darquennes had no idea that Yoram, a big hulking figure of a man who was almost Buddha-like, would have been anything like the polymath that he was; or that he spoke French like a Parisian native. I only discovered then that when he was much younger, he had lived in the city for some years.

'Have we been dealing with a Soviet agent?' I asked, expecting a candid answer.

'Without a doubt, but don't ask for details,' he replied, which was one of the reasons why I always suspected that the meeting of the two might not have been quite as fortuitous as I'd imagined. Possibly there had been others looking into the background of an enterprising and capable young French photographer who had made unusual headway in embracing a number of sensitive contacts in a comparatively short time.

Mulling over things later, I concluded that counter-intelligence in Salisbury had probably tapped his phone because, as I learnt years later, they listened in to mine. This was long before cell phones, and Darquennes must have concluded that the Rhodesians simply weren't up to it; 'A bad, seriously bad mistake', as Julia Roberts said at some point in *Pretty Woman*.

I saw the 'Frenchman' only once more, at my office in the city late the following afternoon. He arrived at my door unannounced, glowering, which was when I stood up at my desk because I sensed trouble. South African media or not, I almost always carried my Colt Government on my belt, but not that day. Suddenly I felt quite naked, which was why I faced him side-on, my empty holster on the far side, away from him. Several times I noticed that he tried to catch a glimpse of whether I was 'carrying' or not; he didn't succeed.

That was when he launched a tirade, warning me that it was all lies and that I would pay, no matter how long it took. I had only a few words in reply, two of which were 'Fuck off.' 'François Darquennes' turned on his heels and left the building.

Neither I nor anybody else who had been linked to the man in southern Africa – or for that matter in Britain – ever heard from him again. Nor did Karin Pretorius.

Discussing the event with Hamizrachi long afterwards – he left South Africa for Israel a day or two later – he told me that Darquennes's departure was a sensible move. He intimated that had he stayed, either the South Africans or the Rhodesians would have iced him 'pretty damn quick'.

I then asked Yoram how they knew that he was a foreign intelligence agent. It certainly hadn't come from me, because I was taken in by his geniality and friendly aplomb, just like everybody else.

The Israeli just smiled…

Yoram Hamizrachi, a famous public figure in his own country – paratrooper, journalist, broadcaster, and author – but disillusioned by contemporary Israeli politics because he believed himself to be the ultimate pragmatist. Throughout an illustrious career, he battled Arab fundamentalism in Israel and in Europe and eventually Canada, to where he had emigrated.

Few are aware that he fought with distinction in the Six-Day War, where he was decorated for several brave actions under enemy fire. On 7 June 1967, the day after that war started, Yoram advanced from the American district to the Damascus Gate, before reaching the Western Wall. He was among the first Israeli troops to capture the Old City of Jerusalem and celebrated that enormously historic event by praying at the holy Kotel Ha'Ma'aravi.

The National Library of Israel holds a collection of photographs put on display from to time, so Yoram is hardly forgotten by his people. I went back to Metullah a few years ago and discovered that he remains a hero among those who had anything to do with him. Few would know that he destroyed the career of a young Eastern Bloc spy who might have moved up through the ranks had his intentions not been thwarted by a seasoned and perspicacious operative. The goal score for us in the West was one: for the Soviets zero.

It had been suggested that Yoram might have had ties to Mossad, even if he was not one of them. But then, like anyone working in intelligence, they never talk about such things. Yoram certainly did not.

He and Beate eventually divorced, but by then they had made a place in this difficult world for themselves in Winnipeg, where he died in October 2010.

Over the years, I'd lost touch with Karin Pretorius. My work was taking me increasingly to other conflicts: a spell covering the war in El Salvador, the Tanzanian invasion of Idi Amin's Uganda, a contract to produce a television documentary on the fifth anniversary of Moscow's invasion of Afghanistan in 1985 for the CIA and so on. That meant that I was giving Rhodesia a miss, which by then had become Zimbabwe.

To me, the Darquennes episode was history because the name turned out to be fictitious, as well as its owner. I surmised too, that Karin had moved on but, as I discovered, that was not so.

Our paths crossed again in 2021 when she contacted me and I was able to put her in the picture regarding the elusive 'Frenchman'. Not a single soul that we knew had heard from him in forty years.

Karin, of course, was delighted with the news about the Yoram connection and my explanations, yet flummoxed by the numerous intelligence-linked suppositions I raised. She admitted that she'd had a few suspicions of her own but attributed her lack of action to the trust she'd had in François and the wonderful relationship they shared.

Still, hearing about him brought her some comfort because she was now able to put that part of her life behind her. To quote Karin:

> You don't know what your email has meant to me. For the first time now, I have peace as to what happened to him. For years I had visions of François sitting in Paris, comfortable with the money he'd have inherited from his parents' antique shop and their vacation home at the coast (if that were ever true), possibly with a wife and family, all the time enjoying the kind of social life that only Paris has to offer.
>
> All that has been bothering me until now, because for the first time, I realise that none of it was ever real.
>
> I know too that he cannot be in Paris because surely, someone, somewhere, would have sniffed out his presence. At the same time if he is in Russia – or sitting in prison perhaps – then well and good, because he deserves it after all the wrong and hurt he did to the people working with him and trusting him.
>
> Thank you, Al. I feel a lot better.

Things went quiet between us for a while, until I was interviewed by Nigel Farage on Great Britain News in early 2022, when she wrote to me again:

> I haven't seen the interview, Al, but I thought you might have mentioned François again. It brought to mind the terrible realisation – shock really – that after such a truly wonderful

relationship, the man would have disappeared from my life so abruptly. And with not a single word spoken.

Even today, so many years later, I still seek closure and that hurts because some kind of explanation would have helped immeasurably.

Just yesterday I went onto the Internet again and googled to see if there was anything I could pick up. But all I got were his photos of the Viscounts shot down [by ZIPRA[4] guerrillas] in the war. I have established that there are two other Darquennes in France and I've been speculating whether they might be family.

And then, in another exchange of emails more recently:

François played an important role in my life – too important. I am not sure of the espionage connection, but I do know that he was brilliant at manipulating people for information, ostensibly for the work he said he did. I know too that he used me, hid behind this Afrikaans girl with little experience of the world, to hide his real intentions.

I recall quite clearly that he was someone with mixed emotions. One moment he was the most loving person in the universe and the next his mien had totally changed, with a kind of wordless iron curtain that came down between us. And before that, there were the secretive telephone calls that forced me to accept that something untoward was going on.

There was also the question of money. I recall him being helped in Johannesburg by a Frenchman by the name of Lejenne and things would be OK for a while. Then he would suddenly receive another pile of cash, which certainly didn't come from his photo agencies in Paris because he wasn't earning that much.

Karin spoke volumes of his visit to the United Kingdom, where he was apparently run ragged by Lord Cecil to meet his friends and family:

That's where he met Richard's parents, Lord and Lady Salisbury, at their Hatfield House home – a palace actually, for that is what it had been in the past. He was also taken to Parliament where he met British notables, steadily broadening the scope of his brief. I later also met Robert, Cecil's older brother who inherited the title, as well as his sister, Rose. They both came to Salisbury after Richard had been killed... Lady Rose was married when we made contact, then divorced and married again: you can look her up on Google. She was a lovely person, very friendly.

Karin suggested that I try and contact them all, though she wasn't sure that they would want to talk about events that were probably best forgotten.

Then, she went on, reflecting on the disappearance of François Darquennes and used the most appropriate Afrikaans expression about him vanishing into thin air: 'Hy't soos 'n groot speld verdwyn.' (He disappeared like a needle in a haystack).

---

4 ZIPRA (Zimbabwe People's Liberation Army), the military wing of the Zimbabwe African People's Union (ZAPU), a Marxist–Leninist political party in Rhodesia led by Joshua Nkomo.

CHAPTER 19

The safari capital of the world

In those early days, Kenya became one of the more attractive destinations for both small and large wallets because Nairobi and the interior catered for both.

The 'heavies' had the Muthaiga and the Mount Kenya Safari Club, while we settled for small hotels, usually owned and run by the country's Asian community. They were secure, too, with no unwarranted visitors after dark, cheap meals, and you could leave your things in your room and be confident that all would be there on your return. Do not try that today.

That former one-time British colony seems always to have been a delightful place, as chroniclers like Elspeth Huxley, Karen Blixen, Kuki Gallman, and others have told us.

We called it the world's safari capital, though most backpackers who transited Nairobi could rarely afford anything like the expensive outings in the wild offered by travel agencies. Those trips into the remote bush country to Maasai Mara, Serengeti or the more distant Selous Game Reserve in southern Tanganyika (even then, the most extensively protected game park on the African continent covering an area almost twice the size of Belgium), have always been popular. However, most tourists arrive by charters, beyond most people's vacation budgets.

In the early days, safaris were both expensive and expansive and almost always multi-vehicle expeditions that could last a month, never without attendant staff to cook and serve, while the guests – each evening freshly bathed and appropriately clothed after a day in the bush – sat around open fires with the requisite gin and tonic in hand.

Also, the Kenyan capital was smaller, a lot less sophisticated than Johannesburg, and more popular than the distant south, which had become embroiled in racial issues due to the apartheid regime.

While neither as big nor as affluent as some South African cities had become – even if white wealth was juxtaposed rather sharply with impoverished townships on the outskirts of them all – Nairobi boasted many of the attributes of modern society. Indeed, from the 1930s, the Kenyan capital was regarded – perched (as it was) on the fringe of the so-called 'Undeveloped World' – as the ultimate in 'doing something different'. It had the additional attraction of the Nairobi National Park in its backyard, just half an hour's drive from the town centre. And the Donovan Maule Theatre, where many British thespians did their thing for a few months before moving south to the Union, usually for a contract spell at Johannesburg's Alexander Theatre.

The Thorn Tree Restaurant spanned the front portal of the New Stanley Hotel, which has dominated Nairobi's casual al fresco social scene, complete with an enormous acacia emerging incongruously out of concrete for decades.

After hours, the Norfolk Hotel took over, the Delaware Terrace being the preferred watering hole as part of the old colonial establishment. Hemingway used to drink there, and so did his compatriot Robert Ruark of *Uhuru* and *Horn and the Hunter* fame. Long before that, Denys Finch Hatton and his good friend, the Honourable Berkeley Cole, an Anglo-Irish aristocrat whose namesake today lives on Scotland's Isle of Bute, were regulars.

Interestingly, the Norfolk Hotel was the base from which many adventurers kicked off their East African adventures. It was from there too, where American President Theodore Roosevelt strode out on his world-famous safari in 1909, all extravagance and pomp as was the big money tradition, when most of Nairobi's roads still had to be surfaced.

His extraordinarily large party – about 30 African servants who attended to their every need while in the bush – headed off into the wilderness for several months in one of the first Model-Ts from Henry Ford's newly constructed Detroit factory the year before. All they needed were trumpets to herald their departure.

Over the years, I spent many good times in Nairobi, which became a second home whenever I needed to base myself in Black Africa for assignments; first, with Amin and his wife Dolly, and then with the delightful Sally Church.

The crude Hog Ranch that the American adventurer Peter Beard and his companions called home was close by. Visits were typically by appointment only, despite the fairly primitive surroundings and makeshift tents. Peter's setup was a short trek along a bush trail – where my son Luke was bitten by a night adder. We didn't bother with an antidote because it was only a minor strike, even though his foot had almost turned black by morning.

Peter Beard, in theory Sally's tenant and always the maverick, was the son of an American tobacco magnate and first came to Kenya as a teenager in the mid-1960s. By his admission, he was 'infatuated with the romance of Africa'.

I got to know him quite well, but the entourage and the sometimes damning of Peter Beard's ups and downs, were often more disturbing than pleasing. Usually, there would be Gilles Turle and his Somali girlfriend, permanently ensconced in an adjacent tented camp that became the backdrop of Sally's colonial-style home. However, the gang eventually shifted base to Lamu.

Peter had some habits that could be disconcerting, including being an enthusiastic drug user who always seemed to have a joint lit unless there were magic mushrooms, cocaine, or more potent stuff available. He'd been married to American supermodel Cheryl Tiegs and had the reputation of being the lover of many famous women, including Lee Radziwill, sister of Jacqueline Kennedy Onassis. The original jet setter, Peter was friends with many famous characters, including Andy Warhol, Truman Capote, Salvador Dali and the Rolling Stones.

All that might have been expected as his family – by Peter's account – threw their money about, and he was never short. Consequently, there were always lovely girls flitting in and out of his tent on the 45-acre estate, which was within walking distance of the Denys Finch Hatton grave.

Beard's worst excesses were twofold; the first from his propensity towards taking chances, something he did with abandon, and which could result in serious injuries, not always to himself. The other was his remarkable ability to embellish any event in which he may or may not have been involved, which meant that you afterwards spent involuntary time unpicking his lies.

His often-stupid bravado also became a feature of his many excesses, with one incident involving Terry Matthews, one of our mutual hunting friends. Terry took Beard along on a game-viewing trip and was almost fatally gored by a rhino because Peter, hot-headed as usual, was showing off. Then he almost copped it in the mid-1990s while photographing a herd of elephants on the Tanzanian border: he'd riled a cow elephant, and she charged.

The American monthly *Vanity Fair* recorded it as follows:

> As the elephant tried to impale him, Beard – attempting to evade her tusks – hung onto her leg. She crushed him with her head, pressing him to the ground, fracturing his pelvis in five places, and slashing his thigh. Other elephants crowded around, nosing him with their trunks. When Beard arrived at Nairobi Hospital, doctors warned that he was bleeding to death from internal injuries, and when he was wheeled into the operating theatre, he had no pulse.
>
> But, after a lengthy operation to piece his pelvis back together, an external scaffold pinned to hipbones through the skin stopped the bleeding. The most immediate danger was the risk of infection; Beard would face weeks in the hospital and up to a year of recovery. As shocking as it was, the news proved less than surprising to his East African friends, who long watched Beard's antics with a mixture of fascination and horror.

Terry Matthews said at the time, 'Peter was playing the fool with elephants twenty years before, back when he was married to Cheryl. Everyone knew he would either hurt somebody or get hurt himself. Now he's done it.'

Always impulsive, the 'dreaded Beard' was eager to accompany me to Uganda in March 1979. He'd overheard me saying I was heading there to cover the Tanzanian invasion and, hopefully, the toppling of Idi Amin Dada. Undoubtedly, it was a dangerous venture, the Ugandan president having already murdered several journalists. The ogre was eventually ousted, but at that point, Beard's often irrational actions had already made him suspect among us hacks, which was when I declined his offer with thanks. Possibly it was just as well because there was no saying how he would have reacted to the presence of 100,000 Tanzanian troops on the rampage.

Peter was in the news again when he died; by all accounts, it became an appalling scenario. By then, 82 years old and suffering from multiple ailments, including dementia, he disappeared from his cliffside compound in Montauk at the tip of Long Island, his body was only discovered in an isolated area three weeks later.

His obituary notices in *The New York Times* – and others – equated him to one of Africa's great explorers: if they only knew…

Sally Church's house lay at the heart of most goings-on in the shadow of the beautiful Ngong Hills. Beard and his friends – some disreputable, some not – became part of the 'rural furniture'. Though she never used 'substances' herself, it surprised me that she tolerated their presence so magnanimously since hard drugs were as illegal then as they still are.

In later years, I stayed at Sally's home in Nairobi; it was a mixture of delight and surprise to meet her guests who would arrive for weekly soirées. Her guests included ambassadors and diplomats, Kenyan leaders like the indomitable Charles Njonjo (he was appointed Attorney General in the Kenyan post-independence government) and poets and writers from near and far. Movie and theatre personalities were regulars; she hosted William Holden and Stephanie Powers (when she was not at her home-from-home at the Mount Kenya Safari Club).

There was always bound to be a professional hunter about, usually from 'Down South' after the Kenyan government banned hunting, some of whom, I was told, had worked with her ex – long since departed for the United States on the arm of one of his wealthy clients. Sally never had a harsh word for anyone, not even old man Church – though she'd had to pick up the pieces when he ran off – leaving her to care for and educate their two daughters.

I was filming in East Africa quite often at the time, and Sally would always rise to the occasion when there was a need. She even handled everything for our long hike up Kilimanjaro – three days up, two down – that my crew and I completed one memorable year. Some claim that the trudge up to the 19,000-foot summit is relatively easy. I can assure you from personal experience, it isn't!

Sally, a scion of a prominent settler family, was also the person to go to if you wished to meet someone that mattered in Kenyan society. She knew them all, including the entire Leakey clan – indeed, she had been the lover of one of them and talked fondly of those days – as she might have done about this old *Kaburu* who had briefly come into her life.

There were very few Kenyans had not spent some quality time with this quiet-spoken woman who ran the best-known antique auction house in East Africa. In the decades before she died, she gathered even more friends: the likes of George and Joy Adamson, Mo and Dolly Amin, Armand and Michaela Dennis, Harry Selby (before he high-tailed it to Botswana), Alan and Joan Root, Errol Trzebinski, Kiki Gallman and a host of 'creatives' who either lived in or visited East Africa at that time.

Sally took me to view the grave of Denys Finch Hatton. His love for the Danish author Karen Blixen was immortalised in *Out of Africa* – one of the great films to emerge from Kenya in the late 1900s because it was painstakingly authentic. (Blixen wrote under the nom de plume, Isak Dinesen.)

Sally had carefully planned the visit to the site in the Ngong Hills above her house – it lies about eight kilometres to the west of one of the entrances of the present-day Nairobi National Park – taking lunch in a basket that included a bottle of wine in a cooler. It was a memorable experience, indeed.

The Finch Hatton family initially positioned a simple plaque at the grave site – it is still there – which just about says it all:

DENYS GEORGE FINCH HATTON
1887–1931
He prayeth well who loveth well both man and bird and beast

Sally told me that Karen Blixen had chosen the original site. She had written in her notes: 'There was a place in the hills, on the first ridge in the game reserve that I, myself – at the time I thought that I was to live and die in Africa – had pointed out to Denys as my future burial place... One evening, while we looked at the hills from my home, he remarked that he would also like to be buried there. Sometimes when we drove out in the hills, Denys said, "Let us drive as far as our graves".'

I produced some memorable films in that cherished period about a quarter-century after the Mau Mau emergency in the interior had ended, for no better reason than Kenya was one of the safest and most secure African countries.

Things have changed since then, but the memories persist, like driving to the coast, not on the main highway that links Nairobi to Mombasa, but rather, hiving off to the left well before Voi. A bush road would take us to Malindi through what were then still some of the largest herds of wildlife in the world. That was before Somali Shifta poachers laid the region to waste.

I did the trip a couple of times and rarely encountered any other traffic, which was just as well because the elephant population ran into thousands. We sometimes had to pull over to let a large group of tuskers pass. Also, there were rhinos – always within sight – which we preferred to give a miss; with their eyesight being poor, they would sometimes charge. They, too, have now been poached.

Another time I linked up with Renaldo Retief, whom I had met earlier when his family farmed on the edge of Rift Valley at Thompson's Falls (Nyahururu today). Following in the tracks of a large Afrikaner 'trekker' group that arrived in British East Africa decades before, the Retiefs eventually decamped to Malindi. There, Renaldo started a somewhat unusual business of harvesting mangos along the Tana River and selling them on the London market in fruit crates airfreighted from Nairobi. He paid a shilling for every mango gathered by the locals living along the river, and they were marketed at about a pound each in Britain. Naturally, he couldn't have done that had he not been able to communicate with his clients in fluent Swahili.

Renaldo's craft was a classic riverboat named *African Queen*, which was appropriate, and while she boasted a funnel, his was steam driven. Moving along the lower reaches of the Tana was an experience because you saw more crocs than you believed possible to congregate in one area. It was also the densest mosquito-infested tropical region I have ever visited: deadly to those who didn't have anti-malarial prophylactics.

Kenya in the old days was a marvellous place to savour everything that a newly independent African country had to offer. There was no gainsaying the excitement, prospects awaiting the adventurous few, and challenges to be faced.

In much of the continent where new dispensations had taken over from their original colonial authorities – for a while yet, entrenched and intransigent – you could hardly miss the new order of things that made black people their own masters – to which at last, they were fully entitled. Destiny was theirs to cherish and make the best of what London and Paris had handed down. In terms of modern-day national infrastructures that included everything that made modern economies tick, it was to be expected that foreign investment followed and most of these nations thrived.

I'd spent weeks in Nairobi three years before Kenya got its independence in 1963. When I returned a few years after that historic event, I found a nation that was not only economically enthusiastic but powerfully confident of the future. There were still many whites around, and the large Asian community brought initially across the Indian Ocean as skivvy labourers to till the land, was self-assured, confident, and relatively prosperous.

In fact, with all these attributes in mind, there were great hopes for the country, even though African people often still addressed whites as *Bwana*, which was as much a colonial leftover as it was a respectful appellation. Our women were always called *Memsahib*, which was courteous. Kenya's Asian community was large even then and more down to earth: we men would be addressed as 'Mister'.

Then, in the Kenyan capital, you could hardly miss the kind of purpose one hardly ever sees in Africa today: hope, a genuine gusto for what lay ahead and a new camaraderie between the races I had never encountered before, certainly not in such abundance. Undeniably, the transition from a dependent British colony to a nation running its own affairs made a significant difference, with crime down

50 per cent, for the simple reason that the reality of this new-found independence brought with it joy and confidence in was the future held.

I'd borrow a car from my old pal Mohamed Amin and head down to the coast. On Kenya's north shores up Malindi way, I'd spend a week or a month diving off Watamu Beach, a stretch of tropics that even today remains the epitome of splendid isolation. At that time, it became my chosen hideaway. I was never disappointed, even though there were mambas and cobras in the overhangs and foliage – far too close for comfort.

Turtle Bay was a favourite too of Jack Bloch, another old diving buddy. Many regarded him, with his brother Tubby, as the Conrad Hiltons of the original colony. They put Kenya's hotel industry on the map. Jack had a house on the beach there, and we'd dive the Big Three Caves, where the groupers were the size of VW Beetles. We never stopped to think of who knows how many bull sharks were hovering along the fringe of that stretch of reef, and while we were never attacked, others were.

That entire region along the coast was secure in those dreamily delightful fun days, and in the traditional sense of the word. You could walk for kilometres on open beaches without being hassled by touts or pickpockets. After dark, we'd stroll the length of those stretches of crystal sand in search of wayward moray eels that would lie, head and body out of the water, on top of the coral at low tide – as seen on tourist posters – free of the fear of being mugged. No longer. These days, holiday homes in the region are plundered by the week if left unprotected.

Nairobi, in contrast, several hundred kilometres into the interior – at the other end of one of the most dangerous roads on the continent – was undoubtedly a convenient base for foreign correspondents from which to cover the rest of Africa, which suited me fine. Being South African-born, I should not even have been allowed into Kenya. Still, my British passport cleared my pitch, which was great since I was writing for a host of publications and news agencies on several continents.

The real bugbear was apartheid, an abhorrent political system that had created enemies for South Africa from the 1950s on. Consequently, it was almost impossible to head out from there to what the Fourth Estate liked to refer to as 'Independent Africa' unless, of course, you held a more acceptable passport or were on the staff of one of the Fleet Street majors, *The New York Times* or a prominent American news magazine like *Newsweek*.

My old friend, Jim Penrith, was hired by the Argus Africa News Service; he and Tatu, his lovely South African-born artist wife, made Nairobi their permanent base. With them in tow, life within the ex-pat community in the Kenyan capital was a thrash, and it stayed that way for quite a few years.

So too with Peter Younghusband, a big name in Fleet Street in his day, who taught me the fundamentals of some of his newsroom tricks when we worked together in Cape Town. On the staff of *Newsweek* and the London *Daily Mail* – reporting for both for decades – we often crossed paths in East Africa, and no question, I owe him a great deal because I could never have managed without his tutelage.

Like me, Peter was of Boer stock – baptised into the van der Westhuizen family (as was British actor Richard E. Grant whose father was also an Afrikaner by the name of Esterhuizen). Peter's mother went on to marry a Younghusband, and with a British passport stuck away in his safari jacket pocket, 'Youngers' – as we know this marvellously jovial raconteur – encountered few problems moving his six-foot, five-inch frame about independent Africa. Very few British heads of diplomatic missions in African capitals did not invite him to dinner when he passed through.

Things were very different for the rest of us scribes, especially simpler souls from South Africa, where most of Africa's press corps was based. Most could not cover African developments north of the Zambezi, one of the reasons why Nairobi became a magnet for news-gatherers on a continent that was starting to experience its versions of growing pains.

On the positive side, there were nightly flights to Nairobi out of Johannesburg – direct and non-stop. It was easy to fly in both directions, even though passengers from the 'Racist South' had to have a good reason for disembarking in Kenya. Nairobi had a solid grasp on the burgeoning tourist trade and did little to interrupt the flow. Still, British passport or not, there were times when I was questioned, sometimes vigorously – and with considerable scepticism – about my so-called 'actual place of abode'.

That was when I initiated a bit of subterfuge of my own.

If your journey started in one of the former British protectorates (that included Swaziland, Lesotho and Botswana), or questions were asked on arrival at Embakazi Airport (later renamed to commemorate President Jomo Kenyatta) I made it my business to have several recent Swazi immigration stamps – arrivals and departures – in my passport.

I'd done some homework and persuaded somebody in Johannesburg to make me an 'official' set of Swazi immigration imprints, complete with moveable date facilities. That meant each time I left the old Transvaal for the north, I'd stamp my passport with one of my newly created Swazi seals, which worked like a charm. That ruse went on for years, though were these deceptions blown, I'd probably have ended up in a Kenyan clink or even in its notorious Kamiti Maximum Security Prison.

In my profession, you soon get to know the names of some of the prisons in which you never wanted to find yourself: Mugabe's Chikurubi and a hellhole called Black Beach outside Malabo in Equatorial Guinea. According to Freddie Forsyth, there was also Lagos's Kirikiri Prison, probably the worst of the lot.

Moving easily within the Kenyan expatriate community, the word eventually got out. Quite a few Kenyan youngsters at South African schools and universities would pop into my house to have their passports 'stamped', usually before they were due to return home. This tally included Angela, the delightful daughter of Daphne Sheldrick. The venerable Dame Daphne, honoured by the Queen for her conservation efforts, headed the trust named after her late husband David, a remarkable facility which, for many decades, was a haven for orphaned elephants and rhinos.

From Nairobi, most of us newsmen and women would shoot off into nearby trouble spots to report on whatever was happening: that included the Congo, then in a permanent state of confusion and almost always violent. Tanzania, then at war (though not formally) with the Portuguese presence in neighbouring Mozambique, also entered the picture, as did the entire Horn of Africa, which included Somalia.

Some journalists would expand their brief and head into the Sudan, which fringes northern Kenya, but that could be dodgy because there were almost always armed dissidents along the way. The last time Peter Younghusband went in, he was stuck for a while along the Upper Nile and went down with blackwater fever, which is usually fatal. The appellation refers to your urine which turns dark because of blood. Peter conceded years later that he was lucky to have pulled through.

These, unfortunately, were some of the perils that we had to deal with in the wild. I contracted malaria numerous times during my travels through Africa (even though I took anti-malarial medication), as well as hepatitis in Nigeria and typhus in Uganda. Tick bite fever, bilharzia, also known as schistosomiasis (an infection caused by a parasitic worm that lives in fresh water in Africa), and amoebic dysentery were still more issues dealt with.

For the news-gathering fraternity, Uganda – Kenya's nearest neighbour and lying to its immediate west – was always a place where there was something untoward happening. Kampala had celebrated its independence, also from Britain, a year before Kenya. But unlike Kenya, conditions in Uganda were different, with the newly elected Prime Minister Obote – a hard-line Socialist – trying, as we have already seen – to impose an alien brand of political ideals down the gullets of his African people at political rallies throughout the country.

'Africa for the Africans' was his credo, only he was not targeting whites but his sizeable Asian community who economically all but ran the country. Not that that prevented President Obote from smuggling gold with the help of Idi Amin Dada, his trusted deputy army commander and the same man who eventually ousted him. That was in January 1971, and the portly former army boxing champ promptly kicked out his Asians.

I entered Uganda a score of times from Nairobi, sometimes by road or, when push became shove, by charter, usually by small plane with another hack or two to split costs. It might have been expensive, but it was worth it because you could always claim some of it back on expenses. Occasionally I'd grab a berth on board the lake steamer out of Kisumu. It was never boring because we'd almost circumnavigate Lake Victoria (Africa's largest body of freshwater) along the way, including several Tanzanian ports.

Very rarely would I enter Uganda on a commercial flight because Entebbe Airport had more government goons than any other air terminal on the continent. Still, there were times when news broke, and things became urgent, so one simply had to.

For much of President Idi Amin's brutal and authoritarian rule where he dictated who lived or died, his appointed thugs could be as vicious as their similarly minded associates in Moscow. It was a curious anomaly that puzzled most of us journalists who were able to enter Uganda that, while the man was regarded as a buffoon by the rest of the world, his impositions became fiercer the longer he remained in power. There was good reason why many observers equated Idi Amin Dada to Haiti's equally notorious 'Papa Doc' Duvalier. Nobody can guess how many people he murdered: that tally is well into five figures.

Also, the absurd racial privations to which Uganda's Indian population were subjected are largely forgotten. It got so bad that the British government eventually permitted almost 30,000 Ugandan Asians to settle in the UK following that tyrant expelling his entire Asian community.

Many prominent people – now half a century later and proudly British – were to emerge from that group. These include financiers, scientists, entrepreneurs, medical specialists and politicians.

One of them, two generations later, was Priti Patel who, some say, was undoubtedly the most effective and demanding Home Secretary in recent memory.

The expulsion of Uganda's only thriving community contributed to Idi Amin's demise. The system started falling apart during his rule when it took some severe downturns – not only within the Ugandan Asian community but also among the expatriates living there permanently. These included both Africans and whites, the majority of whom were routinely accosted and insulted.

At one stage, the word went around that, after having the Ugandan Archbishop Janani Luwum murdered, President Amin removed his body to State House in Kampala. The esteemed cleric's corpse was kept in the deep freeze and served up for dinner at a diplomatic function. I'd mentioned that episode in *Barrel of a Gun*, one of my earlier books, and though I've had my detractors that Africa was really 'never like that', the story was corroborated by a Washington report after Idi Amin had died in exile in Saudi Arabia.[1]

That statement was clear: 'Henry Kyemba, a former justice minister who fled Uganda, said Amin had bouts of insanity and ate human flesh. Accounts of the dictator keeping the severed heads of actual or perceived opponents in his refrigerator were reaching London. In one reported instance, human heads were cooked and served in covered silver dishes to his cabinet ministers, several of whom ended up fleeing the country when the truth leaked.'

---

1 'Butcher is Buried', *Washington Times*, 20 August 2003.

After that, the wife of the French ambassador was sent home under controversial circumstances. That diplomatic residence was on Nakasero Hill and, like State House, overlooked much of Kampala. The suburb also included Amin's notorious State Research Centre, his personal 'Lubyanka', where suspects were imprisoned, tortured and killed. I went through those dungeons soon after the monster was deposed. It was horrific. There was blood on many of the walls and a torture chamber, which I took photos of, wires on the armrests still protruding. There was no denying what the inmates endured – screams were heard from a distance as well as by those residing in the French Embassy. The ambassador's wife eventually declared that she'd had enough and demanded to be sent home.

It is impossible when experiencing such evidence first-hand to take it lightly or be dismissive of some fanatic's excesses because I am still reminded of that visit when his name comes up.

I made good use of my time each time I visited Kampala before and after Idi Amin was forced to flee following the Tanzanian Army invasion. Sticking close to one of the men coordinating security, I was one of the first to enter the tyrant's living quarters in State House, a revelation indeed. On his bed lay an empty box that had held a Smith & Wesson revolver, a .357 Magnum stainless steel Model 66, if I remember correctly. In one corner of the bedroom was a safe that had already been blasted by somebody even more enterprising than me, with a large pile of what appeared to be gold coins lying scattered on the floor. They weren't coins but gold-plated medals embossed with the head of the dictator. I grabbed a bunch and headed back to my hotel to unload, and that afternoon went back for more. I gave them to many of my friends in South Africa, as well as to Elize, wife of President P. W. Botha. Madelon also had a few and kept one for herself.

The next day I went with a small group of about half a dozen people – most purporting to be journalists (I had never met or heard of any of them before, so they couldn't have been East Africa regulars) – to a building adjoining Idi Amin's State House.

That house, we were told, had been a Palestinian bomb factory. The rooms were packed with explosives and bomb-making apparatus, including detonators, timers and much more. Some of the explosives were in liquid form in large vats, and I was at a loss to know for what evil project that lot was intended, so I took all the photos I could and still have them on file.

What caught my eye almost immediately were metal fittings ready to be shaped into pipe bombs, like the one that killed former Kenyan minister Bruce McKenzie on his way back to Nairobi after visited Idi Amin. The bomb detonated over Ngong, after the plane had taken off from Entebbe Airport on 24 May 1978. And as the Ugandan tyrant told one of his ministers, McKenzie was murdered in retaliation for Nairobi's involvement in the Israeli Entebbe raid two years earlier.

Arguably the most interesting items lying around the 'bomb factory' were dozens of envelopes being prepared as letter bombs. It was a tidy and delicate process because the intention was to have them explode while being opened by whoever received them.

One of these letter bombs, obviously ready for mailing, had been placed – probably by someone working at the house – on a window ledge near the entrance. After we'd walked through all the ground floor rooms where most of the potent stuff lay, we headed upstairs to see what else there was. On our return to the main working area again, I noticed that the envelope was missing, taken by somebody in our little party. Evidently, not everybody was media.

In hindsight, the bombing of Bruce McKenzie's plane is worth mentioning. South African-born Bruce, a delightfully ebullient man with a penchant for rugby who I'd met several times, was a sad loss and is still mourned in East Africa. One of the closest friends of this white Kaburu (though he was Jewish) was Charles Njonjo, a black Kenyan who eventually served as the country's attorney general. He was regarded by many of his people as the ultimate African Englishman, referred to by some jocularly as 'The Duke of Kabeteshire' (Kabete being one of a dozen electoral constituencies within Kenya's Kiambu County). Indeed, their backgrounds couldn't have been more diverse.

The Honourable Charles Njonjo, with his brother James, became one of Kenya's wealthiest landowners and financiers. He was educated both at Fort Hare University in South Africa – which meant that he had personal experience of the indignities of racial separation – and at the University of Exeter. The grand old man died recently, in January 2022 having just turned 102.

Looking back, one realises that while the dreaded Idi Amin was still in control, those were never easy times for us foreign types. If any of us were even suspected of doing something out of the ordinary, he or she could be arrested. Indeed, several were, including the American Nicholas Stroh and two Scandinavian journalists who tried to enter Uganda by small boat across Lake Victoria, illegally as it transpired. They pushed their luck because they'd been warned before leaving Nairobi that it would be dodgy. Idi Amin's stooges murdered all three. Stroh's son subsequently went to East Africa in search of his dad's grave, if there ever had been one. It emerged later that most of the victims' bodies had been incinerated.

In Uganda, and to a lesser extent in Tanzania, when Nyerere still called the shots, you always knew that those characters were around. You could hardly miss the bastards with their army-type swagger sticks and signature shades.

Speaking from experience, it could be tricky.

CHAPTER 20

Banned from Rhodesia

Working in Africa in those uncertain times after the chimerical independence of most of that vast and often changeable continent, was a lot less difficult than some journalists would have liked or, for that matter, have their editors believe.

For some, it was a cushy number. I would return to base after traipsing around West Africa or having spent a week or two in Uganda and Tanzania, and my friends would be amazed at my 'daring' and frankly, I wasn't inclined to disabuse them. They all thought the work was dangerous. 'All those unwashed, uneducated and violent people...all those revolutions. You'll catch it one of these days!'

I never argued. It took a few years, but I seemed to have attained a marvellous independence and the kind of flamboyant confidence that went with it. Although life in countries like Liberia, Ghana, Rwanda, Somalia, Nigeria and Libya could be rough, we generally did our own thing. We acted much as we did elsewhere, though obviously Africa had its moments.

After the first full-scale African revolution in Togo on 13 January 1963 – when President Sylvanus Olympio was assassinated at the behest of *Osagyefo* Kwame Nkrumah – many other black rulers were overthrown in rapid succession. Four decades later, there are few countries in Africa where there had not been at least one revolt or attempted coup, usually by the army.

There were some good reasons why I enjoyed working and sometimes living north of the Zambezi. In the first place, it was a rather limited field, as attention was increasingly drawn toward what was happening in Vietnam and secondly, I was getting paid for doing something I enjoyed, even if I did set out in my new career without the benefit of a month or two in the newsroom. That meant that I had to learn on the hoof, though each assignment meant that new intricacies of the game were being revealed.

In this regard, I was fortunate because I had a few tutors who were not only instructive but enjoyed living the life they promulgated. These were journalists and writers who had muddled their ways through successive and demanding undertakings, and most were quite happy to let me hang onto their coattails and do the dog work if

I produced acceptable copy. Peter Younghusband's name has come up often enough, but he was one of the first and eventually I became the other half of his compact two-man team in Cape Town because we shared space behind the *Cape Times* offices.

I was also helped by Johnnie Johnson, one of the most irascible newsmen I'd ever encountered in the decades I was active. Johnnie was a South African editor, and if his administrative style was off-putting, his professionalism as a newspaperman was exemplary, and I appreciated his role as a boss. The trouble for me at the time – going in and out of assignments, some of which were precarious – was that he believed I was a spy working for some foreign government.

'*Moi?*'

'Fingers' van der Merwe was another remarkable character from that far-flung period. It was decades before the cell phone era, and emails were something a few Americans were only dreaming about, so we used the telex machine for our despatches, except for those reports that were phoned through directly. 'Fingers', bless his heart, had his telex office right next door, and if we needed him at three in the morning or all of Saturday and Sunday – without a break – he'd be there.

When Peter was somewhere in Africa, or perhaps covering Beirut or the war in Vietnam, I'd process reports to the handful of newspapers and agencies we covered or for which we had strings. His brief included London's *Daily Mail* and *Newsweek*, together with a bunch of general-purpose publications. I was the *Daily Express* stringer in South Africa, though I did work for UPI now and again as well as the BBC. He'd do the same for me when I was out of town.

With time I was bound to advance because any kind of writing improves with practice, or so I was assured, though as a taskmaster Youngers could be brutal. It was hard for a while, but my stuff was getting printed under my own byline and gradually I could expand the scope of my efforts.

After I'd added a BBC string to my belt, and until I was fired, I'd come to answer to Angus McDermid, a plump, carroty little Welshman (some of us referred to him as 'Anguish'), but only when he wasn't around. He was apt to get the vapours when things got hot, and in Africa, which was often, especially with me since I had an inside line to many of South Africa's efforts to penetrate Black Africa. To his credit, as Chris Munnion commented, Angus had two vital qualities as a foreign correspondent: a sense of humour – which was helpful when you crossed borders manned by trigger-happy soldiers usually drunk or doped or both, and the ability to tackle problems head-on. McDermid had the aptitude to tell a government functionary that he was talking crap in such a pleasant way that the fellow thought he was paying him a compliment. We all tried it at some time or other, but few succeeded as well as Angus.

Donald Wise, the eternally sanguine correspondent from London's *Daily Mirror*, came close to it. He once suggested – after listening to a Congolese general spouting drivel – that somebody should give the man a banana. Soldier, journalist and adventurer who survived four wounds and two plane crashes during a life that saw him involved in wars on three continents from the 1940s through the 1970s, died at the ripe old age of eighty. Over the years, Don had fought the Japanese, followed by communist insurgents in Malaya, covered fighting from the Congo to Aden (with the Parachute Regiment) to Vietnam, as well as a string of Arab–Israeli wars. Still, he was never tempted to settle down. Reflecting a ducal detached air, he always maintained, as the *Washington Post* reported in his obituary notice in 1998, that he was a foreign correspondent, a person 'whose job it was to be somewhere foreign and to correspond'.

Chris Munnion called the journalists who covered Africa in those days Genuine Old Africa Hands, or GOAHs as he liked to refer to this spunky little band of professionals in the alcoholic haze of Fleet Street's days of unlimited expenses. Our associates were a colourful lot and sadly, the majority have moved on.

Those African governments with whom we dealt could sometimes raise formidable obstacles to prevent us from doing our job. Some did their best to conceal or distort facts, or to see us tiresome busybodies off the premises and, preferably, all the way out of the country. We all spelled trouble to most of those tin-pot despots.

An unflattering story in a British or American publication could cause difficulties for power-hungry black demagogues, especially when we highlighted financial excesses or the dwindling of money from foreign 'aid'. Or how some former crony's body was dragged out of the river. Amnesty International was not yet fully into its stride.

Curiously, it was Angus McDermid who convinced Chris Munnion that working in Africa could be fun.

We all had our favourite stories, moments that sometimes seemed likely to be our last, when we'd double up in a strange mixture of horror and hilarity while relating the latest calamity. At least we'd emerged alive…

Youngers and John Monks took Weldon Wallace of *The Baltimore Sun* into the Congo war. Wallace was that newspaper's distinguished music critic and had been covering the opera season in Milan when the Katanga crisis erupted.

Having introduced himself, he told the pair that his editor noticed that he was the man nearest the spot 'and asked me to pop down to Central Africa and cover the story'. Wallace admitted to never having been to Africa before, which was when he raised the issue: 'I wonder if I could possibly get a lift with you two to Elizabethville?' he asked the wily pair. Nobody had told the poor fellow that Elizabethville, the Congo's largest city in the south (Lubumbashi today) near the border with Northern Rhodesia, was under a hefty siege and that people were getting killed on both sides.

The three of them bundled into a hired car and headed out into the Congo, were shot at, arrested, and came within an ace of being executed before they were rescued. After returning safely across the border, Weldon Wallace collapsed, but not before muttering something about still having to file his story.

Well, he couldn't write a word because, as Youngers recalls, the American was in lousy shape and delirious at times. So, Wallace was put to bed by the 'Terrible Twins', who then decided they'd better do something for him if only to justify the horrific experience they'd just survived.

Between the two, Younghusband and Monks wrote a well-fuelled report, sent it off to American editors in Maryland, and which was published to accolades of work well done. What wasn't expected was that the story was eventually nominated for a Pulitzer Prize, which the music critic gracefully declined. While he had all the assurances that it was his story – he was told that he'd scribbled it all down before passing out – he wasn't taken in.

They were not the only ones who escaped with their lives. In a senior position at the United Nations, Sir Brian Urquhart had been appointed the UN representative in Katanga, where all this drama was taking place. Travelling with an Australian diplomat to a dinner for a visiting American senator in Elizabethville, they were stopped by a group of drunk troops – thirty of whom followed them into the dining hall where they set upon the guests and broke Urquhart's nose with a rifle butt. After that, they piled several guests into vehicles and took them away, as one of the thugs declared, to be shot.

Everybody was eventually released. After all, their attackers feared that the local Gurkha detachment would take prompt revenge, which they would have done because they were already on their way. The next day, the press corps asked how Urquhart felt about it – the group included both Younghusband and Wise – who replied with the kind of succinct demeanour for which he was renowned: 'Better beaten than eaten.'

There were quite a few more daft experiences. I once tried to take explosives on board an Israeli passenger aircraft, though that sounds much worse than it was. But I have yet to meet another journalist who has succeeded in taking ammunition onto an El Al jet full of passengers. I did so, twice.

A friend in what was then still South West Africa, Colonel Des Radmore, collected head stamps of AK-47 ammunition. It was an unusual interest, and he was said to have accumulated one of the largest private collections of the stuff in the world. Des had heard that I was going to Lebanon and asked if I'd try to get him a few AK cartridges with Arabic head stamps.

I flew from Johannesburg to Israel and then on to Larnaca in Cyprus, where we were picked up by a boat that took us to Jounieh, the Christian port just north of Beirut. While in Lebanon, I acquired a dozen AK-47 rounds, some Syrian, others Iraqi, and a few with obscure markings. They seemed no different from run-of-the-mill Bulgarian, Soviet or East German rounds that the South African forces in Angola were picking up, but my friend believed otherwise.

In Beirut, I promptly shoved the rounds (all live) into a side pocket of my overnight bag and went back to Cyprus by boat (Middle East Airlines in the Lebanon having suspended all flights because of the civil war). Only after I'd been standing in the queue at Larnaca Airport on my way back to Tel Aviv did I see two Israelis frisking passengers and their luggage ahead of me. Cyprus Airport had no X-ray equipment in those days.

The Israelis were nosy, abrasively so, but as efficient as only Israeli airline personnel can be because we were aware that the danger of an Arab terrorist attack in those days was very real. The terror group, the Popular Front for the Liberation of Palestine (PFLP), had blown up three Western passenger aircraft on the ground at Dawson's Field at Zarqa in Jordan not long before. To this day, I don't know how I managed to talk my way past those two women, but I did. The process was repeated a day or two later when I boarded another El Al flight for Johannesburg, this time with the rounds secreted deep in my checked-in baggage.

What inspired me was the knowledge that if they found the ammunition, they'd arrest me, and I would almost certainly miss my flight. However, I just knew that I'd be able to prove I meant no harm. Besides, I was a military correspondent already known to the Israeli authorities since I'd worked with the IDF on several fronts, including Beirut after Ariel Sharon had taken the city.

I would do foolish things like that in those days. Those who got to know me well would sometimes say something along the lines that it was time that I grew up, and I suppose they were right.

The Rhodesian War, or Bush War – also called the Second Chimurenga[1] and, to some, the Zimbabwean War of Liberation followed – having started erratically in the early sixties.

It continued in phases until late 1979 when Prime Minister Ian Smith, with intense British pressure, decided to call it a day. He faced opposition on all fronts, including a blockade of Mozambique ports to halt Rhodesian exports, and preponderant guerrilla numbers were causing too many casualties. At one stage, 12,000 guerrillas were being trained in Libya, Tanzania and Ethiopia, while 10,000 more had infiltrated Rhodesia.

In any event, the whites, who had been in charge of things for almost a century, still only had a population equivalent to a city the size of England's Bournemouth. For all that, the Rhodesians had held out. They fought hard for 13 years, quite an achievement considering that the Soviets and Chinese were handing the insurgents all the military hardware they needed, mainly channelled through Dar es Salaam (ironically named 'Harbour of Peace').

---

1   *Chimurenga*: war of liberation (Shona). The First Chimurenga occurred in 1896, so so-called Shona Rebellion.

South Africa gave material and military support to Ian Smith's government, which had unilaterally declared Rhodesia independent from Britain in November 1965. By then, my predilection for conflict took over, having survived and enjoyed my brief Nigerian sojourn, which meant that I went on to cover the Biafran War quite soon after returning to South Africa from West Africa.

Other times, I would go north of the border from South Africa (by then I had moved from Cape Town to Johannesburg) doing so scores of times in a dozen years. Sometimes I'd fly or travel by road, which was often enough, occasionally with my wife, traversing the lonely road between Bulawayo and Beit Bridge without another car in sight for hours at a stretch, just hoping to hell that we didn't run into trouble.

Along the route, there would be much evidence of the low-key insurrection that gripped the country: burnt-out vehicles abandoned by who-knows-who in the bush that had been raked by gunfire and others that even on surfaced roads had tripped landmines. It was pre-IED, and some of these bombs were manually activated.

Once Madelon and I travelled on our own across a dirt road to an army base in the remote bush country in the south, another lonely journey of about a hundred miles, and we didn't see a single car; the only villages we passed had been abandoned. There was not a soul along the route.

It was her idea to visit a friend whose husband was then serving in the Rhodesian Army, and it was mid-afternoon when we set out from Fort Victoria. Halfway there, I realised we had possibly made a bad mistake because we could be waylaid at any time. The road was in bad shape, with swathes of low-hanging tree branches and foliage partly covering it in places. Somebody described it as ideal ambush country – all we had for protection was her little .38 Special snubbie and my Colt .45 ACP – no match even for a lone AK.

We got through in the end and spent a few days in the local officer's quarters quaffing beer for Africa, and then headed back on a Sunday morning with an escort for part of the way. We did that kind of thing in Africa in those days because we were young and in love and believed implicitly that the fates would protect us.

Another time, shortly after we met, we drove through Botswana to spend the New Year with the great white hunter Harry Selby and his family at Xugana on the eastern fringes of the Okavango Delta. This was wild Africa in the traditional sense – lions shuffling around our tents after dark – and one afternoon Harry took me out about a mile into the bush to shoot a buffalo. It was a spectacular camp, almost hidden in a most beautiful part of the Okavango, where tourists would easily be charged $2,000 a night per person today if not more.

We swam in a huge lagoon on the banks of which the camp was perched, even though we were aware that there were crocodiles around because there were dozens of little ones in the shallows. As if that wasn't enough, we'd lounge in the sun while lying on inflatable mattresses in the middle of that magnificent stretch of water as big as three or four football fields, surrounded by papyrus. It was crazy; we realised afterwards because people were being taken all the time – if not by crocs, then charged by the occasional hippo.

Then, on the trip back to civilisation, again by road, we had a bit of a run-in with a small group of insurgents on the main road between Francistown and Ramathlabama, not purposely aggressive but hardly sociable either. They were all Zimbabwe People's Revolutionary Army (ZIPRA) guerrillas and displayed their weapons to stop us along another lonely stretch of road.

The group of fighters meant no harm because all they wanted from us – about six or eight of them – was a lift to the next town. I said we'd take two. No, they countermanded – we had to take them all. It was impossible, so I told their leader to get fucked and drove off. I was pretty sure they wouldn't gun us down in a country that was playing uneasy host to their forces – and as it turned out (because the alternative was too ghastly to contemplate) – I was proved right. Nonetheless, the risk was enormous. If asked to do that today, I'd probably offer to take the lot and buy them all two or three rounds of beer.

War or no war, these were magic times in Africa in the 1970s. By then, I was working for Republican Press, or 'RP' as we all referred to the company, the largest magazine group in Africa, and it helped that all its foreign assets in Rhodesia had been frozen. It also meant that none of its money could be repatriated. But that didn't prevent me from spending much of it each time I went to cover the war.

With a phone call to the local representative of RP, I'd let her know that I would be heading in her direction. On my first morning in Salisbury, we'd make contact, and she'd hand over bundles of Rhodesian cash, usually thousands of dollars at a time. I made the best use of it: 'location expenses', it was called. The trouble was that I couldn't take any Rhodesian dollars home because they were worthless abroad.

That suited me just fine – for the best part of a decade, I was able to cover that insurgency almost continuously – and gain an astonishing amount of experience in matters military. And that from somebody who didn't know the difference between an RPG and an RPD when first I set out.

Throughout this period, I was able to feed a host of publications abroad – including a Swiss magazine group in Geneva and photos to Gamma Presse Images and its opposition, Sipa, both in France. With these other interests, I eventually earned the kind of money that allowed me to build a rather beautiful home in Noordhoek, one of Cape Town's better suburbs along the Peninsula. Working abroad, it was all tax-free and that helped.

Using company money in Rhodesia, with no oversight whatever, I'd hire cars, stay in the five-star Monomotapa Hotel (which local forces had dubbed 'The Claymore' because it had the curiously concave shape that resembled that device), ate like an epicure at Meikles, and moved about the country as and when I pleased. When I moved beyond Salisbury's reasonably secure security bubble – I did that a lot – there were obvious risks, but I accepted that it was part of the job.

By then, I'd started communicating with several Americans, many with good experience of their own wars in Southeast Asia and quite a few were eager to experience an African conflict for themselves. I played host to many of these young fellows, courtesy of Republican Press, and I'd usually ask them, as a recompense, to bring along a handgun or two, which I'd started to collect.

Each one of these Americans toted at least one large-calibre 'piece' on arrival in Rhodesia, and some even became members of the only recognised media centre in the country, the Quill Club, which was as much a hangout of local and foreign journalists and spooks as the inevitable 'guns for hire'.

It also helped that quite a few Americans were serving in the Rhodesian Army. Among the best-known was Bob MacKenzie, who operated with distinction in the Rhodesian SAS, even though he had been invalided from the Vietnam War with a crippling arm wound. Once that conflict ended, Bob was appointed second-in-charge to former Selous Scouts commander Colonel Ron Reid-Daly in the Transkei Army.

Major 'Mike' Williams found himself a useful role in a mounted combat unit. Following some unconventional stints in Asia, Mike served as the tactical commander of the Grey's Scouts, the country's famed mounted infantry. Others included Chris Johnson from Houston, Texas, who'd initially served two tours with a Marine Recon Battalion, and Airborne/Ranger-qualified Bob Nicholson from Fortune, California, both of whom eventually found a home in the Rhodesian Army.

All these mercenaries saw a good deal of action in a war being tackled daily at the 'sharp end', usually led by Fire Force elements whose combatants went into action as airmobile detachments. Major Nigel Henson, who commanded Support Commando, Rhodesian Light Infantry (RLI) for thirty months, reckoned that his guys were called out hundreds of times, of which only six operations resulted in no contact with the enemy, or 'lemons', as they were dubbed.

Their complement also included quite a few adventurers – British, Germans, French and South Africans, as well as American veterans of foreign wars who, having come to Rhodesia in search of some form of befuddled excitement that involved guns, preferred not to join the army. Salisbury didn't object – every additional potential combatant, freelance or not – meant an armed presence in a potentially hostile zone.

Some managed to ensconce themselves with numerous others guarding farms or in anti-stock theft units in the country's interior. Almost all had done stints in Vietnam, including former US Marine Bob Miller, ex-Special Forces Roger Barnes and Joe Harcourt, who'd spent time with the 173rd Airborne. There were quite a few others who'd rather keep their names to themselves, including a few intelligence operatives, I'd imagine.

One of the most notable of that crowd became a good friend with whom I am still in regular touch. That's Dave McGrady, who ended up as a mercenary in South Lebanon for the mainly Christian South Lebanese Army. He'd worked for a while as a bounty hunter in a Rhodesian Tribal Trust Land midway between Victoria Falls and Bulawayo – and at one stage, I and two other crazy adventurers from Johannesburg joined him on one of his exploits. To no one's surprise, we came damn near to getting ourselves killed.

The ZIPRA troops that we were targeting were a lot more seasoned, tough and better-armed than our tiny bunch of civvies. They were also equipped with the kind of firepower that made that war tick, not the little Mini-14 and three grenades that I carried or Dave's much more efficient M15 – small wonder then that the guerrillas eventually ended up hunting us instead of the reverse. In fact, we were lucky to get away alive.

Though I was only able to garner details about the behind-the-scenes brouhaha of that effort more than a year later from friends in the Rhodesian Army, the guerrillas – a force of several dozen – were apparently right on our tail towards the end of a sojourn that lasted less than a week, only we didn't know it. They were perhaps half a mile behind us by the time we used an old pontoon to take us back across the river from where we had initially set out and to safety. For that effort, I was finally banned from entering Rhodesia as a correspondent. On a personal level, it didn't matter much because the security situation north of Limpopo was falling apart.

The war in Rhodesia started slowly. Having infiltrated the Centenary area, most insurgent groups were primarily intent on laying mines and attacking the occasional vehicle not travelling in convoy. There were raids on farms, like the one in which another old friend – Arthur Cumming – was murdered, but the most significant effort was to subvert the locals. This wasn't difficult in the bush, where few Shona people had actual contact with Europeans.

Significantly, their support in the cities was muted, though clearly, in a bid to portray the war as white against black (even though black troops far outnumbered white units), they had some success.

For their part, the Rhodesians reacted by initiating a lesson they had been taught in Malaya, with rural people essentially relocated into protected villages – a process designed to cut the enemy off from food supplies and the kind of succour they'd formerly enjoyed.

In 1974, the RLI Fire Force concept emerged after a few hard lessons, using French-built Alouette III helicopter gunships – some obtained legally, but many bought 'under the counter' from Spain and other countries – as well as antiquated C-47 'Gooney Birds'. Over time, the RLI's Fire Force yielded impressive results[2] as did the RAR Fire Forces.

The Rhodesian Light Infantry went on to field all the commandos involved in those operations that lasted almost to the end of the war. RLI and RAR troops were

---

2   Chris Cocks, *Fire Force: A Trooper's War in the Rhodesian Light Infantry*. Amazon KDP: 2020.

sometimes sent on two consecutive missions a day, three on rare occasions and often dropped by parachute, virtually onto the heads of those they sought. Occasionally they were dropped from heights of as little as 300 feet, which barely allowed time for their parachutes to open.

Though foreign observers (and the enemy) perceived that the Alouette III helicopter was a frail machine, that was not the case. The Rhodesians proved in their bush war that those modest machines could take a good deal of punishment. A notable shortcoming was that the little chopper gunships didn't have the rocket capability of Russian helicopters or the French Gazelles.

Built by France as an interim measure, there's hardly a European, African or Asian air force that hasn't deployed the Alouette in a military or police role in the past half-century. Relatively easy to maintain, this is a copter that typically burns jet fuel, though in emergencies it will fly on petroleum, but only for short duration.

In brief, the 'Alo' – as aficionados call it – is a rugged and well-built little craft that can absorb its share of fire. On occasion, this gunship would survive hits from anti-tank rockets. In Rhodesia, for instance, Ted Lunt's K-Car (command gunship, armed with a 20 mm MG 151 cannon) took an RPG blast in his tail section, and he could still fly the old bird home.

Not long afterwards, Dick Paxton's K-Car was peppered with automatic fire when he flew over a well-camouflaged insurgent camp. With all his instruments shattered and a rotor blade punctured, he ignored the damage, climbed to an operational height of about 800 feet and put down a curtain of suppressive fire before heading home. This was Dick Paxton, who, after the war, served for a while as a mercenary pilot in Sri Lanka.

Then came the incident involving the celebrated Mike Borlace – still on choppers and not yet transferred to Ron Reid-Daly's Selous Scouts – the same man who hired Bob MacKenzie to fight in Sierra Leone a few years later. After an action against a guerrilla detachment in the bush, Borlace brought his Alouette safely back to Fort Victoria with its tail rotor drive shaft severed. If an Alouette takes a hit in the engine or main rotor gearbox, the show is over, but somehow, he'd managed to nurse his machine – and himself – back to safety. The chopper was flying again a week later.

The 'Alo', the mainstay of the Rhodesian government's reactive strike force could carry a pilot and five fully equipped troops, depending on fuel and ammo loaded. In practice, the Rhodesians would load four troops plus a technician/gunner, which resulted in the strength of the average Rhodesian 'stick' being limited to four troops who would sometimes stay out in the bush on anti-terrorism patrols for weeks at a stretch, usually without backup.

During casualty evacuation runs (referred to in the southern African wars as a casevac), the wounded were customarily laid out flat behind the pilot. If the action took place in the northeast, they'd be airlifted to the Andrew Fleming Hospital in

Salisbury. There was also provision made in these choppers for external slings that could transport cargoes up to about three-quarters of a ton. Some nifty machine!

Many incredible stories emerged from the war, and sadly a good deal more have fallen between the cracks because those involved have passed on.

Historian Richard Wood tells the story of Vic Cook, who, with a medic on board on the way to a local church mission station, was flying an Alouette at 800 feet when a volley of AK rounds straddled the helicopter. Below, operating from an insurgent base camp – as security forces were to discover later – were 30 insurgents trying their best to bring the chopper down. A hasty survey of the damage told Cook that his tech was semi-conscious after being hit by two rounds that penetrated his body armour, and that his tail rotor shaft had been all but severed. The pilot took his craft down to treetop level, still under fire because he was almost on top of them.

> A lot more rounds hit us, and it was fierce. I felt the controls going, there was vibration, and I realised that one way or another, I had to try to bring the machine down in a single piece… More rounds were coming in, and when I lost tail rotor control, the helicopter began swinging violently, to and fro. Because it would have cart-wheeled had I done nothing, I pulled the Alo up on its tail to knock off forward momentum…and while speed came down, we continued to yaw. It's then that I saw them – they were about two rugby teams strong and just kept on firing.

At that point, Cook saw a group of five or six enemy ahead and decided to aim his helicopter directly at them. 'We thumped in nose first, and I lost sight of them for a little while, just as a piece of the control column came off in my hand.'

The impact on hitting the ground jerked Cook forward, knocking his jaw onto the top of the control stick, cutting his chin and stunning him. His foot was also gravely injured: only when he looked down did he see a deep gash in his leg with the bone protruding. Worse, his Uzi sub-machine gun had taken a hit and was inoperable.

Aware that the engine was still idling – which led the opposition to think they were okay – Cook realised that if he were to survive, he'd need a weapon. One of the guerrillas lay ahead of his wreck. 'He'd been hit by a rotor when we crash-landed, and alongside was his AK… I knew then that we'd all be killed if I didn't get to that weapon and fast. Though the tech had come to, he said he couldn't move, so it was up to me.'

Victor Cook went on to do what he never believed would have been possible. He recovered the Kalashnikov and started firing at the rest of the insurgent group, who were about a hundred metres away, all the while moving from one bit of cover, one clump of rock to the next in what had suddenly become a very personal war.

Meantime, the Rhodesian Army call sign that had called Cook from Rutenga (in southeastern Rhodesia) and had heard the crash – and the subsequent firing – summoned help. That came almost an hour later in the shape of a Rhodesian Air Force Cessna FTB, which laid down a curtain of fire around the crippled chopper. The RLI dropped its Fire Force into the area not long afterwards and immediately launched a follow-up, the guerrillas having grabbed their things and fled.

For his efforts, Vic Cook was awarded the Silver Cross. His comment at the time was that he didn't deserve it. 'I only did what was needed to keep us all alive.'

At best, the Rhodesians were never able to field more than fifty Alouette IIIs (many on loan from South Africa) throughout the war, with Agusta-Bell 206s (the latter bought illicitly from the Israelis) arriving towards the end of hostilities. In addition, the Rhodesian Air Force had perhaps a dozen former RAF Hawker-Hunter fighter-bombers and a handful of Canberra bombers. That wasn't much when one accepts that the country's entire army, apart from Special Forces, consisted of a single armoured car regiment, one artillery regiment and three regular infantry regiments (one RLI and two RAR), one mounted regiment (Grey's Scouts), backed up by ten battalions of territorial and reserve troops.

Except RLI, all these units were multiracial and included whites, soldiers of mixed blood (called 'Coloureds' locally), and Asians. In addition, the paramilitary British South Africa Police or BSAP played a significant role throughout the war, usually in conjunction with the military. Its Special Branch invariably emerged with intelligence gathered while working close to the ground in the interior.

CHAPTER 21

Pen-pushing pals

Ultimately, most roads in those distant days seemed to lead to Ian Smith's Rhodesia. Mozambique and Angola were already embroiled in guerrilla wars. It was only a question of time before hostilities jumped the fence into what had previously been known as Southern Rhodesia.

Unlike most other African states then undergoing some of the problems that followed *Uhuru* – slow trickles that eventually became floods – Rhodesia, in contrast, was always a fascinating country. Tourists came and went, some on vacation, others possibly buying a house to live there permanently. War or no war, they couldn't resist the allure of the county. Life was comfortable (if you did not have to do military service), property was affordable (compared to Europe), and to top it, the country boasted some of the best game parks on the continent, as well as the magnificent Victoria Falls and Lake Kariba.

And, yes, to paraphrase the old aphorism, Rhodesia in its glorious, impetuous heyday – as old-timers like to recollect – was the best of times. Sadly, because lives were being lost, it was also the worst of times. Furthermore, for the duration of the guerrilla struggle until Britain was forced to hand over the country to Robert Mugabe, the hacks of the world made it their business to be there.

We went in singly or in groups, each intent on getting our stories out. I spent nearly as much time to covering the Rhodesian War as I did to reporting on Portugal's forces in Angola, Mozambique and Portuguese Guinea. That meant being constantly on the move; as a result, home life suffered, and the children didn't see enough of me, nor I of them.

Yet, it was an exhilarating way to earn a living. Though we weren't shot at all that often – or not at all if you weren't with one of the operational units – Rhodesians involved in maintaining the status quo or trying to do so came under fire.

Salisbury, the capital, rarely came under direct attack and few of the reporting squad experienced any combat. A tiny handful became casualties, usually because they were in the wrong place at the wrong time.

Unquestionably, there was always an element of risk when leaving the city precincts. Travelling on gravel roads that days before (and often after) might have claimed their share of victims from Soviet TM-46 and TM-57 anti-tank mines was always of concern. So were explicit pictures of farmers, their families and black civilians who had accidentally tripped them.

While we saw our share of vehicles that these bombs had blasted; let's just say that most of us who ventured into these contested zones and emerged with little more than hangovers were very lucky indeed. We must have been because we sometimes heard from our hosts with whom we'd occasionally stay the night that a landmine or two had been lifted along the same road we'd travelled.

Rhodesia's war started slowly. There were minor guerrilla incursions into the country in the early 1960s, mainly from Zambia, and these were promptly dealt with. The Rhodesian Army was already well prepared to cope with the expected insurgencies; their nearest neighbour, Mozambique to the immediate east, had started battling guerrillas not long before – a threat that entered the Portuguese colony from Tanzania to its extreme north.

Then things started to deteriorate, a gradual process after groups of Rhodesian insurgents, having been trained in the Soviet Union, Tanzania, Ethiopia, Libya and elsewhere, infiltrated across the Zambezi to plant landmines in otherwise sacrosanct wildlife reserves such as Wankie (Hwange today), Mana Pools and Gonarezhou, north of South Africa's Kruger National Park.

Militarily, the conflict in this African state spread from the northeast and then southwards. Eventually a new rebel organisation called the Zimbabwe People's Revolutionary Army (ZIPRA) entered the war from Zambia, opening a new operational region and using Lusaka as its operational staging post. For all that and their vaunted claims, the guerrillas could never capture or even properly infiltrate a single town. Instead, the real problem for the defenders was the insurgents' superior numbers: there were just too few government troops on the ground.

Essentially, the war was initially contained by that country's minuscule armed forces. Still, after years of fighting and enormous demands made materially and time-wise upon the tiny white community, many of these people voted with their feet. This resulted, in part, with the disaffected claiming some regions that were formerly tribal, labelled 'no go' areas, and many bitter battles followed.

However, the guerrillas were rarely a match for the professionals, even though their numbers were disproportionately superior. In the final phase of the war (between the Rhodesian elections of the Muzorewa government in April 1979 until the ceasefire arranged by Britain in December of that year), the RLI's four Fire Force commandos killed almost 1,700 enemy soldiers.

In one of my last discussions with former Rhodesian Prime Minister Ian Smith at his home in Harare – before he moved to Cape Town, where that 80-year-old former Battle of Britain pilot died in an assisted living establishment – he disclosed that it was what he called 'the numbers game' that got to him in the end.

'Once I started getting figures that revealed – it was all secret, of course – that I was losing the equivalent of a company of fighting men a month, I knew that I wouldn't be able to sustain the war indefinitely. I was then aware that I had to settle hostilities…I had no option but to talk with those people, which, in the end, London facilitated,' he told me.

By 1979, the last year of actual hostilities, about 2,000 whites were leaving Rhodesia each month. With nobody moving the other way – except the occasional mercenary who had been reading *Soldier of Fortune* and the odd mainstream press report – the country had become seriously stretched due to the relentless loss of skilled and trained manpower.

At the same time, the former prime minister admitted that the outcome was close run. 'The guerrillas were taking some mighty losses in the final stages of the war and had thousands of their comrades killed in combined cross-border strikes into Mozambique,' he declared.

The first major cross-border raid into enemy territory in August 1976, for example, was headed by the Selous Scouts at Nyadzonya, Mozambique, a ZANLA[1] guerrilla base and resulted in about 1,200 recruits killed. Morale plummeted, and the leaders, Robert Mugabe, Joshua Nkomo and Rex Nhongo, told this sizeable insurgent army that such losses were the price that had to be paid for success, and that Salisbury would soon capitulate. But it wasn't happening, not then, anyway.

Initially, the surrounding states were eager to assist in what Dar es Salaam termed as 'The Liberation Struggle' (that had already seen off Lisbon's ragtag armies in Angola, Portuguese Guinea and Mozambique). They were becoming increasingly nervous about being dragged into a full-scale war with the 'White South' (as South Africa was referred to). Their fear was valid since Pretoria had served the Allies well through two world wars and by the late-1970s had become the best-equipped and most efficient fighting force in Africa.[2]

Zambia, already host to 25,000 guerrillas – over and above Joshua Nkomo's ZIPRA troops – included forces from South Africa's ANC and Namibia's SWAPO,[3] powerfully supported by the Soviet Union. These foreign fighters outnumbered the

1   ZANLA (Zimbabwe African National Liberation Army), the military wing of the Zimbabwe African National Union (ZANU), a Marxist–Leninist political party in Rhodesia led by Robert Mugabe.

2   Few people know, even in Britain today, that the highest scoring Royal Air Force and Commonwealth fighter ace of World War II was a young South African by the name of M. St. J. Pattle; his final tally of kills in aerial action (almost all Luftwaffe) numbered in excess of fifty. An excellent book on his exploits has just been republished, titled *Ace of Aces: The Incredible Story of Pat Pattle – the Greatest Fighter Pilot of WWII*. Silvertail Books, UK: 2020.

3   South West Africa People's Organisation.

Zambian Army by something like two to one. This disparity made President Kaunda nervous, especially since large numbers of these guerrillas were housed in bases that surrounded Lusaka, his capital. Kaunda felt that if things didn't go as expected, the rebel presence – and the daunting amount of hardware these irregular armies had acquired from Moscow – could ultimately threaten his country's political stability.

There was another factor which concerned the major powers more than the guerrillas: the secret development by South Africa of nuclear weapons. Not many people know that the Pretoria regime had started building atom bombs – six of them by the time that remarkably successful programme was discontinued.

Preparing for a major survival-orientated confrontation made good sense to the South Africans. The country was being directly threatened by a Soviet and Cuban force that was five or eight times larger than all the troops Pretoria had deployed in Angola in the 1980s, and no question, the threat became the biggest the country had faced in modern times. What better deterrent than a handful of nukes to make Moscow and Havana think twice about invading southwards? Documents released after the collapse of the Soviet Union made that clear – the ultimate objective was Cape Town – which would make them dominant across one of the most significant trade (including oil) routes on the globe.

By then, the major powers were aware of South Africa's nuclear potential, and it did not take long for the Americans to speak directly to the Russians about the implications. The upshot was peace talks – successful as it transpired because the 23-year-long Border War ended a short while later – and Pretoria dismantled its nuclear weapons potential.

Under the auspices of American and British scientists, coordinated by the United Nations International Atomic Energy Agency (IAEA), it was a hugely complex two-year process but ultimately successful.

Effectively, South Africa became the first nation to surrender its nuclear bombs voluntarily. It was perhaps the biggest scoop of my career, as detailed in the four books I have written on the subject. These include *How South Africa Built Six Atom Bombs*; *Nuclear Terror: The Bomb and Other Weapons of Mass Destruction in the Wrong Hands* and the seminal *Iran's Nuclear Option* published by Casemate in the United States and which for me, initially set the ball rolling in 2005.[4]

Obviously, the Rhodesian War must have played a small but potentially potent role. With an aggressive and unfriendly political force taking power in Rhodesia (later renamed Zimbabwe), South Africa and South West Africa (soon independent Namibia), were surrounded by hostile countries, except for Botswana. The entire

---

4   Al J. Venter, *Nuclear Terror: The Bomb and Other Weapons of Mass Destruction in the Wrong Hands*.
     Pen & Sword: 2018.

region could eventually be enveloped in a cauldron of fire, especially since we all knew that the end was approaching fast for Rhodesia.

Politically, Smith conceded that while his country didn't actually lose the war – not in the military sense – Rhodesia finally surrendered at the negotiating table at Whitehall in London. That came after weeks of negotiations that were both bitter and recriminating and ended when Britain handed Rhodesia to the man hailed by Fleet Street as one of 'Africa's great emerging leaders'.

How ironic, especially when one accepts that this was the same tyrant that the world, for decades, recognised as Robert Mugabe, President of Zimbabwe.

He was also the man who drove out most of the farmers from their land, bulldozing many hundreds of squatter camps in his cities, led his people – previously the region's biggest grain producer/exporter – into starvation (and ultimately dependence on United States food aid) and for many years cuddled up to Libya, China, Cuba and North Korea to deliver him from his mind-boggling intransigence.

Although the opening shots of the guerrilla campaign had been fired in 1965, Rhodesia's Operation *Hurricane* was the principal start of it all in 1972 when an intensive series of counterinsurgency campaigns were launched and as phrased by the military spokesman in Salisbury, 'to wipe out this insidious menace'. As far as the Rhodesians were concerned, hostilities gradually progressed towards fully fledged ground and air operations. These spawned the kind of terminology that eventually became commonplace: Fire Force, chopper gunships and four-man combat 'sticks', all of which lasted six difficult years.

As a result, Salisbury, the Rhodesian capital, became the focus of global media interest, though not on the same scale as Vietnam at the time. Nor was that African war nearly as intense as what was happening in Southeast Asia, but what did emerge were some rather noteworthy developments: several firsts for Africa.

Of all the foreign correspondent postings, Rhodesia was considered by the majority of war reporters and TV crews as the most desired posting abroad because, simply put, the country was superlative in many respects. It enjoyed an excellent standard of living, several notches up from what most of those professionals had enjoyed in their home countries, and effectively they found themselves 'in the pound seats'.

Foreign news-gatherers permanently operating out of Salisbury lived like proverbial 'peers of the realm' with some employing strings of servants that included cooks, housekeepers, babysitters and gardeners – all that coupled with cheap liquor (even if some of it was 'home-grown' – the local whiskey was awful).

Together with the media, dissident Americans and other foreigners with indiscernible accents, there were arguably more spooks gathered there than elsewhere in Africa. There were more soirées and outdoor social gatherings than most would experience at any other time in their lives. Rhodesia, as they would tell you if asked, was tops.

As *The New York Times* correspondent Michael T. Kaufman reported from Salisbury in an article titled 'From an Embattled Land', published on 11 July 1976, Rhodesia was a very unusual place. I quote:[5]

> The place arouses passions and inflames prejudices, but most of all, it confounds notions of time and logic. Tom Mix is on the telly, the band at Meikles Hotel plays ersatz Cole Porter and men in dinner jackets and women in long dresses dance nightly as if cruising on the *Titanic*. Black militants, urging all-out war, say they cannot go on strike because they will lose their jobs. Jews are not admitted to the Salisbury Club, and Polo is played every Sunday…

Kaufman's report is unusually forthright for the firmly left *The New York Times*. He took the initiative on several issues, including heading out deep into disputed areas and overnighting with some white farmers, fully aware that many of the roads he ventured on were mined. Overall, he reported the good, as well as the ugly and his comments about the capital were insightful:

> On the surface, in Salisbury, there is no tension. The city's well-kept, crime-free core radiates into a sprawl of white suburbs, with their large plots, large homes and some 20,000 private swimming pools. The whites, feeling more English than the English, are devoted to 'maintaining the standards'. And so too, in an odd way, are the blacks.
>
> When the government permitted a demonstration of perhaps a thousand black nationalists in the centre of town earlier this year, there was a make-believe quality about the signs that screamed 'War, not talks' and 'Rhodesia will be won in blood'.
>
> After about an hour, an unarmed white policeman in knee socks walked towards the milling crowd and said, 'All right, chaps. I think it's time you went home.' Without a murmur of protest, the crowd dispersed.

Kaufmann did add a guarded, 'that's all on the surface. Underneath, something else may be at work.'

The reality of what was going on throughout the war was that Salisbury's affluent suburbs were basically white, with the black population relegated to townships on the outskirts (as in the South Africa of the time), though this disparity weakened somewhat towards the end of Ian Smith's tenure.

Most importantly, communications were good. You could lift the phone and call just about anywhere. For most news folk living there semi-permanently, you couldn't ask for better, even if some of these notable characters ended up literally drinking themselves into early graves.

As Kenyan journalist Aidan Hartley phrased it in one of his columns for the British *The Spectator*, 'Budgets were fat, as were the opportunities for fiddling expenses, and in those days, African scoops got plenty of column space in the foreign pages.'

This novel bunch came from all over the world to report – the majority understandably outspoken for the black African underdog and not afraid to say so – though some were deported for taking too strong a line in their daily despatches.

---

5   Michael T. Kaufman, 'From an Embattled Land', *The New York Times,* 11 July 1976.

There were some famous names involved, some not entirely forgotten, and others no longer with us: Xan Smiley of *Africa Confidential*, Bill Deedes, James McManus, the irrepressible Donald Wise (tall, lean, and possessed of a bristling moustache), Ernie Christie, Mike Knipe (who travelled to Mozambique and spent time with me along the Zambezi during that colonial war), Derek Ingram, Martin Meredith, François Marais, Peter Niesewand and more.

Another character was Holger Jensen of *Newsweek*, a remarkable man of adventure who is reputed to have been wounded numerous times while covering the Vietnam War. Holger did have a predilection for getting into the thick of things when they got nasty. An American of Danish extraction, Holger was born in Japanese-occupied China and went to school in South Africa. He was outspoken enough to have been 'let go' as Foreign Editor of Denver's *Rocky Mountain News* because of his uncompromising stance on Israeli–Arab issues. Ian Colvin, who began his career with the *News Chronicle* in Berlin (the Nazis expelled him in 1939), was another professional much in demand for his news reports.

The 'tribe', for they were precisely that; proud, disdainful of those who did not share their sentiments, and often arrogant, displayed a fascinating cornucopia of talents in the main. Most were high-flyers who had earned their spurs in a few of the globe's trouble spots, Vietnam included. Don Wise was a multifaceted former Special Forces operative and adventurer who charmed all with his trenchant wit and gift for storytelling.

'Elegance was Donald's middle name,' said Pulitzer Prize-winning war correspondent Bill Tuohy. 'He had courage, talent, and a zest for showing us how to report and live.' Long before he came anywhere near Rhodesia, he was already referred to by his colleagues as 'The David Niven of Journalism'.

Bill Deedes was another raconteur ahead of his time and blessed with a wicked but subtle sense of humour. He had his own view of these goings-on, which he usually shared towards the end of a lengthy liquid lunch, heralded when the first calls of night jars rendering their distinctive and frequently uttered calls of 'good-lord-deliver-us' sounded in nearby hedges and trees. Bill once declared that were Evelyn Waugh still alive and set his delightful satire on news-gathering in southern Africa – instead of in pre-war Abyssinia – quite a few of these zany characters would have been appropriately featured in a later version of *Scoop*.

The *Telegraph*'s Chris Munnion always managed to capture a marvellously evocative recollection of those times in his book *Banana Sunday* – as did Peter Younghusband – with one of the best works to emerge from the epoch, *Every Meal's a Banquet, Every Night's a Honeymoon*. If you can get your hands on either of these two titles, hold onto them tight because they are classic interpretations of that genre.

John Monks, who reported for London's *Daily Express* and Peter Younghusband of the *Daily Mail*, were, as previously mentioned dubbed 'The Terrible Twins' by us insiders, mainly because they went where few other journalists covering the African beat dared to venture, but there was much more. Though in fierce competition with one another, representing as they did two of Fleet Street's biggest-selling tabloids, the link-up probably made good sense because the one could then keep track of what the other was up to.

Peter risked his life several times in the Congo's wars and subsequent army mutinies. He even flew over North Korea in a United States Navy F-4 Phantom II from a navy aircraft carrier.

Monks had an equally stimulating career. Australian-born, he was the son of Noel Monks, one of the famous correspondents of the European conflict who was inducted into the Australian Media Hall of Fame and something of a celebrity in his own right. His stepmother was Mary Welsh, one of his father's wartime colleagues whom Hemingway, not as discreetly as some would have liked, wooed and won while her husband was reporting from the front.

The American author Robin Moore of Green Beret fame established his Crippled Eagle Club as a kind of unofficial United States Embassy in Salisbury – in response to Washington's acquiescence in the face of Soviet encroachment in Africa – which he regarded as rampant.

Another regular visitor was Colonel Robert K. Brown, who founded and ran the controversial military-orientated magazine, *Soldier of Fortune*, today a shadow of what it was in the old days. Love it or hate it, this 'Journal of Professional Adventurers' as it was called, had a significant following both in the US government and the military, though no self-respecting career officer would ever admit to having read it.

I first met Brown when he flew to South Africa from Boulder, Colorado, the idea being to meet and discuss the founding of his fledgling mag. Because he'd been involved with Fidel Castro during the Cuban revolution, the South Africans refused to allow him into the country. Having experienced the consequences of Cuban-style socialism, it mattered little that Brown had done a political about-face and become vehemently anti-communist. He and I talked for an hour in a restricted area, and I was appointed the magazine's first foreign correspondent.

While it would be simplistic to label him an unmitigated adventurer, Bob Brown vigorously pursued his anti-Soviet cause, to the point where Moscow's KGB eventually labelled him an imperialist propagandist. That pleased the man, and interestingly, there was a time when his favourite lapel button read, 'I'd Rather be Killing Communists'.

Meanwhile, though he'd mellowed some, Bob's mindset was always intractable and contradictory. He'd coined a maxim by paraphrasing Winston Churchill's words during the Boer War: 'The most exhilarating experience in the world is to be fired at with no effect,' to which Brown added, 'and to fire back.'

Bob Brown came to Southern Africa often enough to seek adventure, and we'd drive up from Johannesburg to Salisbury or wherever we wished to see a little action. When in Rhodesia, he was a regular at the Quill Club, a private bar in the

Ambassador Hotel maintained by the Salisbury Press Club. As with the University of Rhodesia, it was a sanctuary where blacks and whites could come together and where membership was open not only to journalists but to lawyers, politicians and businessmen. There was always a plain-clothes Special Branch presence, the intelligence unit of the Rhodesian police.

Another aspect of life in Rhodesia was that you could arrive at Salisbury Airport or any of the country's frontier posts with guns and ammunition and be allowed entry, no questions asked.

Just about everybody not in uniform carried a weapon, including a good few of my pen-pushing pals. We would arrive in the country through Beit Bridge or Salisbury Airport, and all that was needed – if you had a pistol or rifle in your possession – was to declare it. Sometimes you were even asked to let the local (white) official examine it.

Soldier of Fortune's Bob Brown and his clutch of vets would arrive with minor armouries, of which little was left by the time they left Rhodesia, the guns and ammo having been traded for enough cash to pay for their stay. While with them, I always carried my Colt .45 ACP, which had originally been Bob's: he handed it to me after I'd ferried him to Rhodesia and back from Johannesburg in the company car.

Eager to push the envelope, as was my wont after a bash with the boys, I pulled it out one night while staying at the Monomotapa Hotel with Colin Ainsworth Sharp, a British journalist then living and making a good deal of money in Johannesburg. Together, we attempted to shoot out streetlights on the road below from my hotel window. We stopped when someone on our floor warned that the cops were on the way. Looking back, it was juvenile, but quite good fun if you weren't caught. At the same time, there are few countries where you can get away with something like that in wartime: imagine trying the caper in Kyiv today.

CHAPTER 22

Betrayal!

On one of our last visits, Bob Brown and I spent some excellent time in Rhodesia's Matetsi area, hosted by Giorgio Grasselli, an Italian-born professional hunter. We'd branch out from his lodge, as Bob would phrase it, 'hunting, and looking for gooks.'

We never encountered any guerrillas even though we were all aware, judging by a strong security force presence. On that final safari, they almost found us – as events that followed our safari transpired.

We'd been scouring the bush on the farm of one of my old friends, Arthur Cumming, a dapper, brave individualist and a veteran of his country's bush war. Dubbed 'Gentleman Jim' by his unit, the Rhodesian Light Infantry, he was always impeccably turned out, whether in civvies or the distinctive mottled green camouflage gear worn by Ian Smith's 'rebel army'. We'd spent almost a week on the Cumming farm, and the routine was roughly the same each morning.

Before dawn, we'd go out in Arthur's Land Rover, and though we had to use gravel roads to get to our destination, which was troubling, we weren't deterred. Landmines had also been laid in much of that area over the years, but only a handful on the Cumming hunting concession – all of which had been lifted. In contrast, there were several instances nearby where insurgent mines had blasted vehicles and some occupants, children included, were killed.

We'd also been told that a few weeks before our arrival, guerrillas active in the region had used a couple of TM-57s to boost an explosive charge that dropped a span of the bridge across the nearby Matetsi River, all of which suggested vigilance. The ten-day hunting safari went off without a hitch though no enemy was encountered – so we all went our separate ways – the colonel and his boys back to America.

Bob was two hours into his flight to New York from southern Africa – we had spent a few hours the previous night in the Quill Club – when a flight attendant brought him a message from the cockpit. I'd persuaded an official at South African Airways to pass on by radio the news that Arthur Cumming had been murdered.

First details of him having been killed – which took place at the Cumming ranch two days after we'd left him – were sparse. We'd been hosted by Arthur and his wife Sandy in a region that had endured its share of hostilities, so we could relate to the little we'd heard.

Our tracker on this that leg of our Rhodesian adventure was Tickey, a Matabele tribesman who had been with the Cumming family for more than thirty years. Small, with a pinched face and wiry, he could read the bush like some people scan newspapers. Tickey could follow a trail through thick, mopani brush-covered country and tell you how many animals had used it, what they were, whether they were moving in haste or passively, and how long since they'd passed that way. As a man of the bush, this little African could spot a lioness in the long grass even before she knew he was there. As Arthur said, he was the best in his league, and his boss was justifiably proud of his ability: 'Part of my family,' he would say.

When asked about Tickey's loyalty, considering that so many tribal folks had been subverted, Arthur was unequivocal: 'I've grown up among his people, so did my dad and his dad. Consequently, *his* people are *my* people.' He went on to mention something about a bond of understanding between the Africans living on his ranch that he'd seen demonstrated repeatedly. In fact, the family was on such good terms with its staff that the Cumming family declined a government offer to erect a security fence around their farmhouse.

So who were we to argue when Tickey rode shotgun on board the four-by-four while we hunted the big stuff? What we didn't know – which only surfaced later – was that Tickey was already a fully paid-up member of the active guerrilla force in the region. Had he been a bit smarter, he could probably have led us into an ambush, and his associates might have bagged themselves a prominent pair of Americans because John Donovan was also part of the team. I'm not sure what they would have done to me had we been taken alive because I carried a British passport.

The supposed insurgent could undoubtedly have done so had he wished. Subsequent reports spoke of a squad of ZIPRA guerrillas, some 30 or 40 strong, having crossed the Zambezi River from Zambia into Rhodesia. Furthermore, they were armed with some of the best of what was available in the Soviet armoury, including the usual infantry squad weapons and RPG-7s.

Ultimately Tickey waited until the visitors had left, and a few nights later, he led his fellow guerrillas into the Cumming home. That occurred shortly after Arthur's brother Lawrence had left for Bulawayo earlier in the day.

At about nine that evening, Sandy Cumming, Arthur's pregnant wife, got up to lock the outside doors. Moments later – she recalled during her debrief at police headquarters – three black men wearing Rhodesian Army uniforms, complete with camouflage cloth caps entered the room from the kitchen. Her first words were, 'Arthur, what's the army doing in the house?'

All that Arthur could do was shout, 'Run, Sandy! Run for your life!' Seconds later, all three intruders opened up on him, and he crumpled in a heap on the cement floor. By then, Sandy, almost nine months pregnant, had slipped out through one of the side doors. Thirty seconds later, she heard more shots, some ricocheting off the concrete. The attackers, she knew, had delivered the coup de grâce.

She hid in a clump of foliage at the bottom of her garden, thereby surviving the attack, even though her husband's killers spent a while searching for her. Eventually she was able to sneak back and activate what was known as the AgricAlert system that had been installed as an alarm device in many farmhouses. And, though she played hide-and-seek with these killers a while longer, a nearby army patrol rushed to her rescue.

But even that took time because the favourite insurgent ploy in that war before an attack on a farmhouse, as with the Malayan Emergency some years before, was to lay a pattern of landmines – usually one anti-tank, surrounded by a cluster of anti-personnel mines – on the approach road. If nobody checked, those rushing forward would detonate one or more of these explosives.

What was particularly sad about the attack was that Arthur Cumming, though critically wounded, did not die immediately. For a radius of more than a hundred miles, the entire farming community of the northwest was connected to the same radio-based security system, so they could follow this spectacle – horrific as it was, first-hand.

They all heard Sandy's first call for help once she'd emerged from outside. They knew she'd have to hide again when the killers returned to the house after their search for her. Finally came the words, terse and poignant: 'Arthur is dead.'

Some years later, my hunting pal Giorgio Grasselli, gave us his impressions about what had happened:

> In Matetsi, disaster struck suddenly one night in November. As we did every evening, we switched on our AgricAlert two-way receiver at 7 o'clock and were waiting for our turn to check in. Our code was 'Whisky 30', the last of a long list, which meant that another 29 isolated households had to call the army base before us, one after the other. We were only allowed to jump the queue if there was an emergency.
>
> Every report was critical, from the sighting of people (mostly harmless) to firearms discharged (to be reported as soon as possible after the event, if hunting and, before, if shooting practice), and anything else considered suspect.
>
> That night everything seemed quiet, and within just ten minutes, all calls ended with a 'Good night, over and out.' That was usually followed by the usual routines of going over the grounds outside and locking up. The dogs followed me, wagging their tails and the horses in the stables gave no sign of being nervous.
>
> I went indoors and checked the state of the battery charge on the radio receiver, knowing that in case of an emergency, our lives might depend on it. We had supper at eight and usually went to bed at half past, but we stayed up for an hour longer that night.
>
> I turned off the gas lamps and checked again that all the doors were locked and then perceived, rather than heard, a feeble, anguished woman's voice repeating, 'Help, help!' I turned up the volume, but the tone seemed even lower, and then I heard nothing more. I sat on the floor with my wife next to the radio, our ears glued to it, both of us frozen in horror. Who could it be?

Suddenly, a professional-sounding, low-toned man's voice broke the silence and asked who was calling, repeating the question at short intervals. It was security forces headquarters, and a few minutes later, a woman's voice, still very low and interrupted by sobs, said, 'Help, this is Sandy Cumming...we have terrorists here. They've shot Arthur, and they're looking for me.'

Then another long agonising, never-ending silence. We sat there listening to the drama, unable to do anything about it. After what seemed an eternity, during which we were sure she'd been killed, we heard her voice again. 'Please come and help me!' It was heart-rending. We were 40 kilometres away with an Africa in total darkness between us but could do nothing.

Sadly, the press could hardly be considered to have excelled during the Rhodesian war; many came short, dismally so. Some of the names mentioned previously did what they were required to do despite stringent restrictions on what the media could or could not do. But then, as in most wars (Vietnam excluded), there are rules, sometimes involving access and, more often, censorship.

While I was fortunate to have covered several conflicts and managed to emerge with a reasonably intact reputation for telling it like it was – for many scribblers gathered in the Quill Club, this was their first real war. Some had seen action in Vietnam and knew the ropes. Others, short on scoops, made up their own, very much as foreign journalists had tried to taint South Africa by throwing chocolate bars into a bin and photographing kids scrambling. The headline on one of those images was: 'Starvation'.

I ran a few of these excesses in the series of articles I did on the war in *Scope* magazine, and these included:

- A TV sequence widely distributed in Europe showed Africans asleep in Salisbury's Cecil Square, an everyday occurrence after lunch. These were victims, the commentator said, shot dead by security forces.
- Another clip shown abroad included Soviet tanks 'rolling down Jameson Avenue in Salisbury'. Closer inspection revealed some distinctive Luanda landmarks.
- A German TV team visited Rhodesia at the same time as I did and filed a story on the 'Collapse of the Smith regime'. It showed shots of the Umtali Tattersalls with African punters viewing the runners on a notice board. These were labelled 'Africans looking at war casualties'.
- Another photo was taken in the city centre on a quiet Sunday afternoon. It depicted a deserted town with the commentator declaring that Umtali had been all but abandoned by its white residents.
- One that didn't take the cake was a demolition sequence to make way for some reconstruction at Salisbury's famous Meikles Hotel. That was depicted as the result of a guerrilla mortar attack.

After returning to town from our trips to the bush, sometimes searching for stories, or other times hunting, we writing types would gravitate to the Quill Club. There would invariably be quite a crowd, most of the journalists looking for a 'peg' which might please their editors abroad.

Most of the nightly simply had to accept that Rhodesia in a state of war (although you rarely heard a shot fired in anger in the country's capital) a situation that would sometimes attract its share of oddballs as well as a spook or two travelling under some guise or another.

For the duration of that guerrilla struggle that ended with Britain handing the country to Robert Mugabe – a man who was to become the tyrant of his age – hundreds of freebooters arrived from just about every other conflict on the planet to get 'a piece of the action', British and American veterans predominating.

There were even a few hopefuls from the Seychelles Islands fighting for who-knows-what in the Rhodesian Light Infantry and not one had been actually been recruited. Like all the other foreigners, they were volunteers, earning the same pitiful salaries as Rhodesia's conscripts.

Though Rhodesia became a regular destination for me as the war progressed, once I'd made my mark, I reported on wars in other parts of Africa, the Middle East and even El Salvador. While in Rhodesia, I generally operated alone while on assignment; for me, it was easier than trudging about with a disorganised squad of almost-permanently half-pissed journos.

Others, primarily freelancers who had already experienced war for themselves elsewhere, would follow, usually in concert. These were characters like 'Big John' Donovan, a retired reserve major and demolitions expert in the US Army and a *Soldier of Fortune* pro; 'Fat' Ralph Edens; Dave McGrady (who later fought for an Israeli cause – the Christian South Lebanese Army) and my old pal Dana Drenkowski, a former United States Air Force pilot who had flown 200 missions over Vietnam in B-52 bombers and F-4 Phantoms. In Rhodesia, Dana spent time, his M16 in hand, searching for 'gooks', as he termed them – before he became the only American ever to be hired as a mercenary by Libya's Muammar Gaddafi. I devoted a chapter to Dana's adventures in my book on mercenaries titled *War Dog*.[1] What was astonishing was that he survived that episode, doing so against the most incredible odds.

Curiously, Dana's boss – the man who enticed him to go to Libya as a pilot – was former CIA operative Edwin P. Wilson, found guilty in 1983 of selling arms to the Libyan leader, but he was finally released from prison in 2004 after a judge threw out the conviction. He died in 2012. In recent years – he is retired now – Dana went 'all respectable' and worked as a district attorney in California. As they say, it takes all kinds...

Another prominent Vietnam vet I took into Rhodesia was Bob Poos, erstwhile editor of *Soldier of Fortune*. Not a big man, Poos had filed from Vietnam for several

---

1   Al J. Venter, *War Dog: Fighting Other People's Wars*. Casemate: 2005. Chapter Nine.

years and would often drink half a case of beer in an average day, followed by enough Scotch after dark to drop any seasoned imbiber.

The illustrious Bob Brown – for whom Dana Drenkowski occasionally did a turn – was the original manipulator of circumstances, unconventional governments, and those with whom he came into contact in any one of many 'operational areas', Rhodesia included. He made no secret that he followed his own brand of what he called 'participatory journalism'.

Much of Brown's effort went into creating what he referred to as 'counters' – some quite outrageous – to radical causes. He either personally led 'unofficial' combat groups of his own people into these forays (it is against American law for Americans to fight in foreign wars) or independently, sending them into places like Afghanistan, the Sudan, El Salvador, Uganda, Rhodesia, Angola, the Congo, Lebanon, Mozambique, Burma, Laos, Nicaragua, Sierra Leone, Croatia, and a good few others that he'd rather I didn't write about.

The first time I emerged from the chaos that became Beirut's hallmark during that country's predominantly Christian–Muslim civil war, I told Brown about some of my experiences when I visited him at his offices in Boulder, Colorado. Within days he had American academic-turned-war correspondent Jim Morris (the movie *Dumbo Drop* was his creation) on a plane headed to the Eastern Mediterranean to cover that war. Jim had been lecturing at an Arkansas college and threw it all in within hours of accepting Bob's offer. As he likes to admit today, he's never looked back.

From the late 1960s, I spent almost as much time covering security developments in Rhodesia as I did with the Portuguese Army in Angola, Mozambique and Portuguese Guinea (Guiné-Bissau). Those were also exciting times. Though we didn't come under fire that often, we had our moments.

On two occasions, years apart, the guerrillas – aware of a media presence at a nearby military base – tried to plant anti-tank mines along the tracks we were scheduled to take the following morning. Both times, while inserting detonators, the mines exploded, and after breakfast, we were greeted with human entrails splayed across quite a large area and over some of the trees nearby.

No reasons for these 'accidents' were ever given. However, many of our local friends believed that it was Colonel Ron Reid-Daly of the Selous Scouts who perhaps did the dirty. He'd often have some of his men 'doctor' ammunition caches that had been fingered by insurgents captured in battle. By 'Uncle' Ron's admission, the duties of his Scouts included destabilising the detonators of some of the mines uncovered in weapon searches. As he elucidated, they would appropriately 'tamper' with ammunition and any liquor uncovered in the cache – lacing the latter with arsenic – and everything was then carefully concealed again so that the guerrilla group replenishing supplies would not be aware that Rhodesia's security forces had been near the place.

As they say: all's fair in love and war.

During my second or third visit to Rhodesia, I was drawn to the idea of crossing the border into Mozambique, or what I'd heard my parents refer to many years before as Portuguese East Africa. Similar to Angola, another Portuguese colony where there was a ferocious war on the go, most of the action in Mozambique happened in the north of the country, adjacent to Tanzania.

That conflict started in September 1964. It was only a few years later that Zambia entered the fray by allowing insurgents to enter Mozambique from the west into the Tete Province, creating an extensive second front. Very effectively, that stimulated my interest – I wanted to see it all for myself, or as much as I might be allowed to by Lisbon. We all knew that the Mozambique rebel army FRELIMO (Front for the Liberation of Mozambique) was now increasingly active close to the Rhodesian frontier.

The consensus among those in the know in the Quill Club was that if I was to head out from Salisbury towards the northeast and enter Mozambique through the Nyamapanda border post, there was a good chance that I might encounter something that might provide a story, not guaranteed though. Most of these ready-made fonts of erudition were wrong: a good deal of the action involving the Portuguese Army in Mozambique, apart from the country's extreme north, was taking place along the Zambezi River.

According to John Edlin, an Associated Press correspondent, if I travelled to Tete, a historical trading post that apparently dated back a thousand years and lay about 160 kilometres north of Nyamapanda, then things might be different. Even better, he suggested, 'cross the river at Tete and continue on the road to Malawi and you're certain to come under fire, or maybe worse.'

John, of course, was referring to the proliferation of landmines in that south-east African war. But he didn't tell me until after his fifth ale that the fighting along the final stage of that journey was so bad that nobody dared venture through what had become a 'no man's land' – a region that, without strong convoy protection, favoured the guerrillas.

While Portugal fought its military campaigns in Africa, the town of Tete – a sizeable sprawling place that is still dominated by the massive suspension bridge across the Zambezi River mentioned by Edlin – came to represent one of the last embattled outposts of an imperial tradition that had lasted five centuries. That epoch was about to close when I went there in the late 1960s.

I'd gone from Salisbury through Tete with Michael Knipe – then the London *Times* man in southern Africa – in a beat-up old Land Rover, and we discovered an archetypal Portuguese-style town similar to those found in all Lisbon's possessions on the continent. Those were critical times because most of us knew that if those wars weren't successful in halting the Soviet 'deliverance' thrust southwards, the next stop would be South Africa.

So, Michael and I pushed on, and the experience was unique, for few newsmen or -women ventured into the Portuguese territories. But for the river, Tete could easily have been Luso in Angola or Cacheu in Portuguese Guinea – where the first of Prince Henry's navigators made landfall on African soil in their search for fresh water in their quest to discover a sea route to India.

At that time, however, the town of Tete was going through particularly difficult times. The guerrilla war started on the edge of town, quite often as soon as the sun disappeared over the great river and the jungles to the west, with landmines taking an immense toll. I was forced to hang around there for half a week, waiting for the convoy that would take me north. Michael had other things to do and wanted to return to Johannesburg.

My prospect was to head through the Tete Panhandle; first to Malawi and then on to Lusaka in Zambia – also technically at war with the 'White South'. My destination this time round was the Congo.

While waiting in Tete, there wasn't a day when we didn't spot vehicles being towed in from the countryside or hauled back to town on low-loaders after they'd been ambushed. Many more civilian trucks carrying cargo to Zambia and the Congo (then Zaire) were blown up by landmines. Most times, their cargoes were either removed *in situ* or, if too big – like mining equipment – destroyed and the damaged vehicles abandoned.

Moving through this corner of an embattled Mozambique during wartime was very different from anything most newcomers had experienced. Our first impressions were that, compared to Rhodesia, the level of activity in this Portuguese battle to survive was far more intense. It was the sort of place where you could end up dead if you took too many chances.

Wrapped around a dirty crossroads on the banks of Africa's third-largest river, Tete could easily have passed for a film set depicting the early years of the great American trek to the west. The only real difference would have been a very occasional modern building and tall communications aerials clustered on a well-protected hill south of the river that overlooked all.

Anyway, since I had no alternative but to wait for the next convoy heading north, Tete became my temporary base that involved an unpleasant little sojourn in the town's only hotel, the Zambezi. The plumbing didn't work, and meals, such as they were, became an unappetising and often unsanitary grind where you competed with the flies on your fork. There was little to do after dark because the only movie house didn't work, and even if it did, whatever might have been on offer film-wise would have been in Portuguese anyway.

Tete's Barracks Square was where most military activities were coordinated. Writing about the place, James McManus of *The Guardian* recalled that it looked 'absurdly Beau Geste'. From there, patrols would set out in army trucks, trailing endless mini-sandstorms in their wake before dawn each day in a bid to check all routes for mines, often responsible for the first casualties of the day.

Security in and around Tete was tight, and journalists weren't welcome. In my case, I was fortunate because I'd been given a letter of introduction to the local commander, which worked in our favour. Michael and I were invited to fly in the governor's private plane on a short hop to the heavily defended Cahora Bassa Dam, then being built on the Zambezi River. It was to become Africa's second biggest man-made dam (after Egypt's Aswan High Dam).

Throughout that brief visit – and even the rare Portuguese Army officer who was prepared to talk to us – we found that the general approach to the war differed somewhat from what you'd encounter in other conflicts. One got the impression that the Portuguese liked to think – and some believed – that it was all a relatively temporary business. They'd tell us that it would 'soon' be over.

'Soon' never happened, and when the war finally ended in 1974, the Portuguese had to pull back to Europe. It was an ignominious departure, a bitter ending to what Lisbon always believed was a proud colonial tradition. At the same time, that historical event cut deep into the psyche of several generations of Portuguese in the European Metropole. It remains something that, even today, they don't like to talk about, the entire nation suffering a kind of communal amnesia.

More recently, there has been a spate of books on those African wars, and I'd like to think that with my own books on Portugal's Wars in Africa, I kind of helped to set a trend.

CHAPTER 23

Undersea realm

I chose to make Cape Town my home for several reasons, after having qualified in London; firstly, the magnificent Table Mountain forms its backdrop and just viewing it, even once a day is an inspiration. Secondly, the city nestles around one of the most beautiful settings of all the world's oceans. Small wonder then that the *Daily Telegraph* in July 2023 ranked Cape Town as the best holiday city in the world.

Settled first by the Dutch more than 300 years before and then captured by the British during the Napoleonic Wars, evidence of both cultures remains strong. Many streets are cobbled (some only wide enough to take a single ox-cart at a time), old buildings are well preserved, and natural sites like Kirstenbosch Gardens, situated on Table Mountain's slopes are proof that not all gardens were created equal. It now contains more than 7,000 species of plants from southern Africa and is a UNESCO World Heritage Site.

As a city, Cape Town is situated on both sides of an elongated peninsula that separates the Indian and Atlantic oceans by only a few kilometres in some areas at the southern tip of Africa. On one side, the water is icy cold and curiously, pleasantly warm on the other. The initial appeal was that both oceans would be accessible in winter and summer. That soon became integral to my world; I'd joined the fledgling British Sub-Aqua Club (BSAC) while still working in London.

Those who remember some of the goings-on of the early period will recognise the names of a few of the original British stalwarts: Reg Vallintine and Bernard Eaton, both forerunners in their day of underwater pursuits that took across the planet. Bernard started a dive magazine in the UK, and that a time when the world was much younger, and we were all still beautiful.

It was the great environmentalist, Professor David Bellamy, who once declared that while Cousteau opened the eyes of the world to the wonders of scuba diving, Bernard crafted 'pages that led people of all walks of life to take their first steps underwater'.

In my London days, we occasionally met after work at a West End pub, The Victory, for drinks – used by the London Branch of the BSAC from about 1960 – as it was near their pool at Seymour Hall. A Greek amphora, probably a couple of thousand years old, made it notable, standing inauspiciously in a corner of the public house. It had been brought back by club members after diving around Giglio Island, just east of Corsica. In 2021, when Reg and I discussed these events, his recall – at age 90 – was phenomenal; in fact, the only thing he no longer does is dive.

All those memories lingered, and one of the first things I did upon arriving in the Cape was to join the Atlantic Underwater Club. The diving environment around the Cape Peninsula remains one of the best anywhere. Apart from accessible wrecks and a diversity of marine life that has kept marine biologists active for more than a century, there are kelp forests that camouflage a multitude of unknowns, including the occasional shark, in the inappropriately named False Bay. I did my initial wreck dives in that bay and wrote my first book on the sport, *Underwater Africa*.[1]

Several more underwater books followed, including a significant work on free-diving with sharks, which meant spending time in the water with these beautiful creatures – and not from the safety of a steel cage.[2]

During this early period, the late 1960s, French underwater pioneer Jacques-Yves Cousteau visited Cape Town in his converted wartime minesweeper, *Calypso*. The not-yet-so-old Frenchman – who had invented the aqualung (as it was then called) – spent time with us at the original Atlantic Underwater Club, adjacent to where Cape Town's Waterfront now is. To top it off, he chose underwater cameraman Gary Haselau to join the crew on the next leg of his exploratory journey.

Free-diving with sharks in the early days eventually got me going in that always-awesome undersea realm. It is interesting too that despite having been involved with sharks in hundreds of dives worldwide, I have yet to be attacked by one. Granted, there have been a few close calls, but my basic philosophy is steadfast: sharks need to be more fearful of man than we of them and the worst culprits there is Beijing.

Chinese fishing boats have been removing eighty or a hundred million sharks annually from the Indo-Pacific Ocean basin for decades, and the consequences are catastrophic. They do so solely for the fins – sliced off to make shark fin soup – with the rest of the carcass discarded back into the ocean. The damage to our maritime environment is wilful.

Take one example: I have been diving off the Mozambique coast for half a century; all 2,500 kilometres of it from Ponta do Oura to the immediate south of Maputo all the way north to the Querimbas Archipelago close to the Tanzanian border (the

1   Al J. Venter, *Underwater Africa*. Purnell: 1969.
2   Al J. Venter and Friends, *Shark Stories*. Protea Books: 2012.

last time about 2018). I did a few good dives just south of Vamizi Island, one of the choice diving spots in the region. Before that, my destination of choice was Bazaruto, another island with some of the best resorts on the western shores of the Indian Ocean.

On both trips, I spotted a single immature white-tip male some distance offshore. There were no adults of any shark species around, and I'd been looking because I spent hours underwater.

For all that, things were very different in days gone by. I did have two run-ins with great white sharks, both unintentional. The first was diving in shallows seas off Fish Hoek in South Africa – an area notorious for shark deaths. I was in about 30 feet of water with a buddy. Suddenly, a giant great white – easily 13 or 14 feet long – charged past us from behind and disappeared into the murky depths ahead. It ignored us as if we weren't there. The reality is that this huge 'man-eater' could easily have chomped either of us had it so intended.

The other time I encountered a great white close up – which meant within touching distance – was while wreck diving off the Cape. It was a well-organised turn-out with four or five others on the wreck of a British steamer *Maori*, which sank off the western cliffs of the Cape Peninsula at about a hundred feet at its deepest more than a century ago. The bow lies in shallower water close to shore.

After about 30 minutes, I surfaced and returned to our tender, the last of our group to reach the boat. The dive had been uneventful because visibility was bad – perhaps five or six feet at best; looking down, you could barely see your fins.

I reached the boat and pushed up my scuba tank to the skipper, and had just started to mount the ladder to the deck when an enormous great white surfaced right alongside me, little more than an arm's length away. This was a monster, its upper body easily the size of one of those old VW Beetles. The shark stuck its head vertically out of the water and completely immobile, eyed me carefully with its huge black eye for about three or four seconds, then sank silently back into the depths and disappeared.

That great brute must have been in the water with us, probably during the entire dive, but not one of us spotted it, which meant that none of us was spooked – which might have led to a different outcome. Like all predators on land and in the sea, sharks can sense fear. Anyway, had we spotted it, the lousy visibility in the water would only have allowed us to see a part of a leviathan that was at least 15 feet long.

Again, if it had been looking for a meal, it could have gobbled up any of us in a moment. But it did not.

For the record, most great white shark attacks at Fish Hoek over the years have been on swimmers, almost all of whom were warned that fins had been spotted earlier. Still, they persisted in going into the water, and I don't have to elaborate…

Always searching for something new and adventurous, I discovered the whereabouts of a British ammunition ship, the *City of Hankow*, a steamer that had gone onto the rocks along the West Coast north of Cape Town after having made contact with a U-boat. The ship – owned by Ellerman Lines with the call-sign GMDZ – was an attractive, single-funnel ship registered in Liverpool. I could initially ascertain that she was carrying 'war cargoes' destined for British forces fighting Rommel in North Africa. Her destination was to have been Port Said.

No one is sure what took place on the night she was lost, though we know that there was an exchange of fire with a German submarine. This information was gathered after the survivors had been brought ashore. London's Lloyds List carried a series of comprehensive reports, all dated from mid-December 1942 to June 1943, and as is the custom, documenting the incident and the fate of the ship and its cargo.

Intrigued, 30 years later, I tracked down Paul du Plessis, an old mate with wreck-diving experience – and four of us, all underwater enthusiasts – went out from Saldanha Bay; he and another diver in his little dingy, and me and a pal by road. We met up with the boat after swimming the 500 metres or thereabouts from the shore – a dodgy venture because that stretch of unfriendly coast was rocky and unpredictable because of the weather. But what the hell, I thought, this is what diving is all about.

We went down in pairs, me and Paul going down first to establish conditions and what a sight that was. It was summer, the weather had been clear, so we had excellent visibility. In our approach to the *City of Hankow*, we found the wreck spectacularly spread about over an area the size of a soccer field. The only problem was that the old ship, over decades, had been pummelled and churned into a mass of rusty, jagged metal with very little remaining intact. In places, we could see parts of winches, an armature from a long-forgotten turbine or generating set and several large artillery pieces.

We found hundreds of crates, almost all smashed open in storms that customarily ravage this coast, their contents strewn across the rocks below. Some had disgorged hundreds of large-calibre shells and a short distance away, more cases that had probably contained millions of rounds of rifle ammunition in crazy, zigzag patterns of belts and cartridges. After years of submersion, they still looked quite lethal. The cordite in the larger shells, some of which we took to the surface with us in a sack, was still useable. We set some of it alight, the black explosive taking fire after about six match strikes. It burned with a roof-high fury and was one of the reasons why a week later, the navy declared the area restricted, after having sent their divers to investigate. They later asked the air force to bomb the site in a bid to detonate all the remaining explosives, though whether that worked is problematic.

After the dive, three of us swam ashore this time. Paul's little boat, with its single outboard engine, was too heavily loaded to take the extra hand. I wouldn't try that today; the weather had turned, and a heavy swell was running. Also, this was great white shark territory, but we do such things when we're young and think we're invincible. I took one of the large shells home with me – the only one brought up with the crease of a firing pin on its detonator – and kept it for many years.

Apart from learning to present a story to an editor on another continent properly, the world under the sea's surface soon became a positive focus in my life. There were wrecks like the Dutch East Indiaman *Huis te Kraainsteen* – which lies in shallow water off Oudekraal Beach – and beyond that, the British freighter, *Maori*, which was loaded with goods destined for the British Army in India. The *Maori* went down in 1909 at the base of an almost inaccessible stretch of rocky cliffs near Cape Town's Hout Bay. For years we were bringing up stirrups and other gear for horses, crockery by the bucketful and hundreds of bottles of champagne, none to be enjoyed because the sea had penetrated the corks. Some of this booty is still there for underwater exploration even today and without any restrictions.

There is also the Portuguese liner, the *Lusitania*, which foundered off Cape Point about the same time as the *Maori*. She lies in fairly deep waters that can present problems to the inexperienced because of strong currents.

In one reasonably compact area off the western shore of False Bay off Buffels Bay, five ships were purposely scuttled to create a unique ships' graveyard for divers. One included the SAS *Transvaal* (the frigate on which I first went to sea) and which today lies intact and in reasonably good condition at a depth of about a hundred feet. With that in mind, you need to know what you're doing if you dive in exposed Cape waters because the weather is changeable and some areas are notorious for treacherous currents.

In those early days, I joined the Cape Town police dive unit because I worked from home and could respond almost immediately. It was voluntary work and sobering as it involved bringing up bodies from the water, primarily people who had drowned on inland dams and rivers. I felt that I was giving back something to the sport that had come to mean so much to me.

After dozens of callouts, I called it a day when I was taken with two or three other divers to a wrecked bus lying in a fast-flowing river. It had gone over a bridge at Riviersonderend, about 160 kilometres from Cape Town. More than 30 people died, mostly young men from the Hawston rugby team near Hermanus.

We had to attach a steel wire to the chassis to tow the bus out – in freezing water with zero visibility – which made it particularly hazardous. After several hours in the water, we brought many of the dead to the riverbank, where their families were waiting. That experience affected me so profoundly that I resigned from the rescue unit.

One of the highlights of what was quite an active period was the visit of the Royal Navy light cruiser, HMS *Blake*, to Cape Town, where some of us were asked whether we would take out an RN dive team 'to gather a few tails' (meaning crayfish) or what they call lobster in the northern hemisphere.

The cruiser's dive officer, Lieutenant Peter Bruce, wished to use his ship's boat for the venture, which suited us fine because he would supply fuel and crew. But the nearest crayfish lay around Robben Island, where Nelson Mandela was incarcerated; thus, the offshore areas were restricted. Peter thought he could handle the problem, so with three or four pals, including international spearfisherman Tubby Gericke – who was thoroughly familiar with those perilous waters – we set off in a white-ensign adorned rubber duck to enter the forbidden area. He was right; our presence wasn't challenged.

However, there were other problems, the first being that we dived within a few hundred metres of a huge steel wreck that was probably an oil tanker. There were jagged, rusty sections protruding above the swell through which the sea literally boiled. Also, it wasn't a shallow dive, and it took a little while to get to the bottom – where, to our delight – the ocean floor was black with crayfish. It then struck us that the current was moving us towards the wreck at a rate of knots. We ascended immediately, only just in time.

On reaching the surface, we had perhaps 30 or 40 feet to spare before being sucked into the wreck, but the rubber duck's skipper – evidently, an old hand at the game – reversed towards us, having pushed out several lengths of rope which we grabbed, and he pulled us clear. Looking back, it was fortunate that we had professionals at hand to assist. More notably, they did so without having to think about it.

Peter made the rank of commander before moving on, and we stayed in touch, telling me the last time we spoke that he'd dined out often enough on that little episode. He recalled moving away from the wreck on our next dive and surfacing half an hour later with more than a hundred crayfish. That kept the *Blake*'s wardroom happy for a few days, and undoubtedly, Lieutenant Bruce was in good standing with his Jimmie.

Always the seafarer and a sailing ace of international repute, over decades, Peter Bruce achieved a string of victories in his own yachts, making him one of the top Corinthian skippers in the world. He has twice been in Britain's winning Admiral's Cup team and has taken part with distinction in most of the Fastnet races since his first in 1961. In that unusually arcane world, Peter Bruce has also raked in his share of golds and written several books: his best, *Heavy Weather Sailing*, is known worldwide and has gone into four editions.

Then, unexpectedly, having been back in South Africa from Nigeria for barely six months, I woke up one morning to the news that set the seal on turning my back on shipping and to start writing for a living.

A flamboyant South African cardiac surgeon named Christiaan Neethling Barnard, better known as Chris Barnard, performed the world's first heart transplant at Cape Town's Groote Schuur Hospital on 3 December 1967, a worldwide, life-changing event. The heart of Denise Darvall – a road accident victim – was transplanted into the chest of 54-year-old grocer Louis Washkansky by Barnard.

Originally from Lithuania, the patient had arrived in Cape Town with his family as a boy, accepted South African nationality and ended up in middle age with a terminal cardiac condition. Following the transplant, he lived for 18 days and died of pneumonia because the anti-rejection drugs that suppressed his immune system couldn't counter the infection.

Our modest group of news-gatherers quickly swung into gear, some having been called from London or New York to immediately get their butts to Groote Schuur and see whether the indescribable had actually taken place. It had. For days, very little hard news filtered out, apart from the fact that a successful heart transplant had taken place and that Washkansky was alive, complete with photos in the *Cape Argus* showing him in his hospital bed. To my mind, I thought at the time, he looked a lot more dead than alive.

While Chris Barnard had many detractors, the transplant was scientifically way ahead of its time. His second transplant patient, Philip Blaiberg – whose operation was performed in early 1968, also at Groote Schuur – lived for 19 months and 18 days. He was able to go home from the hospital, having intimated to friends that he was again living a normal life, which included regular sex. Of interest here is that Barnard, as a young doctor experimenting on dogs, developed a remedy for the infant defect of intestinal atresia. This technique saved the lives of ten babies in Cape Town and was subsequently adopted by surgeons in Britain and the United States.

A few days after the first transplant on Washkansky, Peter Younghusband called and said that we should get together because Peter Hawthorne, then *Time* magazine's man in Africa, had come up with an idea. We met at a small Portuguese restaurant in the Victoria & Albert Waterfront, where we had a permanent table booked every Thursday for a lunch that often lasted three hours. Like Youngers, Hawthorne was a bit of a maverick, blessed with the gift of the gab and the propensity to stay cool under fire in conditions where others might be dying.

Once we were gathered around the lunch table and the famous chef from Cascais was preparing a substantial dish of *camarão* (prawns), Hawthorne shared his idea with us. It involved us working as a team to rush out a book on the heart transplant. To make it happen, each of us would have a designated task: he and Younghusband would tackle Chris Barnard because the surgeon would talk to heavyweight international publications like *Time* and *Newsweek* (which, as it transpired, the surgeon did with aplomb).

Cloete Breytenbach, the photographer in our little clique, would grab images, and my job was to talk to both the patient and the donor's immediate family, and, if possible, I was to get some pictures. This was a tall order for somebody suddenly immersed up to his brow in a craft that usually requires years of practice. It took us about a week, and we were finally ready to roll.

Youngers and Hawthorne, having gained access to the by-now-famous surgeon for their respective editors, asked for more meetings with the man and found him remarkably helpful. I met several times with his brother Marius, also a cardiac surgeon and a transplant team member. It had been his job to remove Denise Darvall's heart and prepare it for insertion into Washkansky's chest.

Marius's debriefs, which comprised a hoard of useable material for the book, were invaluable, and so was this quiet-spoken, communicative and almost self-effacing surgeon who was the antithesis of his verbose and colourful sibling. While Chris Barnard moved into the public eye and would soon start enjoying his renown – including the attention of some of the most beautiful women in the world – Marius simply went about his work and, by all accounts, was totally immersed in the work to which he had dedicated his life.

There was no shortage of takers for the book, eventually published in Cape Town under *The Transplanted Heart*. There was also an edition in the United States put out by Rand McNally. I'd expected to be paid for my efforts, but being the novice, there was little I could do when nothing was forthcoming. Peter Younghusband suggested that I consider it all an incredible experience, which I did and, despite the 'no deal', acquired a healthy infusion of some of the tricks scribes are prone to use to achieve their aims; sometimes honourable, sometimes not.

That Cape Town squad of entrenched cronies became an essential backstop to my life. There was always something on the go, and I was never short of writing commitments, either as a stringer or being asked to head out to some remote corner of the country and check out a story that had caught Younger's or John Monks's attention.

Yet, in 1967, there was much happening elsewhere in Africa – Nigeria and Ghana especially – and a spate of mercenary wars in the Congo. I was drawn to the Middle East, but had not yet found my measure as a scribbler and while I was close to some Israeli diplomats and offered a visit, I thought it could wait.

Another of the high points of my time in Cape Town was the books I wrote while resident there, first in Tamboerskloof and then in Peter Younghusband's lovely home (that I bought when he moved to Paarl) in a quiet side street a five-minute stroll from the Mount Nelson Hotel.

It was Portugal's wars that first caught my interest. While those African liberation wars had been ongoing for years – having started in Angola in 1961 and followed by Mozambique three years later, they might have been happening on the moon for all the interest the South African public displayed, which was astonishing. While both guerrilla conflicts might not have been as intense as what was happening in Southeast Asia then – the potential threat to South Africa was manifest. As I wrote in an article at the time, what was taking place virtually in our backyard was only a hop, skip and a jump from our frontiers.

That was basically why, having returned from a lengthy spell with the Portuguese Army and Air Force in Angola, I offered a book to Purnell, the South African subsidiary of a British firm, and they grabbed it. Unfortunately, *The Terror Fighters* was a poor production and not something I'm proud of. Still, it did create enough interest for me to present to a large audience of primarily military people as a backdrop to what was then going on in a war a couple of hours flying time from Pretoria. What was notable was the number of serving generals seated in the front row immediately ahead of the screen where I displayed my slides.

A couple of underwater books followed; one was published in Britain. After my return from Biafra, I approached Purnell again and asked whether they would consider a book on the Coloured people of South Africa.

Ostensibly, the subject was innocuous at the time because this community, then totalling about two million, was settled throughout the Cape and had been for centuries. The city wouldn't have functioned without them, but sadly, Coloureds suffered the same indignities as Africans under restrictions imposed by apartheid laws. They could not send their children to white schools or tertiary students to white universities, what professions they would be permitted to follow and among other restrictions, who could or couldn't be classified as white. It had something to do with hair and fingernails, though I'm not sure who worked out that idiotic conundrum.

Also, the law told them where they were to live, which was why the government of the day created the racial monstrosity called the Cape Flats, having unceremoniously pushed out the entire community living in District Six near Cape Town's CBD, and then levelled the area.

I could go on, as I did with the book *Coloured: A Profile of Two Million South Africans*, all 561 pages of it. Unfortunately, while I spent three good years gathering material and then putting it together, the book received a cool reception. For a start, I was disowned by a section of the white community, some of whom labelled me, in Afrikaans, a *verraaier* (traitor), pointing to my Boer name and family origins as having let the side down. I was personally attacked in Parliamentary debates for daring to suggest that historically whites had been intimate with people of colour as if my subject matter – two million people of mixed blood – had magically appeared out of nowhere.

The reception of the book by the Coloureds was even worse: the book was hardly welcomed, and the consensus was along the lines of 'Why is this "whitey" involving himself in our affairs?' I was cold-shouldered by old friends who had worked with me while bringing the book to fruition – eminent folk like Dr Dickie van der Ross, one of the community's leaders, who never spoke to me again.

I suspect the ruling National Party might have had something to do with it because even getting the book published was a grind. Purnell had commissioned me to produce the book and gave me a solid royalty advance and a range of published historical titles needed to complete the book. Yet, when I finally finished the manuscript, it was Gerald Gordon, one of Cape Town's upstanding legal minds and on the Purnell board of directors, who quashed it. He told me that I could market my book elsewhere because Purnell would not publish it.

When I asked why, Gordon – ironically a member of the South African Communist Party in his youth (and axiomatically, somebody I believed to be an ally to the cause of highlighting the iniquities of apartheid) – said that the book would jeopardise the sales of schoolbooks in the country. It was a highly lucrative market, and he intimated that his company was not prepared to risk it.

Naturally, I was shattered, but aware too that it would have been almost impossible for a young writer to battle the system – if only because I didn't have money to challenge that final decision in court. So, I did the next best thing and sought advice from Koos Human, an old publishing friend and managing director of Human & Rousseau, one of the largest Afrikaans publishing houses in the country. He asked to see the manuscript and came back a week later to tell me that they were happy to publish and that I would again be given an advance on royalties upfront.

As with President F. W. de Klerk a quarter-century later – the man who released Nelson Mandela from prison and handed over his government to a black majority, another historical first – it was another Afrikaner who had come to the rescue.

CHAPTER 24

Intelligence work: a quagmire of nuclear intrigue

Investigative journalism – which often enough involves uncovering devious motives or uncomfortable truths that individuals, and very often governments, would prefer to remain hidden – can result in disturbing outcomes.

In 2018 in the Central African Republic, three Russian journalists reporting on the activities of the mercenary Wagner Group – also Russian – were lured to a remote village in the jungle, ambushed and executed…a Wagner speciality. I must have come close to being 'taken out' while investigating South African–Iranian nuclear links in 1997, less than a decade after Nelson Mandela had taken over the rigours of leading his country to full independence.

Curiously, I was only to discover that truth a quarter-century later when I met the man who had headed a protective surveillance unit that for three years had watched my every move within the close confines of Sault Sainte Marie, a medium-sized city on the shores of Lake Superior in Ontario, Canada. Having been introduced to 'Eric', an amiable, powerfully built, and uncompromising Special Forces veteran who had formerly served in Britain's Special Air Service, he shook my hand and declared in a low, friendly voice: 'I know you, Al Venter, better than Al Venter knows himself.'

'Eric', if that was his name, was dead serious when he gave me the backdrop of keeping track of my movements during those secluded 36 months I spent in Canada, as well as those of anybody who came anywhere close to me. I spent a lot of time in the city's gym, always crowded, so he must have had his work cut out.

Astonished, though I suspected that I was under some kind of observation by the authorities because I was writing another non-fiction book on weapons of destruction, I was never made aware of the presence of either 'Eric' or any other members of his squad.

'The threat factor must have been severe,' I ventured, once I'd managed to gather my thoughts again because clearly, this was an unexpected event. I asked the man whether he would tell me more, but my putative guardian just shook his head. We weren't even able to share a couple of pints in the aftermath of that disclosure.

All that stemmed from me accidentally uncovering one of the major news stories of the day that never really made the news, except for short excerpts published after I had released a string of revelations to Jane's *International Defence Review* and my story was picked up thereafter by the London *Times*.

It revolved around Iran's quest for nuclear weapons, which subsequently appeared in my book *Iran's Nuclear Option: Tehran's Quest for the Atom Bomb*, published by Casemate in the United States in 2005.

Interestingly, my brief encounter with 'Eric' took place in the presence of Floyd Holcom, a Special Forces operator while still in the military. Active and enterprising (he spoke Mandarin, Farsi and Arabic), Floyd went on to do quite a bit of mischief and undercover work, much of it in China while working for one of Washington's three-digit intelligence agencies.

It was also Floyd who told me that while undergoing training for that august body, one of the first books placed before him was my Iranian book. I'm surprised that it was never accorded better attention by the public at large: at least my royalties would have been a lot better. I repaid that debt to Floyd by dedicating one of my more recent books to him: *Combat: South Africa at War Along the Angolan Frontier.*

Of interest here is that *Iran's Nuclear Option* was the first of four books I wrote on the proliferation of nuclear weapons. That was followed by the definitive *How South Africa Built Six Atom Bombs*, with the subtitle, *And Then Abandoned its Nuclear Weapons Program*. The book got mixed reviews from the pundits because much of that effort was conducted under the strictest secrecy and even today outsiders don't know the whole story.

What I was able to uncover was that only South Africans born and bred in the country were allowed access to those august scientific chambers and that there were never more than a thousand people involved in the decades-long task, compared to more than 30,000 Pakistanis engaged subsequently in their successful quest for the bomb.

The third book in this range was the 336-page *Allah's Bomb: The Islamic Quest for Nuclear Weapons*, published in 2007 by Lyons Press in the United States. I was mightily annoyed when it was suddenly withdrawn from the company's distribution list only a few months after its release, which was when one of the editors with whom I had become friendly told me it was because of a strong protest from the South African Embassy in Washington.

It is 'all a bunch of fabrications', one of the diplomats told Lyons, especially the Iranian links which I dealt with in considerable detail because I became enmeshed in some of the intrigues on the periphery of it all. So, the publishers had the book discreetly removed from the shelves and I was never to write for them again. Also notable was that I was never given an opportunity to respond to those charges.

Nobody is sure – or rather, no one in South Africa is prepared to say – at what stage Tehran finally decided to grasp the nuclear nettle and put forward a case for some kind of cooperation between Pretoria and Tehran. It was a clandestine link that would never have been made in public.

Iran's own nuclear physicists, as with the Iraqis before, had not taken long to be flummoxed both by the astronomical cost of these newfound scientific disciplines, as well the multiple engineering intricacies that any nuclear enterprise entails. Issues would have been compounded had they started from scratch, as they were clearly obliged to do.

Like their South African counterparts, they too would have had to get past the complex principles related to subjects like nuclear physics, uranium enrichment, stabilising the HEU core in a gun-type atom bomb, building moulds for an implosion device and many other obtuse necessities. They would also have had to grapple with issues associated with things as arcane as spherical geometry, a highly complex detonation device where timing is measured in millionths of a second and, of course, delivery to target.

South Africa had already been through that mill and when you speak to some of their nuclear scientists today, they admit to having been seriously bedevilled numerous times by some of the skills they needed to inculcate. Despite problems and setbacks – and there were many – the South Africans eventually mastered the complex technology of nuclear weapons construction, if only enough to produce six atom bombs. The Iranians, we now know, wanted a share of it.

It was perhaps to be expected that with Nelson Mandela's new government in place in Pretoria after the African National Congress had taken over from President F. W. de Klerk that South Africa would turn its political back on the West. Three decades later, South Africa remains demonstrably anti-American, and in some respects socialist, and it's no secret that some of this knowledge might have been garnered by the Iranians, if not by coercion, then 'for services rendered', possibly as a trade-off for oil.

Looking back, there were several reasons why South Africa believed that it needed the bomb, the first being the ongoing war in Angola. While nowhere near as intense as what was going on in Southeast Asia at the time, the threat factor was grave.

Though relatively low-key, the Border War could sometimes be hectic and end up fringing on conventional warfare involving armoured vehicles, tanks, artillery as well as heavy air strikes, especially during the annual Soviet and Cuban summer offensives of expanding hostilities into regions adjoining South West Africa. Also, the war lasted an inordinately long time – 23 years – where sons often stepped into their fathers' boots, serving in the same units. The possibility of a Russian-led invasion southwards was real enough to alarm Pretoria into raising the stakes and giving serious consideration to developing a nuclear option.

Bill Keller of *The New York Times* phrased it well in an article titled *'South Africa Says It Built Six Atom Bombs'* published in March 1993, when he declared that the country, then under the apartheid government, pursued research into weapons of mass destruction, including nuclear, chemical and biological weapons. He went on: 'South African strategy was, if political and military instability in southern Africa became unmanageable, to conduct a nuclear weapon test in a location such as the Kalahari Desert to demonstrate its capability and resolve – and thereby highlight the peril of intensified conflict in the region – and then invite a larger power such as the United States to intervene.

It was in late May 1997, quite by chance, that I asked for and was given an opportunity to meet the man who was then in charge of South Africa's nuclear programme. When I arrived in Johannesburg, while on a visit to South Africa from the United States, I called Dr Waldo Stumpf's office for an appointment. I asked for advice regarding an article I was doing at the time for Britain's *Jane's Information Group*. It was all nuclear-related, I explained, something technical about Iraq and how Saddam Hussein had gone about trying to build the bomb, comparatively easily accessed on Google. I was after the devil in the detail.

The half-dozen South African atom bombs that had been constructed by South African nuclear physicists in the 1970s and 1980s were history, but Dr Stumpf, a quiet-spoken, round-faced academic had been in the industry for many years, and if anybody could help, he certainly could. At the same time, when I called by phone, he was somewhat surprised by my interest in those matters because run-of-the-mill journalists are not usually into such arcane issues.

My timing was difficult, he averred because he was leaving for Syria the next day. 'But come along anyway and let's see what I can do.' I wasted no time in rushing to his offices from Johannesburg. The drive to Pelindaba, on the outskirts of Pretoria, should normally have taken me 50 minutes. I got there in less than half an hour.

After stringent security checks at the gate, I was ushered into the office of the man who was the chief executive officer of NECSA, the Nuclear Energy Corporation of South Africa, a position he held from 1990 to 2001 (when it was still called the Atomic Energy Corporation).

Because of time constraints, I had expected the meeting with the man who had worked in the nuclear industry for three decades to last perhaps ten minutes. It was an hour before I finally left Pelindaba.

Dr Waldo Stumpf, a Fellow of the South African Academy of Engineering, had an impressive academic record. He held a B.Sc. Eng (Metallurgy) from the University of Pretoria and a PhD from Sheffield University, apart from a string of other qualifications, mostly engineering related. After completing his studies in Britain in 1968 (on microstructural aspects of ferritic chromium steels during hot working), he regularly taught within the department, including a postgraduate course on phase transformations in solids. Professionally, his area of interest lay in the optimisation of physical properties of metals and alloys through microstructural optimisation by the design of heat treatment or hot working processes or by alloy design…quite a mouthful.

Our business done, Dr Stumpf questioned me at length about my own activities as a foreign correspondent, particularly about what I was doing in the United States. He knew that I had already published more than a dozen books and was clearly familiar with my interest in chemical, biological and nuclear proliferation, mostly done at the behest of *Jane's*. Had he not been, I probably wouldn't have got through the door, since Dr Stumph was a very busy man.

He was especially curious about my forays into some of the Arab countries since I had only recently returned from Damascus, a saga on its own because I was under constant surveillance having entered the area around the prohibited Kuneitra 'stronghold' (today little more than an unoccupied village) in the shadows of both Mount Hermon and Golan, the latter fortified by the Arabs with countless landmines. I would have liked to take photographs but didn't dare because they were watching me.

It was at that point that the doctor's mood turned conspiratorial. Almost off-handedly, he admitted that a few months earlier he'd played host to a group of Iranians at the Pelindaba nuclear establishment. Among them, he confided, was Iran's deputy minister of atomic affairs, Reza Amrollahi. Intriguing, I thought at the time, but I didn't interrupt.

He went on, 'I got a call from the President's Office in Cape Town soon after arriving at work that morning, not from President Mandela himself, but one of his aides, and was told that a high-level Iranian party, including Amrollahi (who I already knew from international meetings that we'd both attended), was already on its way to Pretoria. There were no ifs or buts – they would be here by noon.'

What was immediately troubling, Stumpf confided, was the haste with which it had all been arranged. Nothing was according to form. If there had been adequate time, he would have liked to have had one of the international observers present, someone from the International Atomic Energy Agency.

'However,' he added, 'my time is limited, and in any event, the IAEA has a monitoring role in South Africa and does not have personnel permanently stationed at Pelindaba. But I knew that I had to have somebody of consequence in the office while discussions with the Iranians took place. More to the point, these were sensitive issues, and it wouldn't be in either my or Pelindaba's interest to meet alone with an Iranian deputy minister, especially someone involved with matters nuclear. So, I called Pik Botha, who, until a short time before, had been my immediate superior.'

Botha, a veteran South African politician, had no qualms about accepting a post in the cabinet of his erstwhile ANC 'enemy' as South Africa's Minister of Energy and Minerals Affairs, a position taken over by Penuell Maduna. Fortunately, his former boss was in Pretoria that day, and as Stumpf explained, Pelindaba had once fallen within Botha's bailiwick.

'I phoned him, told him what was taking place and asked that he be there. Pik Botha responded by saying he would be with me within the hour,' Stumpf told me.

The Iranian party arrived on time, just as Cape Town had said they would and, according to Stumpf, the encounter was formal but friendly. For a short while they talked about Minister Amrollahi's visit to South Africa, what he had seen and what he had planned.

'Then the man handed me a file, and I knew exactly what was taking place. It wasn't a big pile of papers, just a few lists.'

The documents, he explained, contained a catalogue of items needed for the manufacture of a nuclear weapon. There were several advanced things asked for like blueprints, industrial, chemical and laboratory equipment, and other essentials required for going nuclear.

'Obviously, we were stunned,' Stumpf said.

The two South Africans rejected the request out of hand, Stumpf telling the Iranian minister that in accordance with the provisions of the Non-Proliferation Treaty (NPT), there was no way either he or members of his staff could comply. He pointed out that not only had South Africa recently signed the NPT, but as everybody present in the room knew, the country had destroyed its entire nuclear weapons arsenal. Additionally, every document relating to the manufacture of atom bombs had been shredded in the presence of British and American IAEA officials.

'I informed him that since Iran was also an NPT signatory, he would be familiar with the kind of restrictions that were in play, and the nature of the visit was compromising. I went on to add that we South Africans were being asked to break international law.'

Stumpf admitted to having been completely nonplussed by the Iranian's effrontery, as well as embarrassed by the charade. What surprised him the most, he said, was that it was almost as if the man had been primed to expect him to comply with his request. It was a bad call whichever way it was viewed, he reckoned.

Both Pik Botha and Stumpf used the opportunity to remind their guest and his high-level party of what had happened not very long before in Iraq following Operation *Desert Storm*, adding that once the names of German scientists recruited by Saddam Hussein to work in his nuclear weapons programme had become known in the weapons strip-search by the IAEA action team and UNSCOM, several warrants of arrest had been issued through Interpol.

Two of those involved in the Iraqi effort had been charged with treason. One was still in jail.

'With deference, I made it clear that it would simply not be possible for us to help. Besides, there were international safeguards in place to prevent exactly that from happening.'

Aware that he might have exceeded his brief in telling me, a foreign correspondent who was acutely aware of the implication as well as the potential political repercussions if any of it was made public, Dr Stumpf – sitting at his desk, and me facing him – pulled himself erect and insisted that everything we'd talked about was to remain off-record.

What to do, but comply…

For a month or two, it stayed that way. At the same time, I was deeply troubled, specifically because of long-term international security implications. I couldn't help feeling that this was too potent a matter to let rest. Back in London thereafter, I mentioned my meeting at the Pelindaba nuclear establishment to Clifford Beal, the American-born editor of *Jane's International Defence Review*.

Now it was my turn for confidences. I was extremely perturbed by what I'd been told, I said, suggesting that if it was true and Iran was seriously interested in building nuclear weapons, the ramifications were incalculable. In my mind's eye, the lives of untold numbers of people could be at stake if this thing ever got to fruition stage. Not only that, but the new South African government would have been complicit in helping an aberrant Islamic state develop a device that could inalterably tip the balance of power in a region half the size of Europe.

'The world has a right to know,' I said, explaining to Beal the nature of my meeting with Dr Stumpf.

On the last point, the American's perspective was that I should follow the dictates of my conscience. He knew my style, as well as the way I worked, always ferreting for more info because I'd been contributing to IDR – first in Geneva, and afterwards in Coulsdon, Surrey – for almost a quarter-century.

Looking back, I am aware now that though my actions might have been considered insidious by some members of the Fourth Estate, it was a long and difficult decision to expose this charade. Inchoate, to begin with, the issue took time to harden into something tangible. At the same time, I was no agitator manque discreetly incubating something seditious. Rather, this was a matter that, in the interests of the international community, demanded action. Nor could I ignore the reality that, in the longer term, there were real implications of nuclear war in the Near East. Frankly, I was faced with a situation impossible to ignore.

My article covering the meeting with Dr Waldo Stumph was published in the September 1997 issue of *Jane's International Defence Review*, which came out in late August. Days later it was picked up by the London *Times* under the headline 'Iran Sought Pretoria Nuclear Deal'.

In the interests of veracity, and because I knew that I'd betrayed a trust, I went a step further. Just before IDR went to press, I contacted Phillip van Niekerk, an old friend from Sierra Leone's mercenary days: we had covered the activities of Executive Outcomes together while working in West Africa. At that stage Phillip ran South Africa's most politically outspoken weekly, the *Mail & Guardian*, then still partly owned by Britain's *Guardian* newspaper. His job as editor gradually evolved into something of a personal crusade, assuming a role as an aggressive watchdog in covering polemical government activities.

I was in a desperate quandary about the matter, and I told him so, taking the trouble to explain why. Up to that point my report of the Stumpf interview was solely based on: 'I said, he said'. What I needed was help to back up my report.

Phillip agreed to investigate the matter. If it added up, he said, he'd run the story a week after it appeared in London. In retrospect, it was good that he did. Van Niekerk immediately tasked Mungo Sogget, the *Mail & Guardian*'s senior investigative journalist to look into what had taken place. Sogget was a good choice as someone had once referred to him as having 'the demeanour of a pit bull', though probably not to his face.

Consequently, when Botha was asked by Sogget in a phone call to his home in Pretoria a day or two later whether Amrollahi's visit had in fact taken place and whether the learned Dr Stumpf had been presented with a nuclear 'shopping list,' the former South African minister replied that he was not only aware of the event but declared emphatically: 'I was there when it happened.'

Once the articles were out, the South African government reacted with the kind of vigour that was not only consummate but aggressive. Within days the issue was raised in Parliament in Cape Town, and I was branded a liar.

In answer to a Parliamentary question, Stumpf declared that 'the entire story is fiction…Venter made it all up.' He told lawmakers that the only time he had ever met with any Iranian official was at a dinner in the presence of a large number of people. Dr Stumpf also denied that Deputy Minister Reza Amrollahi had ever visited South Africa. Clearly, he had been well primed.

Nor was Pik Botha ever so forthcoming again. Shortly after returning to America, I related the saga to another old friend, Dr Jonathan Tucker, head of the Chemical and Biological Weapons Nonproliferation Program at the Monterey Institute of International Affairs in California. I also gave him Botha's personal phone number. Only later did I hear that the South African minister had slammed down the receiver as soon as Tucker raised the Amrollahi issue. Jonathan was a good friend whom I visited from time to time in California and he gave it to me first-hand.

Pretoria went into overdrive. The South African government issued a statement on 11 September 1997 stating that 'The country's Atomic Energy Corporation (AEC) has never been involved in business transactions with Iran. Nor were any being considered at present,' said Mineral and Energy Affairs Minister, Penuell Maduna.

In a written reply to National Party member Johan Marais, when the issue was tabled in Parliament, he declared that the Atomic Energy Corporation CEO, Dr Waldo Stumpf 'had never held a meeting with Iran's deputy minister of atomic affairs, Reza Amrollahi, as claimed by local and foreign news media'.

In turn, Stumpf swore that the only meeting that he, or any other AEC official, had ever had with any Iranian government official took place in March 1995 at a public restaurant in Cape Town with Iranian petroleum minister Gholam Reza Aghazadeh.

'Stumpf had been asked to attend the courtesy dinner by former Mineral and Energy Affairs Minister Pik Botha during Aghzadeh's visit to South Africa in connection with a possible oil storage deal at Saldanha. Though Botha did not attend the dinner, Iranian petroleum officials and other South African officials were present,' Maduna said.

If all this were true, one needs to ask, why would Dr Stumpf choose to be evasive about such a sensitive issue, especially at a time when it must have been clear to him that Tehran was covertly committed to building the bomb? That things were exacerbated by Pik Botha – irrespective of what he told Mungo Sogget – coming out in strong support of his statement only compounded the fraud. More pertinent still, why did both men, respected professionals in their own spheres of influence, choose to lie about something so critical?

This was an issue that could ultimately result in the course of history being irrevocably changed in the most volatile region in the world. Both men must have known the answer, and so, I am sure, did the entire South African cabinet.

There is no disputing that Reza Amrollahi had been in South Africa at the time in question and that the meeting took place, if only because the circumstances were verified, first by Stumpf himself (to me personally) and afterwards by Pik Botha (to Mungo Sogget) who, though a colleague, is somebody I've never met.

Most salient of all is the fact that Tehran admitted in 2022 that it had been trying to build an atom bomb for almost two decades. That fact, alone, totally vindicated my argument. What also emerged years later, was a candid admission by the professor that yes, he had met with Amrollahi and his entourage in his office (and not, in fact in a restaurant as had claimed), but never went so far as to explain the nature of the subterfuge. Also notable is a subsequent article in the *Mail & Guardian* that at least one of South Africa's nuclear scientists made redundant by the scrapping of its nuclear weapons programme had been hired by Iran. I was to eventually discover that that was just the start of it.

Unquestionably, both Botha and Stumpf must have been put under severe pressure by the South African authorities to recant. One must ask why should they have been forced to do so.

It is worth noting that though I was vilified in Parliament, the entire issue – thoroughly controversial – was allowed to rest right there. For his part, Stumpf – highly regarded in his day by his peers – had every opportunity to test my claims in court had he wished to do so. He could have levelled defamation charges and claimed damages from both *Jane's* and the *Mail & Guardian*, as I would certainly have done were I in his shoes and believed to have been wronged. Instead, he did nothing.

Nor did the South African government take further action, even though nuclear weapons issues in that country are still subject to restrictions. There is also the matter of something as disputatious as my making public information relating to weapons of mass destruction. The Official Secrets Act remains in force in South Africa and there have been numerous people arrested over the years for disclosing much less 'incriminating evidence' than I had done. One can only speculate whether the reticence of both men might have had something to do with their state pensions being withheld if they refused to cooperate, or if the government used some other form of leverage. In any case, they are going to have to live and eventually die with the truth of the matter still under wraps.

Interestingly, the issue was taken up not long afterwards by Washington. On 4 December 1997, James Rubin, spokesman for the State Department, issued a statement in his daily press briefing that dealt with the establishment in 1977 of *Vastrap*, a potential nuclear testing site in the remote Kalahari Desert where Pretoria had hoped to conduct an underground nuclear test.

Preparations being made at the time were for a dummy run, which he explained was an 'instrumented' test without an actual nuclear core. Preparations for this event were detected by Soviet satellite surveillance and were subsequently abandoned after, it has been suggested, Washington threatened to prohibit sales of commercial aircraft and parts to South Africa, which would effectively have grounded South African Airways' mainly Boeing fleet.

Though the country never intentionally moved beyond phase one, some officials have said that they believed that once Western or Soviet intelligence discovered that the South African Armaments Board (Armscor) had checked the condition of at least one of the shafts at *Vastrap* (for a possible underground test during the mid-1980s), this exercise convinced both major powers that South Africa was deadly serious about its nuclear capability. In turn, it resulted in the US putting pressure on the Soviet Union and Cuba to withdraw from Angola. Whether the weapons and the strategy ever served this purpose has not been proven and is consequently impossible to determine.

A bit of background as to how South Africa, with relatively limited resources (even if the country had a massive industrial infrastructure) managed to go nuclear. According to an article carried by *Risk Report*, titled 'South Africa's Nuclear Autopsy', its nuclear programme was run by the Atomic Energy Corporation in conjunction with Armscor, whose scientists routinely culled open-source literature, including US Navy manuals on nuclear weapon systems, safety and design.

Essentially, Pretoria's quest for a bomb did not, as some pundits are quoted, begin in 1971. The initial reason for the building of a nuclear explosive (in the days of the old Atomic Energy Board) was from the point of view of a peaceful nuclear explosion, in line with the objectives of the Ploughshare Project in America.

The Nuclear Non-Proliferation Treaty, which entered into force in March 1970, makes provision in Article V for peaceful nuclear explosions (though never applied in practice) which could potentially be used for the excavation of dams, in mining, clearing navigational channels and so on. It is significant that the approval of the first R&D project to investigate the possibility of an explosive device was given by the Minister of Mines in 1971 and not by the South African Minister of Defence. Further, Armscor only took over in the actual construction of the nuclear devices after a change of emphasis from peaceful to military uses in 1978.

For its role, the newly renamed AEC was charged with its most difficult task, producing highly enriched uranium fuel, or HEU in the argot. This substance, lethally radioactive and produced by the Uranium Enrichment Corporation (UCOR), was sent to the Atomic Energy Board on the Pelindaba site where it was converted to metal. This, in turn, was used to produce the nuclear cores for the weapons or for the manufacture of HEU for the SAFARI research reactor (due to the American boycott of exporting nuclear materials to the apartheid regime).

Tasked to build the actual weapon in its nuclear programme was the mammoth state-owned organisation Armscor that handled all projects of military significance such as rifles, artillery, armour and the rest, the majority catering specifically to the needs of the country's ongoing wars within and beyond its frontiers.

Once the country had decided to 'go nuclear,' it took only seven years for its scientists to build an atomic bomb like the one the United States dropped on Hiroshima. The effort required about a thousand experts, but, according to Dr Stumpf, the man who inherited South Africa's nuclear establishment, 'Less than five or ten people had an oversight of the entire programme.' Top secret clearance was only granted to persons born in South Africa and with no other citizenship. For some tasks, says the report, more sophisticated equipment was needed, so Pretoria resorted to smuggling.

'I am not at liberty to divulge anything that we import…we do not identify our suppliers.' This was all that Dr Stumpf, CEO of South Africa's Atomic Energy Corporation, would say when he fielded questions during a 1993 meeting at the South African Embassy in Washington.

He declared categorically that South Africa 'had no help from anybody on nuclear weapons technology…we gave no help to anybody and we received no help… 'On other things, yes…[but] not on enrichment technology, not on nuclear weapons technology.' Stumpf admitted that South Africa had imported nuclear materials over the years, including low-enriched uranium, but he would not say from where it originated, though Israel has been mentioned many times by independent observers within that context. As Dr von Wielligh reminded us in his book *The Bomb* the imported LEU was never part of the nuclear weapons programme but intended for use in reactors.

Less secrecy accompanied South Africa's guided missile programme.

According to *Risk Report*, Israel was South Africa's hands-down most important missile supplier. Pretoria got most of what it needed from Tel Aviv and much of it was a two-way street. Exchanges included testing Israel missiles on South African soil as well as the transfer of approximately 50 tons of South African yellowcake (uranium ore concentrate) in exchange for 30 grams of tritium, the heaviest hydrogen isotope customarily used to boost the explosive power of atom bombs.

Incorporated into the core of the bomb, a tritium plug can quite substantially raise the yield of, for instance, a 20 kT bomb by four or five times. Pakistan claims to have an H-bomb, or thermonuclear capability, but in the view of American nuclear physicist Dr Bogdan Maglich, at one stage one of the heads of CERN in Geneva, as well as having an involvement in the Indian nuclear programme, 'That's a clever bit of disinformation in a bid to counter Delhi's advances in this field. Islamabad,' explained Maglich, 'uses tritium to boost its fissile weapons (atom bombs) and apparently does it well enough to produce some impressive results.' Others are not so sure.

The tritium received from Israel never found a home in the South African nuclear weapons programme. Instead, with a half-life of 12 years, much of it had deteriorated by the time a halt was called to weapons production. At one stage some tritium was commercially used to illuminate advertising billboards.

The secrecy surrounding its A-bomb efforts often forced Pretoria to make do with low-tech equipment. 'These guys were immensely proud of what they achieved under sanctions,' said a US State Department official once Pretoria had opened its door to IAEA and American inspection. 'They came up with their own home-spun technology,' he added.

From the late 1970s through early 1990, South Africa produced HEU at its pilot-scale enrichment plant at Pelindaba. The key technology claimed an American-based report, was called 'split-nozzle gaseous diffusion', which was rumoured to have been supplied by West Germany in the early 1970s. But this is incorrect.

Dr von Wielligh stated that there is no enrichment process with that name. Rather, the different types of enrichment processes are:

- Gas centrifuge (the most common method today)
- Gaseous diffusion (originally used in the US for the Manhattan Project during and after World War II)
- Aerodynamic methods (separation nozzles or vortex tubes)
- Chemical or ion exchange (not really used in practice)
- Laser-based enrichment (AVLIS or MUS)

By mid-1977, the AEC had completed its first bomb package, but the enrichment plant at Pelindaba, known as the Y-plant, did not begin producing the high-enriched uranium fuel until 1978. A second package was built in 1978, and by late 1979 the Y-plant had processed enough enriched uranium for a single bomb core. Pretoria built six nuclear devices between 1977 and 1989 and the design for each was essentially the same.

A constant recurring (and controversial) theme while South Africa's nuclear weapons programme progressed, was whether a fully fledged nuclear test ever took place. While Soviet satellites detected preparations for a test site in the Kalahari Desert in 1977, Washington and Moscow pressured Pretoria to shut it down. In September 1979, however, an American Vela satellite detected a distinctive double flash off the southern coast of Africa. This data offered strong evidence that the flash had been caused by a low-yield nuclear explosion.

In June 1980, the CIA reported to the National Security Council that the two-to-three-kiloton nuclear test had probably involved Israel and South Africa. US intelligence confirmed it had tracked frequent visits to South Africa by Israeli nuclear scientists, technicians and defence officials in the years preceding the incident. They concluded that 'clandestine arrangements between South Africa and Israel for joint nuclear testing operations might have been negotiable'.

Such speculation was fuelled in 1986 when Israeli nuclear technician Mordechai Vanunu was interviewed by the London *Sunday Times*. Vanunu said that it was common knowledge at Dimona that South African metallurgists, technicians and scientists were there on joint technical exchange programmes.

The truth is more compelling. Firstly, says Dr von Wielligh, South Africa's Y-plant produced enough HEU for its first bomb only toward the end of 1979. This was confirmed by Vienna's International Atomic Energy Agency (IAEA – a UN body) in their subsequent study and forensic analysis of the operating and production records of the Y-plant. Secondly, the very heavy first devices (exceeding one ton) were designed and built for underground demonstration tests or such jet bombers as South Africa possessed. At the time, he declared, there was simply no means available to deliver such a device for an atmospheric explosion over the southern Indian Ocean.

Furthermore, he states, 'In discussions on a personal level with high-level officials involved in the project [including Dr Wynand de Villiers, at one stage head of South Africa's nuclear project] it was categorically denied that Africa had been involved in such a test for all the above reasons.'

Due to circumstantial evidence (for example, the unexplained tardiness of the US to do atmospheric tests after the alleged explosion), the theory was advanced that the test could have been some kind of cooperation between the US and Israel on an Israeli test vehicle. Dr de Villiers told von Wielligh that he believed that this is what might have happened and that to blame South African involvement afterwards was a rather useful smokescreen to avoid implication. As Dr de Villiers stated, 'In the apartheid era, who would have believed South Africa anyway?'

All of which brings me back to my involvement in the South African nuclear weapons programme, all very cursory and very much on the fringe of what took place in building the bomb: I am an ink-slinger, not a scientist.

My role was strictly limited to writing about a single event following my meeting with Dr Waldo Stumph in his Pretoria office and his telling me about his contact with an Iranian nuclear-linked delegation. On the face of it, that was a simple truth. What was not was the list of requirements pushed before this scientist, asking for a string of items directly linked to building the atom bomb.

More damning, in the almost quarter-century since, Tehran has consistently denied that it was ever interested in developing a nuclear weapon: it has done so vigorously at hundreds of private and public venues, including the UN Security Council when called to do so.

But once on the trail of such an interesting conundrum, I became mightily intrigued by the truth and set about exposing not only the South African–Iranian link in nuclear matters, but also the full implications of Tehran's weapons of mass destruction programmes. In this, I was assisted by many specialists both in the United States and elsewhere.

Here, much of the credit must go to David Albright, a dear friend and a regular face on international TV networks for many years, and the one individual to whom I am eternally grateful for guiding me through the loops and bounds of a multitude of related issues linked to nuclear weapons proliferation. David founded the Institute for Science and International Security (or what he calls, 'the good ISIS') and the truth is that without his help, my book *Iran's Nuclear Option*, published by Casemate in 2005, would never have reached fruition. While hardly a bestseller it made an impact and is still around, even though I was castigated by a bevy of American academics for daring to suggest that Iran had even the vaguest intention of going nuclear.

The mullahs finally admitted the truth – after decades of obfuscation – in the summer of 2022, when Kamal Kharrazi, an adviser to the Iranian Supreme Leader Ayatollah Ali Khamenei told Qatar's Al Jazeera TV that his country is 'technically capable of building a nuclear weapon'.

The West has been aware of these shenanigans for decades, but for reasons best known to their governments, they have never gone public. That did not prevent the Iranians from coming after me, which they did with aggressive intent – one of the reasons why I was kept under protective surveillance by a multiple-person security team for the duration of the three years I was living in Sault Sainte Marie, Canada.

The denouement – or in quasi-espionage terms, the *pièce de résistance* – followed not long afterwards, in part because Casemate in the United States published my book *The Chopper Boys*, a classic on helicopter warfare in Africa which has gone into several editions over the years.

Since I was regarded as something of a buff on chopper warfare, I was contacted by a director of Denel, a South African state-owned aerospace and military technology conglomerate, the largest on the African continent. There were people at Denel who believed I could help with publicity, so I was flown from Seattle near where I lived to Johannesburg for a three-month stint to add my two bits' worth in a bid to create international awareness of this remarkable machine that has seen good action in several African conflicts in the past few decades.

An issue at Denel at the time was the Rooivalk (AH-2A) attack helicopter, considered by some as roughly on par with the American Apache, which was not getting the attention it deserved: the helicopter had never sold outside its home base. Simply put, the South African product, while excellent value, could not compete on the international market because Denel lacked the kind of investment needed to provide support and back-up capability offered by both American and British aviation companies. So, I decided to give it a go: it was winter in the northern hemisphere, and I could do with some sun.

On arrival in Johannesburg, I was settled into a good hotel and for the next few months reported for work each morning at the Denel headquarters, adjacent to the country's biggest international air terminal. Sadly, nothing was to come of that venture, except that among many contacts made at Denel was 'Joe', a rather flighty, highly intelligent character who for reasons of his own came to regard me as the ultimate 'ideas man'. Joe was the sort of individual who saw a 'spook' behind every bush. He believed that Denel was riddled with spies, which it probably was, because there were several reports in later years of documents, plans and blueprints being stolen by foreign agents.

I took little notice of his ramblings, until he sidled up to me one morning and said that he had been in touch with a foreign embassy, which caught my attention. Was he trying to set me up? I thought.

'Why?' I asked him, perplexed, in part because he was working for a government-owned company and that sort of thing was rare. Moreover, security for the weapons-related products that Denel produced – including the Rooivalk – was a top priority and everyone who worked there had to sign documents to that effect.

It was then that he pulled me aside, lowered his voice and became manifestly conspiratorial, a condition so farcical that I feared would have attracted the attention of anybody watching. 'Some serious things are going on here,' he declared, adding that he was worried, both his eyes had narrowed to slits.

'Are you able to tell me about it?'

'Not really, but what I can say is that some bad things are happening here.'

'Like?'

The issue stalled there.

While I continued to work at Denel, even producing a quality 24-page colour brochure on the Rooivalk which was intended for international distribution (the project was called off with no explanation given by management before its reached printing stage) nothing more about the real or imagined 'intrigue' emanated from Joe.

Things changed quite suddenly shortly before my services at Denel were terminated several weeks before the allotted term and I was sent on my way. On one of the last evenings Joe approached me, obviously disturbed.

He had to talk to me, he, declared, his voice an octave higher than normal, which was when I thought it better if I led him to my car. I didn't need a repeat performance of the previous runaround.

Settled in the passenger seat, Joe began slowly, after apologising for the intrusion which I didn't mind, though it went on a while.

'What is it?' I finally asked.

'Well, you know I've been seeing one of the girls working in the travel office…' He didn't need to explain because I knew that Denel had its own travel division; the ticket to fly from Seattle had come from there.

'Go on,' I prompted.

Then it all came out. While I had been doing my thing at Denel, he explained, the travel office staff had been talking about the inordinate number of South African professionals heading off to Tehran. There was no disputing where they were going because they were writing the tickets. Then one member of staff recognised a family member's name among the prospective travellers, the only difference being that she knew that he had worked at Pelindaba as a nuclear physicist. When she raised the issue at home that evening, she was told by her father not to question. Which was when her mother interceded, and it was made clear that the entire family was in on what was going on.

'Well, truth is, it was staff members who handled the tickets, and not being under severe security strictures socially, not yet anyway, they tended to talk. They could do so because though all were sworn to secrecy, it was generally accepted internally as referring to not speaking to people beyond Denel's security fence.' As one of them commented when chided by an associate: 'This isn't Iran…not yet anyway.'

When I interjected that there were people from all over the world travelling to Iran, Syria and other Middle East countries, Joe's response was brusque: 'Yes – very few – but those from South Africa, are scientists who have worked on nuclear weapons projects…and in any event, almost all their tickets are for a three- or six-month duration in that country.

His final words on the subject were something along the lines of 'Who the hell knows exactly what they're doing there?'

CHAPTER 25

Mayday

As a correspondent, I covered Portugal's colonial wars in Angola, Mozambique and Portuguese Guinea early in my career. I wrote several books on these wars, some of which were translated into Portuguese. Someone in Lisbon commented recently that I was probably better known in their literary and military circles than in London.

In those early days, I seemed to have gained a trust that allowed me to access those conflicts. Unlike most Western journalists, who were not so fortunate, I was able to report on the events because the bureaucrats in Lisbon had an implacable xenophobia towards both domestic and foreign scribes.

Salazar had always opposed a free press, but since I wasn't Portuguese and lived in South Africa, I sort of got away with it. I was critical in my war reports – of what had become an ineffective Portuguese Army fighting in Africa (Mozambique in particular), and a human rights record that had been tarnished long before I came along.

Still, Africa's wars were very much a reality to just about every family in Portugal because conscription was mandatory, and if it wasn't a son who had been called up, then someone from next door. Eventually, so many young men slipped across the border into Spain (and from there on to Europe and North America) that the situation became farcical. The gag was that by the late 1960s, more Portuguese were waiting on tables in France than anywhere else.

Ultimately, economic factors were destined to play as significant a role as politics in the outcome of Lisbon's colonial conflicts as the wars themselves. Lisbon wasn't losing its battles but wasn't winning them either.

A debilitating malaise seemed to have crept into the ranks, mainly because the nation had become war-weary after more than a decade of fighting in Africa. By then, almost everybody regarded those hostilities as a lost cause. You couldn't miss it in the fatalistic mien of the troops in the field who had become scruffy and unmotivated. It wasn't long before they emulated American troops in Vietnam by wearing the iconic peace symbol around their necks. It had taken Portugal a decade to get there…

There were many reasons, including the reality that those were exceedingly tricky economic times; after Albania, Portugal was the second poorest nation in Europe. By 1971, reckoned one source, it had committed almost nine-tenths of its military resources to its African wars.

Captain John 'Jack' Cann, a former United States Navy aviator who served in the Pentagon, wrote *Counterinsurgency in Africa: The Portuguese Way of War 1961–1974*, one of the definitive books on Portugal's African campaigns, and he had much to say that was instructive.[1]

He wrote: 'Portugal, in 1961 – to have mobilised an army, transported it many thousands of kilometres to its African colonies, established large logistical bases at key locations there to support it and then equipped it with special weapons and materials, trained troops for a very specialised type of warfare – was a remarkable achievement,' and continued:

> It was even more noteworthy that those tasks were accomplished without previous experience, doctrine, or demonstrated competence in either power projection or counterinsurgency warfare; therefore, they were without the benefit of any instructors who were competent in these specialities. To put this last statement in perspective, other than periodic colonial pacification efforts, Portugal had not fired a shot in anger since World War I, when Germany invaded northern Mozambique and southern Angola.

He also stressed that all three wars were great distances from the Metropolis. Portuguese Guinea (today Guiné-Bissau), is almost as far from Lisbon as Nairobi is from Johannesburg.[2]

So too, with Luanda, Angola's largest city and the central major resupply point for the war in the interior. It lies more than 7,000 kilometres from Portugal or, roughly speaking, the distance between Washington and Berlin. Mozambique, twice the size of California, is situated several thousand kilometres further towards the east, fringed along its entire coastline by the Indian Ocean.

Look at the facts: Portugal, a tiny nation of fewer than nine million people, fought in Africa twice as long as the United States did in Vietnam. Moreover, they did so in regions where populations aggregated roughly 12 million, spread over areas half the size of Western Europe. Today, only a few generations later, less than five or six in a hundred Americans are even remotely aware that Portugal had colonies in Africa and was involved in a series of military upheavals on that continent. Moreover,

---

1   John P. Cann, *Counterinsurgency in Africa: The Portuguese Way of War, 1961–1974*. Hailer Publishing: 2005; *Brown Waters of Africa; Portuguese Riverine Warfare, 1961–1974*. Hailer: 2007; *Flight Plan Africa: Portuguese Airpower in Counterinsurgency, 1961–1974*. Helion: 2015.

2   Personal correspondence with John Cann, 2016.

it was guerrilla warfare on a massive scale. Lisbon's armies had one more singular advantage that Dr Cann delineated, and I quote:

> Those young men could fight under conditions that would have been intolerable to other European troops. They could go for days on a bag of beans, some chickpeas and possibly a piece of dried codfish – all to be soaked in any water that could be found.
>
> They could cover – on foot and through elephant grass and thick jungle – sometimes distances hundreds of kilometres over a three-day patrol period and quickly learned how to fight well. They did so successfully for over a decade across three fronts in remote regions of Central Africa.

What was clear from the beginning was that the Portuguese were obliged to fight their wars very differently from how other nations handled theirs. For a start, it was the age of the whirlybird but Lisbon could never afford the kind of helicopter support that the Americans enjoyed in Southeast Asia.

The Lusitanians had Alouette gunships to start with, the same machines that the Rhodesians flew, hardly comparable to the utility Bell UH-1 (Huey) choppers fielded in vast numbers by the Americans in Vietnam.

Towards the end of the war, the Portuguese Air Force acquired Sud-Aviation SA330 medium-lift Pumas, but those troopers only saw cursory service in Africa and never flew in Portuguese Guinea. They lost a dozen of these larger helicopters when a militant communist group operating out of Lisbon – all Portuguese nationals – launched a destructive raid at the air force's Tancos Air Base.

Cumulatively, over the course of more than a decade, I spent many months travelling between the three colonial wars. In Mozambique, I did so unofficially and usually with some inquisitive government official peering over my shoulder.

In Portuguese Guinea, probably the most intense conflict of the three African wars, I was attached to units constantly under attack, mainly because the colony was both small and compact. The guerrillas could slip across unmarked frontiers after dark, do their deeds and be back in their Guinean or Senegalese bases before dawn.

Things were tough in that embattled enclave – it had almost been taken by the guerrillas earlier because of inept military leadership. Then Lisbon appointed General António de Spínola, a specialist in counterinsurgency tactics, to take command. It took that veteran of foreign wars only months to get things back on track.

I spent time with him at his Bissau headquarters, and we got to know each other quite well. I found him a remarkably insightful military man who fought the enemy by always planning three moves ahead, almost like a game of chess.

He was not shy to send me out on operations of my choice, which is why I ended up on one of the most challenging assignments of my life at Tite, a contested military base about 20 minutes out of Bissau by Alouette. The drama started on my second night there when we came under a mortar attack. I wasn't hurt, but others were.[3] Not long afterwards, I went out on patrol with a marine unit, and we were rocketed, though thankfully, those responsible were poor shots.

Portuguese Guinea was also where the Soviets allowed the guerrillas access to SAM-7 anti-aircraft ground-to-air missiles, with the result that several Portuguese Air Force Fiat G.91 jets were shot down, other aircraft too.

Possibly the most eventful adventure was going out from Tite on an extended patrol with one of the best commando units fielded by the Portuguese Army in its colonial wars – *Comandos Africanos*. Its all-black unit was as tough and resilient as old boots, commanded by one of Lisbon's war heroes, a Fula tribesman by birth named Captain João Bacar. The irony was that he was Muslim, fighting for a Christian colonial hierarchy.

Though Bacar was still a comparatively young man, he'd received many awards for his leadership and bravery. He took me under his wing when we went out – on foot during daylight hours – and at night we waited in ambush along jungle tracks for the enemy. A brilliant operator, he had rarely been caught short by his sworn enemies who despised him and his allegiance to a foreign flag that they jeered was not even African.

Bacar was idolised by his men – he could lead them through purgatory had he wanted to. We were together for about a week and became fast friends, which is why I was knocked sideways when he was killed on his next patrol a week after I'd left him.

The death of Captain Bacar was deemed a national disaster, and João was mourned in the farthest reaches of the Portuguese Empire.

One of my more sobering experiences came when I left Bissau on my journey home again, this time in an air force DC-6 crammed with war wounded. Two of the aircraft's engines went on the blink after we were well over the Atlantic en route to our first refuelling stop in the Canary Islands (Lisbon had a clandestine arrangement with Madrid by then).

After my session in the wilds with Captain João Bacar, I was scheduled to depart from Bissalanca Airport on board a lumbering old four-engine Portuguese Air Force transport that would take us back to Europe. It was a lengthy series of hops in those days if you weren't on a commercial jet.

We were loaded to the gunwales. That meant that all passengers and their baggage were weighed, not once but twice, the idea being that the engineer would then be able to accurately compute his maximum take-off weight. There could be no mistake in Bissau's oppressive heat – the plane needed a certain runway length to get off the ground, and Bissalanca wasn't the biggest airport in Africa. Part of the problem involved the number of war-wounded on board. There were about twenty

---

3   Tite in this West African colony is not to be confused with Mozambique's Tete, a city on the Zambezi River.

patients, some critical, accompanied by several medical staff. One casualty wasn't expected to survive the trip.

We left Portuguese Guinea late that morning, and it took what seemed an age to get off the ground. There was a ten-second phase when I wasn't sure we'd clear a bunch of palms at the far end of the runway. We made it, and finally, the DC-6 was up and away. Minutes later, we were over the open sea, which changed colour from a dirty, ochre-brown to an almost incandescent hue of tropical blue. Roughly about then, I propped my head against the bulkhead and fell asleep.

Every farewell in Portugal is an event, such things can sometimes be headily celebrated. It's the same almost throughout the Iberian Peninsula, and I hadn't had much sleep the night before. All I knew was that I'd been plied with brandy, 20-year-old Constantino, no less. It must have been an hour or two before a set of jarring vibrations caused me to open my eyes: the aircraft was shuddering.

The first thing that caught my eye was that one of the two propellers in my view of the port wing had stopped turning. We were at 20,000 feet, and there they were, motionless. That was followed by somebody rattling off a string of instructions, none explicit but delivered in a high-pitched voice that suggested it emanated from somebody as disturbed as I was. The cockpit had spoken, and frankly, I understood none of it – except that we had a problem.

The soldiers around me were uneasy, and since I was the only foreigner on board and, in their minds, a 'world traveller', they looked to me for advice. I had none to give – because this kind of thing had never happened to me before. I was as terrified as they were – though I did my best not to show it – stiff upper lip and all that.

One or two made their way to the cockpit; for all the good that was likely to do.

Turning towards my window again, my heart sank still further. Rolling plumes of white smoke were emerging from under the wing, and my immediate reaction was that we were on fire!

We were not. The flight crew was dumping fuel – standard procedure – only I didn't know it. Aviation fuel vaporises at altitude, and when the cocks are opened, giant swathes of steam-like vapour emerge. It must have looked impressive from the sea, and since we were over one of the main sea lanes between Europe and Africa, there must have been quite a few reports transmitted by radio of an aircraft on fire. The trouble was, there was still more to come.

Moments later, the plane's right wing dipped, and as we banked sharply towards the African coast, somebody muttered something about another engine starting to splutter. What a predicament!

One could hardly miss the implications – with all the sick and dying on board, any prospect of ditching in the sea would have meant more blood being spilled. In these tropical waters, it was axiomatic that there were sharks galore, which I knew since I'd just recently published my first underwater book.

An abundance of instructions poured though the intercom, and I finally got someone to explain to me exactly what was happening. One of the nurses said we were heading back towards the coast. Not Portuguese Guinea, where we'd come from because we might not be able to get that far; we were already losing altitude. Instead, she said, we'd set course for Dakar, in Senegal, which was still quite a distance away. I didn't feel it necessary to tell her that Senegal was one of several African states technically at war with Portugal.

Anyway, a string of Maydays had gone out, and air traffic control in that West African city would have been aware by then that we were on our way, she happily reported.

As we got within sight of Goreé Island, in Dakar's broad oceanic bay, the pilot again turned sharp right, and instead of landing, our aircraft headed down the coast. We were close enough to Dakar Airport, but why risk the diplomatic brouhaha that would likely follow should a Portuguese military aircraft be forced to land in enemy territory? After that, the plane kept flying farther south once we got over Banjul in the Gambia, and we kept at it until we reached Bissau.

It was close, too damn close, the pilot told me when I sought him out later that evening, 'But we made it back safely.'

It was a harrowing experience, hopefully never to be repeated. Not eager to board the DC-6 the next day, though I was assured it would have been repaired, I was able to coax General de Spínola into getting me on board one of the bi-weekly TAP Boeing flights to the Metropolis, which he did with a smile. His government paid for the ticket as well.

While I've had a few narrow scrapes while moving about Third World countries, I'd so far – touch wood – never experienced an absolute disaster. It has been close, like flying out of the former British colony of Aden in the Arabian Peninsula in a decrepit Dakota DC-3 that seemed to be kept together with masking tape. I'd watched one of the planes take off after arriving at the airport for my flight, and sheets of flames emerged from the engines' exhausts as it trundled down the runway. Ominous…

My flight was from Aden to Djibouti, then still under French control, and the airline was the Brothers Overseas Aircraft Corporation or BOAC. That was a sharp move because the Arab government didn't need to remove all the original British BOAC billboards cluttering just about every road in and out of the capital. After a wait of five hours, we were ordered to board by a squad of soldiers and settled down to await our departure.

The pilot had started gunning his engines for take-off when two Arabs in the seats immediately in front of me decided that they needed to smoke, something I only became aware of after one of them had already lit up – the idiot!

I wasted no time, unbuckled and thrust forward to knock the man across the face, extinguishing his fag in the process – the entire episode, punctuated by a squeal of pain that reverberated throughout the aircraft, even above the roar of the engines. We were not playing games.

Nothing ever came of it because one of the cabin crew rushed forward and gave the man hell in his own language, and the flight took off without further incident. In retrospect, nothing serves the purpose better than a *harde klap* (a solid smack).

As I was to learn about 48 hours later, the flight that followed mine out of Aden to the French colony a day later crashed into the Red Sea. There were no survivors.

In the Angolan War, once I got to cover it, I didn't spend as much time flying with the air force as I'd hoped, but they did take me on the occasional foray.

I was flown to Cabinda, the enclave north of the Congo and later, to eastern Angola, both times in an air force Nord Noratlas, and then back again in a small plane out of an army base on the Zambian border.

My first sortie with an air force detachment in Angola was long before I even got to Bissau. This is a record of that experience as it appears in my first book, *The Terror Fighters*. I quote verbatim:

> The bulky Portuguese Air Force transport plane swung inland from the sea minutes after take-off from Luanda's Presidente Craveiro Lopes Airport. We levelled off at about 150 metres.
>
> In the early morning haze, the Angolan capital disappeared fast behind us. Coastal swamplands and civilisation gave way rapidly to rough, uneven jungle country below. We'd been airborne only a short while and were already deep into wild country, continuing at almost tree-top level for five minutes before the plane slowly lifted for higher ground towards the north. Occasionally a palm broke through the heavy, felt-like jungle canopy as we passed close to some of the taller leviathans.
>
> We were still only minutes out of Luanda when the four paratroopers on board started to prepare for a supply drop.
>
> 'So close to Luanda,' I asked, having been given a pair of cans and a mike which I'd adjusted over my head so we could talk.
>
> Captain José Moutinho, our pilot, shrugged. 'We've come a long way since the war started in 1961, amigo. However, we still have our problems,' he replied, adding that our objective was Quicabo, a Portuguese Army position in mountainous terrain only minutes away.
>
> Below, the topography had become splintered, grey-blue fingers of granite outcrops emerging out of the jungle, roughly 60 metres tall and that stood out silent and erect. All were mute sentinels to the insurgent campaign being fought around them. I later learned that they made excellent observation points for the enemy.
>
> For all that, viewed from the air, this was an astonishingly beautiful region, typical of the African bush country that had awed visitors from every continent for centuries. Now it was being ravaged, and the war wasn't the only pestilence because people who customarily lived there were constrained from working, and the region was going to waste. There was the occasional plot of land, but that barely served the needs of those who tilled them.
>
> 'This area is thick with *terroristas*,' Captain Moutinho declared, using the accepted phraseology of the time for insurgents. 'The enemy brought terror,' he said... 'they are a poor example of the kind of guerrilla you find in other wars.'
>
> I didn't argue. I could have pointed to the obvious: his adversaries had kept Lisbon on its toes for the past five or six years, and many lives had been lost on both sides. Also, if the guerrillas were *that* ineffective, what were they doing virtually on Luanda's doorstep?

The pilot made clear that we were flying over the disputed *Dembos*, local lingo for a vast jungle region in the north of Angola that was probably two or three times the size of his own country back home.

The notorious Sector D starts here, he ruminated, casually waving an arm across the terrain ahead. We'd been briefed about the war before take-off from Luanda, but nobody told us that hostilities started seventy or eighty clicks north of the capital.

'Like Vietnam, heh?' the captain chuckled. I didn't respond.

Lights flashed on an instrument panel next to him, at which he turned his attention to the drop – the paras in the rear were ready, and I unbuckled to join them. Each of the four men wore a safety harness, a precaution, as one of them was to explain after we'd landed. The straps were there because, in the event of being dragged out with one of the bundles we were dropping or becoming disorientated, they would be lifesavers. That sometimes happened, he averred.

With the rear aircraft door open, wind furiously swirling within the narrow confines of the fuselage and engines roaring, it made talk difficult, so I pulled back and observed.

The captain had earlier detailed that there would be seven crates and some mailbags to be dropped during three runs over a short runway that lay between a pair of hills: two crates each on the first two run-ins and the last three on the final approach with the post going out intermittently. It was a relatively simple assignment for the Noratlas, which could carry 35 fully equipped paratroopers and, if necessary, haul them 2,500 kilometres at about 400 kilometres an hour. Those were reliable planes, of which four hundred were initially built in France, with few being lost in Lisbon's wars.

Captain Coutinho: 'Our approach will be at about 165 metres, but this varies because of the hills: more importantly, we will have little opportunity to manoeuvre.'

We'd been told earlier that most of the fresh supplies came in by air because the roads were terrible and, as might have been expected, the guerrillas were active. It sometimes took a convoy 24 hours to cover a 100-kilometre stretch and twice that in the rainy season. Road convoys were attacked several times during an outward journey and more often on return: by then; the insurgents would be waiting.

It's a bad war, the captain commented to nobody in particular…all this business to drop a few parcels to a camp…we stick our necks out every time…

Captain Moutinho was a veteran of Portugal's wars in Africa. He'd flown jets in Guinea further up the West African coastline and only recently been transferred to transport command and hated it. 'Now I drive a taxi in the air,' he joked.

The Noratlas dipped sharply to port to avoid a row of granite peaks, and Quicabo stood out sharply against a jungle backdrop like an ochre-coloured mine dump in a world of speckled green.

What happens if something goes wrong? I asked.

'Ah well, perhaps a helicopter will reach us before the *terroristas*,' he laughed. And anyway, where do we land in this kind of jungle country? The pilot and his co-pilot were armed with a 9 mm service pistol and a bush knife under each armpit. They carried them in specially designed camouflage service waistcoats that Portuguese aviators wore on operational duties in Africa.

Moments later, the military post loomed ahead, and we were approaching fast. Captain Moutinho sounded a buzzer that flashed a green light in the rear, and the drop began.

Three times the plane passed over Quicabo. It seemed as if all 200 men that manned the base had turned out to watch because we were sometimes close enough to see their faces as we passed. A group at the far end of the runway near the jungle waved.

Fifteen minutes later, the Noratlas landed on the long, uneven airstrip at Santa Eulalia, further towards the north and not far from the Congolese frontier, where more stores were unloaded. We'd been told we'd eventually visit the place because the war around that army base was severe. But next time, we'd come in on the weekly convoy from Luanda because there were other things the Portuguese military wished us to experience.

The captain told us we'd had it easy on those runs after we'd touched down back in Luanda. It could be much worse when the camp was covered in a low cloud called a *cassimbo*, as the locals referred to the mountain mist. And then again, he added, they sometimes came under fire – nothing serious because the insurgents had not yet succeeded in crippling one of the transports. But it could be unnerving, he admitted.

CHAPTER 26

Lisbon

After covering the wars in Rhodesia and briefly in Mozambique, my first experience in Angola was when I decided to cast my net a little wider. I did so for several reasons.

To begin with, what had happened while I was in Nigeria had started to haunt me, Biafra in particular. I'd observed death up close many times, and while working in Lagos, it was clear to me that a full-scale war was brewing. That country's civil war erupted shortly thereafter, and in the course of three years, a million people died – mostly women and children – the majority starved into extinction.[1]

The situation in the Congo – then and now – is one of constant turmoil, with people slaughtered every day. Even then, I couldn't help feeling that South Africa might be on a long-term tightrope. In West Africa it was all tribal, of course. Nigerian Christian tribes ranged against Muslim ones, and as we regularly see in news reports, the bloodletting continues.

With the Biafran War having gone the way of all conflicts, I had concerns that a similar situation could arise in South Africa, the country of my birth. There were many tribes in South Africa – the whites, then politically dominant, followed by Africans, Coloureds and the Indian community. Though it took a while – a fellow named F. W. de Klerk seemed to have shared those sentiments – only he was in a position to do something about it. He started by releasing Nelson Mandela from his 27-year-long incarceration.

On my way home from West Africa, I travelled through Angola again, this time taking the road from north to south. It was only a couple of years since I'd first traversed that terrain, but it was clear that the Portuguese, while being able to handle the ongoing military situation in Angola, were in trouble up to their craw.

My view, not all that perspicacious because it was apparent to anybody who really knew and understood Africa well enough following the 'Liberation period' (as some refer to it) in other parts of the continent, was that Lisbon might be able handle

---

1   Al J. Venter, *Biafra's War 1967–1970: A Tribal Conflict in Nigeria that Left a Million Dead.* Helion: 2015. Also, *Biafran Genocide – Nigeria: Bloodletting and Mass Starvation.* Pen & Sword: 2018.

one insurrection. But with the guerrillas opposed to a Portuguese military presence in Africa in all three of Lisbon's African possessions and getting everything they needed from the Soviets and Chinese, as well as Cuban backing for their *Guerras do Ultramar* (foreign wars) – which included manpower – that European nation would not be able to hold out indefinitely.

Granted, the Portuguese Army and Air Force had great fortitude but it was battling those three wars simultaneously, all being fought thousands of kilometres from home. Simple logic told one that Lisbon lacked the resources and versatility of the United States, a nation that could support a much bigger conflagration in Vietnam by flying in troops whenever it wished, thousands at a time. In contrast, just about everything Lisbon needed to fight a series of guerrilla struggles in Mozambique, Angola and Portuguese Guinea, including troop movements from Europe to Africa, had to be brought in by ship. That took time and effort.

As one rebel leader told me when we met in Addis Ababa a few years later, the Portuguese did make excellent mileage of their problems, but as far as time was concerned, the guerrillas had oodles more. More salient, one didn't have to be clairvoyant to see that these colonial insurrections were exhausting the nation to the point where something had to give. Nobody needed to be reminded that such hostilities almost always ended ignominiously.

Paris's exit from Indochina in 1958 and then Algeria a few years later were still fresh in everyone's minds. The consensus among rebel leaders was that if a much wealthier and better-equipped nation like France could be beaten in the field, then Portuguese forces should be a pushover. Well, they were not. By the time I returned to cover the Angolan liberation struggle, the war had already lasted six years. Effectively, I needed to spend time in that conflict to understand why.[2]

I returned from one of my visits to Rhodesia, where I managed to inveigle my way to the sharp end, and I again wrote to Colonel Bettencourt Rodrigues at the Portuguese Embassy in London asking whether it would be possible for me to spend a month covering his country's war in Angola.

Once more, he replied promptly: 'Send me your passport.'

From the earliest days of the revolutionary uprising, the war in Angola was more intense in the undeveloped region that lay across a vast, disjointed expanse of the country north of Luanda – forests and swamps swept across the land from one horizon to another. It was, and still is, a remote, heavily foliaged area, much of it suited for growing coffee. But farms were sparse, isolated and with tracks in the bush for roads. Most of the owners had fled the war, which was why the rebels had such success in the early days.

---

2   Al J. Venter, *Combat: South Africa at War Along the Angolan Frontier.* Helion: 2019; published in South Africa by Ex Montibus Media: 2020.

South Africa's Border War lasted 23 years and eventually involved the Soviet Union, China and many African countries. But while Pretoria held fast it was always a demanding war to cover, which I did from the start.

After the Portuguese had been ousted from their African colonies, Rhodesia came under fire in a war that lasted six years. I went in there on assignments many times while hostilities lasted.

Counterinsurgency operations in Africa always involved aircraft and helicopter gunships, a tradition that has continued with today's Jihadist wars in West Africa. Seen here is a Rhodesian Air Force Alouette III helicopter preparing for a bush sortie.

Recce squad with whom I went in near Chipinga in the east of the country.

I took Colonel Bob Brown and his boys into Rhodesia to cover the war several times. He is seen here, centre, in the bush north of the capital with 'Big John' Donovan (on his left) and 'Fat Ralph' who came along for the ride.

French, South African, British and other nondescript mercenaries – particularly those able to fly vintage warplanes – became a feature of counterinsurgency operations in the Congo in the early 1960s.

French mercenaries in the Congo.

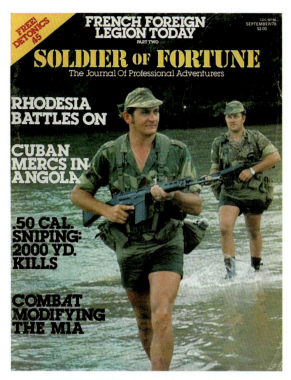

One of my many covers for Colonel Robert Brown's *Soldier of Fortune* magazine, this one on the Rhodesian War, printed in September 1978.

Me (centre) with Colonel Bob Brown (right) and 'Big John' Donovan in El Salvador's civil war. Bob MacKenzie can be seen, right background.

Neall Ellis prepares for an Mi-24 sortie in the African jungle.

Freetown from Neall Ellis' helicopter gunship in 2000.

American mercenary Dave McGrady worked freelance as a 'Bounty Hunter' in the Rhodesian war. I accompanied him on one infiltration in a particularly hostile area near Wankie in the north-west and us 'hunters' soon became the hunted. We were fortunate to have scarpered to safety.

With a United Nations contingent in Lebanon on the icy slopes of Mount Hermon in winter. We could sometimes see Damascus in the distance on a clear day.

I accompanied an Israeli strike force commanded by General Arial Sharon when the IDF invaded Beirut in the summer of 1982. There were some grim battles fought.

My then-wife Madelon went with me into the South Lebanese war, with Israeli Colonel Yoram Hamizrachi, who controlled South Lebanese operations in the disputed zone.

There were few buildings in the Lebanese capital during the civil war that did not display prominent battle scars, like this former apartment building in downtown Beirut.

The so-called 'Green Line' which separated opposing forces in Beirut was unquestionably one of the most dangerous places on the planet while hostilities lasted. I spent good times with the largely Christian Lebanese Force Command.

Tyre in Lebanon – I flew over the city in a helicopter approach to Beirut and although photography was prohibited, I took this picture anyway.

Looking at jihadi forces across the Green Line.

These small strike/patrols were called *Daburs* and operated mostly out of the southern Lebanese port of Sidon while the Lebanese invasion lasted.

With a couple of Israeli-led South Lebanese Army officers along their northern front in what is today referred to colloquially as 'Hezbollahland'.

Peter Beard gave me this classic shot of himself on the shores of Lake Turkana, it went viral!

Shark diving, one of my favourite pursuits. I have been diving with these predators for half a century and never been purposely attacked, though I have had my 'moments'. (Photo courtesy of Walter Bernardis)

Gun club where I shot competition with my favourite handgun, a Colt .45ACP pistol. I am kneeling bottom right.

Karin Pretorius, the South African journalist with whom the Russian KGB spy – so-called Frenchman Francious Darquennes, was involved before he was exposed.

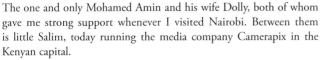

The one and only Mohamed Amin and his wife Dolly, both of whom gave me strong support whenever I visited Nairobi. Between them is little Salim, today running the media company Camerapix in the Kenyan capital.

I operated for a month during the Balkans War with the United States Air Force, working from a variety of planes that included military refuelling aircraft from where this image emerged.

I sat in the rear of a USAF aircraft flying over the Balkans to get this and other pictures.

With members of the Portuguese Army's Rapid Reaction Force in the Central African Republic in 2019. (Pedro de Avillez)

Guerrilla-held village in interior comes under Hind attack in the Sierra Leone rebel war.

Luanda airport with Sukhoi SU-27. Most of these Soviet planes were flown by South African mercenaries who soon brought the guerrilla war to an end.

A French Special Forces operator aboard one of their helicopters heads into action across an embattled Mali. More recently that insurgency became a tough option for Paris and they withdrew all their forces from that country in August 2022.

Sidegunner over Timbuktu combating al-Qaeda rebels

A French Foreign Legion operational base in the disputed heartlands of Mali. Observe the Puma helicopters in the background.

Mali is an enormous African state today wracked by Jihadist terror. When the French were still ensconced with their forces they would run lengthy convoys to the north, always with helicopter 'Top cover' if needed.

I went into the Central African Republic twice, in 2019 and 2022 and spent more time dodging Russia's notorious Wagner Group than any guerrillas operating out of often impenetrable jungles in the interior.

Burkina Jihadists allow a rare photo.

Farewell parade for the world's oldest, still-active war correspondent while embedded with an operational NATO tactical air detachment on the outskirts of Bamako, the Mali capital for a month in late 2021. Lieutenant-Colonel Duarte Soares and his troops took good care of this ancient warrior.

As a result, I was surprised that the base where we dropped the seven crates was only 15 minutes flying time from the capital. Until then, I (and almost everybody else not familiar with the complexity of this colonial war) had been led to believe that hostilities were taking place hundreds of kilometres to the north, adjacent to the Congolese frontier (though the rebels had also opened up a new front in eastern Angola). Naturally, it was in the interests of Lisbon's high command to remain vague about most things related to the insurrection, and being candid about distances was one of the anomalies.

When we finally put down at Santa Eulalia, much of the country to the north of the camp – which stretched towards the west and the coast – was either impenetrable jungle or low-lying arboreal terrain, an unhealthy environment in which to fight a war. If malaria didn't get you, the guerrillas might.

Because it was an equatorial region, there were rivers everywhere. Almost all the bridges had been blown at one stage or another; first by the retreating Portuguese and then – government forces having gained the upper hand once more – by the insurgents. That suggested a measure of sophistication and possible foreign involvement that was only briefly touched on – and then strictly off the record – during the few briefings I was able to attend.

With time, the Portuguese rebuilt most of them – without bridges, movement into the interior would have been impossible. These structures had to be protected, which meant the need for blockhouses, requiring still more men for guard duties – a perpetual cycle…

One of the first things to happen on my arrival at the Santa Eulalia base, headquarters of Sector D, was a briefing by the unit intelligence officer, which – like most order groups – was thorough. But, as I was to discover as our fact-finding tour progressed, it was often spliced with occasional snippets of disinformation – an axiom as old as man himself: truth is war's first casualty.

With about two dozen trucks and a couple of helicopters on hand for emergencies – continuously operating out of Luanda and not permanently stationed in the interior it seemed to sometimes become a precarious contest of wills: who would give way first. Because the base often came under mortar fire, its garrison was reasonably mobile, the Portuguese seemed to be able to hold their precarious jungle fortifications. But then again, could they do indefinitely because casualties, while low, were a constant. Thereafter, I was taken on an inspection tour where I learned that like several other Portuguese Army units in the region, the army's primary task, apart from running convoys, was to protect the local African population. Consequently, Santa Eulalia had its own clinic, surgical theatre and dental unit. Soldiers further into the interior who needed advanced attention, such as root canal treatment or an appendectomy, were flown in by light aircraft or helicopter. More serious casualties were airlifted to the military hospital in Luanda, usually on special litters fitted to an Alouette helicopter or possibly in a single-engine aircraft like the Dornier Do 27. Helicopters would land on a concrete slab behind the clinic – which became an 'after-hours' tennis court for the officers – a lot more than the insurgents had to offer their fighters.

I was also to discover there were many more female combatants in the guerrilla ranks than most observers initially realised. As the war progressed, evidence of women combatants in some units became more apparent.

Much of the briefing provided at Santa Eulalia centred on the two main enemies that the Portuguese Army faced in its African combat zones: the jungle in the north and the semi-desert in Angola's southeast. These areas are located in an enormous African country that is twice the size of Texas.

The first rebel group that had entered the country from a newly independent Congo had been linked to forerunners of the FNLA (the National Front for the Liberation of Angola) and headed by Holden Roberto (he also called himself Roberto Holden). A profligate drunk and prone to using American foreign aid for his own purposes, the man was a rogue – but we news-gatherers did not dare say it. He was smart enough to be virulently anti-communist and very effectively played America's interest during the Cold War phase and became a CIA stooge.

Likewise, his FNLA military wing was useless: their soldiers fled the first time they faced Cuban resistance, and from then on, the Front was a spent force.

The FNLA did have a few efficient, more or less independent units in the distant interior, one of which was headed by a former MPLA (the Soviet-backed The People's Movement for the Liberation of Angola) turncoat, Daniel Chipenda. Known as *Chipa Esquadrão*, the contingent – some hundreds strong – eventually sought refuge with the South African Army. Colonel Jan Breytenbach, one of South Africa's most distinguished combat commanders, remoulded it into the crack, white-officered 32 Battalion during the Border War.

Portuguese speaking, this unit became 'a beneficial adjunct to South Africa's Special Forces operations within Angola', and I could go out on patrol with their boys once they had donned South African Defence Force uniforms. Interestingly, 32 Battalion patrols, usually compact at about a dozen men at a time, were preponderantly black, with two or three white officers or NCOs.

As a volunteer rather than a mercenary (I was never paid a cent), I served briefly with *Chipa* while the unit was countering MPLA attacks in and around Nova Lisboa (Huambo today), complete with an FN FAL rifle and six magazines. I was also handed my FNLA identity card, basically going against stringent Geneva Convention mandates, but it was one way to get my story. After that, having handed in my rifle, I made tracks southwards.

Far more effective was the MPLA, a protégé force already ensconced in Luanda as a consequence of some of the machinations of a communist senior command headed by Admiral Rosa Coutinho, appropriately referred to by his peers as 'The Red Admiral' (in Portuguese, *O Almirante Vermelho*).

MPLA guerrillas had been forged into an excellent combat force by their Soviet instructors fought hard from the start. They proved to be competent, well-motivated and disciplined, even though they made little headway against the South African Army in the almost quarter century that the Border War lasted. Yet, with independence when it was all over, it didn't bother the West that while the MPLA had promised free elections, it simply went ahead and grabbed power, with brilliantly manipulated Soviet and Cuban support. That, essentially, became one of the reasons why Pretoria ended up fighting a 23-year insurgency along the Angolan and South West African frontier.

Headed by Agostinho Neto, a mild-mannered revolutionary, he was one of the few black Angolans chosen to attend a university in the Metropolis during the colonial period and studied medicine at Portugal's Lisbon and Coimbra universities. He combined his academic life with covert political activity as a member of the Portuguese Communist Party. Very early in the developing war, this subtle but strong-willed revolutionary leader called on Fidel Castro for military help to mould his movement into a cohesive and well-coordinated revolutionary force. In 1989, by the time that civil war ended – or was supposed to have – Cuba had more than 100,000 of its soldiers deployed in that African state, its most significant involvement in a foreign war.[3]

The briefing session following our arrival at Santa Eulalia in a road convoy lasted well into the evening. It was initially handled by a baby-faced lieutenant with his left arm in a sling, his shoulder having been 'creased' by an AK bullet in an ambush the week before.

'It could have been worse,' the youthful officer admitted, 'We were caught in an ambush in some difficult bush country, and the bullet ricocheted off a Panhard gun turret that I'd commandeered as a command post…during a routine convoy run south of here.' In reasonably good English, he elaborated on some of the problems faced by the Comsec D Command:

> The enemy came into northern Angola from an area along the Congo frontier, roughly between Matadi [the Congo's biggest port] and the capital city Leopoldville [later Kinshasa]. The guerrillas had developed another front in the tiny enclave of Cabinda, which lies north of the Congo. The guerrillas came in from Congo-Brazza and crossed the river in shallow-bottomed *pirogues*, usually after dark, and though we had problems in the past, naval patrols have successfully stopped some of these infiltrators. But once you've seen the river for yourself, you'll know that the Congo is wide, many kilometres across in places. Also, endless numbers of floating islands are constantly carried downstream by the current.

---

3   As detailed in Chapter 12 of *Combat*, it emerged only years later that while Havana always maintained that its Angolan force numbered only about 50,000, the real figure was at least double that.

So, it's easy for them to hide in those matted reed or papyrus islands when they see the lights of a patrol craft approaching. From our perspective, it's physically impossible to inspect everything that floats…that would need thousands more men.

Once across the border and on Angolan soil, it took the average insurgent about six weeks to reach Sector D.

He stressed that it was very different in the early 1960s when the war first started. Then, insurgent groups simply walked through the jungle from the Congo because there were no barriers, not a single demarcation line to show which country was which. There were perhaps half a dozen Portuguese administrative or customs posts and a few more, possibly a few hours' march towards the rear, in a region that stretched six or eight hundred miles. The result was that there were many places in that dense jungle terrain where the rebels could infiltrate.

We were shown our position on a map of the area. Other camps in Sector D included Zala pinpointed to the north, Zemba further south, and the pivotal crossroads settlement of Nambuangongo lay strategically in the centre – the prime reason it had become a territorial prize to both sides.

There were four other Portuguese military bases in an area probably the size of Scotland, each responsible for the security of quite large territorial segments; in total, perhaps a couple of thousand government troops for the task.

Nambuangongo, he told me, was probably the most interesting place because it came with a history that went back to the earliest days of the war. 'Nambu', as the troops called it, had been the original headquarters of the rebel army in Angola. They'd taken it by force and killed everybody there, including several logging crews. Their families had taken refuge at the home of the local *chefe do posto*, and everybody who survived the initial onslaught was fed lengthwise into industrial circular saws at logging plants, the local political administrator included.

Fighting in the vicinity of the camp had been fierce and brutal, and it had been that way since March 1961, the lieutenant said. At this point in the briefing, Captain Ramos de Campos took over and told us that the guerrillas still tried to retake the hilltop base from time to time. They had come close to succeeding several times, he reckoned, 'especially when they know that some of our troops are away from base, either on patrol or on convoy duties.'

It was at Nambuangongo, too, that the rebels had achieved some of their best successes. Their political commissars, he said, would talk about 'Our glorious victories against the Fascist colonial forces', an expression routinely used on the guerrilla radio station broadcasting out of Brazzaville.

Apart from terminology, said de Campos, you couldn't deride that notion. Early on, the rebels had pushed everything the government could muster at short notice, to the very outskirts of Luanda. He revealed that there were several months in the early days when they were masters of just about all they surveyed…from the Congolese frontier southwards.

'But no longer…these days, we have a grip on the war and its solid. However, that doesn't mean that we can simply sit back…'

It was integral to the insurgent 'master plan' to recapture Nambuangongo, 'and snatching it from under us again would be a significant victory.' He admitted that were that to happen, it would be an enormous defeat, adding that Portuguese losses in the environs of the camp remained comparatively high, 'and they're still at it, literally as we speak.'

Another officer at the briefing was Captain Virgil Magalhan. His job was to outline guerrilla tactics and called for a display board to be brought into the command centre.

Using a pointer, he detailed how the war had entered a new phase, how the insurgents liked to lay their ambushes, the types of weapons and mines with which they were equipped – all Soviet origin, including RPG-2s (predecessor to the ubiquitous RPG-7 today) – and where their main operational bases were situated.

His section experienced about four or five actions a week. Most involved ambushes on patrols or convoys, some of which were intense, invariably resulting in casualties on both sides. As opposed to the early days of the invasion, when the rebels attacked in groups often 200 strong, the insurgents had recently tended to concentrate in smaller groups of about 20 or fewer, which was the situation at the time of my visit. Notably, some of the guerrillas that had come through from the north had spent time in Russia, Cuba, China, Tanzania, Algeria, Egypt and elsewhere, while some had been in Eastern Europe for so long that they were fluent in Russian or German.

'As for fighting ability, they're a mixed bag, which holds for most of Africa's liberation wars,' he stated. 'The majority of fighters are difficult to categorise… they might be reasonably well trained, but many among their ranks lack focus or purpose. Nevertheless, some section leaders were reasonably sharp about tactics and the use of more advanced weapons like heavy machine guns, rocket-propelled grenades or mortars.

'The balance, thankfully, is dismal…they've been taught, that is obvious, but they've learned nothing… Still, they persist, and recently they tried a new gimmick,' he elaborated. 'While they'd previously restricted their attacks on campsites to the dark hours, they've resorted to making an occasional daylight mock attack on a particular area.' He explained that a small group would make a show of strength near the forest, perhaps a kilometre from one of the bases, then snipers hidden on higher points would attempt to pick off the officers, a tactic also used by the Viet Cong.

'However, their aim has always been deplorable – although not all of them are bad shots because we've had some men killed.

'Fortunately, they are rarely accurate at anything more than a 150 metres, which is one of the reasons why our casualties have been somewhat light.' He reckoned that things could change radically, but that was the situation at the time of my visit.

To my surprise, I noticed that Portuguese officers – in all three services – often displayed rank in the various operational areas, despite the threat. When you are likely to be shot at, especially in the bush, one would think they would have discarded their epaulettes and gold braid or used muted shades. That would have made it difficult to distinguish who was who from a distance, very much as other Western military forces function in hostile areas. That was not always the case.

Granted, they removed all ranks on patrol or convoy duty, but the insurgents could identify officers and NCOs because they were the ones issuing commands. Additionally, the insurgents had their own means of monitoring activity in Portuguese Army military bases. No doubt, they also used some African domestic staff as informers, as has always been the way in these African conflicts.

Captain de Campos told us of an ambush he'd experienced a short time before in northern Angola. 'Just before I was promoted to captain, I was based in a village a few kilometres from Terreiro, a small coffee-producing area in Sector F north of here,' he said.

'The area had been reasonably active, but it was calm at that stage and had been so for a while. We thought the main enemy force might have passed us and tried to move closer to Luanda, which happened from time to time. Anyway, it was a Friday morning, and it was my job to go into the village to shop for fresh provisions. In the Catholic tradition, we try to eat fish on Fridays, not too difficult because the rivers are full of them.'

The captain chose seven men and set out in two jeeps, his own leading the way along a rough bush road. Driving into town, he kept his foot down on the accelerator. The route through that kind of rugged, mountainous country was fair, and he was eager to return to his camp for lunch.

'We came round one of the many bends in the road, reasonably close to town, and as we turned sharply and dropped into a dip in the road, the enemy – perched above us on a knoll – opened fire. They let rip with everything, and I remember thinking the noise was terrible. In retrospect, I thought it a pretty good spot for ambushing us...a shrewd move, indeed.

'This is when you start reacting instinctively; I had only a few moments to get us out of that mess. All eight of us simultaneously jumped off our vehicles, firing into the grass immediately ahead.'

It was standard procedure, he stated, a precaution that often resulted in some of the insurgents lying next to the road being hit. 'But you had to know what you were doing,' he warned. 'On your own in heavy bush country and away from the vehicles, it could quickly become a one-on-one issue. The ambushers would sometimes slash at anybody nearby with their machetes.

'It lasted only seconds – an inordinately long time when you're taking fire – but we eventually got clear of that lot after emptying a few magazines and hurling grenades.'

'Only when we were in the comparative safety of the surrounding elephant grass did I call for a casualty count from my two corporals. I'd heard the whistles used by the enemy officers and knew the attackers had pulled back.'

Details of the attack were interesting, and the captain answered questions, especially about extricating his men.

One of his soldiers in the second jeep had been hit in the thigh – a serious wound that bled profusely. A dum-dum bullet had blown most of the flesh away, exposing the bone, and that meant that he had to get the fellow back to base, or he would have died right there.

'Now I had some terrorists still hanging about a little longer with harassing fire, and I knew they could have done some real damage. But fairly quickly, they shot their bolt after we'd retaliated and were off.'

The captain estimated the attacking force at about two-dozen-strong. They were well dug in about 30 metres along a rise above the road, and though their position was not easily defensible, height gave them an obvious advantage. They'd been able to see where all the Portuguese troops that had emerged from the vehicles were positioned.

'All we had for protection, if you could call it that, were clumps of tall elephant grass ahead and the road behind,' said the captain, commenting that they hadn't used the opportunity as well as they should have.

'We saw afterwards that they'd initially broken a path through the thick bush and were able to disappear down this jungle trail when things got tough – leaving one of their number behind – an African irregular who had taken a blast from one of the grenades. Several blood trails indicated that one or more had been wounded. More importantly, they hadn't removed any of their used cartridge shells.

'It's the unwritten law among these rebels – Russian influence, I suppose – that they return to base with all their empty shells…if they can do so, of course.'

The Portuguese were initially puzzled about their adversaries collecting spent brass after an action. Captured rebels admitted that they were only issued with more ammunition if they could produce their original casings, which prevented them from throwing away good ammunition and claiming they had been in an action. It would have been challenging to achieve that much had government forces gained a quick advantage.

Interestingly, the spent shells were used again, often many times over. Back at base, they were reloaded and reissued. The captain mused: 'It's a question of economics.'

Another aspect of the ambush, the officer noted, was that the attackers had abandoned a dead comrade. He suggested they probably didn't have time to move the body. 'In any event, we were coming up fast.'

De Campos reckoned that if the enemy didn't leave their casualties behind, the Portuguese would have nothing specific to show for their efforts in action…it was all psychological.

'Often, after an action, we'd find blood traces where one or more of the wounded had sheltered. Unfortunately we weren't always able to establish whether it came from someone killed or possibly wounded.'

CHAPTER 27

You'd be lucky to be hit

When I arrived in Sector D, the rebel army in northern Angola was estimated at about 6,000 regulars. Their numbers were more dominant than the strength of the Portuguese Army, though with conscription having taken effect, conditions were improving. Apart from an insurgent presence, there were two or three times that number of African civilians who lived in the jungles and mountains of the sector, many involuntarily caught up in the crosshairs of conflict.

Though not part of the regular insurgent movement, non-combatants were required to provide valuable support when needed, customarily acting as porters or bearers. They'd also be tasked with burying the dead and tending to the wounded in their villages if a casualty could not be taken back to their lines.

Though these irregulars might have been innocent bystanders initially, that was no longer the case. Early rebel successes had given many of these tribal people the desire for more of the same – often due to ethnic or familial associations – or simply because they were sympathetic to what the rebels regarded as a 'just' cause.

Living permanently in the wild, they could also provide succour to rebels passing through. They'd feed and hide those operating near their villages, called *sanzalas*, which were often big enough to house makeshift field hospitals and which saved many lives, partly because quite a few foreign doctors crossed the border to 'help the cause'. They came from all over the world: African countries, Cuba, China and even Vietnam. Medical supplies came mainly from Europe, the Scandinavian countries and Canada.

For all that, it was an exceedingly difficult war. Life in the primeval forests in northern Angola had evolved over millennia. Locals could grow relatively large crops of their popular cassava root (manioc) in any one of thousands of jungle clearings, the root pushed a few centimetres into the soil by hand. Fertile soil coupled with abundant rain and a hot tropical climate saw the crop through to maturity, which could often be harvested every other month. Sometimes the tubers might be left in the ground for lifting later by the villagers or the rebels.

Locals also grew small quantities of corn, beans or sorghum to supplement their diet, which they would share if a rebel group stayed in the area. Meat was always scarce, especially in wartime where a rifle shot could be heard for miles. Snares would be set but nobody knew where anyone would be the next day.

'We see these communities from the air from time to time, but we're rarely in a position to do anything about it apart from reporting to the intelligence people on returning to base,' the captain stated. Yet curiously, he wasn't overly critical of the role played by civilians caught up in the confusion of war.

They had little option but to help when ordered to do so by a group of armed newcomers, though whether their hearts were in it was another matter – if they didn't assist, they might be accused of siding with the government. Then it was not only the individual at risk but his entire extended family, including grandparents. Still more salient, those pointing fingers, like someone holding a grudge, needed little proof – a bullet behind the neck would end it all.

'We have precisely the same [situation] the Americans have been facing in Vietnam and what the British experienced in Malaya with the civilian population… the guerrillas are now doing the same thing here – trying to win the support of the locals.' For various reasons, he added, they'd succeeded quite well. Others referred to the situation as winning hearts and minds…

It took us almost a day to travel to Madureira on our way to Zala in Angola's tropical north, much of it triple-tiered jungle in the raw.

The country between the two military posts was, as tourist brochures might have phrased it, 'a rather spectacular steamy African hideaway', with bush and undergrowth sometimes straddling the road. In other parts, the elephant grass that overhung the route was twice as tall as our vehicles. 'Hideaway' it certainly was because there was not much movement in those remote parts because almost all its former inhabitants had fled. Some had disappeared into the Congo, and others to seek the government's protection against the 'ungodly invaders'. Most were appalled by the brutality that had become a feature of rebel tactics, with heads sometimes lopped off before questions were asked.

Serried rows of mountains, interspersed by an occasional granite strongpoint – some as tall as skyscrapers – fringed the skyline. Everywhere in between was forest, forbiddingly verdant. Each time we came over a hill or entered a valley, fast-flowing streams would cut across the road with many of the bridges newly built, the old ones destroyed by retreating insurgents.

The country is admirably suited for waging a guerrilla struggle, said Captain Ricardo Alçada, our escort officer, on his second tour of duty in the *Ultramar* and loving it. Dr Alçada – a banker by profession from Lisbon – was a rather unusual individual who played a good game of chess and whose regular tipple each evening was *Aguardiente*. For a born-and-bred city dweller, he relished the bush and the possibility of initiating a scrap, having already been twice wounded by the time I first met him.

The captain and I shared quite a few experiences and ended up fast friends, even visiting each other after the war. He also had a few opinions about what was happening in Angola then.

'This is the closest we've come to Vietnam-type conditions in southern Africa,' he declared. The insurgents had become masters of jungle warfare, especially when they held the high ground. 'Like this,' he said with a wave of an arm towards the surrounding hills. He conceded that the terrain was too overgrown for helicopter deployment. However, the gunships were helpful if they were around because, as in all African insurgencies, their very presence intimidated.

Because of the heat, we travelled from Santa Eulalia on top of – rather than inside – one of the lumbering old Panhard armoured personnel carriers that the army used to protect civilian trucks. We sat perched atop the turret and enjoyed the view, hardly an unpleasant experience. The bulk of the men in the convoy – a couple of dozen soldiers – followed in their troop carriers and sat crouched, eyes intent and weapons at the ready. We were assured that ambushes happened, but that didn't prevent some from dozing off.

There were three APCs in the column, one each at the two extremes and another towards the centre for our use. My photographer and I wore regular army camouflage. We'd been advised to do so, as anything unusual drew attention, and without doubt, a couple of gringos in civilian garb would have.

'You must look and act inconspicuously,' said the captain. 'If they think you're important, their snipers will go for you…not the best shots, but then you don't want to take chances. Nor do we.' He commented on it being difficult terrain to bring in a chopper to haul out the wounded.

Another of the wags in our party who spoke good English said that if 'those guys were actually aiming at us, we were quite safe. They're terrible shots – you'd be lucky to be hit; the fellow next to you should be worried.' By all accounts, guerrilla snipers were more of a problem than the Portuguese were prepared to concede.

Captain Alçada told us later that they constantly targeted officers if they had the chance and, as in any war, people improve with practice. He'd become a target several times, even though he'd removed his epaulettes, and while he always travelled at the van, it was obvious who was in charge. I sensed that my beard worried him because all our escorts were clean-shaven, and my appearance was out of character. Only then did I realise I was the only person in any of the camps we'd visited who had one.

It is worth mentioning that none of us wore helmets or battle jackets, probably because there weren't any. Even with only T-shirts covering our backs, we were covered in sweat within minutes of getting underway.

Although the area we moved through was a part of northern Angola and immediately adjacent to the Congolese frontier, the nights were unusually cool for the tropics. Getting up in the morning was almost as bad as a London dawn; it could be cold, misty and miserable.

It was the altitude – much the same as Eldoret in Kenya, on the Equator – where, over the years, I spent time with Hoffie Retief and his family before they decamped to the coast. On the edge of the Great Rift Valley, not an evening passed without the staff lighting a log fire; once the sun dipped, temperatures plummeted.

That part of Angola differed from East Africa in other ways because, unlike the plains and tracts of savannah and scrub at Serengeti, Amboseli and parts of Tsavo, the Angolan undergrowth encroached everywhere. It had to be constantly kept in check if roads were to remain passable because the foliage all but devoured open clearings used as campsites and, if left to it, even buildings. This could occur within months of not being regularly pushed back.

The entire region was characterised by a distinctive mist which the locals call *cassimbo*. It often envelops the countryside by early evening in what they called the 'cool season'. It was anything but…

By nine in the morning, those shadows would be dissipated by the sun, but until then, nothing moved. It was noon before the last of the previous night's dew had evaporated, and each time we passed under a cluster of overhangs, drops would rain onto our shoulders. After ten minutes or so, we'd be soaked.

Damp permeated everywhere and everything. Leather straps on my cameras turned mouldy within days, and no matter what I did, it stayed that way until we returned to Luanda.

Apart from our Panhards and the accompanying troop carriers, there were about a dozen trucks in convoy hauling an assortment of arms, munitions, supplies and replacement troops to outposts in the interior. The captain said we were travelling relatively lightly because much of the equipment had already been off-loaded further south, at Cage, Canacasalle, Nambuangongo and elsewhere. What was left would be delivered to Madureira and Zala.

'Zala is the end of the road – thank God,' our driver commented. He was relieved that we were almost there. It had taken him two days to get that far from the city – about 150 kilometres and thankfully, there had been no mines. Not yet…

He said they picked up all the coffee harvested from surrounding farms on the way back and that his group did the run five or six times a month, but less in the rainy season. 'Then it's hell…some roads just disappear…and sometimes it can be dangerous.'

We'd arrived in the middle of Angola's dry season, and the roads were atrocious. Under normal circumstances, they would have been graded every few months, but the war was preventing that. Tropical downpours and the constant movement of heavy traffic would create holes and culverts that could swallow a jeep, and of course, there were landmines.

Our column fared no better. There were times when we'd be reduced to a crawl; then, we'd amble alongside our vehicle until the convoy picked up speed again. In several places, we skirted hefty boulders in the road. It was worse when some of the men searched ahead for mines.

'We should really do something with what's left of these roads,' the captain suggested. However, the rebels intensified their activity each time they spotted heavy equipment coming in from Luanda. Then there would be mines all over the place and obviously, casualties would mount.

'The war has been getting hot again, so the authorities haven't been able to get around to it this season,' he confided. In the other sectors, they'd managed to keep roads in a reasonable state – as I was later to see in Cabinda and the east – but the *Dembos* and its jungles had problems all its own. Meantime our column progressed, one kilometre at a time. Almost like clockwork, our vehicles would be ordered to halt, and we'd wait for the stragglers. The officers would order perimeter defences to prevent an attack. Every third or fourth vehicle was a German-built Unimog (Mercedes) personnel carrier with Portuguese soldiers sitting back-to-back. The troops faced outwards, almost reminiscent of famous Robert Capa photos of the Spanish Civil War.

I could see that in Angola, with its distances and undeveloped interior, convoy routine was tedious and almost always, boring as hell. Each troop carrier had a sergeant who sat next to the driver, and we constantly heard orders being barked.

At one stage, the captain raised a hand; one of the NCOs was ordering his men to keep their heads up, which meant that some were asleep. 'It happens all the time,' Alçada explained. The dreary road, monotonous jungle terrain and the dust became soporific, and for some, even in the heart of the war, sleep came easily.

Our transport was more casual than most. Either by accident or design on the part of the colonel-in-charge at the base we'd just left, most of the men on our transport could speak some English. It was clear that they enjoyed the change as much as the challenge, posing for the camera whenever our lenses appeared; a pair of *estrangeiros* thrown in among them taking photos, asking questions or, more likely, voicing smart-arsed comments.

There were times when the trip could actually be quite pleasant. Conversation along the column line was interrupted every fifteen or twenty minutes by a radio operator in one of the Panhards calling up another section of the convoy.

'Echo…Lima…Nove…Dois…Zero.' His staccato voice would echo across the forest and probably deep into it.

If there were enemy about, they'd have heard his voice, not that it would have mattered as there seemed to be more wisecracking among the men than sitreps.[1] It helped to ease the tension. Then the men would shout from one vehicle to another, and several times, almost as if on cue, they would start singing, and the rest of the column would follow in perfect unison. They'd had a lot of practice.

---

1   Military jargon for situation reports.

The musical 'hit of the day' – even in Portuguese Africa – was Tom Jones's 'Delilah'. Surprisingly, everybody seemed to know the words and melodies that might not have been unfamiliar to many of the insurgents in the surrounding bush. That ditty would be followed by 'It's Not Unusual' and other songs made famous by the talented Welshman. Then shots would ring out from somewhere near, and in a blink, everything would change.

After five minutes of intermittent radio talk, the convoy rolled out again. Captain Alçada reckoned that somebody had fired a clip into the first Panhard, and he'd sent a patrol out to scout around.

'That's precisely what those clowns hope for,' he stated after things had gone quiet again. 'They fire a few shots, we send in a patrol – and it's slap-bang into an ambush. They're waiting for us – I've taught my guys never to follow any tracks, to spread out, stick close to the bush, make their own paths if the foliage allows.' From what I could observe, it was not always possible because the bush was not only dense but impenetrable in places.

'They've learnt about the jungle, but it's the AP[2] mines that I worry about,' he declared in low tones, 'and those bastards have a lot of them.'

Though circumstances would vary, the insurgents would never hang about after a contact or an attempt at one had been made. When things didn't go according to plan, they'd pull out, principally because of fear of encirclement, which, considering the undergrowth on both sides of the road, I thought unlikely.

I was only to learn later about the terrible cost both soldiers and civilians were paying in that war because of the indiscriminate use of mines. There wasn't a Portuguese Army base that didn't have at least one victim who had lost a foot or had his leg blown off. The blast had killed others outright, especially if their torsos took the full impact. And that, more than half a century ago, was only the start of what was to spread throughout southern Africa in the decades ahead.

Once we had Madureira almost in view, Captain Alçada showed us where he'd made his first actual contact with the war.

It was a remote spot in a valley on the outskirts of what had once been a logging settlement – the reason the military base had been established. As with the rest of Angola's north, the forest crept up and it was inexorable, all the way to the road. Nearby stood the burnt-out remains of an old farmhouse where we could still spot patches of whitewash against the few crumbling moss-covered walls that remained. The images were foreboding.

It was late April 1961, he told us. He was a young *alférez* then in charge of his own platoon. 'We came down this stretch of road towards the town of Nambuangongo in the early hours, a bunch of us travelling in a column of three jeeps.

---

2   Anti-personnel.

I'd been ordered into the first vehicle by my superior, and I couldn't argue. We knew there were landmines, but someone must lead the way, and that's usually the junior officer.

'As we came out of the jungle gloom to this spot, I felt uneasy. I still don't know why, but I'd asked our driver to slow down. Then we emerged from around *that* corner,' he said, pointing at a cluster of palms, 'and in the road ahead was the head of a woman on a stake.' In Alçada's mind, he admitted, this was symbolic, a warning of sorts. The head, with long black hair matted with blood, had been purposely placed there by somebody, and it definitely wasn't the Portuguese Army.

'They were audacious in those early days: that face, pitted by rot and detritus with insects and flies clinging, took us all by surprise...I'll never forget it. I can still see the dark cavities where her eyes had been; what was left of her jaw was hanging askew.'

The woman had been Portuguese, and it didn't take the patrol long to discover that she'd been the farm manager's wife and that he'd also died in that first attack.

'No one ever found her body. God only knows what medicine they used it for. Her husband, we learnt later, and a couple of young kids were also missing – presumed dead – as more civilised Angolans phrased it.'

That night, Captain Alçada really got going in that war – his first real baptism in a conflict that ultimately claimed many of his contemporaries. Later, over a couple of beers, we talked about the event, and the young officer admitted that nothing else had shaken him up quite like that experience, either before or after.

'There have been other brutalities since – some far worse, but for me, that single event had a special significance – revolting.'

He also intimated that his immediate response was hatred, even revenge. 'I suddenly wanted to murder – to kill everything black – man, woman or child. I wanted to do to them what they had done to our people. But then I had to pull myself together because I had three black soldiers under my command, one of whom was an outstanding tracker.'

Captain Alçada admitted that managing his instincts had been difficult in the early days. To put his mind at ease and find a measure of acceptance, he needed to still an atavistic lust for blood. 'So, I did it another way,' he said in a quiet voice.

'I took an oath. I knelt and made the sign of the cross, very much as the Spanish Conquistadores probably did when they first went after the Incas, though for very different reasons. I swore that I would avenge those deeds and do so with enough courage to become a name to be feared among these people.

'I would become a deadly hunter of people and go after those who had started the war. However, I would retain my integrity and that of my flag to the best of my ability.

'Also, because this had become personal, I would fight my war justly and fairly. Unlike some of my colleagues, I would take prisoners and not shoot them out of hand. I also promised myself that I would kill more *terroristas* than any other Portuguese officer who served in my command.'

Not usually an effusive individual, Captain Alçada's revelations were instructive. I found it encouraging how one man coped under powerful emotional pressures. In the process, the captain had achieved some of his aims and earned a reputation that followed him back to the Metropolis.

In fact, by the time I met him, Captain Ricardo Alçada was quite the war hero. He had probably done more than his share of killings, though he was never to talk about it with me afterwards. I heard from others that he had been awarded a medal or two for bravery.

There was no question that the captain was an efficient, if a ruthless, fighting man. He was also tough but fair to his men. He'd managed to balance how he might have reacted and how he actually responded when faced with critical problems. Several times in the years that followed, we'd meet, both in South Africa and in Portugal. Once, when I travelled on a South African Airways flight to Europe with Madelon that stopped over in Lisbon, he pulled some strings and came on board to say hello while we refuelled.

Invariably, he'd be reasonably forthcoming about what new experiences he'd had, but he wouldn't tell me everything – only enough for me to ponder on, sometimes for a while afterwards. While many of those events involved bloodshed and some were quite horrendous, he told me that he'd always managed to keep his emotions in check.

He'd call it 'keeping my cool', which was when I told him he'd been reading too many American books about Vietnam. He responded by admitting that he had.

I recall him confiding that eight years after seeing that woman's head on a stake, insurgent headquarters in Kinshasa had put a price on his head. 'Not the highest bounty for some of the men fighting this war,' he declared with a smile, 'but enough to tell me that I might have accomplished what I'd originally set out to do.'

After arriving at Madureira, we discovered the base to be one of Sector D's smallest mountain-top military camps. The road to the garrison wound two or three times around a huge, bald granite outcrop before you reached the gate of the encampment. It was topped by two machine-gun turrets that had covered our approach all the way from the base of the incline. All surrounding slopes were swathed in neat rows of metre-high coffee bushes, with the ordered pattern of the plantations standing out vividly in contrast to the jungle below, much of which had recently been cleared of undergrowth up to the barbed wire and adjacent minefield.

This Portuguese Army post was possibly one of the most beautifully situated in Angola. Like Santa Eulalia, it had previously been a coffee estate, the old farmhouse standing at the very pinnacle and dominating the countryside for almost

50 kilometres in all directions. One of the officers joked that on a clear day, you could see forever…

The jungle splendour might not have been primal in the immediate vicinity of the camp, but it was enchanting. In the distance, bright greens blended almost imperceptibly with blues, yellows and purples. The evening brought out a shower of reds and oranges in abundance. Unnamed mountaintops toward the horizon provided more ragged contrast. Had this been Kenya or Sarawak, the setting would have been a tourist attraction of note. The sunset alone compared with anything I'd experienced in Africa.

The war that had blighted these images was stamped on the scene, almost indelibly. Four trucks stood on the central parade ground, and troops with an assortment of weapons – rifles, automatic weapons, grenade launchers and mortars – crowded around, all being briefed. Completing a Malayan Emergency-type scenario, there were more heavy machine-gun turrets on the periphery.

'This is where the action is,' said the young captain who commanded a company of soldiers that had been posted to Madureira for two years. 'You have come to the centre of the war,' and adding a welcome, he suggested we move to the mess.

A patrol of 40 men was going out that afternoon. It was nothing definitive, but some of his trackers had picked up the trail of a large enemy squad that had entered from the Congo, probably overnight. They weren't after the men as much as the stuff they were reported to be hauling through the jungle, probably on their way south. One captive spoke of about 30 or 40 mines, all metal, which headquarters had deduced were anti-tank, probably TM-46s.

In the insurgent group, it had been reported, there were also about a dozen mysterious parcels, carried in slings between pairs of men. The contents hadn't been identified, but it was Madureira's job to search and destroy. If possible, they were to discover what new 'secret weapon' the guerrillas were introducing into Angola.

'They'll try rockets next, probably 122 mm Katyushas, like the Cong have been using around Saigon,' Alçada commented. He added that there were already RPGs galore – the enemy deployed them in every possible contact. The RPG-2 of Portugal's wars in Africa, as we have seen, soon gave way to the more sophisticated RPG-7, both of Soviet extraction.

Though the 'bark' of the RPG-7 is worse than its 'bite' – unless it is armour-piercing and the target is a vehicle – these rocket-propelled grenades have been used to good effect by just about every insurgent army in the world. South African scientists had subsequently reverse-engineered several versions to produce their version of the rocket-propelled grenade in quantity.

RPG-7s were also used to good advantage by the Jihadists in the Battle of Mogadishu in October 1993. Thousands had been secretly shipped from Yemen to the Somali warlord Mohamed Farrah Aidid (by al-Qaeda, one report maintained).

He deployed them to ambush an assault force of about 160 American soldiers travelling in a dozen vehicles.[3] Of the almost twenty aircraft involved – including several Black Hawks – two were shot down by concerted RPG-7 fire. I should mention that while living in America, I exchanged notes with Mark Bowden, who wrote *Black Hawk Down*, and he was not surprised that the RPG had become so widely used in a spate of African conflicts.

That situation remains current in every ongoing modern war, in Africa today, all across the continent.

---

3   Several hundred RPG-7s were used, almost like artillery barrages, to bring the US Army Black Hawks down in the Mogadishu contact that crippled two helicopters and eventually left eighteen American servicemen dead.

CHAPTER 28

South Africa invades Angola

Portugal's colonial wars were over, and I found myself in Luanda in the third week of October 1975, or roughly 18 months after the Portuguese Army had dropped everything and beat an inordinately hasty retreat to the Metropolis.

The Angolan capital, by then, was firmly in the hands of the MPLA. Headed by an Angolan-born academic who all but deified Lenin, the party was decidedly Marxist. It included its version of the hammer and sickle on what became the country's national flag.

I was doing work at the time for various publications, including the *Express*, Geneva's *Interavia*, and *Scope*, a South African news magazine that sometimes liked to emulate *Playboy*. For all that, they paid my bills, so why complain?

I flew into the Angolan capital ahead of the final transition to freedom and joined a large body of scribblers who had arrived to report on the handover. What should have been a happy, historical event, a brave young country – joining almost 50 other African states that had earlier achieved their sovereign independence – was already showing cracks.

Apart from the MPLA, there were two other political movements in Angola vying for dominance, and each was doing its best to either discredit or destroy the other. Some parts of Angola had already devolved into a state of war, undeclared but intense. Even Luanda was not secure.

We were strolling along the city's Marginal one afternoon with Allen Pizzey – a CBS veteran with decades of experience in dodgy places – and had to take cover when a machine gun opened up from somewhere on the heights that overlooked the city. It could have been meant for one of us or somebody else uncomfortably close to where we'd found ourselves.

We all stayed at local hotels because currency issues – and a lot else besides – had not yet been sorted out. We were required to pay in US dollars, which we didn't mind, except that it made a bottle of Scotch hellish expensive.

But even those conditions became uncertain. Almost overnight, there were scores more 'journalists' joining our throng; only these came from Cuba and a good sprinkling of Soviets, Poles, Bulgarians and even North Vietnamese. Some really menacing people from Cairo represented Africa, Dar es Salaam, Algiers and Ghana, and we newsmen concluded that many of them were spooks.

I couldn't retreat into an unobtrusive shell because, British passport or not, everybody around me knew that I came from South Africa. That had gone down well enough when Lisbon still ruled, but with Portugal out of the African political equation, I suddenly had to answer questions about apartheid.

Because I had been covering the Africa beat since the mid-1960s, I could handle that, except that things took a serious turn when I was approached by a couple of enthusiastic young journalists who asked whether I knew that South Africa had invaded Angola. Frankly, that was news to me, and I told them it didn't make any sense.

My reply was direct: why would Pretoria be that stupid to invade a neighbouring country? I reiterated that I knew nothing about it, but their eyes told me they thought otherwise.

The following night, I was again cornered by half a dozen putative colleagues and questioned about the 'invasion'. One of them mentioned that the 'Boers' had taken Pereira d'Eca, a provincial administrative centre I'd visited several times in previous years. Someone else came up with the word 'Savannah' and then qualified it by asking if I knew the meaning of 'Operation *Savannah*'. I did not, I replied truthfully.

At that moment, alarm bells started to ring. Something was going on in South Angola that I knew nothing about. Everybody I mixed with knew that I lived and worked in South Africa – and things started becoming a little uncomfortable – especially after someone on the fringes of our social group had been found shot a few days previously. We were told it was suicide, but...

Worse, there had been several battles in the streets of Luanda during the week. It was nothing serious because guns were fired every night in this great city – though successive volleys of automatic fire adjacent to your hotel are somewhat different – and tend to focus the mind. Were it not that I started to pick up a few unfriendly vibes from some of my colleagues, including distancing themselves when I approached them in the clubs and restaurants we all frequented, I might have stayed longer.

The most palpable thought had crossed my mind several times; some thought I was linked to South African intelligence. Under those circumstances, 'agent' would have been equally damning.

It didn't take me long to consider my options. I was not ready to return to South Africa because I hadn't yet gathered enough material to justify the trip. Also, every one of these scribes with whom I had been associated knew that there was a reasonably hefty war in the interior, with one group of fighters – the FNLA – opposed to the future government. Their irregulars had already occupied Nova Lisboa, the country's second-largest city in the central highlands. There were no 'front lines', but people were getting killed, though the real war between the factions was still to come.

Meanwhile, scheduled flights between most urban centres in the country – sporadic for the most part – continued. So, I made a few discreet enquiries and discovered that there was a plane leaving Luanda for Nova Lisboa each night at about nine. Whether there would be a seat available was another matter, I was warned.

The following evening, without telling anyone, I quietly paid my bill, slipped out one of the rear entrances of the hotel and got a friend to drive me to Luanda Airport. There I joined a queue well over 1.5 kilometres long, with just about everybody trying desperately to get to Nova Lisboa. It didn't help that the Angolan airline offering this service was equipped with high-wing Fokker F27 Friendships, which at max, could take something like 40 passengers.

So, there was I at the airport, very much aware that almost everybody around me was desperate to leave what most feared would soon become a cauldron of horror. Angolan independence was scheduled for 11 November, only weeks away – and since fighting in the adjacent hinterland had intensified – most believed that the city was about to become a battlefield. That never happened, but with a civil war threatening, who could be sure?

Camera secreted and bag in hand, I waited in a long queue of hopefuls, aware that I was at risk just by being there. It was rumoured that MPLA political commissars – backed by Soviet agents – were monitoring movement at the airport. The presence of this six-foot-two bearded honcho, not being the most inconspicuous type, would almost certainly have been noted. The reality was that I simply had to get onto that plane, so I made my move.

With the kind of determined, poker-faced purpose that suggested that I had a confirmed booking in hand, I strode towards the check-in counter, and in the best Portuguese I could muster – I didn't ask but *demanded* to know – who was in charge.

'I am,' said an officious youngster with gold braid on his shoulder, distinctly displeased at my approach. Under any other circumstances, he probably wouldn't have given me the time of day.

'Well,' I said, 'my name is Venter, and I am pleased to meet you.' With that, I thrust out my hand, which he couldn't ignore since my outstretched paw was almost in his face.

Reluctantly he took it, and I knew immediately that he'd felt that rustle of a banknote in my palm. It was the oldest trick in the book; moreover, he was familiar with accepting a bribe – a $100 bill – which he accomplished fluently without anybody knowing that a transaction had taken place. He took my passport and went to the back for a moment or two, probably to check the amount.

That night I slept in Nova Lisboa.

The flight itself was not entirely uneventful. Because so many military factions were involved in Luanda's transitional 'freedom' process, more weapons were floating around than even during the colonial period. Consequently, somebody was constantly emptying their AK magazines at some real or imagined target, including low-flying aircraft. Even South African Airways Jumbo jets attracted attention: I have a photo of one of their Boeings with bullet holes in the fuselage.

That meant that after the pilot lifted the Friendship's wheels off the ground in Luanda, he had to make an extended, lazy circle over the airport to gain enough height, just in case anybody started shooting at us.

I was seated next to a pleasant young fellow who said he was off to visit his mother in Nova Lisboa. He told me he lived in Johannesburg and was intrigued to hear that I had just spent a couple of weeks in the Angolan capital because he had only arrived from abroad earlier that day.

He expressed fears about the upcoming handover and quizzed me keenly about conditions in the big city, the East European presence especially, which I thought a bit odd. I confided that I was pleased to have moved on and was blunt about fears for my safety had I stayed in Luanda. The 500-odd-kilometre flight went quite quickly, the two of us sharing half a bottle of Johnny Walker. I'd heard that Nova Lisboa was not only cut off from the sea but almost under siege, and I'd made it my business to ensure that I wouldn't be caught short.

On arrival at our destination, the pilot told us to remain seated because a certain unnamed VIP had to disembark first.

The Fokker taxied to a stop, and through the aircraft window, I saw a relatively smart military escort group on the apron waiting for the steps to be brought alongside. My newfound friend quietly excused himself and made his way to the back of the plane. As he appeared at the door, the troops outside stood to attention, and their officers saluted.

Only afterwards was I to discover that my companion was one of the senior military commanders of the FNLA force, then in command of Nova Lisboa. He'd successfully slipped past the goons at Luanda Airport, and I am pretty sure that once they'd learned who had boarded the F27, they would seriously upgrade airport security. As it was, civilian flights between Luanda and Nova Lisboa ended shortly afterwards.

Before we parted, one of his last gestures was to suggest that I give him a shout once I'd settled in. He said I'd find him at the local military headquarters.

A day or two later, we met for lunch at my hotel, one of the few restaurants still functioning in a reasonably large city preparing for war. The first thing he did was apologise for telling me he was visiting his mother…his family were all in Portugal, he said, but he did live in Johannesburg, adding that getting back to Nova Lisboa was vital because hostilities had already started.

Interestingly, though he knew I intended to write about my experiences, he was candid about what was going on. There were daily clashes in the hills to the west of the city, where some MPLA elements had tried to make inroads. Though these were still low-key, things would soon escalate, he intimated. As it was, he had some of his forces deployed on all the roads leading towards the coast and contacts with the enemy were a daily event.

Many of his troops were irregulars, with a sizeable body of ex-Portuguese Army soldiers and a few foreigners (who 'believe in our cause') forming the bulk of the FNLA Army; I chose that moment to ask whether I could join.

'*Join*, Al? What do you mean?' he asked incredulously. After all, he added, I was supposed to be a *journalist*. I replied that I wanted to move in with his troops. He hesitated briefly before adding that his people had no money and everybody in his ranks was there because of their political convictions.

'Well,' I said, 'I'm not in favour of a Soviet takeover of Angola either, so count me in.' He smiled and told me to report to the barracks the following morning to pick up a uniform and some hardware.

I'd already told him while still on the plane that I'd covered quite a few wars and was thoroughly familiar with firearms, having spent three years in the navy and was also a member of a gun club in Midrand, north of Johannesburg, where I regularly competed with my Colt .45 ACP pistol.

So it was that a day later, I was issued with a camouflage uniform and what I thought was a brand-new Fabrique Nationale FAL of 7.62 mm NATO calibre. Had I looked at it more closely, I'd have seen that it was not a Belgian-made rifle but a standard-issue R1 rifle in everyday use by the South African Army. Lyttelton Engineering outside Pretoria had manufactured it. Also, I did not yet know that an entire South African battle group was in the process of leapfrogging halfway up the length of Angola as part of what would become known as Operation *Savannah*. More significantly, my flight companion was a major player in an event I knew very little about.

My fellow combatants in Nova Lisboa could hardly be described as 'great guns'. The majority were Angolan nationals, split between the country's three racial groups; mostly black, some white and quite a few more of mixed blood or *Mestiços*. All, if asked, would tell you that they regarded themselves as the country's new breed of *Angolanas*, and proudly so. The few officers I met were primarily European and had served in the Portuguese Army.

Though the unit was strictly military, many of the men had grown up in the Angolan highlands and spent most of their lives outdoors. They had their own hunting rifles, which they preferred to either AKs or the newly arrived NATO-calibre rifles.

Their reasons were simple, one of them told me. 'When we go out, we go straight into military mode and never bunch up along the road. Some of us head toward the high spots, where we wait for those bastards to show themselves. All we need to see is a head,' he declared, fondly patting his Holland & Holland .375 Magnum rifle fitted with a high-power scope. I queried his success rate, to which he reckoned he'd killed quite a few of the enemy at ranges over 500 metres. Nor was he shy to use soft-nosed bullets, which, under the oft-quoted Hague Convention, was illegal.

It was the African military component that, to my mind, held the most promise – those black soldiers who formed the bulk of the force. A shadowy bunch of experienced guerrillas who had already seen a good deal of action, they were commanded by Daniel Chipenda, a disillusioned former communist. Several hundred strong, the squadron started fighting the Portuguese by proclaiming fealty to the MPLA's Agostinho Neto. They then switched to the FNLA, financed by the CIA – it was the money that did it – maintained Chipenda's detractors.

However, there was no doubt that the driving force behind this unit was Chipenda himself, whose background was almost as complex as the war in which he was involved.

A testy but competent military man, he had fallen foul of the elders of the founding party while serving as the MPLA representative in Dar es Salaam. His job had been to coordinate training and supply programmes with other liberation groups in southern Africa. This was a significant role because a large proportion of the military hardware used by the MPLA – and Mozambican and Rhodesian liberation groups – was channelled through the Tanzanian harbour. However, his time within MPLA ranks was often contentious, in part because he constantly griped that his party was 'too white' because the top structure was composed mainly of *Mestiços*.

Things came to a head in 1973 when he was involved in an assassination attempt on his boss, Agostinho Neto. The Soviets got a whiff of it and warned their protégé, but once Neto had taken over the country, he'd become weary of all the stringent socialist constraints imposed on his people over several decades. Like Mozambique's Samora Machel, Neto wanted closer ties with the West and ignored Moscow's advice about Chipenda.

Notably, Samora Machel died in a still-unexplained plane crash, while Neto succumbed undergoing relatively minor surgery in a Moscow clinic under circumstances that have never been properly explicated. The Soviets (and Putin today) have always done things their way.

By the time Chipenda defected, he had used his position as head of *Chipa Esquadrão* to good effect. The word got around that he was also working for South African Military Intelligence. If nothing else, this man wore a diversity of hats – shortly after Operation *Savannah* had ended, he took his merry band of *Chipa* veterans almost *en bloc* over to the South African Army.

Colonel Jan Breytenbach moulded this unit into the crack 32 Battalion.

I found it curious that some former Rhodesians and their families were also in Nova Lisboa, 'on call' should things get out of hand, as it was phrased.

Many of these fellow African expatriates had seen combat in Rhodesia and left the old country to make new lives in a 'Promised Land'. It all looked good when they first arrived because the Portuguese had regained control of the country. They were offered as much fertile farmland as they could use – all there for the taking because the original owners had fled. As one of the Rhodesians declared, they had been made to feel quite comfortable by the locals in their new environment, but then Angola had welcomed new settlers for five centuries.

Quite a few of the 'Rhodies' had built lovely homes in the city's surrounding hills, and there was even talk of starting an English school and a 'Club Rhodesiana'. Just then, all those good intentions went onto the back-burner because contact with MPLA units and the occasional UNITA guerrilla group looking for a scrap became more regular and intense.

Whenever a firefight took place, those involved, primarily Portuguese, would return to the city with their wounded and the occasional irregular killed in action. The news would ripple through the community like a torrent of doom. Then most locals would start telling each other that things were getting serious. A day later, everything was forgotten, and things were back to normal.

Until the next time…

Though I stayed on at my hotel – my magazine was picking up the tab, so any expense didn't come out of my pocket – everything centred on one of the houses in town being used as a headquarters. If we were not out in the countryside, we'd wait for instructions or help with training. The 'Home Guard' as they called it, was mainly wives and girlfriends of our *compadres* who would do the washing and cleaning and always had meals ready for their men when they returned.

This concerned me as it was obvious that these limited hostilities were primarily daytime affairs: I felt that the unit was too set in its routine. When I enquired whether defences and roadblocks were manned during the hours of darkness, eyebrows were raised.

One of them collared me afterwards and asked why I wanted to know. I told him the logic was simple: if the MPLA cottoned onto the fact that we were settling into a routine, they might launch attacks after dark and wait in ambush for our people to return in the early morning. The fellow scoffed.

He said I shouldn't worry my little mind with inconsequential things; it was all being dealt with.

Well, it wasn't. Forty-eight hours later, on an off-duty day when I remained at base, several of the pick-ups rushed back into town from the front while we were having breakfast. One vehicle had been caught in an ambush and badly shot up – it had brought back the body of one of our fighters.

Pandemonium followed. The women started wailing like banshees, and just about everybody within earshot came to see the corpse. I thought that odd; Nova Lisboa had seen its share of violence over the previous year when many people were killed.

The following evening, at a morbid dinner with a few of our guys at my hotel, a boy – an *umfaan* – not older than five or six – came in off the street to give me a note. It was pretty informal, but the message was clear. '*Go Home! If you do not, you will die.*'

The kid was collared and said he belonged to somebody in the immediate area. On being questioned, the youngster admitted that one of the soldiers in town had given him the note. The soldier had even walked with him to the restaurant door, where I was pointed out. He was told to give the letter to 'that white man with the beard' and got a few escudos for his effort.

This was a new development, and it was troubling. While most of my colleagues laughed it off, I took it seriously enough to barricade my hotel room door with a chest of drawers before I went to bed.

When I got a second letter a few days later telling me that I wouldn't be warned again and would be killed if I stayed in Nova Lisboa, I figured the time had come for me to head south. Some of the Rhodesian farmers had decided to pull out – I was given an opportunity that might not come again soon. I upped sticks and headed out with them on the long road to Caprivi, where more adventures awaited us.

Only years later did I learn that while all this buffoonery was happening, a relatively large South African force – part of the Operation *Savannah* that had been bandied about when I was still in Luanda – had been delayed from entering Nova Lisboa, partly due to my presence. The last thing Pretoria wanted was for its clandestine military presence in the interior of Angola to be exposed to the world by a maverick journalist. Somehow, they had to get rid of me, and I suppose that bogus 'death threats' seemed to offer a solution.

In truth, that irregular band of fighters that held the city could have bundled me off into the bush and shot me. But then, there is a measure of honour among men in uniform, whatever their political hue.

What underscored these events is that I must be one of the few contemporary journalists to have joined an army to get my story and, no question, that event made for quite a bit of excitement.

Some of our colleagues were making headway in other directions. Mike Nicholson of ITN had already achieved a breakthrough by reporting to London that he had seen South African soldiers in southern Angola. Others spoke of mercenaries attached to UNITA forces, but they had no proof. Mike had wandered into a forward South African position at Silva Porto, now Menongue.

Not long afterwards, Fred Bridgland – the Reuters man in Lusaka – boarded the Lonrho jet on what was to have been a tour of 'Unitaland' – otherwise known as Savimbi country. One of their stops en route for Benguela was at Rundu, a South African military town and strongpoint near the northernmost border of South West Africa.

Once the aircraft was stationary on the runway, the two journalists saw rows of Eland armoured cars, stacks of ammunition ten metres high, artillery pieces and hundreds of khaki-clad South African soldiers. On the apron, South African Air Force C-130 transports were loaded with the stuff, taking off and landing in relays.

To be sure, this war materiel was being despatched to Angola to support South Africa's war effort.

CHAPTER 29

Getting to grips with the CIA

I expect that the Americans would have taken notice of my goings-on a long time before Washington approached me to handle 'a little something' for them in Central Asia. Judging by their initial inquiry, it sounded intriguing.

I wouldn't have touched it had the concept not been mutually rewarding. But once those men in grey suits started talking about making a film on the war in Afghanistan in 1985 – then approaching its fifth year of a Soviet invasion that was starting to unravel – I jumped at it.

Also, the money was good. When asked what I wanted for a fee, I replied that a quarter million of the green stuff would do fine. They didn't argue, though there were still a few things we needed to discuss: access, food, communications, my team, the protective role of our putative hosts – the mujahideen, once the film crew was across the frontier – medical concerns, including the possibility of extrication if events went belly-up (zero, as it transpired), precisely who to contact in Islamabad if that were needed and, finally, how to make that initial connection, and so on.

I was assured it would all be routine, though it did occur to me that a few office johnnies in the American capital – intelligence-linked or not – wouldn't have a notion about what was happening on the ground in that distant, dirty conflict. Nor was I informed that my film crew would enter hostile territory from Pakistan *on foot*: that revelation only came immediately pre-departure.

Naturally, there were assurances given that we would get solid, unstinting support from Pakistan's MI, as the country's military intelligence is colloquially termed.

They assured me that their secret services would work closely in our interests, which, until then, had been my single biggest concern: Westerners simply cannot go prancing about the countryside of an embattled province (that covered the entire zone north of Peshawar) in the hopes of making contacts, never mind sneaking into a neighbouring state from one of the larger conurbations.

Other issues needed clarification. An initial hitch was my insistence on travelling first class on all intercontinental flights, which was when my two Langley 'minders' sidled off into an adjacent room and went into a huddle. It took a little while, but when I suggested that my financial situation would have been thoroughly examined before the initial approach had been made (or I wouldn't have been offered the job), they relented.

I surmised they had probably done as much with everything else, so I wasn't surprised to learn afterwards that they had.

That travel stipulation, they warned, would be only for the current project, which sounded promising; it seemed to suggest that there might be more such adventures in the offing, especially were I to pull this one off.

It took a good deal of effort to resolve the rest of my concerns, and by the time everything was on the table early in May 1985, it was pretty damn clear that I was faced with a humdinger of a task that would take me and my crew to the other side of the planet. Curiously, that only added to the allure, even though none of us mentioned the possibility of coming under Soviet fire once we had crossed into Afghanistan.

The odds were about even that we would be shot at some time or another, and there wouldn't be anyone we could call to send in a chopper to haul out the dead and wounded.

There was another issue of concern. To begin with, I could hardly tell the crew members that I intended to hire that the job they were on was being sponsored by the CIA. I kept that under wraps for years, maintaining throughout that it was a Saudi project; after all, the Russians in Afghanistan were into the wholesale slaughter of Islamic dissidents, so it made sense and the agency concurred.

Then there was the time factor, an immediate issue. I had only months to get everybody involved with the film in and out of the beleaguered country before the routes were obliterated by snow. The use of vehicles would be minimal, and then only while we were still on Pakistani soil.

Once across unmarked and sometimes vague and uncertain frontier lines, it would have been crazy to cadge lifts or even consider using local transport. That meant that almost all movement, including traversing the mountains, would involve legwork. We couldn't risk being stopped at a roadblock manned by Soviet or government troops.

Outcome: there was to be no compromise on getting across the western reaches of the largest mountain range in Central Asia, though Langley assured me that the team would get solid help from groups 'inside', who were ambiguously referred to as 'friends'.

More to the point: we must have been one of few groups during that precarious timeframe ever to have referred to the mujahideen as their 'buddies'.

Essentially my job involved infiltrating one or more TV crews into the Afghan war, filming what was available (movie equipment generally had not yet gone digital) – hopefully remaining unchallenged and undetected – until everybody was able to pull back into Pakistan and head back home again. It was a call that was both precarious and tough for the few summer months left.

If the teams couldn't get clear of the mountains on their return by late September – when the snows started – they might have to winter in a region where the rebels were known to switch allegiances like some of us change our jockeys.

In the end, two film crews were deployed to complete the clandestine film. One crew went in twice – that meant three entries into a fairly expansive war and three exits. In spite of many close calls and what I'd prefer to call 'incidents', all returned safely back to base.

We agreed from the start that I would not cross the border into Afghanistan with the boys. If I were wounded or killed, the object of the exercise would have been defeated. In any event, history has shown that in this business, just about everything that is likely to matter – unless you are a field worker – is customarily conducted from the rear. The CIA wasn't prepared to test that premise.

What emerged rather sharply was that – simply put – this very unusual expedition was beyond sensitive and involved critical splodges of subterfuge. To begin with, the film crews would be working closely with several guerrilla groups whose external 'outliers' were then ensconced in and around Peshawar, one of the largest cities in Pakistan's north and my people would even dress like them.

Once 'inside', the film crews would be passed on to other groups – whose trustworthiness, one would have surmised, would already have been put to the test – but most importantly, there would be no contact with any civilian Afghan groups. Also, no scouting of towns where, we were warned, the populace might already have been corrupted by infiltrators and informers to whom the Soviets paid good money. Moscow, I gathered, always tended to be tight-fisted, but they would pay well for the kind of information that a group of foreigners wandering about would certainly generate, even if they were escorted by anti-Soviet insurgents.

Lastly, there was to be as little movement along regular tracks or roads as possible – partly because the landmine threat was omnipotent – which meant that movement and the where and how that the teams could get their heads down could sometimes be brutal.

I was never asked by the agency whether individual members of my teams might be physically strong enough to handle those envisaged hardships. Usually, faced with demanding imponderables, one was inclined to take that sort of thing for granted. In any event, being in good shape myself, even though I was already into my forties, I was a fairly good judge of physique and never asked any of them to have a medical.

Much of what took place inside Afghanistan was on high ground – of which there was plenty but having been warned what lay ahead, the crews accepted that conditions would be trying, and on occasion, almost impossible. However, my American contacts assured me, their/our 'friends' knew their business and were as interested in success as I was because they too would be getting paid, probably a lot more than the roubles promised by their adversaries.

Chosen by an unnamed authority (with close links to my Washington-based interests), bunches of mujahideen fighters would accompany the teams across the mountains, weapons and all. There was little time to get any of them militarily orientated or trained, though several, including the cameraman, had spent time fighting in Rhodesia, so they were familiar with most Soviet squad weapons, AKs especially.

That the group might be attacked was fairly certain: Afghanistan was enmeshed in a difficult and unpredictable war. More salient, neither side could be absolutely sure of loyalty. Apart from the money, there were family and tribal issues, often obscured by long-standing grudges or personal jealousies.

The biggest single hurdle, it was generally accepted, was Soviet air power, with Hind Mi-24 helicopters predominating. There were more than a dozen enemy army bases adjacent to the Pakistani border in the south-eastern quadrant (through which most recruits to the anti-Soviet campaign had to pass), and chopper gunships were operating from them all.

I was assured that the Afghan 'heavies' looking after the team could and would handle all ground-based threats. Moreover, they had done jobs like this before, and every man-jack in tow was a seasoned guerrilla fighter, some with a decade or more of combat experience to draw on. But enemy airpower, in contrast, was something else.

If it sounds like a complex mission, it was, and as that became apparent I thought I might have sold myself short. But by then it was too late to do anything about it.

What did emerge only after the crew had returned from its first sortie – the first camera team went in twice – was that they were buzzed by a gunship fairly early on. Spotted by the pilot of a Hind, he circled the group but didn't go in on the attack. The mujahideen leader told me later that the aviator had probably exhausted his ammunition and might have been on his way back to base. Had the pilot been able to strike, he reckoned, he certainly would have done so…

This raised a more immediate issue which crossed my mind several times early on; why me?

The answer came in stages: firstly, because American media (journalists, camera crews, et al) are prohibited by law from engaging in intelligence matters linked to the United States government. In simple language, that means that the CIA was (and still is today) off limits.

Secondly, Washington had been keeping tabs on me, as they, the British, Russians, Chinese, Canadians, Israelis, South Africans and one or two other governments probably still do. By 1985, I had seen a good deal of action in the Middle East, Africa and elsewhere. There were many intelligence agencies following the progress of various African conflicts and had probably seen my work, which by then included *War on the Border*, an hour-long documentary on the South African conflict in

Angola which I produced and directed in 1981. A truncated version can still be viewed on YouTube.

There were several more TV films, including the even more dramatic *Into Angola,* where my cameraman and I followed a South African Air Force helicopter strike on enemy camps across the frontier from what is known as Namibia today. Before that, I'd covered the Tanzanian invasion of Uganda in 1978, followed by *Africa's Killing Fields,* a 40-minute documentary ultimately broadcast nationwide in the United States by PBS.

I should also mention that Africa in those days – as we have seen with some of my peregrinations – was fairly 'open door.' In other words, you could go just about anywhere with few questions asked and (unlike today) in relative safety.

Working as a correspondent in Africa and the Middle East, I was regularly bumping into foreign spooks just about wherever my meanderings took me. It said a lot that there was usually healthy respect between the intelligence operatives of almost all the nations involved in that more civilised epoch. I was on nodding terms with quite a few, including the CIA's Larry Devlin, whose home base then was Leopoldville (before it was renamed Kinshasa). His book, *Chief of Station, Congo,* is still one of the most comprehensive works of the period.[1]

In his day, Larry exemplified some of the old-guard CIA operatives working in remote parts, and was regarded by those who ran into him as a true professional under the conditions we all encountered while working the Africa beat. He was also one of the nicest guys around: sharp, erudite, willing to stick his neck out and, most importantly, was thoroughly familiar with many of the conundrums that Africa tended to hurl at us. We would bump into each other in the early days, and though he was aware of my South African connections (and that I used a British passport to move around), Larry was as discreet as they came.

There were also a few British and French news-gatherers, mostly men back then, whom we believed – through one quirk or another – were reporting back to their governments which, after all, might have been expected as they were going places where few ordinary folk would venture. In later years, I was to bump into some of the women who were so discreet about their roles that nobody would have imagined that espionage was their game.

One of the men included the prolific Polish author and journalist Ryszard Kapuściński who had been identified as working for the Soviets in the decades that he remained active in Africa. The fellow was affable, but distinctly devious and if I was aware of his secret service links, then so were many others, as well as his tendency to 'colour' some of his reports with more than a few rather blatant 'porkies'.[2] Pleasant

---

1   Larry Devlin: *Chief of Station, Congo: Fighting the Cold War in a Hot Zone,* Public Affairs: 2007.
2   Ben Quinn, 'Polish Journalist's Legacy Under Threat "because he was a commie",' *The Guardian,* 16 September 2016.

enough when we had drinks together, you never knew what was going through Ryszard's head, which meant that most of us kept the Pole at arm's length.

At his request, early on, I gave him one of my photos to use on the cover of a book he wrote about the Angolan war – a beautiful sunset shot of a South African Army Buffel troop carrier framed by one of Ovamboland's famed Makalani palms. The book was published in Polish and English, but the bugger never reciprocated, either by paying the agreed fee for my photograph or crediting its origin.[3] I am still waiting for my copy of the book.

Back to the Afghan project, personal connections concerning my new venture on the other side of the world gradually came into play. Most were initially tentative because a good friend was involved, in fact, had been from the start and without whose help the venture would never have gone ahead.

I had been working for a while with Bill Kyriakis, a New York-based film producer and editor – and while he knew very little about Africa he was enthralled by my adventures, though he did stop short at accompanying me on one of my assignments, which would have taken us to Nigeria. What he did suggest was that we do a TV series, possibly for the likes of Discovery Channel (which only came later) or one of the British networks, but I was never around long enough to get anything going.

What Bill did have was Ed, a friend and business partner – also media orientated – who had served in Europe during the war attached to the Office of Strategic Services (OSS), the forerunner of the CIA. Ed's role in that war was something he never talked about, but Bill was aware that he'd helped direct the activities of continental spies from London and, as a result, became a close friend of his boss from that London posting, William (Bill) Casey, the same indefatigable nonconformist who had played a prime role while involved with OSS activities after he became head of its Secret Intelligence Branch in Europe.

A maverick at heart, Casey's talents again came to the fore when he was awarded leadership of the CIA in 1981; it was on his watch that covert United States intelligence action increased in Afghanistan, Central America (where the notorious Iran-Contra affair took place) as well as in Angola. By the time Kyriakis and I were talking, Afghanistan had become a prime focus of attention.

Though I was never entrusted with details, I'm aware that Bill Kyriakis spoke to Ed who, in turn, suggested to his old pal Casey that I might be the man to do something timely on Russia's ongoing war in Afghanistan.

With the Cold War still running hot, the idea acquired legs, because 1985 was the fifth anniversary of the Soviet invasion of that Central Asian country. Indeed, what better way than an insightful documentary to highlight Moscow's escalating problems in a subversive struggle that was going nowhere?

---

3   I cannot recall the title of the book, which was published in Polish and English, but the image was distinctive because it was snapped behind *his* enemy's lines.

A short while later – still unbeknown to me – Langley started checking my bona fides in Britain, South Africa and elsewhere, and, from what I gathered (never directly, but always third-hand), responsible people linked to the agency took my background apart, which would almost certainly have included my books, television documentaries, politics, finances and even my family background.

The penultimate item was significant because it had to be shown that I was financially independent and not actually in need of work (I wasn't), and in this regard, my lifestyle would have featured prominently. The company also had to be sure that I wasn't into using mind-altering substances, something they were tough on – though, judging by recent events at Langley – I'm not so sure that tradition still holds.

An approach was made to me shortly afterwards, indirectly to start with, because it wasn't made clear that it was to have been a project sponsored by the Central Intelligence Agency. That disclosure only emerged later, by which time I was fairly certain who I was dealing with.

The first real step in this direction was an invite, all expenses paid, for me to fly to the United States, where I was to meet a 'Mister Freeman' in the main bar of The Algonquin, just up the way from New York's Grand Central Station.

That message came from Bill, who told me that at a specific time – late afternoon – I had to be there and look for a man who had a copy of *Le Monde* under his arm. Though it was a French daily, the foreign touch was distinctive enough to allow for the connection to be made. Looking back, I rather enjoyed that rather subtle touch of intrigue.

'Mister Freeman', I discovered soon enough, was one of those inconspicuous multilingual individuals that the CIA might have hired to give a potential employee a thorough going over; his personal approach, bearing, attire and, I suppose, his table manners (if any). And yes, he spoke fluent French. Bear in mind that up to that point, I'd had no personal contact with anybody from Langley.

Anyway, 'Mister Freeman' didn't keep me for very long as it was 'drinks only' and no dinner. I did inquire about the newspaper under his arm, and he admitted that he'd hoped it would provoke a short chat about Tangiers which he knew well, though he didn't elaborate.

He also gave me my first real communications pointer. I was to head for Washington DC immediately, he instructed, where I would be taken in hand for the next phase. At the same time, he handed me a phone number with a California dialling code: 'Call that number if you have any questions and ask for Mister Freeman. I won't be taking the call,' he declared, 'but you will be patched through to somebody in DC who'll take over.'

Over the next few days, once ensconced in the Jefferson Hotel, a few blocks up from the White House (I specifically asked for a hotel with a pool because I needed my daily workout), I met and got to know the two agency men who had been designated overall responsibility for the project, literally from start to finish.

Like others involved in the assignment, they would be unhappy to be identified as having been linked to Langley for most of their professional careers, so I'll refer to them as Jim and Joe.

Money details and a timeline having been dealt with, I was then told that a lie-detector test would follow – there were no ifs or buts, said Joe, it was mandatory. It was also an ordeal for someone who had never been subjected to something quite as intimidating as a polygraph, but I couldn't argue.

It went something like this: Jim and Joe picked me up at my hotel, and we drove to Tyson's Corner close to the main highway to Dulles International Airport. Once there, we checked into the Marriott and were met on a prearranged landing by a faceless functionary who was to decide my fate: no introduction, no handshake, not even a formal greeting.

I was ushered into a room and told by the operator to take a seat next to an electronic device with so many protruding wires that it could easily have passed for an ECG – only this one was not assessing any presupposed heart condition.

In a low voice, the anonymous one said he would ask me five simple questions. He stressed that he wanted nothing more from me than a straightforward 'yes' or 'no' each time. Nothing more, just a yes or a no...

'Do you understand?' he asked.

'Perfectly,' I replied.

'Incorrect,' he thundered. 'I want only a yes or no,' to which I nodded.

The first question was whether my last name was Venter. I both nodded and answered yes. He went on with three more, all fairly mundane questions about secrecy and intelligence work, finally asking something peculiar, which, I decided later suggested a British input: 'Do you hate the British?'

I responded with a 'no'.

Both Jim and Joe clarified that issue for me over lunch an hour later (fortunately without the dreaded operator).

Washington and London, they explained, have an age-old tradition of informing each other (through their respective intelligence services) if either intended to use a national of the other country for a job. In my case, as a British national, I was going to be making a film for a United States intelligence agency on the war in Afghanistan and Whitehall needed to be accordingly informed. I never did get to the bottom of that last question, or the motive involved. My Boer antecedents might have had something to do with it.

I stayed in DC for the rest of the working week, spending several hours a day with Jim and Joe giving me the lowdown on what might or might not happen.

There was much to impart about Pakistan and, in particular, Peshawar. Once in that large city, somebody else from the agency would take over but it was never made clear whether or not he or she would identify themselves as operatives, or even if they were American nationals. Essentially, I would be on my own.

I was questioned about who would be part of my film team: they needed names in advance so that they could be checked out, though that was a formality.

Once in Pakistan, security would be provided for our safety, but how this was to happen was never explained, though we were all aware that once checked into the old Deans Hotel, where there were mysterious and constant comings and goings in the corridors that ended up unsettling one or two of my squad, especially since they'd been told by then that the target country was 'Stan.

So too with contacts that had been arranged with several Afghan insurgency groups and which complicated matters still further. Those tasked would be in touch with us, not vice versa. Also, we would all be thoroughly briefed on the war by Pakistani officials who would also arrange transport, but only as far as the mountains, by then well into the Himalayan foothills.

Additionally, we were lectured on the possible encounters the crew might expect once across the border; ambush potential, weapons, landmines, as well as security in general, air strikes especially.

We spent a day in a military camp near Peshawar with numerous weapons on display, some of which were fired to familiarise the crew with what might be expected. Nobody ever raised the likelihood of them actually coming under fire, which was an unspoken given.

On our third day at Peshawar, two Soviet soldiers – captured not long before we arrived in the country – were brought to our by-now regular meeting place and we were invited to ask questions through a Pakistani interpreter who spoke fluent Russian. It was hopeless; both men were heavily drugged, heroin probably, to keep them sedated. They could barely keep their eyes open.

'They're the lucky ones,' our Pakistani escort told us. He intimated that the pair had been part of quite a large Soviet squad that had been ambushed, and most had surrendered almost immediately. Almost all were executed, with the 'druggies' kept alive for some inexplicable reason.

'Just as well,' he said, 'before the others were killed, they were horribly tortured, some having their eyes gouged out – there's a lot of bitterness in the war you are all going to…'

Before leaving Washington to get on with other tasks such as recruiting my team and several other pre-departure necessities, I was handed a quality hard-backed case similar to those that artists are fond of when moving their creations around. That one held six or eight large-scale maps of Afghanistan's south, roughly the area to be traversed by the team once they had finally entered the country.

Incredibly detailed, each had satellite origins, with all roads, tracks, high points, and Soviet encampments carefully detailed and labelled. Notably, none had any indication of where the maps came from and nothing about origin or copyright.

'Keep them safe,' said Joe. 'They're classified…and you didn't get them from us.'

Curiously, in 2022, going through one of my storerooms where I kept many of my books, I discovered two of the original charts: they appeared to have hardly been used on location.

There was a final pointer about likely problems arising once we were all on location: no satellite phones were allowed because the Soviets by then had electronic tracking systems in place that could locate the source of calls by simple triangulation. Nor, once we were in Pakistan, was I ever to call the United States Embassy in Islamabad, 'not for any reason, no matter how serious,' warned Jim, adding that as far as the crew was concerned, there was no United States connection.

'If you need to make contact with us,' he explained, pushing a small sheet of paper in my direction across the table in the hotel room, 'then this is the number you call.'

He went on: 'Say or explain absolutely nothing. Your making contact will indicate to us that something is wrong.'

'And then?' I asked.

'Then you go to that hotel, the name you see alongside the Islamabad number, and that you do that the following evening at about seven. You need to have a copy of *The New York Times* under your arm – and that's the signature connection – you will be able to meet and talk to somebody in authority, not necessarily from the embassy.'

'And if I can't find a copy of the *Times*?'

'You will…their quality bookshops stock most major American and British newspapers: they're brought into the country by air, direct,' was his response.

Once the preliminaries had been dealt with, I headed home to get the show moving – a long and complicated job.

Communications between Washington and Cape Town went well, all by phone. There were no cell phones or much Internet in those days, though satellite calls were an option but hellish expensive.

I was given two options: if I needed a quick answer to an issue raised, someone from the American Embassy in Pretoria would fly down, and we would discreetly meet in one of the local Cape Town pubs. But that only happened once; my contact felt I was too well-known in South Africa not to be spotted and possibly compromised because he sometimes had to shake off a tail. That individual 'dry-cleaned' his every move.

The alternative, which we used a couple of times, was for us to meet in London. I'd fly across Africa and my two handlers would come in from DC on the 'Red Eye'. We'd meet at a Mayfair restaurant, discuss business over lunch (which might last an hour), after which they would fly back across the Atlantic – an enormous waste of money on both parts, but I couldn't argue.

Overall though, things went smoothly, with me detailing expenses as things progressed, something Langley was rigorous about. They were paying me a packet but any expected outlay was to be used solely to achieve objectives, not profits.

From my South African base, numerous ancillary issues needed attention: my crew, or rather crews, their kit (which would have to be good quality if the guys were to be hiding out in the Afghan mountains while making the film), a specific type of food (that could withstand rough handling and travel), medical supplies to cover all emergencies, and the rest.

One of the more difficult problems was food. The crew had to be adequately fed, and because contact with locals was to be kept to a minimum, I had to devise a way for them to take along what was needed. Also, they might be inside for as long as a couple of months, so volume was always a prime issue since everything had to be carried – either by packhorses, porters, or themselves – essential when hauling camera gear.

According to my research, one of the issues encountered by NASA during the early days of their space programme, was how to feed the astronauts during their time away from Earth. Food had to be shelf-stable and long-lasting: also, it needed to be packed, small and light and be easy to prepare. That was when freeze-drying appeared to offer a solution: compact, longer shelf-life and better nutrition than dehydrated food. In particular, NASA's advances made freeze-dried meals easier to rehydrate without boiling water.

Unfortunately, there were few companies offering that kind of product to the general public and I was eventually pointed in the direction of Boulder-based American Outdoor Products who answered my call. It was expensive, but batches of meals came packed in cartons, so I ordered forty boxes, a rough equivalent of two months' supply and asked for the consignment be air-freighted to London to await our arrival.

All were handed over at Heathrow when we arrived for our flight to Islamabad. I reckon we broke records with the amount of excess baggage we were charged for.

A sidelight here involved the packaging of the meals: each one had the supplier's name stamped on the labels. Once inside Afghanistan, the boys would discard this packaging, with the result that some of this trash landed on the desks of Soviet intelligence officers, and then even more, as the filmmakers' trail across the country widened. Had things continued, it might eventually have been possible for the Russians to track the route the guys were following and take action, but fortunately, they were never in-country long enough.

Medical equipment was the next priority and the bugbear there, I realised early on, was moving across continents with fairly substantial quantities of drugs, including morphine, a Class A, Schedule 2 banned substance. Since we were transiting Britain to get to South Asia, I could not take the chance of not declaring possession – that could result in a mandatory jail sentence.

Because I was travelling with a substantial quantity of opiate narcotics that had been medically supplied, the first thing I did on arrival at Heathrow from Johannesburg was declare it. It was lucky that I did, the customs official told me when he confiscated the lot: medical supplies are checked by them as a matter of course and it didn't matter whether I was going to cover a war or not, I could not bring them into the country even though we would be there for a few days only before flying out again.

As it was, we needn't have worried. Morphine and other painkilling drugs were available on the open market in Peshawar, and we could even stock up with a supply of auto-injectors for self-administering painkillers, though it never came to that.

The next priority was saline solution in litre bottles, both for intravenous purposes if one of the crew or protection unit was wounded and – should it get to that – for debridement of damaged tissue. Saline, being isotonic, customarily contains an electrolyte balance similar to plasma in the bloodstream and is in common use in all armies.

In fact, during decades of travelling through Africa when filming, it was a rare trip where I didn't take along a couple of bottles of saline solution, not because I feared coming under fire, but because the liquid could be vital for those (or me) injured in a car crash. There is also a case or two on record of the solution having kept somebody stranded in an arid region alive long enough to be rescued.

To start with though, each team member needed to be shown how to administer a drip intravenously, especially since most people are not aware that the needle is usually inserted into a vein in your wrist, elbow, or the back of your hand and also involves a catheter.

Going into South Asia then, it was brought home forcibly by one of the doctors consulted, that we would be entering amoebiasic territory where, for Westerners, dysentery of the most injurious and awkward type constantly happens. He was right because two of the five-member team on the first shoot went down viciously with Montezuma's Revenge…

I took loads of the latest counter-diarrhoeal medications, but both guys hit by 'tummy tremors' suffered badly, and it continued for months after they'd returned home.

Other items in the small tea chest that contained our medical needs included battle dressings, cardboard splints, towels for padding, bandages (by the score), scissors, roller gauze, tape and much more. We even had strappings for sprained ankles, though who knows what would have happened had anybody been seriously hurt because there wasn't a trained medic among those who went in. It would have been worse if a leg were broken because that unlucky casualty would have to be hauled back over the mountains on the backs of mules or porters. What we didn't take were helmets, which would have been self-defeating: anyone wearing that kind of headgear in Afghanistan would have stuck out like a lily in the desert.

The venture became quite extensive, eventually requiring an additional film crew to cover the Afghan central regions around Kandahar. That team headed out across the border from Quetta after the first crew had pulled out. The new guys were faced with a difficult option because even though distances were more modest than the route covered further eastwards by the first group – about a four-hour drive along the main highway connecting the two cities – they would have to steer well clear of villages because of the Soviet and national army presence.

Matters were further compounded by the huge Registan Desert that lay to their immediate west. Desolate, waterless, and supporting almost no humankind, this barren region stretches for some 500 kilometres from the main road deep into the interior.

The region to their right was a little better – lightly populated with the distinct possibility of any stranger or group passing through remaining undetected. Soviet intelligence would be informed within a day and it didn't help that there were no mountain hideaways in which to seek refuge, even though Kandahar is surrounded by several high points.

What the Kandahar region had in greater abundance than the southeast, were more helicopter gunships, because that military airport was specifically geared for them, as it was when Coalition Forces invaded after New York's Twin Towers were destroyed fifteen years later.

Peshawar will remain etched in the minds of everybody involved with the main crew because – stimulating as a travel destination – the city was a disappointment.

Though thoroughly infiltrated today by Islamic Jihadists, we had none of those problems in 1985. All political focus – on both sides of the frontier – was on the 'unbelievers' – the Soviet infidels that the Jihadists were totally fixated on destroying.

Deans Hotel was chosen as our base by some American diplomatic official in Islamabad, probably because somebody at the embassy had used the place and found it 'quaint.' They would have been aware that alcohol was available, even if you had to get a signed permit from a government official to buy a single bottle of Scotch… the same with beer, in limited quantities.

Somebody writing home described Peshawar as a hideous place; smoke-filled, overcrowded, and arid. I agreed.

It was also an unsightly relic of the British colonial epoch: tasteless, carbuncles of concrete and plaster, all of which were grossly disproportionate compared to the graceful pavilions, typical Indian verandas and classical buildings that once dotted the original cantonment area. That was forty-something years ago, and it's probably worse today.

As a temporary home, Deans – for all its problems and awful food – was the tiny spark that made things different for all.

Built over a century ago, the old hotel was once a centre of great hustle and bustle, especially for foreign journalists during the Afghan Jihad. Among its notable guests of previous generations were Professor Arnold Toynbee, Rudyard Kipling, Sir Winston

Churchill (as a young soldier journalist on his way to Malakand), Quaid-e-Azam, and King Nadir Shah of Afghanistan (in 1929).

By the time we arrived, our team were the only guests, and the place was little more than a cavernous mausoleum. It has since been demolished and a grotesque glass and marble plaza erected in its place.

CHAPTER 30

The Battle for Beirut

It would be remiss of me not to include something about time spent covering wars in the Middle East. In the days before the Hezbollah influence became pronounced, I could travel relatively freely in Lebanon, though there was the perpetual fear of being taken hostage by radical Islamic elements. That concern aside – there were many others, including being sniped at – I often accompanied the Israeli Defense Forces (IDF) in and out of a beleaguered Beirut, then mired in a civil war that many of us failed to describe accurately because it was so brutal and mindless.

To what can one equate the execution of children, something to which neither side ever pleaded? It happened often enough.

Beirut, they used to say when I first came ashore from Cyprus in the late seventies, was a city of shattered façades, bad dreams, almost no prospects worth shouting about and desperately few aspirations. It was impossible not to perceive a practically visceral antipathy towards peace. Worse, it had been going on for a while.

These were times when each dawn was greeted by the unholy trinity of Israeli reconnaissance planes in the sky, mortar bombs exploding at road intersections and muezzin calls from the minarets in the foothills of the Shouf. Then came roadblocks on the outskirts of town, manned by any one of about a hundred factions, almost all of them Islamic.

Moving about the city in the eighties, I was amazed at the inhabitants' resilience. Just about every basement had become a home, with beds and tables placed so that at least two walls separated inhabitants from the outside. The first, it was hoped, intended to absorb a blast. The usual tactic was to hit East Beirut during rush hour. Since the town had been meticulously mapped years before, even the Syrians had the charts, they could drop a bomb within metres of any street corner. Some intersections would be teeming with traffic, and the carnage was always horrific.

For years these people had been subjected to car bombings, rockets, mortar bombs and artillery barrages that continued for days and sometimes weeks. There was no 'getting used to it', but if you stayed, you tried to manage. Robert Fisk, then of the London *Times*, described what was going on in the Middle East as a kind of catharsis for the Lebanese…who have long understood how these dreadful events should be interpreted…

'Victories,' he declared, 'were the result of courage, patriotism and revolutionary conviction. The plot always caused defeats; *mo'amera* – a conspiracy of treachery in which a foreign hand – Syrian, Palestinian, Israeli, American, French, Libyan, Iranian – was always involved.'

Yet it wasn't always so. In its day, Beirut was among the wealthiest of cities: 'The Paris of the Middle East', they called it, with boutiques that rivalled those on Paris's Avenue Montaigne and the best on offer from the world's capitals, including Arab versions of Harrods and Bloomingdales, chic cafés and the finest patisseries east of Lyon. The Lebanese capital had long ago put Cairo to shame as the finest city in the entire region. Still more salient, Beirut was the capital of the Islamic banking world.

The public buildings and private houses that gave the city a Tuscan or Provençal look were still there – at least those that had not been blown apart in the ongoing ground conflict – but just about all had been hideously disfigured. Their original occupants, the ones with the money, had long since moved on. Some had retreated to higher ground outside the city, especially those with children, and others had gone abroad.

Those who could manage it went to 'other' homes in London or Cannes, as it was euphemistically phrased, or perhaps back to West Africa for the diamonds that had made many of these Levantines extraordinarily wealthy. Few people are aware that Lebanon is the original home of the African blood diamond.

Even so, there were diversions to relieve the stress – parties up the coast at Byblos – beyond the range of the guns and the Katyushas. And picnics in the mountains, regular events when fighting and weather conspired to abate. So was fishing at sea (guarded by patrol boats) and endless 15-course dinners that are a feature on any Lebanese social calendar. Christian radio stations helped, though they were primarily French and invariably hip. Some of their DJs could easily have relocated to Brussels or Montreal.

Listening to a French-speaking announcer in some lonely post at Kfarchima, or in my hotel room at Byblos where I stayed on later visits, you might forget that you were on the fringe of what then was one of the most dangerous conflicts east of Algeria. It was a day and night thing, but Byblos was away from it all, roughly 20 kilometres as the blackbird flies from Beirut's elegant Corniche where I often strolled in later years.

On my second or third visit, Jihadist bombers destroyed the US Marine barracks at Beirut Airport. More than 300 American servicemen were killed, soon followed by two more suicide bombs, one at the entrance of the American Embassy and the other at the French diplomatic legation a few streets down. The American Embassy bomb killed many top CIA officers in the Middle East who were there at a conference, a severe loss to Langley.

Only years later were we to discover that this was the work of a new brand of Islamism that called itself Hezbollah – Shi'ite militants taking their orders directly from Tehran and indirectly from Moscow – something dealt with in considerable detail by former CIA operative Bob Baer in his book *See No Evil*.[1]

Half the population had already fled by the time I became an active correspondent in Beirut, the rest fighting a hopeless rear-guard action and in an environment where day-to-day conditions were constantly fringing on the desperate. As one wag said, the future was a narrow tympan of confidence quickly shattered by daily bombardments. Another thought it could sometimes be like something out of a conventional European war: only those who stayed hoped for better.

Over the decade and more that I covered the war off and on – from the late 1970s, well into the 1980s – I most often entered Lebanon through the sealed Israeli border post at Rosh Haniqra – closed to the public. By then, I'd negotiated an arrangement with the IDF Spokesman's office in Jerusalem to allow this *goy* access to enemy territory in South Lebanon. Other times I entered the country by boat from Larnaca in Cyprus.

Arriving by sea, we would usually dock in the port of Jounieh in Christian territory. It was the better option because it lay marginally beyond enemy artillery range and from where the Christian Lebanese Force Command planned operations across the Green Line in downtown Beirut. In between, we still had to run the gauntlet getting in and out of Beirut proper and, in the early days, dodged being shot at while travelling the coastal road from the Lebanese capital to Israel. That route could be dangerous because it periodically came under fire from Israeli warships patrolling offshore, but, as I'd say: 'What the hell, this is my day, not theirs,' and I'd go for it.

Nevertheless, I had some remarkable escapes. Coming in from Haifa not long after the Israelis had invaded Lebanon in 1982 (which eventually forced the Palestinian Liberation Organisation out of their Lebanese bases), I slept in one of the IDF temporary headquarters, having found a cosy corner on the first floor of what was a fairly large building in the port city of Tyre. The PLO knew what was coming and had prepared things for the Israelis earlier. They command-detonated a heavy bomb secreted in the building's basement a day after I'd left for Beirut – dozens of Israeli soldiers were killed.

On one of my visits to that corner of the eastern Mediterranean – I'd usually stay two or three weeks – I was invited to lunch by friends I'd made from G-5, the Christian Forces' intelligence unit. There was a café on a corner three blocks away, well sandbagged and accessible only through a narrow reinforced concrete entrance. Steel plates hung over the door, obstructive but adequate.

---

1   Robert Baer, *See No Evil: The True Story of a Ground Soldier in the CIA's War against Terrorism.* Penguin Random House: 2003.

After lunch, we were strolling back to the office and since we were at least a kilometre or two from the front with multistorey buildings on all sides, there appeared to be no need for caution. Suddenly the first mortar bomb exploded on the road about a hundred metres ahead of us. Seconds later there was another, 20 metres closer. By now, we were in full gallop for the entrance of a large granite residential block nearby: any opening would do if it offered cover. A doorway loomed, and we didn't need to be told it was ideal.

We reached it with about a second to spare before the last mortar bomb detonated in a shower of fragments immediately outside the entrance to our refuge. Nobody was hurt, but our ears rang for days. A shard of jagged steel as big as my hand ricocheted off one of the eaves to land at my feet, smoking hot. I kept that chunk of twisted metal on my desk for years until I moved to America, even though it was an unpleasant recall.

Sobering was the realisation that a piece of shrapnel that size would easily sever a man's arm, his neck, or possibly a foot in full flight. More worrying still, by the time I got to Beirut, there had already been five journalists killed and a dozen wounded.

There were escapes, and some dreadful 'non-escapes' that we old survivors still marvel about after a few toots.

A Frenchwoman – somebody said she was a cub reporter from one of the provincial dailies – was killed by a sniper in a patch of open ground near the port soon after she disembarked in Beirut harbour, as I did on arrival. It was a bad mistake on her part; she was a foreigner and had been warned, but they shot her anyway. Her body lay there for days, and anyone who tried to move her body was targeted. The French Embassy protested every hour on the hour, but nobody listened.

They killed a German whose car had broken down near the Green Line a week later. He'd arrived from Syria, and the Christians felt no compassion because somebody discovered that the man was a freelance military contractor with sympathies for the hated Islamic enemy.

Then, a French television crew was filming in downtown Beirut – close to the Green Line – when a Russian 82 mm mortar bomb hit the curb. It exploded in a shower of shrapnel next to the cameraman – fortunately, the bomb detonated in the gutter and a raised concrete curb absorbed most of the blast. When I looked at the place afterwards, I could see it was remarkable that the man had survived relatively intact. He was spattered by bomb fragments down the length of his body and was taken by boat to Larnaca the following evening.

Afterwards, I saw an Arriflex 16 mm camera at the offices of Gamma Presse Images in Paris. It had a hole in it, a sniper's bullet neatly lodged where the magazine would have clipped onto the body. The trajectory had been straight in line with the side of the cameraman's head when it struck, a reflection of excellent marksmanship which improved as the war progressed. Apart from a whopper bruise above his ear, I was assured that the chap holding it was unhurt.

Snipers of all nationalities were active until the end, but the average journalist seemed to take little interest in these actions – though this was clearly an issue tailor-made for the front page. Why? Because it was an extremely delicate subject, they were told. More than one journalist in the Commodore Hotel got a friendly nudge whenever the topic was raised. Sniping wasn't a good story, they'd be warned. Naturally, they would agree.

Nonetheless, the subject was in everybody's face. The almost blanket silence about sniping in the Western press was strange since these marksmen – among the Muslim fundamentalists especially – accounted for an astonishing number of killings, though few of them were combatants.

While in Beirut, I usually stayed in an apartment near the headquarters of Fadi Hayek's G-5; he later managed the offices of the Lebanese Force Command in Washington DC. Maxim Geahel and Jacques Tabet were his partners, of whom only Max is still alive. They could all speak English, but like most Christians in Lebanon, they preferred Arabic or French (there were quite a few French-language newspapers in Lebanon then).

Fadi was a gracious and generous host. None of us had much money and his hospitality in that dangerous country was abundant and made us feel welcome. He was also a convivial entertainer who could drag a bottle of Château Lafite-Rothschild out of somebody's cellar and moments later produce the best in pâté de foie gras from what passed as the local gourmet store.

Living in Fadi's discreet shadow served two purposes. Mainly, he could keep an eye on us, supposed friends of the Christian Forces, but who could just as easily have been the enemy. Also, by then, all Christian hotels in East Beirut had become designated targets for proliferating crews of Islamic car bombers. With so much activity, their job was made easy. Second, he was our direct access to the war.

As hostilities went on and car bombs – only later was the name changed to Improvised Explosive Devices (IEDs) – became commonplace, that situation changed radically. Although there are few cities anywhere – even in wartime – as clogged as Beirut with traffic (parking had always been impossible, anyway), Christian hotels started using heavy concrete security barriers for protection. Then you needed a permit to get close to the main structure, even more controls. The cycle was eternal, one means of destruction supplanting another as multiple solutions were devised by one side or the other to counter them.

The Commodore Hotel – in the Islamic part of town – was not one of my favourites because I had to pass through a potentially hostile part of the city to get there. However, it was a necessary stage in any journalist's itinerary in that corner of the world, and we all frequented it at some time or another.

I held a lot of affection for the old Commodore, much improved when I stayed there again in 2019. It was shabby and rundown during the war, yet as comfortable as a pair of old slippers. The ebb and flow of events in the Middle East could be gauged by the number of foreign correspondents packed into the round bar on any evening.

We would find diplomats priming journalists and vice versa, strange unsmiling people with Russian passports who were always ready to talk over a beer, UN 'Peacekeeping' soldiers on leave – usually talking tough even though very few had ever experienced a firefight – and, of course, the usual spooks, professional murderers and friendly ladies. It was a congenial watering hole and I often wonder what happened to Younnis and Mohamed, who served behind the bar.

Signing in at the Commodore was a ritual. 'Sniper side or car bomb side?' the clerks would ask new arrivals, almost all nervous. Yet curiously, it felt strangely cosy, even safe, once through those doors. From the top of the Commodore, we would sometimes watch the nightly display of Christian tracer fire.

John Kifner of *The New York Times* described a night after the American Embassy had been blown up for the second time by a suicide truck bomber: 'Suddenly, the windows around the bar [of the Commodore Hotel] shook and dissolved as Shi'ite fundamentalists bombed nearby bars and bingo parlours. Thirty journalists dived onto the floor in a heap. Their glasses were placed neatly on the bar, not a drop spilled.'

'Oh,' someone whimpered, 'surely it is not going to be one of those fucking nights again!'

Then came possibly the narrowest escape of my career during one of my earliest visits to a war-ravaged Beirut, something that I still contemplate in quieter moments because of the enormous – and deadly – consequences. It involved the death of a young man in Beirut with whom I shared meaningful time. During the week that we shuffled precariously along the Green Line, I got to know him quite well, which happens in wartime.

His first name was Christian, a declaration of sorts in a country where religious divisions give rise to fourteen centuries of conflict, much of it spurred by the same Christendom that this youthful, effervescent young man held to be sacrosanct. To my eternal regret, he died a pointless death. Also, a soldier, he was barely 21 years old, having spent a year or two at the Sorbonne and told me that he'd returned home to 'do my bit for something in which I truly believe'.

His job was to be my military escort after I'd returned to cover this utterly futile conflict.

Christian did a sterling job as my guide, interpreter and friend under deplorable conditions. One sensed that large numbers of combatants had lost all reason because they were slaughtering each other with a ferocity that has recently surfaced even more mindlessly – if that be at all possible – in Iraq, Afghanistan and the Ukraine. As a combatant, I'd like to think that Christian held a more balanced view.

The battle in which he died raged for 36 more hours. Still worse, both he and I – together with two more of his colleagues – had, if the truth be told, probably been responsible for the bloody sequence of events that began a few hours before. That 'impromptu' rocket attack of ours from a basement apartment resulted in Syrian Army deaths, though we were never to discover how many.

The Christian Lebanese Force Command had killed some Syrian soldiers in a surprise attack launched by my friend Christian and his two comrades, all three members of the unit to which I had been seconded for the duration of my stay. I was the media guy they were trying to impress, and if nothing else, they were hugely successful because five or six Syrian troops were killed in the rocket attack they had launched.

Consequently, Beirut's Green Line erupted along its length, an avenue of sepulchral ruins that stretched from the water's edge near the port through Chiyah, Galerie Semaan, Quadi Dbaa and on into the foothills of the Shouf. Overall, it was pretty grim as those experiences went. For a day and a half, Christians and Muslim soldiers did terrible battle. They lobbed everything they had at one another: artillery, infantry missiles and mortar bombs and the entire gamut of light and heavy machine-gun fire. If you were close enough to the other guys' lines, you even lobbed the occasional grenade.

Heavy DShK machine guns – more recently much in evidence in the Ukraine – thundered into Phalangist defences. Nor could you miss the screams of volleys of Katyusha rockets that roared in over the rooftops from what we later discovered were banks of Russian BM-21s brought into the city by the Syrians. My friend Christian was not the only one to die during those two terrible days. Many more were ripped apart from bursts of ZSU-23-4 'Shilka' anti-aircraft guns as shells slammed into blocks of apartments, villages, hospitals and schools. It happened simultaneously on both sides of the line, and no one was spared.

Following our mortar attack, it took the Syrians a while to respond. By then, we'd reached a tall, partly finished skyscraper called Sodico – used by the Lebanese Force Command to observe their targets and spot hostile mortars. The structure overlooked the battleground, and after reporting in, we took a builders' elevator up to the top floor, seventeen or eighteen storeys up. It was a metal box fenced in with what appeared to be chicken wire on three sides, and from that vantage, all of Beirut opened up Panavision-style before us as we went higher.

The top half of the building had only a central concrete core and was wholly exposed; only the bottom ten floors had walls. It offered an observation team a splendid view of what was happening below as the city lay spread-eagled before us.

From a height of approximately 100 metres, Beirut – irrespective of the fighting – looked quite different from any other city I had visited. Paris at night from the top of the Eiffel Tower is a blaze of lights. So is Manhattan. In the Lebanese capital, all lights after dark were heavily shaded and intermittent, as if some parts had no electric power. Smoke hung in patches in valleys, and the navigation lights of ships that lay at anchor off the coast were hardly visible, which told you that they were cautious too.

Christian pointed out the place where we had just been. It was eerily black, and I knew there were enemy dead there.

Then, as if by some unified command, the entire front blazed like a firework display. We were suddenly enveloped in a thousand explosions, guns firing everywhere and stunning the senses. It all seemed like a tremendous, incandescent stage spectacle – a *son et lumière* performance that reeked of cordite, with great cannonades emerging from untold positions.

Katyushas screamed past; first to the left and then to the right of our building. A shower of ZSU-23-4 shells – clustered in a massive ball of fire about a 100 metres across – shot past almost within throwing distance of where we crouched. There is no other way to describe it but as terrifying because I had never before experienced anything quite like it. Had the man pulling the trigger of the multi-barrelled heavy machine gun aimed half a degree to the left on his second salvo, we would have been history – because the ZSU is one of the most destructive weapons devised by man.

Of Soviet origin, with four barrels and a liquid cooling system to allow for sustained fire, it pushes out 4,000 rounds of high-explosive ordnance a minute. When it fires – almost always in bursts of about a second or two – it sounds like a bulldozer revving its engines. One ZSU salvo into our building, and that would have been that.

By now, some of the Katyushas were exploding far behind us in the Christian part of the city. Others went into the mountains in the direction of Jounieh. Meanwhile, our mortar men below had opened up. I couldn't miss Jamal, a slight man with three days' beard, giving coordinates over the radio to a command post below.

More Katyushas and more ZSU salvoes, each one perilously close. We had to be hit sooner or later, and I said so. Somewhere near the foothills to our left, Christian artillery batteries of the Lebanese Force Command joined in. Just then, I felt frighteningly exposed, vulnerable.

Suddenly, a loud crack on the half-finished floor below shook us. Probably a rocket grenade, said Jamal under his breath, but loud enough for me to follow his French. If so, that meant we were up shit creek: somebody was aiming straight at us from the ground. RPGs aren't fired randomly. You select your target, aim and fire.

Had they spotted our presence with night-vision equipment? Another blast rocked the landing we were on, and Christian moved back towards the incomplete elevator shaft, which, I expect, he believed would provide some protection.

I'm not sure exactly what happened next, except that a frightful explosion shook the entire building, close to where we were perched. One of the mortar-spotters threw himself flat, away from the narrow parapet he'd been standing on while I got down behind a narrow ledge.

Another explosion, followed by a yell which pierced the night. It was Christian, unmistakable over the sounds and echoes of blasts and machine-gun clatter. We heard it just as Jamal told his men to get back under cover. Christian screamed once again before he hit the ground. Then silence, except for some intermittent blasts below us. Firing from across the way picked up again.

Without speaking, we all knew immediately what had happened. When the last shell hit, Christian had stepped back into nothing but a great black hole of an unfinished elevator shaft that dropped hundreds of feet into the basement. He was probably conscious until he hit bottom.

All I could think of at that moment was that he wouldn't have been on top of that half-complete building if it hadn't been for me. He'd still be alive. I gathered later that his cry of terror was also heard by some of the Christian soldiers operating guns and mortars on the ground, way below us, followed by a muffled thud.

When they lifted that young man's body from the bottom of the shaft – cumbersome, and by the look on his lifeless face, almost unwilling to accept death – it had to be carefully manoeuvred to pull him through the narrow opening, difficult in such a confined space. Anybody who has carried someone dead or unconscious will know the real meaning of 'dead weight' – bodies always seem much heavier than their size would suggest.

I'd made my way down all 17 floors by then, of necessity using the stairs because the power was off and was to observe with horror as they extricated him gently and carefully, at one point, his head touching his heels. His vertebrae seemed to have turned to jelly and one of his eyes had been forced out by the impact, a hideous sight. That – and the scream – will remain with me forever.

Rocky, the commander of the mortar post, laid the blame fairly at my feet. I was the only stranger there. Christian had been escorting me. Ergo, I must be an enemy agent – QED: *I had thrown him down the elevator shaft!*

Even before they had removed the body, Rocky was on his way up the stairs as we were coming down; we met halfway. What I didn't yet know was that he was set on hurling me to my death. A big powerful man with wrap-around combat boots and a 9 mm pistol in a shoulder holster, he could have done so with ease. A year later, when we were having a drink within sight of the same building, he told me: 'If you had resisted, I would have shot you.'

He added that he was stopped by Jamal coming down those stairs with me. 'I asked him why you were still alive, and it took me a minute or two to convince me that when Christian had stepped backwards, you were already behind the same ledge as himself...if you had come down those stairs alone, we wouldn't be here having this drink tonight.'

I knew nothing of all this at the time because I don't speak Arabic.

I spent the rest of that night in the deepest basement garage at Sodico and was thankful for it because shells were constantly pouring down on us. Stalingrad, I imagine, must have been something like that. For hours the Syrians seemed to concentrate on our building as if they knew we had started the crap. At least a dozen 240 mm mortars rocked the tall building's concrete core. Each time one of those monsters struck, plaster and dust would rain down on us.

Sleep was out of the question, though I did fall into an uneasy doze for a few hours as Rocky's men above us were still pounding back. Still, it seemed absurd – firing at what? Empty spaces in looming canyons of fire? In retrospect, they probably were.

Apart from Christian, our tiny group only had a handful of wounded and one more death. One of the irregulars had caught a sliver of steel – jagged and sharp – in his throat, and without anybody realising he'd been hit, he silently choked to death in his blood. They only found him later that day in a half-crouch pose on a landing into which he had crawled.

A few men and one of the female radio operators were slightly hurt by shrapnel, one with a flesh wound in the backside. The Lebanese nurses who shared our ordeal dealt with them quietly and competently.

Dawn came slowly. Christian's broken body remained before me like a vision throughout the night, and it must have shown, for one of the Christian officers came and sat on the edge of my stretcher and told me to get a grip of myself. There was nothing that anybody could have done, he said.

'It's the price we pay for this war…what those savage bastards do to us.' Almost half-heartedly, he cursed his Crusader forefathers for not doing a more efficient job a millennium ago. Then he smiled because he too realised that he was a product, if not of that epoch, then of this one – which was equally as savage.

He suggested I find myself something to eat. They'd got something going at a makeshift canteen at the end of the garage, but hummus and tzatziki at six in the morning – no matter how much pita bread might have been available – weren't on my agenda. Perhaps a bit later because there was nothing else if you didn't count cucumbers. The coffee was welcome.

At ten that morning, we heard bells. Their peals echoed across a landscape of violated and pitted walls and empty passageways between tall buildings. They came from the adjacent Maronite Church that Christian and I had passed on our way to Sodico the previous evening. It was for him that they tolled.

'They're burying him,' said the officer, 'Christian.' He made the sign of the cross, kissing his thumb as he completed the devolution.

Although we didn't see his parents, they were there, though the fighting continued. As a precaution, they'd been called during the night and escorted to wait in the church. These were things that simply had to be done in wartime. 'A precaution,' said another of the men before he went off to comfort a young soldier crying alone in a corner, one of Christian's schoolboy pals.

Jacques Tabet fetched me from Sodico about noon in a Volkswagen and at high speed. So, what's new? He drove into the parking garage and came to a raucous halt in a cloud of dust disturbed by a mortar bomb from across the way. Jacques had a crazy look about him, which I suppose was understandable considering that he'd driven through one of the most challenging battles for a while.

'Let's go,' he said, 'you can't spend the whole fucking war here.' He had an excellent way of expressing himself, but the firing immediately intensified. They must have spotted him racing along the Line.

'You're joking,' I replied. 'We're not going into *that?*'

He wasn't, though I was dead serious when I asked him if he was crazy. There were still some heavy mortars coming in, and frankly, I was happy to wait it out in the basement. 'Give it an hour,' I suggested.

'No. You must come! We've got something else for you,' was his retort, and he walked towards the car without even checking whether I was following. Jacques hadn't time for jokes: he knew the family of the dead youngster.

I squeezed into the front seat of his battered old Beetle beside my old friend from many visits to Beirut, and he shot out of the basement of the Sodico building like a man possessed. It was undoubtedly the single most dangerous journey of my life because we were the only car on a deserted road and were suddenly attracting an awful lot of attention.

Jacques swerved and zig-zagged, which became a constant for the next eight or ten minutes. If anyone was targeting us – and they did so, in numbers – we didn't present an easy target, even though you could see chunks of brick and mortar falling in the road ahead and behind as the buildings around us were pasted. The Beetle, a compact little machine, presented a low profile, though a solid piece of shrapnel would have ended it all.

The relatively quick charge that it took us to get away from the Green Line was the longest ever, and meantime, as if on cue, both sides opened up again. More evidence that we were in a hot zone came when a building was struck by a large shell about a hundred metres to our left. This was a few minutes after Jacques had declared that we were, if not in the clear, then no longer in the direct line of enemy fire.

CHAPTER 31

The murder of a United States Marine Corps colonel

One of the questions most often asked by friends after I'd returned home from some of these exploits was what my wife thought of me putting my life on the line as often as I did.

In truth, we rarely spoke about my adventures. I'd tell Madelon before flying out that I was going to the Middle East, or possibly Nairobi or Cairo and leave it at that, though some assignments left me visibly disturbed. On my return from Beirut after Christian had died falling down the lift shaft, I was distressed but decided that it was best that I kept the details to myself.

I'd keep my pals posted of course and while they were sceptical to start with, they soon enough followed my stories and simply had to accept, as one of them put it, that I was 'for real'. Perhaps just as well because my bosses were occasionally having to fit some fairly hefty insurance policies, like when I lost almost hearing in my left ear after a blast close to my face.

What was strange was that while my activities were initially largely Africa-orientated, I ended up spending a good deal more time in the Middle East than I anticipated, whether it was to Lebanon, Syria or even the Holy Land (where I'd register with the IDF spokesman soon after my arrival). There was always something newsworthy happening. Also, I took my own photographs, which though not unusual, wasn't the norm in Fleet Street where most correspondents had a cameraman or camerawoman tailing them.

It was the murder of an American Marine officer that got me thinking that my luck couldn't hold forever, especially once the occasional 'snatch' or hijack in the early 1980s became a flood.

Commonly referred to as 'the Lebanese Hostage Crisis', this was serious business, with 104 foreigners abducted in the decade following 1982 when the civil war was at its height. Among that number, was Terry Waite, the Assistant for Anglican Communion Affairs for the then Archbishop of Canterbury. He was kidnapped and held captive from 1987 to 1991.

At least he came out of that horrendous ordeal alive because eight hostages are known to have died in captivity, though there could have been more, mainly Lebanese. Some were murdered, while others died from lack of adequate medical attention. Quite a number tried to commit suicide, though that was impossible if you were trussed to a steel bar and only briefly released for ablutions and food. Also, many victims were kept blindfolded.

Nor is it generally known that during the 15 years of the Lebanese civil war, an estimated 17,000 people disappeared after being abducted. I suppose I could count myself lucky for not being one of them because I travelled the country far and wide during hostilities. At one stage, travelling along the coastal road south of Sidon, I was in a car that was targeted by an Israeli gunship patrolling offshore waters. Fortunately, their accuracy was suspect that day…

Veteran BBC correspondent Jeremy Bowen covered the same ground in 1996; he also came under fire on the road between Sidon and Tyre, a lonely stretch of highway from seawards. An Israeli patrol targeted his car as well, and as he relates, he laughed with relief together with his driver Abed when shells exploded on the road rather than on their car.

'It was calculated risk,' he recalled. 'The alternative was returning to Beirut without a story.'[1]

Colonel William R. Higgins of the United States Marine Corps was 43 years old when he was murdered by Hezbollah zealots in 1990. At the time he was Commander, Observer Group Lebanon (OGL), a United Nations body responsible for 'supervising the truce' on the border between Israel and Lebanon, a fairly small unit with whom I spent some good time.

The word 'truce' in the context of this United Nations body is anomalous. In typical Middle East fashion, there might have been something written on paper at some stage or another, but as experience has proved often enough in the past, it's usually as worthless as the peace it was supposed to have guaranteed.

I met Colonel Higgins only once, at a function at Naqoura that I attended while at the South Lebanese UN base. It was a busy occasion, and we were hardly able to connect because of the crush. Only after he'd been abducted and I spotted his picture in the papers – a strong round face, with a receding forehead and the stock grey Marine Corps moustache – did I realise who he was. To the Jihadists holding him hostage, Bill Higgins was a remarkable prize. To Hezbollah, he was a spy, simple as that…

As they described the incident at OGL headquarters at Nahariya on the Israeli side of the border, Colonel Higgins had set out on a blustery morning in February 1988, mentioning to an aide who didn't accompany him that there was a meeting

---

1   Jeremy Bowen, *The Making of the Middle East: A Personal History*. Pan Macmillan: 2022.

planned with Arab leaders about a problem, though he wasn't specific. Overnight, an icy wind had swept in from the Syrian highlands and by all accounts, it was cold, so the American wore his standard UN blues together with a heavy winter greatcoat.

What we do know is that the Colonel intended to raise the question of eight Americans already being held hostage by fundamentalist Muslim groups, the most prominent only later identified as Hezbollah, the Party of God (not yet the most important player in this grubby Middle Eastern game), but nonetheless, it was active and making a name for itself. Colonel Higgins played a significant role in those aspirations because he was to become Hostage Number Nine.

Once in custody, the American was held in isolation for two and a half years, and was murdered early on the morning of 6 July 1990. In this time, in my own usually discreet movements about the region, I only found out afterwards that several times I must have been only yards from his improvised prison. Had I only known…

Subsequent interrogations of Hezbollah prisoners by the Israelis have revealed that the captivity of Colonel Higgins was brutal, indeterminate and often cruel, often mindlessly so. Reports have it that there were times when he was beaten and starved.

Bound, gagged and most times blindfolded, this senior American officer was kept in solitary confinement throughout. In short, the man who had served with distinction in several military campaigns during a rather illustrious career suffered horrible privations.

It's worth mentioning that the Israelis made it known afterwards that his tormentors never managed to break him. He was finally dispatched with what the Nazis called a *nackschuss* (a bullet in the back of the head or neck) in Tyre, the biggest town in southern Lebanon, not far from where the original meeting was scheduled to have taken place.

A spokesman for Hezbollah later tried to dismiss this horrific chapter by declaring that Colonel Higgins was a CIA agent. As such, a spokesman for the movement deduced, he was an enemy of Islamic people everywhere. An immediate result of Higgins's death was that from then on, no member of Observer Group Lebanon ever again travelled alone in Lebanon. These days meetings are held in the presence of at least two members of the team, backed up by a radio check to base every 30 minutes or so. The same procedures are followed when OGL staff travel on the roads in that country, though not when on business in Israel. Even my own movements with members of the group in 1997 were in the company of two of their officers, and sometimes with a member of the UN spokesman's staff as well. The last time I went in, two New Zealand officers escorted me.

We'd drive throughout the region, from Naqoura eastwards towards Shihin where Team Zulu had its observation post (OP).

Our route would take us past Bint Jubayl, where we were regarded with great suspicion. From there we'd wend our way along to Team Victor's position, another concrete bunker fitted with a powerful pair of binoculars on a metal stand. We then turned northeast, where Team X-ray had its base that overlooked the heartland of Upper Galilee, on the fringes of ground that had come under heavy Israeli gunfire during Operation *Grapes of Wrath* the previous April.

We moved cautiously through terrain dominated by Hezbollah, we passed unhindered, even though those members of the Party of God we encountered along the way knew exactly who I was and why I was being escorted by OGL. They'd been formally told so by Naqoura, as is the custom with the UN, and while we were never really challenged, we remained cautious.

Along the way, we passed several South Lebanese Army mine-clearing squads. Each time we'd stop until we were waved on. One of the Australian officers had been fired on the month before after suddenly coming over a rise. He'd unexpectedly run into a group of SLA soldiers. Although his vehicle was white and he was in his usual blue uniform, he was shot at despite his conspicuous UN markings.

He wasn't seriously hurt, although his car took several hits. One lucky Australian!

The most active of the United Nations Truce Supervision Organisation's (UNTSO) observation posts was OP Mar, manned by Team X-ray. It comprised two more New Zealanders and an officer each from France, Canada, Belgium and Finland. The OC was an Australian, Major Frank Kalloway, RAAC, from Tasmania.

The fortifications around this tiny base were essentially a cluster of concrete blockhouses, some of them underground with the entire area surrounded by staggered layers of razor wire. OP Mar had come under fire many times in the last few years, usually from the Israeli side, which Jerusalem would afterwards declare was either accidental or inadvertent fire.

During the course of *Grapes of Wrath,* OP Mar had been hit by two Israeli airbursts at close range, the incidents dismissed as trivial by the Israeli government, which infuriated the occupants. If the observers had been in their usual positions, the base commander submitted at the time, they might have all been killed. Damage had been severe, Major Kalloway confirmed.

'What really pissed us off about the Israelis,' said Captain John Doran, a New Zealand reserve officer from Otago, 'was that the bastards didn't even ask whether any of us were hurt.' Then it happened again, and once more the matter was taken up with the government in Jerusalem.

Doran, like many other UN troops who had come under Israeli artillery fire believed that it was no accident. 'It was fucking intentional', he told me, the intention, he reckoned, to intimidate. 'They're one of the most advanced military nations in the world and that's not the kind of mistake they would make…remember, their own people are around here too, and you very rarely hear about accidental losses from friendly fire among Jewish forces, now do you?'

I afterwards asked several Israeli officers about the stonking. Either they didn't know, or they weren't telling, because those matters were casually dismissed with a shrug and a wave or other offhand gestures of indifference or contempt that remain one of the reasons why United Nations–Israeli relations are as bad as they are. In this regard, little has changed over decades.

At the same time, one must give the IDF its dues. The Israeli Captain Shimon who accompanied me into one of the border camps admitted that his people must have fired at least 25,000 rounds of artillery during the *Grapes of Wrath*. 'So, a couple of rounds fell short…what can we do?' he'd state, adding that this was war. 'What do those people expect?'

Shimon was less forthcoming about the five or six shells that landed in the FijiBatt camp at Qana, east of Tyre; historically, the Bible tells us, the same place where Jesus transformed water into wine.

More than 100 Lebanese, men, women and children were killed in an attack that must have been one of the worst Israeli military blunders. Apart from needless loss of life, it cost the Jewish nation an inordinate amount of goodwill among countries that in past might have tolerated the occasional excess, including many Jewish folk abroad and in the United States. But not on the scale of what happened at Qana. As might have been expected, the American TV network CNN made a meal of it among viewers all over the globe.

I had to pass through Qana a few days after that disaster and the eyes of those who followed my every move while I was there reflected only hatred, a gesture reserved for anyone who was not Arabic. Communally, in their view, we were all guilty of those atrocities.

Situated on the Israeli border about five clicks east of Qiryat Shmona and with the Lebanese hinterland stretching away behind, OP Mar had been the focus of much attention by Hezbollah in the period leading up to Operation *Grapes of Wrath*. All towns in the region – mostly Islamic and pro-Shi'ite – had been afflicted by numerous ambushes, mines and roadside bombs or IEDs.

These included Bani Hayyan (from where the fundamentalists had tried to launch a microlight, which was immediately shot down by the IDF with a six-barrelled Gatling); Markabe (where a car bomb was detonated); and Houele, the source of at least two Hezbollah suicide bombers and still more violence that caused the death of children a few months before I got there.

The region is characterised by a series of wadis – river valleys or gullies – running from east to west, none offering much natural cover of the kind needed for guerrilla operations. They have their uses nevertheless, usually to penetrate as close to the Israeli border as possible. The deepest is Wadi Salaq, referred to by both the UN and the Israelis still today as 'Hezbollah Highway'.

Many of the UN officers that I met during that visit in the 1990s maintained that Hezbollah was making serious inroads wherever it had influence, including its social, political and military domains. They noted too, that suicide bombings had become the norm and since everything was swathed in secrecy, there was little they could do to counter such threats.

One example showed remarkable guile. In its bid to foil Israeli remote-piloted vehicles (RPVs) – which use infrared instruments positioned at 18,000 feet to seek out hostile intruders making their way across the country – Hezbollah commanders had acquired neoprene wetsuits for their men. Not only did the suits reduce heat emissions at night when most of these activities took place, but they also kept their people warm. A Hezbollah attack group, elaborated a Norwegian intelligence officer, might lie in one position for three or four days without supplies waiting for an Israeli or SLA patrol to pass.

'They are totally focused in their determination to get at what they naturally regard as a 'blood enemy'.

Since then of course, that kind of activity has if not stopped, then moderated. With Islamic attrition increasing, the Israeli government finally decided that it would be in its interests to withdraw the IDF to positions behind its borders. The gesture was trumpeted throughout the Arab world as a major Hezbollah victory, which when you examine the consequences, it probably was. Only now, Hezbollah attacks take place directly on Israeli soil, though they are rare because of solid IDF border defences and patrols.

While the IDF was still stationed in South Lebanon – and during my visits to the region – Hezbollah tactics changed in other ways. Besides taking along their own camera crews to record attacks at the 'sharp end', they would invite Lebanese television personalities from Beirut to position themselves at specific spots at designated times.

One such incident involved Israeli troops returning to Israel near the Metullah border crossing. The cameraman filmed footage that was later described as sensation and grabbed by CNN to be beamed all over the world. Pictures of dead and dying Israeli soldiers, some still writhing on the ground had a profound effect on Jewish sensibilities and many expressed horror. As might have been expected, air attacks on Hezbollah training camps in the Bekaa Valley intensified.

Of course, the cameraman involved was arrested by the Lebanese authorities immediately after the attack, but not before he was able to spirit away his tape. Naturally, he denied any prior knowledge of the ambush, which was interesting: it happened near a busy road and a strict policy in force mandated that no casual movement of civilians was allowed on this or any other border road which, in any event was out of bounds.

The cameraman later added his two bits' worth, proclaiming loud resentment of the presence of the Jews on Lebanese soil. On this issue, there were even some Israelis who had to acknowledge that it was his right. The man was held for several weeks by the Israeli General Security Service (GSS) and then released, but not before strong protests by the Egyptian and Jordanian governments had been lodged.

The nearest Israeli fortified post to OP Mar is marked as Four One Alpha on the operational map. At the time it was manned by about 20 IDF conscripts and supported by a couple of armoured personnel carriers as well as a lone heavy tank with an array of electronic sensors and masts on its turret. Four One Alpha was then used for launching nightly patrols against Hezbollah, usually on foot, though sometimes a helicopter would go across the border and pull them out again.

According to the commander, the squads, usually heavily camouflaged, left their base at about eight in the evening and were back before dawn. They often carried mine-clearing equipment, and you simply couldn't miss the night-vision goggles that hung limply about their necks, he said. He also disclosed that it was Hezbollah's purpose to lay mines and set booby-traps in their efforts to hamper these patrols in and around Houele. They also fired at them with their Iranian-supplied Sagger missiles.

Altogether, said the Australian officer, the Israelis had about a dozen camps (Permanent Violations) in his area, which was relatively heavy compared with a few years previously when most of the work was left to the South Lebanese Army. He disclosed that Hezbollah became most active when Israeli forces were preparing for the resupply or relief of their men.

'They don't always do damage, but the very fact that they can attack is a morale boost since it shows the people that they can act in the area, if not with impunity, then at least with much less risk than before. That is a victory of sorts for the guerrillas,' he stated. Major Kalloway made the point that some of the guerrilla strikes were causing serious problems that Israel needed to solve. As we now know, rather address those issues, the IDF was ordered to pull out of Lebanon altogether.

I was shown some of the positions where Hezbollah had laid their roadside bombs (IEDs), including two placed along roads in Houele. According to an OGL report published subsequently, the first bomb exploded in what was identified as 'Echo Road' on the map. Its target was Captain Ali Abass, deputy commander of the SLA 70th Battalion. The first explosion caused no damage, which immediately gave rise to the suspicion that it had been intentionally set off to send SLA officers by another route where a second device had been laid.

What happened next was not entirely clear, but to quote from the report, four children, three of them girls, apparently chased a snake into a hole in a wall about a hundred yards from where it joined Echo Road. This wasn't all that unusual because there are plenty of snakes in the Levant.

They poked about for a minute or so with a stick, and suddenly there was a powerful explosion and three of the children killed outright. All that was left of the only boy, Muhammed Talar Juwad, aged 12, was his shoes. They were still there where he'd been standing.

Very little of the two girls was ever found. The fourth, a 14-year-old and a sister to one of the dead was unharmed, but she was too shocked to speak for days.

About 20 minutes after the explosion, Al Manaar, Hezbollah's radio station in Beirut announced that four 'collaborators' (sic) had been killed by a roadside bomb laid by their guerrillas. When the extent of the mishap became apparent, the story abruptly changed: that evening the children's deaths were blamed on 'an Israeli attack on innocents'.

What had happened was that a Hezbollah group of three men had set up an OP on a hill with a clear view of the bomb site in Shaqraq, the next village to the east. They'd set off their bomb in the belief that it had been found by security personnel who were dismantling it. In truth, they were too far away to be able to see that the 'intruders' were children.

It is one of the tragic quirks of this vicious struggle that the family of 11-year-old Hamama Ashad Hussein had already lost three boys in the war. SLA engineers later produced fragments of remote-control equipment taken from the site of the explosion and a UN source confirmed later that it had all the hallmarks of bombs previously laid by Hezbollah.

Observer Group Lebanon teams with whom I worked were very much aware that roadside bombs presented a danger to their own safety. According to another New Zealander, Captain Charles Smith, also from Otago, bombs were seldom laid singly; there was usually a second charge, which was detonated while the other was being investigated.

'Since it has always been the principal task of the OGL to look into such matters, it is possible to become a casualty by accident,' he said. 'The first is usually set off by a trip wire; the second is command-detonated by radio from a mile or more away. From that distance, all men in uniform tend to look the same.'

I was to experience this for myself the morning when we set out from Naqoura for Majdal Zun. Word had come over the radio that a bomb had gone off in the next village to the east. Smith asked headquarters for permission to investigate; it was refused. Other bombs might have been laid, said his superiors. Let the SLA handle the matter first, was the order.

That premise was correct. It was a Sunday, and nobody went near the place until the next day. When they did start scratching around, it wasn't long before a second charge was found. It hadn't been detonated because SLA units had fanned out into the surrounding hills and they'd probably disturbed those manning the OP who had been tasked to watch the place. It was also confirmed before I left the area that a possible 'armed element' observation post had been found in the hills nearby.

One of the OGL officers reckoned that as the war dragged on, roadside bombs were increasingly being used to settle personal and domestic scores. Conflict had hardened sensibilities, was his view. 'It's often easier to kill a man who annoys you than argue with him…or you'll have an individual who might fancy somebody else's wife…'

Many prisoners were taken in this war while the Israelis remained on the wrong side of their frontier and there were questions raised as to who exactly could be construed as the enemy since all Hezbollah combatants were on their own soil. To the Israelis the conflict was an 'insurrection'; to the Arabs, it was a war, presaged by an illegal occupation.

When was a man a prisoner of war, and when was he a plain prisoner? The issue gave rise to acrimony on both sides.

All 'suspects' were taken to the main SLA prison at El Khiam, to the immediate southeast of Marj'Ayoun, which was regarded as little more than a hell-hole by local inhabitants. Not everybody who went into Khiam, they said, came out alive. It was also general knowledge that El Khiam had been the subject of numerous human rights investigations; and that it was the Israelis who ran the show there.

The difference between prisoners taken by the SLA or the Israelis and those grabbed by Hezbollah is that there was an odds-on chance of being charged or released by the former two if such things happened in Lebanon. With fundamentalists, it was enough to be *suspected* of treason or of being fingered as a 'collaborator' to be killed. Life throughout the area was always precarious.

One of the most interesting towns in the region at the time was Bint Jubayl, almost laid to waste during Israel's 2006 invasion of the region. Quite big by South Lebanese standards in the old days, I visited the place with the two New Zealand captains.

It lay on a series of hills at the southern edge of the part where the Irish Battalion was then stationed. Although it was predominantly Muslim, some Christians were living there, although I've been told that most had since all left, which happened to minorities in a hostile and active region that saw much fundamentalist Islamic support. We have the same thing happening today across the border in Christian Arab towns such as Bethlehem and Nazareth.

Observer Group Lebanon logbooks, I found, contained dozens of entries that indicated Bint Jubayl as being linked to car bombings, roadside bombs, unauthorised arrests of suspects, arms caches as well as attacks on SLA or Israeli positions or patrols. I read that a car bomber had been intercepted outside the main SLA military base in the town shortly before I arrived. Countering this activity, there were Israeli attacks on Hezbollah infiltrators in nocturnal ambushes on approach roads. Some left blood trails that were followed up the next day and it said a lot that many led to Bint Jubayl.

The history of Observer Group Lebanon is interesting. It dates back to the year when the Israeli state was founded, 1948.

As the convoluted politics of the Middle East changed, so did the principal United Nations monitoring body which we all referred to as UNTSO (the UN Truce Supervising Organisation). In the interim, it has cost a lot of lives. Besides Colonel Higgins, dozens more officers had been killed on active service with the force by the time I got there the last time in the mid-1990s. Only six were OGL, including an Australian Captain Peter McCarthy, who was killed on the last day of his tour of duty.

On 12 January 1988, he'd sauntered up to the hill overlooking Naqoura for a farewell look at the area and tripped an anti-personnel mine. For his colleagues, it was indeed a sad goodbye.

The OGL came into its own in 1972 when the government in Beirut demanded that the Security Council of the UN strengthen its presence along the southern border with Israel. The first three units were stationed at Naqoura, Ras (next to the Shi'ite town of Marun ar Ras) and Khiam (where the prison is situated).

Three more posts were added later, although the Israelis never agreed to the presence of the OGL which is why its activities have always remained restricted to Lebanon, even though most of its personnel spend their off-duty hours, or actually live, in Israel. There were 36 observers until the spring of 1980 when increasing hostilities caused its strength to be doubled.

After the abduction of Colonel Higgins, the OGL base north of the Litani River (in so-called 'Free Lebanon') was shut down because it was considered too dangerous to maintain effectively. More abductions were feared. Its numbers were further reduced in 1989.

Although the OGL maintains a headquarters presence in Naqoura, it is rarely manned by more than one or two officers. Most of its duties seem to be carried out in a pleasant villa near the beach in Nahariya where it has a bar, entertainment areas and rooms for off-duty OGL members. The radio room is always manned.

The future of Observer Group Lebanon or even UNTSO, for that matter, is problematical. The UN constantly warns that it is running out of cash. Somehow though, its life is extended year by year – vote by vote – at the UN Headquarters at Turtle Bay in New York.

There was one development however that its officers in recent years started to take more seriously, something I saw for myself during that tour of duty. Whenever we left our vehicles unattended, Captain Smith would clamp a metal locking device to the steering wheel.

'Orders,' he said. 'The UN and the Israelis believe that the next car bomb will be a suicide thing. It could happen in one of the big SLA or IDF bases or the border post at Rosh Haniqra.' The only difference between those vehicles or buses that had exploded in the past and the next one, he explained, was that this one would be white, with UN markings and a man in United Nations uniform at the wheel.

'We know that they already have some of our uniforms in their possession. We're aware too that they have some of our types of vehicles, already painted and fitted with UN markings. What we don't want is for them to steal one of our rigs and turn it into a bomb,' he added.

The Israelis too, were severe about the threat. Every vehicle that went through border control at Rosh Haniqra was searched, inside and out, and that was done some distance from the main control point. I spent an afternoon there once watching the process: some vehicles were driven onto a ramp where a soldier with a mirror at the end of a pole knelt down and peered along the chassis in search of explosives. Nobody was taking chances after the Tel Aviv and Jerusalem bus bombings of 1996.

For all that, many questions were being asked about the United Nations Interim Force in Lebanon (UNIFIL), not only in Israel but in some of the countries with a share in the 'peacekeeping' operation. There are still questions being asked about the so-called peacekeeping body.

Most nations, Holland, Fiji, Norway and Ireland, ended up withdrawing their troops. Others accused UNIFIL of bias in favour of the Arab cause. Some still do.

Over the years I spent a lot of time in South Lebanon with these units. I even made a television documentary on the UNIFIL role in the middle-1980s. While some national units performed admirably, others lacked ability and initiative. There were a few that were downright terrified of even being there, between two powerful and demonstrably belligerent entities that regarded a day without some kind of military action as a wasted 24 hours.

As I was to observe for myself, quite a number of these UN troops would look the other way whenever there was Hezbollah around. The Ghanaians, for example, were constantly being accused by the Israelis of gross incompetence for letting 'armed elements' through their lines. It happened so often that nobody took any notice of such charges anymore and anyway, as one IDF spokesman was heard to comment, 'They shouldn't even have been sent there in the first place.'

The Irish and the Finns were sometimes little better, though there were good, professional soldiers among them all. More than once the Irish took me to task afterwards for highlighting their inadequacies, which, as the saying goes, sometimes included their men looking a little too deep into the bottle.

An American observer made the point that while troops from those countries might perform brilliantly in other conflicts, they were really quite inadequate for the task at hand. Quite a few were nothing but 'time wasters' with 'neither the will nor the stomach for the job'.

In contrast, there were some nationals, the Fijians in particular, who were respected and trusted by all. It was a sad day when these island contingents were withdrawn from South Lebanon. Tough, aggressive and intolerant of any kind of obstruction in the performance of their duties, this is a national army that in this modern day and age is not to be trifled with.

As might have been expected, the Fijians paid a price. There were more Fijian soldiers attached to United Nations units killed in action in Lebanon than any other country deployed there. What they did leave behind was a proud legacy of their activities in one of the most troubled regions of the globe.

Stories about FijiBatt are legion. At the height of Operation *Grapes of Wrath*, one of the fundamentalist groups set up a Katyusha rocket launcher in front of a control post on the main road south of Tyre. A Fijian soldier didn't like it and first asked and then told the Hezbollah soldiers to move. They could do as they liked since it was their war, he told their senior man, but it was his job while he was there, to prevent that sort of thing happening. They simply couldn't shoot at Israel within sight of his post, he declared. The Arabs said nothing. Instead, they carried on with what they were about.

The man from Fiji tackled them again. One of the insurgents drew a pistol and shot the Fijian soldier in the chest. A shootout followed in which quite a few more Fijians were killed or wounded, but almost an entire Hezbollah squad was annihilated.

The Israelis, likewise, have been guilty of infractions. In December 1995 an IDF artillery battery fired several 155 mm shells at four Norwegian soldiers while on patrol along the east bank of the Litani River. This kind of patrol activity was routine at the time and sometimes took place twice a day, once during daylight hours and again at night.

Of the half-dozen or so nations stationed in Lebanon at the time, only the Fijians and the Norwegians patrolled at night. The Irish, the Finns, the Ghanaians and the Nepalese didn't consider it necessary or, as one Israeli officer succinctly phrased it: 'They'd shit themselves if they had to leave their camps after dark.'

All visits to United Nations ground force contingents in Lebanon in those days started and ended at Naqoura, about a mile north of the Israeli border post at Rosh Haniqra; today you have to apply directly to UN headquarters in New York and that has become a tedious business.

Then I'd come straight in from Israel, through the 'closed' border at Rosh Haniqra and Timur Goksell, the UN spokesman at the base, didn't like it.

He'd always suggest that it would suit him better if I entered through Beirut, but for me at the time, it would have meant an additional risk. Hezbollah knew very well who I was and what I was doing there. I was also aware of a UNIFIL communications infrastructure that had long ago been compromised. Some of Timur's messages were seen by Israeli intelligence officers before he read them. I surmised, correctly as it later turned out, that Hezbollah was kept similarly primed of just about anything that the UN did.

Naqoura UN Headquarters is one of the largest such United Nations establishments in the world. For many years it was the biggest, and with almost 15,000 personnel – military and civilian – on the books, it probably still is. The base squats rather than sits along the Mediterranean, with the result that it has something of a holiday air about it. From the air, it might be mistaken for a village on the Côte d'Azur.

Arab Naqoura, in contrast, the original old town, stands isolated on a hill that overlooks the base, the same hill on which the Australian Captain Peter McCarthy was killed.

In the town itself, dozens of little stores line the road and you can buy just about all you need at a fraction of the price that it'd cost you in the Holy Land. Though things have changed a lot in the interim, you can still get a suit made in a couple of days at Naqoura, or buy a range of electronic goods and cameras, all duty-free.

Despite its role in a region that has been marked by hostilities for the past half-century, Naqoura strikes the visitor as being more of a civilian town than a military camp. It has more pubs than anywhere outside Beirut. At the bar in the Irish Compound, you sometimes buy three beers at a time to avoid standing in line. The Irish officers drink in the appropriately named Irish House, a delightful little hideaway a little higher up, towards the main road. Next door the Fijian officers have their own boozer.

There is much movement between all the national clubs and bars. I thought that the Italians at the helicopter port tended rather to keep to themselves, though they were most hospitable to me, probably because I flew with them.

The evening meal at the Italian base was communal, invariably presided over by their commander at the time, the genial, soft-spoken Lieutenant-Colonel Guaccio Aldo, a classicist. When not flying helicopters in Lebanon he visited historic sites in Britain with his wife. It was he who first showed me the small Crusader fort that stands in the base grounds, close to the water and overlooked by the office of the local UN commander.

Having something pre-prandial in the Italian mess was almost like being in one of those upper-class places in Italy where form is dictated by unspoken ceremony; everyone at the base was an officer and there were no NCOs present.

Life at Naqoura in the old days was easy-going and unhurried. The occasional guest like me stayed in austere single quarters that would probably be turned into a sort of Club Med after the fighting is over, were that ever to happen. A first-rate four-course dinner in the officers' mess cost me only $4, without wine.

Since most supplies for camps lying in the 'interior' (though the furthest was perhaps only ten minutes' flying time by chopper) were controlled from Naqoura, the base was – and still is – little more than a transit camp. In a sense, it's a clearing-house for troops moving in and out from the various bases. You headed for Naqoura if you had a toothache, or went on furlough, or had your weekly session with the base shrink.

It was significant that no senior UN commanders or civilian staff lived there. Which begs the question: did they ever?

Whether for convenience (which is improbable because of the hassle of crossing the border twice a day) or doubts about the ability of UN soldiers to defend them, all senior UN officers based at Naqoura had homes in Israel, the majority in Nahariya, the northernmost town along the coast. The commander of UNIFIL on my last visit, Major-General Stanislav Wozniak, a Pole, had a home there. So did all those who came before and after him.

None of these officials sent their children to Israeli schools because, as one Italian officer stated, that might be interpreted as partisan by some of the Arabs in the region. However, Timur Goksell, the UN spokesman at the base, had his two children driven all the way to a school in Tel Aviv every day, more than two hours each way. To do so, Timur confided, the family had to get up sometime after four each morning.

Each UN battalion in South Lebanon had its own rules about length of service, local leave, fraternisation with the locals which, as far as the Fijians were concerned, was just not on. Most of them worked off excess steam in their unit gym and their physiques were commensurately impressive. But then the Fijians have always been remarkably physical as we've seen by what they can accomplish on the rugby field.

The Norwegians were different: they mixed with the local people as and how they pleased. Some of their troops even married Arab women, but then Scandinavians generally tend to be crazy about dusky southerners.

On my first day at NorBatt, we had lunch at a little house outside Clea'a, a mainly Christian village. Outside there was nothing to show that it was a restaurant. Inside, the little lady of the house, a Maronite Christian, lit a paraffin stove. It still took us about 20 minutes to feel the warmth: it was icy outside, even at midday.

Our hostess was dark, friendly and enchanting and, said my escort, a reserve captain in the Norwegian Army on his second tour of duty, she was soon to marry a Norwegian. By that stage already something like 20 Norwegians had already paired off with local women, some of them widows who seemed to be perfectly happy to move to the very different domesticity and climate of Scandinavia.

The restaurant in an Arab village that day was interesting. In a country where health inspectors and veterinary controls barely exist, I was wary of the steak roll placed before me until the officer with me assured me that the unit had its own vet. It also had the only working post office in the area; letters were sent off as if from Norway, with Norwegian stamps and postmarks. It said something that the townspeople also used the service; there were no other means of getting letters out unless they went into Metullah across the border, and that was a schlep because of the controls.

The job entrusted to the United Nations in the Levant is regarded by most of the officers involved as one of the most challenging. In the thirty years that this multinational force has been active, it has lost almost 270 of its men plus a sprinkling of civilian aid personnel as well as locals working for the international body.

Few observers have spent any time in South Lebanon who don't concede that the UN role has always been a ticklish business. The Lebanese say that the UN soldiers are biased against Arabs. Others accuse them of being partial towards the Jews.

Israeli sentiments are well summed up by an Israeli officer who had close dealings with the UN troops: 'Ineffectual, apathetic and often in fear of getting themselves hurt,' were his words. I'd heard the same kind of comment made about other UN 'peacekeeping' troops in Angola, where the soldiers – also Scandinavian – spent more time screwing the local ladies than on patrol trying to sort out problems.

UNIFIL soldiers, almost to a man, had a lot to say about the almost total lack of civic probity among most of the Israelis whom they encountered in their 'dealings' with Jewish people, official or otherwise. In the early days, United Nations troops on leave in Israeli cities left their uniforms back at base – stories about US soldiers being beaten up were regular. It still goes on, I'm told, but to a lesser degree.

What is manifest is that there are very few Israelis who like the UN, and even fewer UN personnel who have any time at all for the average Israeli.

To some of these mercenaries (which is what they are) it is simply a meal ticket, usually tax free. In Norway there was such a demand for six-month, tax-free UN postings, that the system was run on a quota basis. It probably still is.

Yet there is no doubt that if the UN were to pull out of South Lebanon tomorrow, the present low-level insurrection would probably blow up into a full-scale war.

Again…

CHAPTER 32

The bin Laden syndrome in South Africa

Then there was Osama bin Laden, someone I knew as little about as anyone else, which was essentially only what the media told us. The subliminal hack instinct having kicked in, I got involved...

Western intelligence agencies searched for this elusive al-Qaeda commander for decades, but there were few if any, indications of his whereabouts.

They looked everywhere – from Afghanistan to the Americas and just about every country in between. The elusive revolutionary with an enormous following seemed to have disappeared into thin air.

What did eventually surface – circuitously as it happened in a series of tangled security links – was that he was spending a good deal of time in South Africa, sometimes months at a stretch.

Clandestinely, Osama bin Laden was a regular visitor to South Africa – a country that has since emerged as a strong supporter of Moscow in its war with the Ukraine. Apparently, he quite liked the place; partly because he thought the authorities there too stupid to believe that he might be within their ambit, and now and again almost within touching distance.

What is noteworthy is that during the decade that followed Nelson Mandela's accession to power in South Africa in 2003, there were numerous reports – all unsubstantiated – of a tall, bearded Arab, usually wearing distinctive, long, flowing robes wandering around the Cape with small groups of friends or attending local mosques for services.

He was also said to have been seen in Port Elizabeth several times, but none of those reports were investigated.

One should remember that events in Afghanistan after the invasion of that nation by American and Coalition Forces following the destruction of New York's Twin Towers – and then the Iraqi war – got good coverage in South Africa's media. That meant that Osama bin Laden was no figurative or imaginary person: he was as real in the local context as biltong or Ouma's Rusks.

We all remember photos of the man sitting with his acolytes in the Afghan mountains, usually the Tora Bora (his Kalashnikov always within reach), or firing an RPG-7 and then addressing a fighting group. No question, Osama bin Laden was constantly in the news, particularly within his own Islamic circles.

Also, it was no secret that many people – Muslim, as well as non-Muslim – celebrated the revolutionary leader as an elusive hero who had cocked a snoot at the West.

It was common knowledge that Washington and most European nations had launched an international hunt for the man that had almost become an obsession for some. There were searches on almost every continent for evidence of this recalcitrant Arab whose Saudi family by then had disowned him.

Irrespective of suspicions that he might have visited South Africa and even reports of sightings, nobody could get their heads around the possibility that the 'Rainbow Nation' might be playing host to the world's most prominent anarchist. And, as for al-Qaeda having established a presence at the southern tip of Africa, that kind of conjecture was dismissed – by one and all – as absurd.

The main arguments centred around the fact that it would have been physically impossible for him to travel to South Africa on any of the airlines then serving the nation. Coming in from the sea – though feasible – involved distances that made it improbable.

Information subsequently released (with which I deal later) suggested that such a visit was very possible indeed – not only of bin Laden coming to South Africa but also his deputy, the Egyptian doctor Ayman al-Zawahiri. The al-Qaeda deputy spent such long periods in the country that he might have acquired a residence permit, had he applied.

Of supreme importance is that both men, while in South Africa, always moved about incognito, protected by extensive security screens that were only cursorily penetrated, and briefly, the subject of this chapter.

It was then, inadvertently or otherwise, that I came into contact with an intelligence operative that not only knew about the presence of both Osama and al-Zawahiri but had personal contact with many of the people with whom both leaders were associated. As proof, he had reams of documentation he'd acquired as an undercover operative, some of which he was prepared to share with me.

Most puzzling, the main player and source of all this information was an eager and fairly well-schooled secret agent who had been put through his paces by some of the country's most experienced intelligence operatives of the apartheid era. A local Muslim, he was the brother of one of a tiny protective unit that guarded the men whose faces were prominent not only on America's 'Most Wanted' but on every hand-out published by the majority of the world's intelligence agencies. Interpol rated him as of supreme value.

The fact is, if South Africa agencies were made aware of bin Laden's presence, something that was eventually passed on to me, then the eminent Nelson Mandela would unquestionably have been told. So would certain members of his cabinet, especially those of Islamic persuasion. Instead, the government remained shtum throughout.

The cardinal mistake my contact made was that he opposed some of the tenets of a faith that is unforgiving when transgressed. More pertinently, he ignored the fact that al-Qaeda's chiefs were protected by a level of security that was then safer than anything comparable in the West.

The inescapable reality was that while the Mafia might have boasted of the power of their all-encompassing *Omerta* (which is essentially secular and mercenary), Islam, in the minds of its followers, is a far more engaging religious force. Followers not only have those around them as their ultimate strength, but as their Holy Book declares, they must obey their conscience: *Allah u Akbar* – the rallying cry of a billion Muslims says it all.

For all that, my interest was piqued once the broad outlines of what was going on were revealed by someone – even though he was Muslim – who believed that the al-Qaeda 'myth' – as he called it, needed to be exposed. To him, bin Laden was a criminal, and though constrained by the organisation he worked for, he had an idea – strictly personal, of course – that as a news-gatherer, I might put the word out.

That said, it didn't take long to confess to my source that I might not be the man for such work. Just being aware of some of the most sensitive intelligence material – and the names of those involved – was interesting and disquieting, but making it all public was altogether another matter.

That kind of hard news – if your role as a disseminator were to be uncovered, or more simply put, 'somebody *suspected* you of knowing too much' – and I certainly would have qualified because by-lines speak for themselves – I could end up on a slab.

Right now, with Stage Four bone cancer, I couldn't care a damn. In any event, at that time I'd already spent several years under protective surveillance while living in North America following my disclosures about the South African/Iranian nuclear links – I didn't need that kind of experience again. Or did I?

Meantime, I did my own research on Osama bin Laden and his cohorts, and discovered that while there were thousands of pages written about the man and his legacy – as well as that of his deputy, Dr Ayman al-Zawahiri – there was absolutely no mention of either's links to South Africa, that by then was promulgating comforting images of what Mandela's young government was already referring to as the 'Rainbow Nation'.

After all, apartheid was dead, South Africa had cast off its hideous past and, as the expression goes, there weren't supposed to be any skeletons left in the cupboard. Unfortunately, there were.

So, over several months, I searched the web and every possible mainline source for evidence of any kind of South African connection for either al-Qaeda or its leaders.

That hunt included al-Zawahiri. Going back years, I scoured all major international newspapers and agencies of the day and found nothing.

I then expanded my search to include reliable sources such as Encyclopaedia Britannica, Washington's Council on Foreign Relations, GlobalSecurity.org and even obscure, but possibly related entities, like the Egyptian Islamic Jihad website.

Neither man's name nor any presence linked to South Africa ever appeared. There were thousands of mentions of visits by the al-Qaeda leadership to places like the Sudan, the Middle East and even Israel (though Palestine is used throughout) as well as some African countries, but not a word of visits to any country south of the Equator during the al-Qaeda phase. It remained so up to the time that this book went to press.

Osama's visits to South Africa were never detected or even alluded to, but we now know that they happened. These visits remained secretive throughout, with none of the more salient details released by those very few operators within the government who were aware of what was going on, irrespective of the fact that al-Qaeda's presence had become firmly established within the country's hard-core Islamic community.

This situation could obviously not persist indefinitely within Pretoria's National Security Agency, which was roughly when I was sucked into the conundrum.

As any experienced journalist will tell you, those who know the ropes are sometimes approached by total strangers and offered extraordinary stories – scoops actually.

In most cases, especially in some African states, individuals would come forward with information about impending military coups or plots to expose graft or corruption, something that has happened to practically all of us, with most leads proving to be false. However, there are the rare exceptions that could expose remarkable pieces of information, often classified. Access to those Osama files was no different, with more than a hundred in toto.

But this newly acquired al-Qaeda-linked intelligence was not only about fomenting revolt or changes of government. It dealt primarily with the leader's push for influence in a completely new domain that would ultimately enhance his influence over a vast region.

For a start, when Nelson Mandela was voted into power, the country was referred to as the Powerhouse of Africa, which it was; its industries kept – and still keep – the southern half of the continent supplied with every possible need modern societies require, all the way north to the Congo and East Africa.

Also, South Africa was wealthy, well administered, and – unlike the majority of black states, already then in decline – its leaders reflected hope for the future, oodles of it.

At the same time, those who have worked in Africa long enough are aware that there are few countries in western, eastern as well as southern Africa that do not have some measure of potent Jihadist activity, quite often significantly so.

The ongoing insurgent war in West Africa's Sahel is an example. So is northern Mozambique, a conflict involving Islamic guerrillas trained in Somalia to overthrow the Maputo government. It is noteworthy that – though the Jihadist bush fighters had been labelled as untrained and undisciplined barefoot fighters – most soon proved that they were good at what they did. The guerrillas have since proved that they are as good as any in bush war scrap.

In 2019, Russia's Wagner Group went into Mozambique in full force, fitted out with helicopter gunships, infantry fighting vehicles, drones, advanced communications equipment and much more. That bombastic group lasted only four months before they packed their bags and returned home.[1]

South Africa's burgeoning Islamic community – reckoned to be between three and four million strong – is another powerfully motivated community, though you would be hard-pressed to find anybody living there today who will admit that Islam has revolutionary potential.

By then, cadres loyal to Osama bin Laden were inordinately active in the Middle East and Central Asia but, more importantly, my nameless contact claimed that the Jihadist leader had already managed to garner strong support in Africa's deep south.

He told me that training camps were already established on several farms in the Eastern Cape – something I'd already heard whispered in Pretoria's corridors of power. I was also aware that military training of 'volunteers' was already taking place in South Africa, mainly in the Eastern Cape, another issue I'd picked up on the ether.

It was nothing new. In 1996, Israel sent a formal complaint to the South African authorities detailing the existence of five Hezbollah training camps on South African soil. That took place three years after Mandela took over the government, thereby suggesting that he wasted no time bringing his revolutionary buddies in from abroad to establish a South African presence.

The majority of these people had voted with their feet to head overseas when apartheid politics became too oppressive. Some sought sanctuary in Europe; others opted for Cuba, Algeria, Tanzania, Ethiopia, Iran, and other countries opposed to the West. By the time they were called on to return to the country of their birth by Mandela to help run the 'New South Africa', many had transmogrified into fully fledged revolutionaries.

What is not generally known is that the eminent Madiba was a regular visitor to Libya where he was hosted three or four times a year by his good friend Muammar Gaddafi. These flights were very well documented because he was flown there by South African Air Force jets, and being good pals with many of the pilots involved, some from my Border War days, there were some interesting revelations.

---

1   Prof. Hussein Solomon, Lecture on 'Radical Islam in South Africa' during the World Summit on Counter-Terrorism – Terrorism's Global Impact, ICT 8th International Conference, IDC Herzliya, Israel.

This brings us back to the documents I ended up perusing – several thousand words of information that included the names of many South African Islamicists involved – where they lived, the number plates of their vehicles, businesses owned or ran, meetings attended, trips abroad (mainly to the Middle East) and a good deal more that could only be labelled contentious.

There was a host of information detailing visits to South Africa by the leader himself, as well as Dr Ayman al-Zawahiri who was assassinated in a CIA drone attack in Kabul in August 2022. In truth, this information was vast and also specific and detailed and something I wrote about in the British magazine *Air Forces Monthly*, published in February 2023.

This was when I posed two questions to my informant: firstly, what was his purpose in disclosing all this information – almost all of it palpably secret – and, until then, closely guarded?

And secondly, what was his objective, or more pertinently, what did he want cash-wise for playing the intermediary?

'Nothing,' he declared, which in itself was astonishing.

'Then why offer this stuff to me?' I asked.

'Because I think you might have the connections to pass it on and put a stop to a situation that I believe will result in violence,' was his reply. It was a fair answer, and for the moment, I left it there.

The files – hundreds of them – all dealt with events that had taken place and involved al-Qaeda and its South African leadership during the course of about a year during 2003 and 2004, a short time after Mandela was elected President. Some were quite detailed, others just short notes of activities taking place within the revolutionary ambit in South Africa. I discovered some astonishing revelations.

Then, quite abruptly, the reports ended. Only later did I discover that all had been sourced from a single individual, a South African national, also of Islamic persuasion, who had infiltrated the group.

He had been sending his reports to a senior member of the South African security establishment, someone linked to the former apartheid government. However, once Mandela took over government, Madiba could place whomever he pleased in positions of trust.

The Jihadist faction, now part of the ruling establishment saw to it that one of their own took charge; it wasn't long before that valuable source of information was exposed. He was murdered a short while later, with little or any information about his demise emerging.

Nor has it ever…

To say that the contents of those controversial files were compelling is more than ironic. The information provided was explosive enough to change the government had any of it been made public at that early stage.

By way of introduction, it is important to look at a few of those files involving the Supreme Leader and others, including the role of his son, Sa-ad bin Laden, who was then being groomed to eventually take over leadership of the al-Qaeda movement.

The man I was dealing with had direct contact with the source that had infiltrated al-Qaeda's South African revolutionary hierarchy, none of whom were small fry. Some, in their own right, were major players and, once details were out and their South African connection compromised, they went on to lead the movement elsewhere in Africa.

There were many reports, sometimes lone messages delivered either in person often phoned through or passed on by an intermediary, though none of their names were ever made public. Their missives covered not only domestic news about bin Laden or more generally about al-Qaeda operations and also international links or connections.

For instance, in a perfunctory message dated 18 August 2003 that was intercepted, it was reported that the South African wing of al-Qaeda had established close links with the Israeli terror group HAMAS. The document was titled 'Hamas Leaders and Operators from Gaza Strip'. It read:

> A team of eight HAMAS operators arrived [it does not indicate where in South Africa] on Friday afternoon 15.08.2003 [from the Middle East]: four leaders and four operators. The operators had apparently first been sent to Riyadh for the bombing as they are suicide bombers. Their vehicle, which was loaded with explosives, was not called into action, so they are preparing for a new mission.

The message then went on to describe the four more Palestinian leadership figures expected to arrive in South Africa within weeks:

- ABDEL ALI HAMMAD: +/- 45 years. Bald head, brown eyes, long thick bushy beard. Limps on left leg. Bottom section of right leg has several serious scars. Inside lower left arm has a tattoo that has been cut out and grafted over. Slanting scar on right cheek from nose to mouth. Speaks good English and acted as spokesperson for this *Jamaat*.
- FAIZEL BARAT: Early 50s. Engineer. Ameer of the *Jamaat*. Short black hair and beard, brown eyes. Speaks English.
- SALEH ABBAS: +/- 40 years. Dark brown short hair and short trimmed beard open over the cheeks. Speaks some English but prefers Urdu.
- HAMID KHARAZZI: +/- 45 years. Black hair, brown eyes. Has a distinct scar starting on the outer corner of his left eye (claims he fell when he was small). Has a thick black beard, long and thick on the sides. Speaks poor English.

While none of this information can be regarded as inspirational, what is of interest surfaces in the following file, dated 24 December 2003.

It deals specifically with Osama's son, Sa-ad bin Laden. That young man – apparently a bright and enthusiastic individual with indifferent language skills – was then on a clandestine visit to South Africa under the auspices of his Dad. He was said to be 'clean shaven, no beard…age 22 years, likes to converse in Arabic and Urdu. Strongly resembles his father'.

There were also details of close links between named South Africans (SEVERAL NAMES DELETED) with prominent international Islamic leaders. I quote:

> Sa-ad bin Laden went to Durban with NAME DELETED then to PRETORIA and came back to PORT ELIZABETH for one night and left again at *fajir* (dawn) on the 16th or 17th December 2003 for Cape Town with NAME DELETED and two bodyguards (also identified).
> Both Sa-ad and NAME DELETED then left Cape Town to attend a meeting in Iran with Osama. Whilst overseas, (the named South African) was due to meet with:
> - MUAMMAR GHADAFFI, who is currently sponsoring various Muslim-related meetings and conferences. His current image of cooperating with the United States and the IAEA is only a smokescreen. He has no intention of giving up his weapons of mass destruction.
> - AYATOLLAH KHAMENEI, leader of IRAN, also to discuss his visits to South Africa in 2004.

Another comment about al-Qaeda operations in South Africa (edited to make it comprehensible because the language used by the source was inadequate because his first language was Afrikaans) also refers to comments made by Sa-ad bin Laden under the heading 'Important of South Africa to al-Qaeda':

> Sa-ad bin Laden said he had now travelled to most countries where there was an al-Qaeda presence, and of the many countries he'd visited, South Africa was definitely the best. It was his first visit here, and he was very impressed with the country and the state of the al-Qaeda organisation here. He said that South Africa was the ideal country to monitor international news, and because of its accessibility to Muslims it was an ideal operational base for al-Qaeda.
> He said his father had sung the praises of NAME DELETED and NAME DELETED. (Both men were apparently linked to al-Qaeda intelligence). Additionally, he stressed that he was very impressed with the work they were all doing to build the organisation, adding that 'South Africa will soon feature more prominently in the rebuilding of al-Qaeda in Africa and internationally.'

Additionally, there was an earlier communiqué posted on 23 October 2003, regarding a visit to South Africa by Osama bin Laden.

> Sa-ad bin Laden declared that his father, affectionately referred to as 'ABI' (which means Daddy), would be arriving in Cape Town shortly. He will be accompanied by Abu Huzaifa al-Rakishi and Abdul Mohammed al-Masri, who, in collaboration with Dr al-Zawahiri, are already identifying South Africa as a safe place for him to stay.

Several months before, a report dated 11 June 2003 indicated why Osama bin Laden had come to be focused on establishing an operational base in South Africa.

I quote that report verbatim since it has a bearing on subsequent South African (referred to throughout as RSA) links within the operational structure of the Jihadist terror movement:

> The RSA al-Qaeda operation, under the leadership of NAME DELETED and followers, is clearly becoming a very important operational base for al-Qaeda. The RSA allows our movement great freedom of movement, providing no attacks are launched locally. For this reason, all projects there have been shelved.

It would now appear that Osama will use the RSA as a transit route for al-Qaeda operatives and as a training and recruitment facility, together with a conduit for international funding. Al-Qaeda operatives on the run will also find a safe haven here.

Most importantly, it now looks as if the RSA will be used as a base for planning some big operations; certainly one in the USA, where at least 20 South Africans are to be used. Also, NAME DELETED (another South African operative) is involved with receiving SS4 [Soviet] missiles in Sierra Leone [apparently for transit to another destination] and these will probably be used for operations in Africa and elsewhere.

There are many reasons why the al-Qaeda command chose South Africa as a secure base for its future operations in Africa; the main one being that when the newly inducted President Nelson Mandela took over the government from the white-led regime, the country was peaceful and prosperous. Moreover, law and order had been an established factor for generations.

South Africa, at the turn of the millennium, not only functioned well but was also a most efficient and productive country with the largest industrial base in Africa.

What caught the attention of al-Qaeda leaders early on was that, as a post-apartheid nation, South Africa was tenacious in defending civil rights. The Jihadists believed that after all the turmoil their people had gone through in the Middle East and Central Asia, this African state could well be exploitable to develop networks of covert operations.

Additionally, they were made aware that in setting up this base abroad, they would be effectively protected by an entrenched right of free speech coupled with a strong, working constitution.

Still more significant was a succession of permeable borders all the way across the sub-continent. Jihadist tacticians involved had done their homework, and it didn't take them long to discover that South Africa's northern borders are not fenced and are largely unpatrolled and unprotected. That would have been of crucial value for any insurgent movement, with its associates able to infiltrate southwards – at least those that did not fly in – with comparative ease.

They would have been able to enter illegally without appropriate travel documents and certainly no visas – as did a couple of million or more from just about every country in Africa – either through Zimbabwe (by then having been made almost ungovernable by the tyrant Robert Mugabe), and Mozambique, which had just recently emerged from a civil war.

One incident that highlights this point was described by Professor Hussein Solomon in his lecture at an ICT counter-terrorism summit in 2008.[2]

He mentioned the case of a Durban businessman who was arrested after trying to cross the border from Swaziland into South Africa couriering US $130,000 to

---

2 Robert Block, 'In South Africa, Mounting Evidence of al-Qaeda Links', *Wall Street Journal*, 10 December 2002.

his contact. He made the point that the individual had done that trip 150 times over a period of eighteen months.

Regarding the same incident, another man involved and subsequently taken into custody, indicated that the contact man was involved with an exchange bureau managed by a businessman with links to Islamic groups in Africa and the Middle East.

Arguably, the most attractive aspect of operating out of South Africa was its highly developed banking system. By then, the *Wall Street Journal* report included a good idea of what was happening and revealed evidence of a substantial al-Qaeda presence in South Africa.[3]

Various Islamic organisations are mentioned in the report that dealt with laundering money, smuggling gold and diamonds, and the receipt of, or transfer of cash abroad, through South Africa's efficient banking system.

It quotes Gideon Jones, the FBI-trained former head of the Criminal Intelligence Unit of the South African Police Force, saying that South Africa is 'a perfect place to cool off, regroup, and plan your finances.'

To support this statement, one has to look to the case of Abd al-Muhsin al-Libi, aka Ibrahim Tantouche, a senior al-Qaeda member who established two charity organisations as al-Qaeda fronts. Both collected donations for large numbers of orphans who never existed.[4]

In January 2007, the United Nations Council accused two South African cousins – Farhad Ahmed Dockrat and Dr Junaid Ismail Dockrat – of international terrorist activity linked to the Taliban movement in Afghanistan and al-Qaeda leader Osama bin Laden. This was a result of the US Treasury Department's suspicions that Farhad served as an al-Qaeda 'facilitator and terrorist financier'.

According to Washington, he was responsible for the transaction of almost half a million South African Rands (roughly US $60,000 at the time) to the al-Akhtar Trust in Pakistan, which had been identified as an al-Qaeda front. The transaction was made through the Taliban ambassador to Pakistan in 2001.

The last factor that appealed to bin Laden – and of prime importance to any terror or subversive movement – was communications, the quintessence of any clandestine activity that goes global. Anyone who has lived or visited South Africa knows that it has the most advanced and highly developed communications systems that incorporate state-of-the-art high-tech and cellular networks.

For instance, scrutiny of the background to the 7 July 2005 bombings in London led to Haroon Aswat, a British citizen with connections to al-Qaeda who then resided in South Africa. He was arrested after investigations revealed phone calls between

---

3   *Ibid*, Solomon, 'South Africa: Playing Ostrich in the Face of Global Jihad.'
4   African Terrorism Bulletin, *Southern Africa: Strategic base for international terrorism?* (Organized Crime and Corruption Programme of the Institute for Security Studies (ISS): African Terrorism Bulletin, 4th Edition. September 2005.

Aswat and each of the suicide bombers in London, the group of anarchists led by Mohammed Saddiq Khan.

In the overall picture of the South African political changeover following the demise of apartheid, the corruption bugbear features damnably in the insurrectionist mix. In this regard, South Africa is at the forefront of government fraud.

In the article quoted, Professor Solomon stated that 'With lawlessness, government corruption and a wide range of preferred terrorist financing methods available – minerals, gemstones, pirated products and narcotics – al-Qaeda could indeed partake in illicit and unregulated trade in southern Africa to sustain itself.'

He focused specifically on the South African Department of Home Affairs which he accused of allowing illegals to obtain South African passports easily. He stated: 'There is evidence that some of these travel documents were used widely by al-Qaeda and its associates to move about internationally.'

There was also the case, following the London bombings, that the British authorities found genuine South African passports when they raided the residence of an al-Qaeda member.

Another counter-insurgency specialist, the Israeli counter-insurgency specialist Shahar Or, shows conclusively in one of his reports that the modern and developed infrastructure of South Africa has a strong appeal to global terrorist groups. He reminds us of a study conducted by Richard Cornwell of the Institute for Security Studies, where it was argued that terror groups preferred to operate in advanced countries with open multi-racial societies rather than in failed states with unstable infrastructure and poor finance and communications systems.[5]

Shahar Or raises, as has been done numerous times in the past, the fact that in 1998 a Tanzanian citizen by the name of Khalfan Khamis Mohamed – who was responsible for the American Embassy bombings in Dar es Salaam, Tanzania and Nairobi, Kenya in the same year – was turned over to the US Federal Court in New York. He was later convicted and sentenced to life in prison without the possibility of parole.

Khamis Mohamed was a colourful individual, having entered South Africa on a tourist visa only a week after the bombings. He pleaded with the South African authorities for shelter and at the same time was identified with a false name. Before he was uncovered, this revolutionary lived peacefully in Cape Town for over a year while working at a local hamburger outlet.

Of all the Islamic revolutionaries linked to Osama bin Laden who have been involved in Jihadist movements in South Africa in recent decades, the most remarkable has

---

5   Al J. Venter, *Iran's Nuclear Option*. Casemate Publications: 2005. See also David Albright's seminal *Revisiting South Africa's Nuclear Weapons Program*, which he wrote together with Andrea Stricker, and published by Institute for Science and International Security (ISIS) Press, Washington DC, 2016.

to be his deputy commander, the mercurial Egyptian medical man, Dr Ayman al-Zawahiri.

His presence pointed to the fact that while things are changing rather rapidly at the southern tip of Africa, South Africa has always had an appeal to those wishing to establish bases outside their home countries.

It is (or was) stable, prosperous, and had excellent links with the international community (until Pretoria became outspokenly pro-Putin after the invasion of the Ukraine), as well as the reliable banking and communications links mentioned. In fact, it did not take long after Nelson Mandela took over the Pretoria government that revolutionaries from around the globe started to gravitate towards Pretoria.

As a result, South Africa attracted a range of al-Qaeda commanders, Imams, functionaries, recruiters, training personnel, foot soldiers and the rest. But of them all, apart from possibly the Iranians, Ayman al-Zawahiri – with his dynamic, almost overpowering bearing – seemed to exude the most influence.

A tall, striking man, the al-Qaeda deputy commander visited South Africa dozens of times over the decades that he remained active. He probably spent more time embedded within the revolutionary Islamic community in all the main South African cities than any other Jihadist then 'spreading the revolutionary gospel' either in Africa or Asia.

He started young and was only 15 years old when he established a group dedicated to overthrowing the Egyptian government in favour of more fervent Islamic rule.

So be it, and by his own admission, he told some of his followers in South Africa that the only reason he had managed to survive so many wars, insurrections, revolutions and distant military campaigns was that he had learned from an early age how to protect himself: it had become, what he termed 'a way of life...'

That he was exceptionally meticulous about security – demanding exactly the same from his 'minders' – testified to his ability to have survived as long as he did. The Americans tried often enough to liquidate this operative, usually through the well-paid efforts of others. They finally succeeded when they brought in a state-of-the-art killing machine.

No novice to subterfuge, everything about al-Zawahiri reflected years of undercover work, spy craft, effective use of lookouts, safe houses, anti-tracking 'dry cleaning' specifics, concealing attire, covert action, different modes of transport and so on. There was no moral compass in his life as you or I might define the term because, in the process, there were many lives lost. He once executed a man who was only suspected of betraying him: 'It was necessary,' he declared, my source told me.

In terms of pure espionage, the man exemplified the ultimate undercover operative, simply because his whereabouts was never revealed. He travelled widely and freely across southern Africa and met with hundreds of his followers during his many stays that sometimes lasted months.

'The Doctor', as locals deferentially referred to him (or more fully, Dr Mohammed Ebrahiem on some of the documents that refer to his presence in southern Africa) even prayed in the same mosques his people used. He did so with impunity under the noses of that country's much-vaunted security establishment.

The holy places he visited are listed in a variety of reports and were always heavily protected by a bevy of volunteers who regarded their presence not as a job, but as an honour. They demanded no payment and nor is there any question that the Imams where he prayed – and where he sometimes preached – were perfectly aware who was in the congregation with them.

Among the files given to me were the names of some of the Cape Town mosques that al-Zawahiri liked to frequent:

- Mosque on the corner of Chiapini and Church Street in Bo-Kaap. Al-Zawahiri visits a *moulana* who stays up from the mosque, and they walk down for prayers.
- Mosque opposite Westridge Shopping Centre in Rocklands, where al-Zawahiri once gave a sermon.
- Mosque in Bellville not far from the Technikon (near a garage).
- Muir Street mosque in District Six.

There was much embarrassment when this simple fact was eventually revealed through appropriate channels in both Washington and London and, let it be said, things changed dramatically thereafter.

Al-Zawahiri's movements were to become inordinately restrictive in later years – particularly after the death of his mentor Osama bin Laden – and he ended up frequenting friendlier haunts in North Africa, the Middle East and Central Asia.

Interestingly, following the attack on the bin Laden compound on the outskirts of Islamabad by an American maritime task force, he forwent any hospitality offered by his Pakistani 'friends'. He told several of his followers that the South East Asian nation was not to be trusted…

The second al-Qaeda supremo was eventually taken out in a classic drone and missile strike after someone had betrayed his presence in a Kabul apartment block in 2022: it made international headlines at the time.[6]

Whoever was responsible for the actual hit – he would have had a distinct location in hand, provided by the person who had betrayed him – was clearly intent on achieving success and launched two almost six-feet-long missiles simultaneously

---

6   Full details of that historic attack involving a double R9X attack drone strike can be found in an article by the author 'Hunting the Hunters' in the February 2023 edition of *Air Forces Monthly*: Key Publishing UK: Editor Alan Warnes.

from American MQ-9 Reaper RPVs (Remotely Piloted Vehicles). One would have been perfectly adequate, but it seemed that nobody was taking any chances.

Each drone fired the Hellfire R9X missile which, instead of explosives, was designed to deploy six blades a moment before impact. The kinetic energy released destroyed anything with which the 'warhead' came into contact, vehicles included. In this instance, the missiles penetrated the veranda where al-Zawahiri was lounging and he was totally shredded.

His wife and children in an adjacent room were unharmed.

Ayman al-Zawahiri left behind a number of interesting instructions and comments, some listed in the files. One of his statements is self-explanatory, though more comes from a third party charged with recordings. I quote:

- Al-Qaeda intelligence sources report that the CIA, FBI and Israelis are concerned about the situation in South Africa, and will start with a concerted effort through liaison sources to establish what is happening there. Zawahiri says it is essential to plug into police and other sources to try and monitor the progress of the American and Israeli efforts. These people know that there are a lot of Muslims visiting South Africa, and they want to try and find out exactly who they are. Zawahiri says it is essential that activists try and conceal their true identities, and that they are shielded from exposure while in the RSA.
- To this end, a special reception committee will be set up to receive and handle foreign visitors. One of the committee members will be NAME DELETED – the fat *moulana* from Natal. The group will be selected at the Cape Town meeting starting Friday 06.02.2004.
- Osama and al-Rakishi were in the Sudan on Saturday and Sunday and Monday 02.02.2004, and will be arriving in Cape Town on Friday 06.02.2004. XXXXXX and other executive members will be in Cape Town by Friday. (XXXXXX is still driving around in the VW Passat, registration). (Yellow number plates – observed Thursday 5.2.2004 at XXXXXX in Durban Road.)

And another, dated 8 October 2003:

Al-Qaeda is busy with global reorganisation. HAMAS and Hezbollah and other radical groups have all agreed to operate under the umbrella of al-Qaeda, but will retain their separate identities. All the leaders involved agreed on the need for cooperative action.

Al-Qaeda arms caches will be moved to the southern African countries of Botswana, Lesotho and Zimbabwe, but not the RSA at this stage. Caches will come via Egypt, Sudan and the DRC. Iran and South Africa have entered into a trade agreement, and this will be used to move arms to southern Africa.

Al-Qaeda has sent, and is sending, many operatives to Iraq, and in 2004 they will make a big push to get the West out of Iraq and re-instate Saddam Hussein. (before he was killed, remember). Many activists from Sudan and Algeria have been sent to Iraq and some have been trained as suicide bombers.

Al-Qaeda members not killed or captured on missions will be sent to South Africa for a rest period. Some suicide bombers will also be kept here prior to missions.

A second message that week stated:

There is now an urgent need to get training camps in the RSA and Africa up and running again. There is a pressing need to purchase a training farm between Port Elizabeth and Cape

Town and this will be given priority [there had been five Jihadist training camps in that region before they were exposed].

From 10.10.2003 until 20.10.2003 various delegations from India, Pakistan and Arabia will be visiting PE and will be staying at XXXXXX in Malabar, and the top mosque in Malabar.

Saadiq al-Quds from Zambia reported that they have been sending people to Iraq and Palestine. The movement is awaiting an arms cache from Iran that is due to arrive late October, early November 2003.

Epilogue

One could say that the travails involving the life of one individual – and featured between these covers – have not only had their moments but have been a long and often challenging haul. 'By the odds, we shouldn't still be around,' Frederick Forsyth wrote to me a few years ago.

But we are. Freddie has another novel coming out, apart from his regular insightful comments in British newspapers. On my part, I'd like to believe that I still have 'just one more war,' I appropriately tell friends, adding, with a touch of irony, that it could 'possibly be my last'.

Most of our mutual friends have taken the long road, including my old buddy Wilbur Smith whom I first met in Rhodesia; David Cornwell, as well as his lovely wife Jane; the one and only Herman Wouk, with whom I would have loved to have shared a few words but never did, and former SAS Colonel Jim Johnson, the Special Forces architect who, with a tiny force that included French mercenaries, drove the Egyptian army and air force out of the Yemen in the 1950s.

Nor should I forget two more South African stalwarts: Justin Cartwright, who, like me, ended up living in Britain, and Cloete Breytenbach. The cover photo of me – monkey on my back in an Angolan military base in northern Angola – was taken by him near the frontier with the Congo. Cloete and I did many things together in that war, including him showing me how to use my camera effectively.

Most of these illustrious people were ordinary folk who made exceptional contributions to our times. Quite a few, including a few mentioned above, went on to make history.

That said, on reaching the conclusion of this volume, I am aware that there are still many episodes of my rather haphazard career left either unsaid or unrecorded. These include quite a few blunders and an adventure or two that some people (and governments) would rather I did not mention – especially those relating to weapons of mass destruction.

At the forefront stands one of my best books, *Iran's Nuclear Option*, where I exposed several of Iran's efforts to acquire nuclear weapons. It was published in 2005, and many American academics castigated me for daring to suggest that Iran might be trying to build the bomb; in fact, quite a few others believed they were. In this, I was solidly backed by David Albright, whom most of us have seen on major American, British and European networks warning of what could ultimately be severe consequences of not checking Tehran's progress.

My old friend, a former Special Forces operator Floyd Holcom of Astoria, Oregon, told me on our first meeting that he was given my Iranian nuclear book to read by one of Washington's three-digit intelligence agencies while under training.

I have never gone into print about some of the efforts made to prevent its publication, including my being poisoned while still in South Africa. Though there is nothing I can definitively prove, except that before the book was published by Casemate Publishers in the United States, I was in South Africa and rushed into hospital in Pretoria late one night for an emergency MRI following what felt like an explosion in my brain. Hospital staff had to be pulled from their beds, and it took me a good four months to recover; my blood pressure and eyesight have been affected.

Curiously, I had a haircut shortly afterwards and kept some of the clippings. Floyd still has them in a plastic sachet he keeps in my file – a 'routine' procedure with some intelligence operatives. I suppose I could have them tested.

That I was under severe threat, there is no doubt. On a visit to the United States late 2021, I met a former member of Britain's Special Air Service who disclosed for the first time that he had headed the team that kept me under close protective surveillance for three years while I was living in Canada. Still, he was not prepared to be drawn further on the issue, except that I had already learnt some years previously that Canada hosted one of North America's largest expatriate Iranian communities.

Another issue only cursorily mentioned in this volume was my time covering the war in El Salvador with a bunch of American mercenaries. Before that, I was jailed for espionage in Mobutu Sese Seko's Congo.

With a French journalist, Gilles Hertzog, working at that time with *Le Monde*, we were trying to get into Angola through the Congo, but were both suspect the moment we stepped across the border from Zambia: they thought we were spies. We were hauled off to the local secret police headquarters, the *Centre National de Documentation* in Lubumbashi. The one unsavoury fact was that anyone incarcerated in the place in those days rarely came out alive. We could clearly hear the unfortunates being tortured; thankfully, they spared us that indignity.

To cut a long story short, Gilles and I managed to smuggle a message out of prison to the manager of the local Katangese copper mine (scribbled in pencil on toilet paper). Days later, an official from the British Embassy in Kinshasa flew down to check whether we were kosher, or at very least, alive.

I only heard much later that it was Mitterrand, on very good terms with President Mobutu, who used his influence to get us released.

There are many more tales to relate, like when I spent weeks in Somalia during Operation *Restore Hope* with a United States helicopter unit operating out of Baledogle, 15 or so minutes flying time north of Mogadishu.

Situated in desolate, semi-desert terrain, Baledogle always seems to have been at war, was once the largest Soviet air base in the Indian Ocean basin. The Soviets left so hurriedly that they didn't bother to take dozens of fighter jet engines that were left behind lying in a heap with them and which are probably still gathering dust in that severely parched terrain. These days Baledogle is home to Somalia's crack Special Forces unit and is constantly under attack by hostiles.

Before that, there had been my trip down the Nile from Khartoum to Cairo – first by train to Wadi Halfa on the Sudan's northern frontier with Egypt and then a two-day journey by paddle steamer across Lake Nasser (as it was then called) to Aswan. And finally, to Cairo by rail after spending a week exploring Luxor's enormously intriguing Valley of the Kings, staying in the original old Winter Palace Hotel that my Swiss godparents had managed in the 1930s.

That trip through the Sudan and Egypt is probably worth a book on its own. Our train out of Khartoum was caught in one of those monumental Saharan sandstorms that can paralyse African regions half the size of Western Europe for days at a stretch. Since it was only a few years after Israel's Six-Day War, security throughout Egypt was rigorous. I never saw another Western tourist in Luxor, though there must have been a few. On the train that took me to Cairo, I was the only non-Arab on board what would have passed for a troop train anywhere else in the world.

An interesting sidelight here is that once in Cairo, I thought it would be a good idea to pop into the local offices of the PLO, complete with sandbags in front of all large buildings in the city centre area. They were distinctly surprised to see me, a lone Westerner in a city ostensibly seriously threatened by the Israelis. I was made welcome anyway.

Guarded initially, a young Palestinian was appointed to show me around, and for days we travelled the surrounds of Cairo on his old rattling Vespa scooter. Finally, on our last evening together, he dropped me off at my hotel, a decrepit, rundown dump that accorded with my financial status at the time.

As he left me, he called out: 'Shalom, Al' and unthinking, I responded with a shalom of my own.

By then, I had spent so much time in and around the Jewish State that my reaction was spontaneous. More to the point, my newfound Palestinian friends must have been convinced all along that they were dealing with an Israeli.

There have been many more recent exploits, including spending a month covering the Balkans War with the United States Air Force and, after that, clearing landmines in southern Croatia with Richard Davis, the man who invented concealable body armour.

Richard and I had joined a South African mine-clearing team in the south of the country, and, together with a bunch of sappers, we found ourselves in the middle of a minefield. At the time, Richard was exploring the possibility of using the Kevlar that he used in his body armour to devise a new anti-blast system that would prevent mine-clearers taking it in the face.

To cut to the quick, it took a little while to gingerly feel our way out of a rather precarious situation, made even hairier because there were anti-tank mines peppered with AP mines all over the place. The mines had been laid along the length of a long-abandoned railway line, and once we'd been warned about the threat, we had to walk on the rails for almost a kilometre to get out of that predicament.

What is notable is that Richard's invention (though unheralded in his own country) has saved thousands of lives over the past decades, the majority of whom in the early days were wearing his Second Chance body armour. Other companies followed suit, and scores of countries now use Kevlar or similar materials to stop bullets. There are even vests that can thwart a knife attack (another of Richard's inventions), for which two generations of prison officers are eternally grateful.

Of interest, too, is a battlefield sock that will absorb some but not all the blast of an anti-personnel mine. I took the first photos of a blast test at his Michigan home and almost became a casualty myself because my camera was too close to the detonation.

It was Richard's invention that obligated American presidents to don one of his vests whenever they left the White House. The book, *Cops: Cheating Death*, published in 2007 by Lyons Press, emerged from that venture. I gave them sixty well-researched 'saves' – some with photos – and they used only twenty.

The question: why has Richard Davis never been honoured by Washington, though he is regarded as a hero by law enforcement circles throughout the North American continent? Rock stars do better than that.

Perhaps my nearest brush with the inevitable was when I was with a Special Forces team that had to attack an Angolan strongpoint through three lines of trenches at Cuamato in southern Angola. Peter MacAleese led our section, a British mercenary who, while still in the British Army, had served with the SAS and wrote about his adventures in *No Mean Soldier* (originally published by Orion in the UK) with a few of my photos appearing in his book.

Our target was well defended (and consequently not strictly in accordance with the Geneva Convention, I was carrying an AK because you never knew who would rush out of the bush at you and waving my press card about would hardly have been appropriate).

Anyway, when the mortars started coming in (a few of our boys were killed in that two-day onslaught), I found myself in a trench that the enemy seemed to have zeroed in on. So, totally independently and stupidly, I jumped up and moved forward, but there was an explosion behind me, and I was hurled forward onto my gun, which went off in my face. The bullet missed, but the incident left me permanently deaf in my left ear.

Second, must come flying combat with South African mercenary pilot Neall Ellis in the Sierra Leone conflict in 2000 in an ageing Russian Mi-24 helicopter gunship. We took an awful lot of incoming at times, and because I was in the nose of the chopper, I could keep track of what was going on around us.

As assignments go, the consequences of those sorties were pure luck, something most news-gatherers can only dream about. All the details are well-featured in *War Dog: Fighting Other People's Wars*, also published by Casemate.

Not to mention those wonderful overland safaris, which are no longer possible because of a spate of Islamic Jihadist wars that now have left much of Africa embattled. The most memorable possibly was all the way across the Niger Republic from the capital Niamey to the ancient city of Agadez on the southern fringes of the Sahara. I spent a week there with my team, travelled deep into the desert and returned home with some beautiful silver art made locally from centuries-old Maria Theresa Thalers that had been melted down. Madelon still has one of those pieces, now quite rare because of hostilities.

Getting permission to take my film team into the interior was the first obstacle I faced. Without the requisite ministerial permit to move about freely with my crew, it could not happen. I knocked on the door of the head of the country's security services anyway and took my chances and was brought before a quiet-spoken official in traditional white garb seated at a desk that took up almost half of his office floor space.

My French must have been quite good because I made a reasonable case for being allowed to take images of his country which would be screened abroad.

The senior man, as I expected, was a Tuareg, whose origins in those desert regions went back to before Mohammed the Prophet started his crusade.

Early explorers were to find that most of these people were distinctly xenophobic and rarely disposed to social contact with other tribes and he certainly fitted that bill, especially with whites like me who, cap in hand, came begging. I told him that I'd been ordered to report to his office by the Minister of the Interior, and even had the requisite stamped and signed written authority which I'd cajoled from that high authority. He looked me over once or twice, asked where I was going to film and then signed the pass. He was born in Agadez, he said with a dash of disarming courtesy as he led me to the door.

Curiously, I generally found it quite easy to deal with senior government officials in the former French African colonies because most had had their tertiary education in France, as had he.

Equally stimulating some years later was a visit to what had once been one of Africa's outstanding wildlife reserves in northern Mozambique's remote Niassa Province, which adjoins southern Tanzania. That trip was completed only a few years ago before the entire region erupted into a guerrilla war that continues to this day, which is sad because conflict has ravaged a good deal of one of the most beautiful natural regions in the world.

The truth is, Africa has moved on from how it was in the old days, and not always for the better. My goodness, you could travel just about everywhere – and without a firearm.

Apart from Nigeria, Uganda, the Congo and one or two other isolated spots, neither I nor my television crews were ever threatened. There were even overland tours, mainly in converted heavy-duty trucks that started either in London or Paris and traversed the length of Africa to Johannesburg or Cape Town. These experiences, across the deserts of the north and the jungles further south, usually lasted a couple of months where you lived and slept rough. Indeed, they were enjoyed by thousands of young folk in search of adventure.

Another of my experiences include climbing Mount Kilimanjaro (with great difficulty, no matter what anybody says) and travelling across Lake Tanganyika in the motor vessel *Liemba* (formerly the *Graf Goetzen*), the last remnant of the Kaiser's World War I fleet which formed the basis of C. S. Forester's historic 1935 novel *African Queen*. The old veteran still runs a regular service out of Mpulunga in northern Zambia, but I need to warn that conditions on board are not smooth!

Also, I have drowned twice while diving.[1] Both times I very literally lost consciousness, the second time, aged 76, while trying to get down to the wreck of my old frigate, the SAS *Transvaal*. I survived only because having all but passed out at a depth of 30 metres, I was firmly grabbed by a former navy diver and taken to the surface. It was a delicate manoeuvre because he had to monitor both the timing and rate of our ascent to avoid decompression problems.

I'm not sure where I'd place emerging from an ambush laid by a particularly aggressive bunch of rebels in northern Uganda. I had gone in from Kampala with a French television crew from Channel 4, and we were heading back south when the guerrillas that had the town under siege opened fire. My driver did the only thing he could: he put his foot down!

We must have travelled for quite a few minutes before we finally reached the next settlement on a hill – time stands still when people are shooting at you – with the entire populace gathered on the edge of town and watching events go down. The lusty cheers they gave us were inspirational. Parts of that event were used in one of my productions screened nationwide in the United States by Public Broadcasting (PBS), called *Africa's Killing Fields*. I reckon it's still about.

Probably the most serious incident that could easily have gone wrong came when I was with the mercenary group Executive Outcomes, on which the film *Blood*

---

1   The author gives a graphic and disturbing account of this event. He only survived because he was accompanied by two former navy divers who brought him to the surface: *Shipwreck Stories*. Protea Books: 2015. See the chapter headed 'How Not to Dive a Wreck'.

Diamond is based. I was attached to a group of those freebooters in Saurimo, in Angola's northeast, checking some alluvial diggings when I wandered off from the main group to take some shots of a bridge over a river. It was the only crossing for hundreds of kilometres, all the others having been blown.

The next thing I heard was the Angolan colonel leading the group who had rushed off in my direction and shouted that I should stop immediately. I stood dead still when I heard his first call, and he hardly needed to elaborate that all the approaches to the bridge had been mined. It took time and effort, but I managed to extricate myself by jumping from one rock to another, though that exercise lasted a while. It was a stupid move to go off on my own in an extremely active operational area.

Thereafter, a Russian Antonov crash-landed at Saurimo Airport. The plane had come down reasonably intact within the air base perimeter, so the crew decided to walk the 600–800 metres to safety instead of waiting for a vehicle to fetch them – as the unit air traffic control had ordered them to do. All ended up stepping on anti-personnel mines.

Not all the people that I dealt with in many of those operations were mercenaries, but Frederick Forsyth encapsulated it well in an op-ed piece that he wrote for *The Wall Street Journal* on 15 May 2000:

> For the mercenary is a simplistic fellow. Not for him the strutting parades of West Point, the medals on the steps of the White House or perhaps a place at Arlington. He simply says: 'Pay me my wage, and I'll kill the bastards for you.' And if he dies, they will bury him quickly in the red soil of Africa, and we will never know…

Acknowledgements

I suppose one could say that the Boer War was partly responsible for my career choice. John Holt Shipping Services sent me to Nigeria in 1966 – with the original intention that I should take over the job of Harry Whittaker, a Coaster (as we called them) who had worked on the African West Coast for decades and was due to retire.

John Holt's headquarters in Liverpool were unaware that retirement was the last thing that recalcitrant old bugger desired. Therefore, my arrival in Lagos to take over his little domain was an imposition, and he did his damnedest to prevent it. I did not know was that the man had lost two great-uncles in the Boer War and, since I was a South African and of Boer extraction, he considered me his 'enemy'.

The result was that Harry – still in charge of the office – sent me on long hauls all over Nigeria on obscure missions, perhaps hoping that the hazardous conditions on the country's roads would result in my departure. I couldn't refuse, but I did end up exploring that part of West Africa as few others could in the immediate post-independence period. I assimilated much that was linked to both its politics and the army because I was meeting people from all walks of life, including military personnel. Moreover, I had already started writing about what I was experiencing, and my fears of more violence. When the second army coup took place in July 1966 – the so-called July Rematch – its leaders had hatched their plot at Lagos's Ikeja Airport, within metres of my office.

More salient, thanks to my access to international flights (before faxes and other technologies had become commonplace), I had the means to get my stories and photos out of the country to the various international news agencies. My newfound talent as a surreptitious news-gatherer had emerged, an invaluable attribute because the media was banned from entering Nigeria after the insurrection and remained so for some time.

While working in West Africa, I made good use of another valuable contact that had developed after I'd travelled overland from Johannesburg to Dakar. My contact was Colonel (later General) Bettencourt Rodrigues, defence attaché at the Portuguese Embassy in London, who quietly arranged for me to cover his country's insurgency in Angola. It was a rare privilege because, simply put, Lisbon and the media were not friends.

Others helped in that arcane realm of stringing words together, and no one played a more influential role in my becoming a scribbler than the tenacious Peter Younghusband, one of the best journalists on the African beat for decades while reporting for both the London *Daily Mail* and *Newsweek*. He was instrumental in my being handed the *Daily Express* string from his old pal John Monks, who, with Peter, covered developments in Africa for years.

On the editorial side, several more individuals are notable. The first is Klaas Steytler, erstwhile editor of *Huisgenoot* and husband of the illustrious Elsa Joubert. Also, Otto Krause, who owned *News Check*, the best South African news magazine of its day. Both broke my report – in different languages – that suggested a second army coup d'état in Nigeria was imminent. That happened within weeks of my stories being published – which truly set me on the path to a new career.

Likewise, Johnnie Johnson, editor of the Johannesburg *Sunday Express* – sometimes cantankerous, often irascible, but always a professional who firmly believed in the job being properly handled. Jack Shepherd-Smith was of a different calibre: no less demanding, which was why he did an excellent job editing *Scope* magazine. Both men taught me a good deal about preparing good, useable copy.

With David Albright, who founded ISIS (he calls it the 'good ISIS' – Washington's Institute for Science and International Security) – I discovered a man who not only created an international awareness of many of the perils of rogue nations trying to develop nuclear weapons and other weapons of mass destruction but was also willing to help someone willing to learn about those things. I could never have managed without David's help during my early days reporting on these issues for Britain's Jane's Information Group. In the process, he also became a good friend, and I have something else up my sleeve in which he might be interested. But since I will have turned 85 by the time this book is out, don't hold your breath.

In Britain, I owe a good measure of gratitude to Peter Felstead, former editor-in-chief of *Jane's Defence Weekly*, who had been at the forefront of my efforts for decades. In the United States, it was Lieutenant-Colonel Robert (Bob) Brown, a buddy with whom I covered several wars, including those in Rhodesia and El Salvador.

In a career that spans more than half a century, scores of others need to be acknowledged. For now, though, I will thank a few more immediate participants, starting with former SAAF veteran Neall Ellis, with whom I shared many adventures, not only during the Border War but also later, when he went freelance and began 'fighting other people's wars'. And Manie Troskie, of Charlie Company, 1 Parachute Battalion – with whom I was dropped into battle at Cuamato in Angola and where I came close to meeting the man in the white suit.

Parts of this book were written while I stayed with two great friends, Walter and Sandy Bernardis, at their South Coast dive lodge in South Africa. Walter helped temper my frustrations by taking me shark diving over quite a few years: we always did it free-diving (without protective cages) with these beautiful creatures. Often there were times when we had more than 30 black tips and the occasional tiger shark milling around his boat, and he would be the first to jump into the water for the routine filming session. Divers come from around the world to experience those thrills with Walter. He admits to only being 'attacked' four times by sharks.

Others included Cobus Claassens, and Roelf van Jaarsveld, who, with his team of irregular combatants, hosted me in the battle for Sierra Leone's Kono diamond fields. Douw Steyn features prominently in this mix, the only man I'm aware of who commanded underwater demolition teams put ashore by submarines to destroy Russian and Cuban ships in Angolan harbours. He achieved several times what the Americans never managed once in the war in Vietnam. I must include Jonathan Pittaway, an illustrious author in his own right because his military books have recorded much of it.

More recently, in some of Africa's Jihadist wars, Admiral António Silva Ribeiro, Chief of the General Staff of the Portuguese Armed Forces, played a pivotal role in getting this octogenarian attached to some of his units active in Mali and the Central African Republic. So too, with Hannes Wessels, who opened doors for me in contemporary Zimbabwe and Zambia.

I worked closely with Frederick Forsyth for a very long time, both on his takes on the Nigerian civil war in Biafra and later, after he'd gone public in his biography about having worked with Britain's Secret Intelligence Service for most of his professional life. As Freddie admits, we're both pretty lucky to have survived many of the dangerous shenanigans we were involved in.

Floyd Holcom, that distinguished American warrior who has done more intelligence work for Washington than almost anyone I know before he settled down in Astoria, Oregon, gave me a lot of assistance during a particularly difficult period. More recently, he surprised me by introducing me to the protective surveillance unit team leader that watched over my well-being when I lived in Canada's Sault Saint Marie. That period covered about three years, and I was never even vaguely aware that a bunch of professionals were keeping close tabs on me. The threat fact must have been pretty high, but he steadfastly refused to discuss it when I asked. 'Next time,' he said with a smile.

In bringing this work to fruition, Madelon Venter's enterprise and determination have prevailed; let it be said, it has been a monumental task. Without her help, I'd have been sunk. Durban's Bruce Gonneau came up trumps numerous times with many of the images acquired – he has a knack for making something out of practically nothing.

On the technical side, Graham Davis was always there to assist with IT problems that tend to bug the industry, as was Downe's genial communications specialist Steve Barnes, who still assists with the occasional Zoom connection when I give my lectures.

By the time the 'Big C' had hit me – second time round – I couldn't have managed without them. Nor without one of the top oncologists in Britain, Dr Daniele Crawley, and the dedicated staff at Guy's Hospital's Acute Oncology Unit, who have been pulling out all stops to keep me alive. As she told me, the mind is just as important as physical treatment in that ongoing battle.

Emerson Paul and his lovely lady Monika Thaler rose to the occasion each time I needed help: their two boys are blessed with such caring parents. Joan Smith, a close neighbour, also needs a few words of thanks because she's always there for me, as does Robert Herd, one of Downe's stalwarts.

As Freddie Forsyth mentioned in his letter to me on page xx he is pleased that after all my adventures, I am now in the warm embrace of a solid little English community, for which I must give thanks.

Among those are quite a few notables and include Jamie Newman, owner of my 'local' The George and Dragon, his chef Michael Stevens (who is also a bench-press specialist), Hugh Burton, the irrepressible Andy 'The Hat', Denise Jenkins behind the counter, as well as the Braxtons, Andy and Gemma. And never to be forgotten is 'Cornish' Tony, the man who keeps me warm in winter with regular supplies of wood.

I don't really know how to thank the woman in my life right now, Lynn Goodfellow, who spent her entire professional career, first in the Canadian and then, after marrying her late husband Mark, in the British Diplomatic Corps. She and her son Adam reviewed this book several times, and their contributions are invaluable. Adam, ex-Cambridge, is so good we ended up referring to him as 'Eagle-Eye': he would highlight many small things we'd overlooked.

On the editing side, I must thank my old mate Chris Cocks – a warrior like me – who wrote *Fire Force: A Trooper's War in the Rhodesian Light Infantry*, unquestionably one of the best books to emerge from that conflict.

Last but not least, it was David Farnsworth, to whom I gave a rough draft of this work while he was laid low by Covid. To my surprise, he suggested that I 'get on with it' – and that at a time when I thought it might not be worth the trouble as I'd been working on the book for some time. And a massive thanks to Ruth Sheppard, his Oxford-based deputy, who oversaw production and provided support and understanding when I needed it most along with the help of her colleagues Adam Jankiewicz and Declan Ingram.

Thank you all, and *salaams*…

About the author

Al J. Venter has been a military correspondent, documentary filmmaker, and author for over fifty years and, at 85, is currently recognised as the world's oldest still-active war correspondent.

He has had more than 60 books published and reported over more than three decades for several publications in the stable of Britain's Jane's Information Group, including *Jane's International Defence Review*, *Jane's Islamic Affairs Analyst*, *Jane's Defence Weekly* and others.

During this time, he reported on most of Africa's fiercest conflicts, including the Nigerian Civil War, where he spent time in Biafra working for the BBC alongside colleague Freddie Forsyth, who was in the rebel state at the same time. All three of Portugal's colonial wars followed – in Angola, Portuguese Guinea and Mozambique, where he was to go in many times. Then the Rhodesian War, which he covered intermittently, virtually from beginning to end. He was a regular visitor to the front during South Africa's Border War, which lasted almost a quarter century.

Other African trouble spots followed, including the Congo, Uganda under the tyrant Idi Amin and the subsequent invasion by Tanzania. The most notable outcome was a one-hour documentary titled *Africa's Killing Fields*, broadcast nationwide in the United States by Public Broadcasting Service (PBS). His hour-long film, *Aids, the African Connection*, was a finalist for China's Pink Magnolia Award in the documentary category.

Other assignments covered the Lebanese Civil War over several years (a phase that included the invasion of Lebanon and the taking of Beirut while embedded with the Israeli Army). He regards this conflict not only as the most dangerous but also extremely exasperating. One of the senior men with whom he was associated on the Christian side (but with whom he had some severe differences) was later exposed as a Syrian agent. As he admits, 'I reckon that had I hung about too long, he would probably have dealt with me, as he had others, until he was exposed and unceremoniously iced.'

In the early 1990s, Venter spent time with the US Army helicopter air wing at Baledogle and Mogadishu in Somalia (a country which he frequently visited before and after Operation *Restore Hope*) as well as three assignments with the mercenary group Executive Outcomes in Angola and Sierra Leone.

He believes one of his most memorable times came later – during the Sierra Leone civil war – when he spent several months flying combat with Neall Ellis in a Soviet Mi-24 helicopter gunship that leaked when it rained. One of his best books emerged from that venture: *Gunship Ace: The Wars of Neall Ellis, Helicopter Pilot and Mercenary*.

After that, he spent a month flying over the Balkans with the United States Air Force. That assignment included a Joint-STAR operational mission with the USAF over Kosovo and, later, mine-clearing operations in Croatia.

Venter has been featured on the BBC, CNN, Great Britain News and many more, and also involved with Discovery Channel in a five-part series on the phenomenon of the modern mercenary – a subject on which he wrote the book *Mercenaries* for Casemate Publishers.

He also wrote a seminal book on South African politics titled *Coloured: A Profile of Two Million South Africans*. Published in 1974 by Human & Rousseau, that work is a savage indictment of South Africa's racial policies of the time. He condemned the system long before it became fashionable to be anti-apartheid, at considerable risk to his personal safety because the government of the day had its own way of dealing with dissidents. As it was, he was denounced in Parliament as a *veraaier* (a traitor).

One aspect of his life that he hasn't touched on yet is Africa's wildlife. He has made a point of spending time in many of the continent's 'majors' – Kruger, Hluhlwe, Serengeti, Maasai Mara, Tanzania's Selous and the Ngorongoro Conservation Area, Wankie, Chobe, Moremi, Etosha, and the greatest of them all, the Okavango. This will now become a primary focus because he will be working with one of his closest friends, Peter Comley, himself a published wildlife author. Peter, and his partner, the American wildlife enthusiast Bill Given, built up one of the finest lodges in the heart of the Delta – Bushman Plains, prominently featured by National Geographic – and has started another.

As he says, with all these projects on the go, there are just not enough hours in the day to complete them all, and cancer doesn't help.

More recently, already in his eighties and having fought off the disease once, he spent a month in Mali's Jihadist insurgency operating out of Bamako with a NATO tactical air force unit and was twice embedded with a crack NATO Rapid Reaction Force in the Central African Republic, the last time in October 2022.

He has been injured in combat a couple of times, once by a Soviet anti-tank mine while on operations with the South African Army in Angola, an incident that left him partially deaf. His son Johan, attached to 61 Mechanised Battalion Group, was wounded in a subsequent cross-border raid into Angola in an engagement with a Cuban-Angolan military detachment. He believes it was the only father–son combination in which both were wounded in that conflict.

After that, during the Angolan civil war and in a somewhat devious ploy, Venter joined the FNLA's *Chipa Esquadrao* (which led to the formation of South Africa's crack 32 Battalion). He enlisted as a combatant, the only way he reckons he could get his story. Venter was also operational in the guerrilla struggle in El Salvador.

At the behest of the CIA, he made a one-hour TV documentary on the Soviet offensive in Afghanistan in 1985, an event he covers.

He has authored several books on nuclear proliferation, including *Iran's Nuclear Option* (which he rates as one of his best books); *How South Africa Built Six Atom Bombs* and *Nuclear Terror: The Bomb and Other Weapons of Mass Destruction in the Wrong Hands*.

Professionally, before turning to journalism, Al Venter qualified in London as a Fellow of the Institute of Chartered Shipbrokers at the Baltic Exchange.

Index

Books by the same author

Coloured: Profile of Two Million South Africans; Human & Rousseau, 1974
Africa Today; Macmillan South Africa; 1975
Report on Portugal's War in Guiné-Bissau; California Institute of Technology, 1976
The Chopper Boys: Helicopter Warfare in Africa, 1994
The Iraqi War Debrief: Why Saddam Hussein Was Toppled; Ashanti Publishing, 2004
War Dog: Fighting Other Peoples' Wars, Casemate, 2005
Iran's Nuclear Option – Tehran's Quest for the Atom Bomb; Casemate, 2005
Battle for Angola – End of the Cold War in Africa, 1975–1989; Helion; 2021
Allah's Bomb: The Islamic Quest for Nuclear Weapons; Lyons Press, 2007
Cops: Cheating Death: How One Man Saved the Lives of 3,000 Americans; Lyons Press 1986
How South Africa Built Six Atom Bombs; Ashanti Publishing, 2008
Barrel of a Gun: A War Correspondent's Misspent Moments in Combat; Casemate, 2010
Gunship Ace – The Wars of Neall Ellis, Helicopter Pilot and Mercenary; Casemate, 2020
Biafra's War – A Tribal War that left a Million Dead; Helion, 2016
African Stories by Al Venter and Friends; Protea Books, 2013
Shark Stories by Al Venter and Friends; Protea Books, 2016
War Stories by Al Venter and Friends; Protea Books, 2012
Shipwreck Stories by Al Venter and Friends; Protea Books; 2015
Portugal's Guerrilla Wars in Africa – Angola, Mozambique and Portuguese Guinea; Helion, 2013
Mercenaries: Putting the World to Rights with Hired Guns; Casemate 2014
Combat – At War Along the Angolan Frontier; Helion, 2019
Nuclear Terror – The Bomb and Other Weapons of Mass Destruction in the Wrong Hands; Pen&Sword, 2018
Al-Qaeda in the Islamic Maghreb: Shadow of Terror over the Sahel; Pen&Sword, 2020
The Last of Africa's Cold War Conflicts; Pen&Sword, 2021
Portugal's Bush War in Mozambique; Casemate, 2022